The Best Way to Use Th

The Ultimate ACT M

Learn How to Master ACT Math with Perfect Scorer Matthew Stroup

To have the best experience with this book, sign up for the Ultimate ACT Math Course. **It's like having your own private math tutor, only cheaper!** The course includes:

- **3-Point Score Improvement Guarantee** (see full details at preppros.io/3-point-guarantee)
- **30+ Hours of On-Demand Lessons and Practice Question Explanations.**
- **Video Lessons Teaching All 35 Chapters in This Book.**
- **1,250+ Video Explanations For Every Practice Question in This Book!**
- **Proven Score-Raising Lessons, Strategies, and Test-Taking Tips.**

Ultimate ACT Math Course

$29.99/month (with discount code below)

- **3-Point Score Improvement Guarantee!**
- Video tutorials teaching all 35 Chapters.
- 1,250+ video explanation for every practice question in this book.
- 4 practice ACT Math tests & full video explanations.

Answer Explanations Course

$12.99/month

- 1,250+ on-demand video explanation for every practice question in this book.
- Only includes answer explanations.
- Does not include 3-Point Score Improvement Guarantee.

Free Trial & Secret $20 Off Discount Code!

Chapters 12 and 19 are **FREE** in the Free Trial (no credit card needed to sign up). With this book, **you get a lifetime $20 discount on the Ultimate ACT Math Course! Enter coupon code "MP23"** at checkout to make the course **$29.99/month** (normally $49.99/month).

To sign up, go to www.preppros.io/act-math-course.

Preparing For The Entire ACT?

Check out the Ultimate ACT Course! Get full access to the Ultimate ACT Math Course and so much more for **only $99/month!**

- **3-Point Improvement Guarantee**
- **70+ Hours of Expert Tutoring**
- **ACT Math Course**
- **ACT English Course** (book included)
- **ACT Reading Course** (book included)
- **ACT Science Course**
- Study Plans
- 4+ Practice ACTs and Explanations.

We also offer a **FREE trial** that includes 2+ hours of English and Math lessons. To sign up for the free trial or the full course, go to www.preppros.io/act-course.

PrepPros Presents

The Complete Guide to

ACT Math

By Matthew Stroup and Michael Stroup

1st Edition

Copyright © 2023 PrepPros

All rights reserved. Photocopying any portion of this publication is strictly prohibited unless express written authorization is first obtained from PrepPros, www.preppros.io.

Test names and other trademarks are the property of their respective trademark owners. *ACT is a registered trademark of the ACT which is not affiliated with PrepPros.

For more information about this book and additional ACT Tutoring services offered by PrepPros, visit www.preppros.io.

Quantity discounts are available for teachers, companies, and other educational purposes. Please contact info@preppros.io for more information or to purchase books.

About the Authors

Matthew Stroup and Michael Stroup are both master tutors, brothers, and the founders of PrepPros. Together, they have over 15,000 hours of private tutoring experience and have both achieved perfect scores on the ACT. Their students have improved their ACT scores up to 12 points. Matthew Stroup graduated from Johns Hopkins University, where he studied biology, economics, and was pre-med, and Georgetown University, where he obtained a master's degree in biotechnology. Michael graduated from Georgetown University with a degree in Marketing and Entrepreneurship.

Matthew and Michael both work as full-time tutors. If you want to lerarn directly from Matthew and Michael in private tutoring, group classes, or online courses, check out the PrepPros website at www.preppros.io.

Table of Contents

Introduction To The Complete Guide to ACT Math i
- How to Best Use This Book
- Sign Up for On-Demand Video Lessons and Explanations **(Secret Discount Code!)**
- Difficulty of Practice Questions
- What Else to Do?

How Our 4 Level System Works iii
- How To Find Your Best Level
- Level 1 – Core Fundamental (For Students Scoring 23 and Below)
- Level 2 – Advanced Fundamental (For Students Scoring 24-27)
- Level 3 – Advanced Topics (For Students Scoring 28-32)
- Level 4 – Expert Level Topics (For Students Aiming for 33-36)
- How To Best Use The 4-Level System

ACT Math Study Guides v
- How To Best Use The Study Guides

Level 1 Study Guide – Core Fundamentals v

Level 2 Study Guide – Advanced Fundamentals ix

Level 3 Study Guide – Advanced Topics xv

Level 4 Study Guide – Expert Level Topics xxii

ACT Math Equation Sheet xxvii

Introduction to ACT Math xxxiii
- Format of the Test
- Difficulty of the Questions
- Time Management
- Guessing
- 6 Test Day Tips to Maximize Your Score

Chapter 1: Backsolving 1

Chapter 2: Substitution 4

Chapter 3: Geometry Part 1 - Angles 7
- Intersecting Lines
- Parallel Lines
- Interior Angles in Polygons
- Figures Drawn to Scale Trick

Chapter 4:   Geometry Part 2 - Shapes..**14**
        Area and Volume
        Areas, Volumes, and Units
        Volumes of Other Three-Dimensional Solids
        Right Triangles
        Special Right Triangles
        Similar Triangles
        More Triangles – Equilateral Triangles, Isosceles Triangles
        Third Side of a Triangle Rule
        Other Rules You Might Need to Know

Chapter 5:   Lines..**31**
        Slope
        Slopes of Parallel and Perpendicular Lines
        Slope-Intercept Form
        Point-Slope Form
        Standard Form
        Midpoint Formula
        Distance Formula
        Solving for Intercepts

Chapter 6:   Fractions **41**
        Combining Fractions
        Dividing Fractions
        Simplifying Fractions
        Getting Rid of Fractions
        Turn Fractions into Decimals
        How To Use Your Calculator For Fractions

Chapter 7:   Algebra Skills **51**
        PEMDAS
        Negative Numbers
        Negtive Numbers and Exponents
        Combing Like Terms
        Cross Multiply Fractions
        Square Both Sides of an Equation Correctly
        Algebra with Inequality Signs
        Taking Square Roots in Algebraic Equations

Chapter 8:   Number Theory **61**
        Types of Numbers
        Properties of Even and Odd Numbers
        Greatest Common Factor
        Least Common Multiple
        Prime Factorization
        One Solution vs. Infinite Solutions vs. No Solution

Chapter 9: Percentages 72
        Simple Percentages
        Percentage Increase and Decrease
        Percent Change

Chapter 10: Ratios and Proportions 82
        Introduction to Ratios
        Question Type #1 – Ratio and a Total
        Question Type #2 – Ratios as Proportions
        Question Type #3 – Comparing Across Ratios
        Question Type #4 – Ratios and Geometry
        Direct Proportion
        Indirect Proportion

Chapter 11: Functions 89
        Function Basics
        Composite Functions
        Other Function Notations
        Functions on Graphs
        Domain and Range
        Inverse Functions

Chapter 12: Mean, Median, Mode, and Range 102
        Definitions of Mean, Median, Mode, and Range
        Finding the Average
        Weighted Average
        Finding the Median in a Table

Chapter 13: Exponents and Roots 112
        Exponents
        Roots
        Roots and Variables with Powers

Chapter 14: Logarithms 123
        Basics of Logarithms
        Logarithm Rules
        Natural Logarithms

Chapter 15: Systems of Equations 129
        Solving with Elimination, Substitution, and Setting Equal
        Word Problems
        More Complex Systems of Equations Questions

Chapter 16: Quadratics 135

    Multiplying Binomials
    Factoring Quadratics
    "Easy to Factor" Quadratics
    Solutions, Roots, x-intercepts, and Zeros for Quadratic Equations
    How Solutions Appear on a Graph
    The Quadratic Formula
    The Discriminant
    Finding the Vertex

Chapter 17: Trigonometry 146

    Basic Trigonometry – SOH-CAH-TOA
    Using Trigonometry to Find Side Lengths in Right Triangles
    Inverse Trigonometric Functions
    Trigonometric Identity to Know
    Graphing Sine and Cosine Functions
    Amplitude and Period
    Graphing Tangent Functions
    Law of Sines
    Law of Cosines
    Unit Circle and Radians

Chapter 18: Absolute Value 173

    Basics of Absolute Value
    Absolute Value and Unknown Variables
    Absolute Value and Inequalities

Chapter 19: Matrices 179

    What is a Matrix?
    Matrix Dimensions
    Matrix Addition and Subtraction
    Finding the Determinant of a (2 × 2) Matrix
    Multiplying Matrices
    How to Use Your Calculator to Solve Matrix Questions

Chapter 20: Repeating Patterns 191

    Repeating Decimals
    Repeating Patterns with Powers and the Units Digit
    Repeating Patterns with Powers of i
    How to Solve Repeating Patterns Questions

Chapter 21: Circles, Ellipses, and Hyperbolas 198

    Equation of a Circle
    Advanced Circle Questions – 2 Principles to Know
    Ellipses
    Foci on an Ellipse
    Hyperbolas – Vertical and Horizontal Hyperbolas

Chapter 22: Probability 210

    The Basics of Probability
    3 Probability Rules to Know
    Probability and Data Tables
    Advanced Probability Questions
    Expected Value

Chapter 23: Permutations, Combinations, and Organized Counting 224

    Factorial
    Permutations
    Combinations
    Organized Counting
    Advanced Permutations, Combinations, and Organized Counting

Chapter 24: Sequences 235

    Arithmetic Sequences
    Geometric Sequences
    Recursive Sequences

Chapter 25: Complex Numbers 241

    Adding and Subtracting Complex Numbers
    Multiplying Complex Numbers
    The Complex Conjugate
    Powers of i
    The Complex Plane
    Absolute Value of a Complex Number
    Distance Between Complex Numbers

Chapter 26: Word Problems 250

    4 Tips for Word Problems

Chapter 27: Inequalities...256

    Algebra with Inequalities
    Graphing Inequalities
    Advanced Graphing Inequalities with Parabolas, Circles, and Ellipses

Chapter 28: Exponential Growth and Decay..264

    Exponential Growth
    Exponential Decay
    General Exponential Form
    Graphing General Exponential Form
    Advanced Exponential Growth and Decay Equations

Chapter 29: Unit Conversion 271

    Basic Unit Conversion
    Dimensional Analysis

Chapter 30: Scientific Notation **277**
        How to Write Numbers in Scientific Notation

Chapter 31: Arcs and Sectors **280**
        Arcs
        Inscribed Angle Theorem
        Sectors

Chapter 32: Vectors **285**
        What is a Vectors?
        Adding and Subtracting Vectors
        Drawing Vectors
        Tip-to-Tail Method for Adding and Subtracting Vectors

Chapter 33: Shifting and Transforming Functions **291**
        Rules for Shifting and Transforming Functions
        Shifting and Transforming Parabolas, Cubics, and Other Functions

Chapter 34: Statistics **296**
        Description of A Survey
        Shapes of Distributions
        Standard Deviation
        Stem and Leaf Plot
        Sample Proportion
        Normal Distribution and The Empirical Rule

Chapter 35: Miscellaneous Topics **305**
        Venn Diagrams
        Made-Up Math
        Logic
        Pattern Spotting
        Mapping
        Puzzles
        Binomial Theorem and Pascal's Triangle
        Visual Spatial
        Vertical and Horizontal Asymptotes

Practice ACT and Diagnostic Sheet **321**

Answer Key **323**

Introduction to The Complete Guide to ACT Math

The ACT Math Test is a 60-minute section with 60 multiple-choice questions. The questions on the test aim to assess your mathematics skills on a wide range of topics that include those taught in algebra 1, algebra 2, geometry, and pre-calculus along with a variety of other math topics.

Since the ACT Math Test covers so many years of math, the biggest challenge for most students is being familiar with all the topics tested, some of which you may have learned years ago and forgotten and others that you may have never learned in class. Do you remember what a remainder is? Have you learned matrices? Do you know what an ellipse is and how to graph it? In this book, we will review all the topics and equations that you need to know for the ACT. In addition, you will learn proven test-taking tricks and tips for how to properly setup and solve the questions in the most efficient way possible.

How to Best Use This Book

To maximize your improvement, make sure to follow these tips:

1. **Find Your Level.** To make this book as effective as possible for each student, we have split the book into 4 levels. The levels are based on your math ability and scoring goals. The levels are listed below. **Make sure to read the complete description of the 4 Level System on page iii.**

   Level 1 – Core Fundamentals
   - **For Students Scoring 23 and Below on ACT Math**

   Level 2 – Advanced Fundamentals
   - **For students Scoring 24-27 on ACT Math**

   Level 3 – Advanced Topics
   - **For Students Scoring 28-32 on ACT Math**

   Level 4 – Expert Level Topics
   - **For Students Aiming for 33-36 on ACT Math**

   In each chapter, the logos above label each concept, example question, and practice question with its corresponding level. **To have the best experience with this book, focus on the concepts in each chapter and practice questions that are AT AND BELOW your level.** If you are a weaker math student, start with level 1. If you master all level 1 topics, move onto level 2. If you are a stronger math student, make sure that you still know all level 1 and 2 topics before moving onto the level 3 topics. Level 4 topics are for advanced math students aiming for perfect and near perfect scores.

2. **Sign Up For The Ultimate ACT Math Course (On-Demand Lessons and Answer Explanations). The course includes over 30 hours of on-demand videos of expert tutor and perfect scorer Matthew Stroup** teaching all the concepts and showing you how to solve all 1,250+ questions in this book. Start by watching the lessons for each chapter, where Matthew teaches you everything that you need to know and shows you how to apply the concepts on example questions. These lessons are the same ones that he teaches students in private tutoring sessions for $200/hr.

   Next, complete the practice questions at the end of each chapter. Do not watch the video explanations before attempting to solve the question. The struggle is one of the best ways to learn. If you are stuck, look back at the teaching pages in the chapter first. Once you are done with the practice questions, check your answers with the answer key in the back of the book and watch the video explanations for any questions that you answered incorrect or did not confidently know how to solve.

To sign up, go to www.preppros.io/act-math-course. Chapters 12 and 19 are FREE in the Free Trial (no credit card needed). **The Ultimate ACT Math Course starts at $12.99/month for the answer explanations and $29.99 for the full course with discount code MP23 at checkout** (the course is normally $49.99 but with this book you get a lifetime $20 discount! **For even more information on the course, go to the first page of this book inside the front cover.**

3. **Use The Study Guides.** In the next section, there are 4 study guides: one for each level. **The study guides lists the topics and equations that you should memorize based on your math level and scoring goals.** You can use the study guide as a checklist of all the concepts you need to learn and equations you need to memorize.

4. **Work Front To Back.** This book is designed to be completed from front to back. The most commonly tested topics are in the front and less commonly tested topics are in the back. To maximize your improvement, we recommend working through all the chapters. That being said, each chapter is written to be independent of the other chapters. If you are already proficient in certain topics, you can skip around and focus on the chapters that you need to learn to improve your score.

5. **Take A Practice ACT to Diagnose Your Weaknesses.** Take a practice ACT and use the diagnostic sheet (p. 321). The diagnostic sheet lists the topic and corresponding chapter for all questions on the practice ACT. Based on the questions you answer incorrectly, the diagnostic sheet tells you exactly which chapters to study. You can find a free practice ACT at www.preppros.io/free-resources.

6. **Practice Makes Perfect.** We recommend completing all practice questions at your level and below in each chapter. For example, if you are a level 3 student, complete all level 1, 2 and 3 practice questions.

7. **Learn From Your Mistakes.** The students who improve most are the ones who learn the most from their mistakes. We recommend keeping an "Improvement Notebook" where you keep a list of the equations you need to memorize and takes notes when you make mistakes on practice questions.

8. **Mark Questions You Answer Incorrectly and Repeat These Question in The Final 2 Weeks Before Your ACT.** Repeating questions that you answer incorrectly as you lead up to test day helps students review challenging concepts, learn from their mistakes, and maximize their scores.

Difficulty of Practice Questions

In each chapter, the difficulty of the practice questions increases as you work through the problem sets. Just like on the ACT Math Test, the earlier questions are easier while the later questions are much more difficult. All questions are labelled with their corresponding level.

As you work through each chapter, keep your math level and scoring goals in mind. **If you are aiming for a math score of 30+, make sure you understand how to solve every level 3 question in this book and attempt the level 4 questions as well. If you are a weaker math student who is currently scoring below 25, do not be intimidated by the level 3 and 4 questions at the end of each chapter.** These questions are written to challenge top math students. That being said, you can still learn by attempting these questions and watching the video explanation in the Ultimate ACT Math Course if you have time to do so, but do not be discouraged if you find them very difficult. You can still see great improvements in your math score without knowing how to solve the most advanced questions on the test.

What Else to Do?

Take practice tests...lots of them! In addition to this book, you should take at least 4 full practice ACTs. You can find practice tests for free in the Ultimate ACT Math Course introduction videos. You can also download a free practice ACT at www.preppros.io/free-resources.

How Our 4 Level System Works

To make this book as effective as possible for each student, we created a 4 level system. The levels are based on your math ability and scoring goals. The topics included in each level are based on the difficulty of the math topics and how often the topic appears. You can learn more about each level below to find which level is best for you!

How To Find Your Level

The best way to find you level is to complete a practice ACT and use the table below. Go to page ii and read tip 5 to find where to get a practice ACT. If you have not completed a practice ACT, you can use the general descriptions in the table below to find what level sounds like the best match for you.

Level	ACT Math Score	General Description of Student
1	23 and Below	Weak math student
2	24-27	Average math student
3	28-32	Strong math student, often in advanced/honors math courses
4	33-36	Very strong math student in advanced/honors math courses

As your scores increase on practice ACTs and/or as you master the concepts for your level, you can move up to the next level! **To have the best experience with this book, focus on the concepts in each chapter and practice questions that are AT AND BELOW your level.**

The 4 Levels

Level 1 – Core Fundamentals
- **For Students Scoring 23 and Below on ACT Math**

Level 1 is designed for students who find ACT Math difficult and are scoring 23 and below on the ACT Math Test. **Level 1 concepts are the topics on the ACT that are easiest to learn and most commonly tested.**

Learning Level 1 concepts helps weaker math students improve their scores quickly and teaches them how to solve many of the easier questions that appear in questions 1-25 on the ACT Math Test.

Level 2 – Advanced Fundamentals
- **For Students Scoring 24-27 on ACT Math**

Level 2 is designed for average math students who need to review and relearn many concepts they have forgotten from math class. Level 2 also includes some easy-to-learn concepts that students are often never taught in math class. **Level 2 concepts are medium difficulty and are very commonly tested.**

Mastering Level 2 concepts allows average math students to solve more easy and medium difficulty questions that appear in questions 1-45 on the ACT Math Test quickly and easily, leading to much higher scores.

Level 3 – Advanced Topics
  o **For Students Scoring 28-32 on ACT Math**

Level 3 is designed for strong math students aiming for scores of 30+ on the ACT Math Test. Level 3 concepts focus on the advanced topics tested in the questions 45-60 on the ACT Math Test. **If you do well on the first 45 on the ACT and then struggle on questions 45-60, you are definitely a level 3 student!**

Overall, Level 3 concepts include all advanced topics that are commonly and somewhat commonly tested in the last 15 questions of the ACT Math Test. Additionally, level 3 includes other less commonly tested topics that are easy to master for students at this math level. Mastering level 3 concepts prepares students to achieve scores of 30+ on test day.

Level 4 – Expert Level Topics
  o **For Students Aiming for 33-36 on ACT Math**

Level 4 is designed for very strong math students aiming for scores of 33-36 on the ACT Math Test. **You should only complete Level 4 concepts after you have mastered all Level 3 concepts.** Level 4 includes the concepts that are the most advanced and the most uncommon. However, if you want to achieve near perfect or perfect ACT Math scores, you need to know EVERYTHING tested. Mastering level 4 concepts prepares students to achieve scores of 33+ on test day.

How To Best Use The 4-Level System

To have the best experience with this book, focus on the concepts in each chapter and practice questions that are <u>**AT AND BELOW**</u> **your level.** More detailed instructions for each level are written below.

Level 1 Instructions
- **Complete all Level 1 concepts and practice questions.** On chapters you feel confident, try level 2 practice questions as well.
- After mastering Level 1 concepts, start working on Level 2 concepts to keep improving.

Level 2 Instructions
- **Complete all Level 1 & 2 concepts and practice questions.** On chapters you feel confident, try Level 3 practice questions as well.
- After mastering Level 1& 2 concepts, move onto the commonly tested Level 3 concepts (see Level 3 study guide on pg. xv for a list of these concepts).

Level 3 Instructions
- **Complete all Level 1-3 concepts and practice questions.** Many Level 3 concepts are topics that strong math students have never learned or forgotten, so they are important to review to prepare you for scoring 30+ on the ACT.
- Attempt to solve Level 4 practice questions on chapters where you feel confident.

Level 4 Instructions
- **Complete all Level 2-4 concepts and practice questions.** You need to understand EVERYTHING in this book to be ready for a perfect score on test day. You can skip Level 1 questions, as you likely do not need to practice easy questions.

ACT Math Study Guides

The Complete Guide to ACT Math Book can be overwhelming. With 35 chapters and over 1,250 practice questions, it can be difficult to know where you should focus your studying. Not to worry! We have created this ACT Math Study Guide to help you know what topics to study.

How To Use The Study Guides

There are 4 study guides: one for each of the 4 levels. Each study guide lists the concepts you need to understand and equations you need to memorize based on your math level and scoring goals. If you need to find your level, go back to page iii.

We recommend that you the study guides in 2 ways:

1. **Use the study guide as a checklist of chapters to complete in the book.** As you complete each concept and chapter, you can check them off.

2. **Use the study guide to review before test day.** In the 2 weeks before your ACT, go back through the topics you have learned. Make sure that you have all equations memorized, know the concepts you learned, and review any questions you answered incorrectly.

Level 1 Study Guide – Core Fundamentals

Math Level: Easy

Best For: Students Scoring 23 and Below on ACT Math

Prevalence on ACT: Very Common

Level 1 concepts are the most heavily tested topics on the ACT and the ones that everyone needs to know. If you are a weaker math student, start by learning all the topics listed below. Level 1 concepts are the easiest to learn and do not require advanced math skills. Questions in core fundamentals most commonly appear in the first 30 questions on the ACT and sometimes appear in questions 30-44 as well. These topics are rarely tested in the most difficult questions at the end of the ACT Math from 45-60.

As a weaker math student, you should focus on trying to answer as many of the first 44 questions (easy and medium difficulty) correctly. These topics will help you do that! **You will likely run out of time on the ACT Math Test – that is okay!** You should not worry about the more advanced math questions at the end of the test in questions 45-60, as these are designed to stump advanced math students.

2 Test-Taking Tricks To Know

Chapter 1: Backsolving (A Powerful Test-Taking Trick)

Chapter 2: Substitution (Another Test-Taking Trick)

ACT Math Study Guide (Level 1)

Almost Guaranteed to Appear on the ACT

Chapter 3: Geometry Part 1 – Angles
- Intersecting Lines (p. 7) – memorize rules.
- Parallel Lines (p. 7) – memorize rules, understand example 1.
- Interior Angles of Polygons (pp. 8-9) – memorize equation for total interior angles, understand example 3.
- Drawn to Scale Trick (p. 9)

Chapter 4: Geometry Part 2 – Shapes
- Area and Volume (p. 14) – memorize equations, understand example 1.
- Areas, Volumes, and Units (pp. 15-16) – memorize conversions, understand example 4.
- Right Triangles (p. 17) – memorize Pythagorean Theorem, try to understand example 6.
- Similar Triangles (p. 19) – memorize rules, try to understand example 9.
- More Triangles (p. 20) – memorize definitions of equilateral triangle, isosceles triangle, and scalene triangle, try to understand example 10.

Chapter 5: Lines
- Slope (p. 31) – memorize equation, understand example 1.
- Slopes of Parallel and Perpendicular Lines (pp. 31-32) – memorize rules, understand example 3.
- Slope-Intercept Form (pp. 32-33) – memorize equation, understand example 4.
- Standard Form (p. 34) – know how to turn into slope-intercept form, understand example 6.
- Midpoint Formula (p. 34) – memorize equation, understand example 7.
- Distance Formula (p. 35) – memorize equation, understand example 8.
- Solving for Intercepts (p. 36) – memorize rules, understand example 9.

Chapter 6: Fractions
- Combining Fractions (p. 41) – know how to add or subtract fractions with numbers, do not worry about example 1.
- Dividing Fractions (pp. 41-42) – know the flip and multiply trick, try to understand example 2.
- Simplifying Fractions (pp. 42-43) – understand simplifying with numbers, do not worry if variables examples and example 2 are confusing.
- Getting Rid of Fractions (p. 44) – know how to get rid of fractions if you hate fractions!
- Turn Fractions Into Decimals (p. 45) – great trick to make fractions questions easier.
- Use Your Calculator (p. 45) – know how to turn decimals into fractions with your calculator.

Chapter 7: Algebra Skills
- PEMDAS (p. 51) – understand example 1.
- Subtracting Negative Numbers (p. 52) – understand example 2.
- Combining Like Terms (p. 53) – understand example 4.
- Cross Multiply Fractions (p. 53) – understand example 5.
- Algebra with Inequality Signs (p. 55) – memorize rule.

Chapter 8: Number Theory
- Types of Numbers (pp. 61-62) – memorize definitions, understand example 1.
- Properties of Even and Odd Numbers (pp. 62-63) – understand rules.
- Greatest Common Factor (p. 63) – understand example 4.
- Least Common Multiple (p. 64) – understand example 6.

Chapter 9: Percentages

- Simple Percentage (p. 72) – understand examples 1-2.
- Percentage Increase and Decrease (pp. 76-77) – memorize equations, understand example 1.
- Percentage Change (p. 77) – memorize equation, understand example 4.

Chapter 10: Ratios and Proportions

- Ratio and a Total (p. 82) – memorize the "x" trick, understand example 1.
- Ratios as Proportions (p. 83) – understand example 2.

Chapter 11: Functions

- Function Basics (p. 89) – understand examples 1-2.
- Composite Functions (pp. 90) – understand example 4.
- Functions on Graphs (p. 92) – understand example 8.

Chapter 12: Mean, Median, Mode, and Range

- Finding the Average (p. 102) – memorize definitions, understand example 1.
- Finding the Median (p. 105) – understand example 7.

Chapter 13: Exponents and Roots

- Basic Exponent Rules (pp. 112-113) – memorize rules, try to understand examples 1-3.
- Simplifying Square Roots (pp. 114-115) – understand example 5.

Chapter 16: Quadratics

- Multiplying Binomials (p. 135) – understand example 1.
- Factoring Quadratics (p. 136-137) – know how the box method works, try to understand example 2.
- "Easy to Factor" Quadratics (p. 136) – memorize equations.
- Solutions, Roots, x-intercepts, and Zeros for Quadratic Equations (pp. 137-138) – understand example 3.

Chapter 17: Trigonometry

- Basic Trigonometry – SOH-CAH-TOA (pp. 146-147) – understand examples 1-2.

Chapter 19: Matrices

- What is a Matrix? (p. 179)
- Matrix Addition and Subtraction (pp. 179-180) – understand examples 1-2.

Chapter 22: Probability

- The Basics of Probability (pp. 210-211) – understand examples 1-2
- 3 Probability Rules to Know (pp. 211-212) – memorize the 3 rules, understand examples 3-5.

Chapter 26: Word Problems

- Understand 4 Tips for Solving Word Problems (p. 250)

ACT Math Study Guide (Level 1)

Sometimes on the ACT (But Easy If You Know The Rules)

Chapter 18: Absolute Value

- Basics of Absolute Value (p. 173) – understand example 1.

Chapter 21: Circles, Ellipses, and Hyperbolas

- Equation of a Circle (p. 198-199) – memorize equation, understand example 1.

Chapter 23: Factorial, Permutations, Combinations, and Organized Counting

- Organized Counting (p. 226) – understand example 5, do not worry about other examples.

Chapter 24: Sequences

- Arithmetic Sequences (p. 235) – memorize arithmetic sequence definition, understand example 1.
- Geometric Sequences (p. 236) – memorize geometric sequence definition, understand example 3.

Chapter 25: Complex Numbers

- Adding and Subtracting Complex Numbers (p. 241) – understand example 1.
- Use Your Calculator for Complex Numbers (p. 243) – see if your calculator has an i button!

Chapter 27: Inequalities

- Algebra with Inequalities (pp. 256-257) – memorize rule, understand examples 1-2.

Chapter 29: Unit Conversion

- Simple Unit Conversions (p. 271) – understand examples 1-2.

Chapter 30: Scientific Notation

- How To Write Numbers in Scientific Notation (pp. 277-278) – know how to write numbers in scientific notation, understand example 1.

Chapter 32: Vectors

- What is a Vector? (p. 285)
- Vector Addition and Subtraction (p. 286) – understand examples 1-2.

Level 2 Study Guide – Additional Fundamentals

Math Level: Easy, Medium

Best For: Students Scoring 24-27 on ACT Math

Prevalence on ACT: Common, Somewhat Common, Less Common

Level 2 concepts range from very commonly tested to less commonly tested and do not require advanced math skills. These are the concepts, rules, and equations you can learn to quickly boost your score. Many of these concepts are ones you may have never learned in school or have forgotten because you only covered them briefly in math class.

This Level 2 study guide includes some Level 1 concepts that students often need to review and additional Level 2 concepts. **The Level 2 additional fundamentals in this study guide expand your math knowledge and allow you to answer more questions correctly.** Level 2 concepts are of medium difficulty and range from quite commonly tested to less commonly tested, and they are all easy to learn.

Level 2 concepts can appear anywhere in the ACT Math Test, but they most commonly appear in the easy or medium difficulty questions from 11-44. Some topics in this section are "advanced" topics that appear late on the ACT, but they are included in this section because they are not actually too difficult in term of math skills. Instead, these topics are "advanced" simply because they are topics many students are not as familiar with. If you can master these topics, you can answer these questions correctly on test day and boost your math score!!

2 Test-Taking Tricks To Know

Chapter 1: Backsolving (A Powerful Test-Taking Trick)

Chapter 2: Substitution (Another Test-Taking Trick)

Likely To Appear on the ACT

Chapter 3: Geometry Part 1 – Angles

- Intersecting Lines (p. 7) – memorize rules.
- Parallel Lines (p. 7) – memorize rules, understand example 1.
- Interior Angles of Polygons (pp. 8-9) – memorize equation, understand examples 2-3.
- Drawn to Scale Trick (p. 9)

Chapter 4: Geometry Part 2 – Shapes

- Area and Volume (p. 14) – memorize equations, understand examples 1-2.
- Areas, Volumes, and Units (pp. 15-16) – memorize conversions, understand example 4.
- Right Triangles (p. 17) – memorize Pythagorean Theorem, understand example 6.
- Similar Triangles (p. 19) – memorize rules, understand example 9.
- More Triangles (p. 20) – memorize definitions of equilateral triangle, isosceles triangle, and scalene triangle, understand example 10.

Chapter 5: Lines

- Slope (p. 31) – memorize equation, understand examples 1-2.
- Slopes of Parallel and Perpendicular Lines (pp. 31-32) – memorize rules, understand example 3.
- Standard Form (p. 34) – know how to turn into slope-intercept form, understand example 6.
- Midpoint Formula (p. 34) – memorize equation, understand example 7.

ACT Math Study Guide (Level 2)

Chapter 6: Fractions

- Combining Fractions (p. 41) – know how to add or subtract fractions with numbers, try to understand example 1.
- Dividing Fractions (pp. 41-42) – know the flip and multiply trick, understand example 2.
- Simplifying Fractions (pp. 42-43) – understand simplifying with numbers and variables, understand example 3.
- Getting Rid of Fractions (p. 44) – know how to get rid of fractions if you hate fractions!
- Turn Fractions Into Decimals (p. 45) – great trick to make fractions questions easier.
- Use Your Calculator (p. 45) – know how to turn decimals into fractions with your calculator.

Chapter 7: Algebra Skills

- PEMDAS (p. 51) – understand example 1.
- Subtracting Negative Numbers (p. 52) – understand example 2.
- Negative Numbers and Exponents (p. 52) – understand how to enter negative numbers and exponents correctly in your calculator.
- Square Both Sides of an Equation Correctly (p. 54) – understand example 6.
- Algebra with Inequality Signs (p. 55) – memorize rule, understand example 7.
- Taking Square Roots in Algebraic Equations (p. 56) – memorize when to use the $\pm$ sign, understand example 8.

Chapter 8: Number Theory

- Types of Numbers (pp. 61-62) – memorize definitions, understand example 1.
- Properties of Even and Odd Numbers (pp. 62-63) – understand example 3.
- Greatest Common Factor (p. 63) – understand example 4.
- Least Common Multiple (p. 64) – understand example 6.

Chapter 9: Percentages

- Simple Percentage (p. 72) – understand examples 1-2.
- Percentage Increase and Decrease (pp. 76-77) – memorize equations, understand examples 1-2.
- Percentage Change (p. 77) – memorize equation, understand example 4.

Chapter 10: Ratios and Proportions

- Ratio and a Total (p. 82) – memorize the "x" trick, understand example 1.
- Ratios as Proportions (p. 83) – understand example 2.

Chapter 11: Functions

- Function Basics (p. 89) – understand examples 1-3.
- Composite Functions (pp. 90) – understand example 4.

Chapter 12: Mean, Median, Mode, and Range

- Finding the Average (pp. 102-103) – understand examples 1 and 2.
- Mean, Median, Mode, and Outliers (p. 105) – understand example 6.
- Finding the Median (p. 105) – understand example 7.

Chapter 13: Exponents and Roots

- Basic Exponent Rules (pp. 112-113) – memorize rules (especially the fractional exponent rule), understand examples 1-3.
- Simplifying Square Roots (pp. 114-115) – understand examples 5-6.

Chapter 14: Logarithms
- Basics of Logarithms (pp. 123-124) – know how to turn a logarithm to exponential form, understand examples 1-2.
- Memorize Change of Base Rule (pp. 123-124)

Chapter 15: Systems of Equations
- Solving with Elimination and Substitution (p. 129) – understand examples 1-2.
- Word Problems (p. 130) – understand example 3.

Chapter 16: Quadratics
- Multiplying Binomials (p. 135) – understand example 1.
- Factoring Quadratics (p. 136-137) – understand example 2.
- "Easy to Factor" Quadratics (p. 136) – memorize equations.
- Solutions, Roots, x-intercepts, and Zeros for Quadratic Equations (pp. 137-138) – understand example 3.

Chapter 17: Trigonometry
- Basic Trigonometry – SOH-CAH-TOA (pp. 146-147) – understand examples 1-3.
- Using Trigonometry to Find Side Lengths in Right Triangles (pp. 147-148) – understand examples 4-5.
- Inverse Trigonometric Functions (pp. 148-149) – understand example 6.
- Amplitude (p. 151) – memorize rule, understand example 8.

Chapter 19: Matrices
- What is a Matrix? (p. 179)
- Matrix Addition and Subtraction (pp. 179-180) – understand examples 1-2.

Chapter 20: Repeating Patterns
- Repeating Decimals (p. 191) – understand examples 1-2.

Chapter 22: Probability
- The Basics of Probability (pp. 210-211) – understand examples 1-2.
- 3 Probability Rules to Know (pp. 211-212) – memorize the 3 rules, understand examples 3-5.

Chapter 23: Factorial, Permutations, Combinations, and Organized Counting
- Factorial (p. 224) – understand example 1 and factorial with numbers.
- Organized Counting (pp. 226-227) – understand examples 5-7.

Chapter 26: Word Problems
- Understand 4 Tips for Solving Word Problems (p. 250)

Chapter 29: Unit Conversion
- Simple Unit Conversions (p. 271) – understand examples 1-2.

Sometimes On The ACT

Chapter 5: Lines

- Point-Slope Form (p. 33) – memorize equation, understand example 5.
- Distance Formula (p. 35) – memorize equation, understand example 8.
- Solving for Intercepts (p. 36) – memorize rules, understand example 9.

Chapter 16: Quadratics

- How Solutions Appear on a Graph (pp. 138-139) – memorize rules, understand example 5.
- The Quadratic Formula (p. 139) – memorize equation, understand example 6.

Chapter 18: Absolute Value

- Basics of Absolute Value (p. 173) – understand example 1.
- Absolute Value and Unknown Variables (pp. 173-174) – understand example 2.

Chapter 21: Circles, Ellipses, and Hyperbolas

- Equation of a Circle (p. 198-199) – memorize equation, understand examples 1-2.

Chapter 24: Sequences

- Arithmetic Sequences (p. 235) – memorize arithmetic sequence definition, understand example 1.
- Geometric Sequences (p. 236) – memorize geometric sequence definition, understand example 3.

Chapter 25: Complex Numbers

- Adding and Subtracting Complex Numbers (p. 241) – understand example 1.
- Multiplying Complex Numbers (pp. 241-242) – understand example 2.
- Use Your Calculator for Complex Numbers (p. 243) – see if your calculator has an *i* button!

Chapter 30: Scientific Notation

- How To Write Numbers in Scientific Notation (pp. 277-278) – understand examples 1-2.

Chapter 32: Vectors

- What is a Vector? (p. 285)
- Vector Addition and Subtraction (p. 286) – understand examples 1-2.

ACT Math Study Guide (Level 2)

Less Commonly Tested

Chapter 4: Geometry Part 2 – Shapes

- Special Right Triangles (p. 18) – memorize triangle proportions, understand example 7.

Chapter 8: Number Theory

- Prime Factorization (p. 65) – understand example 7.
- One Solution vs. Infinite Solutions, vs. No Solution (pp. 66-67) – memorize rules, understand example 8.

Chapter 10: Ratios and Proportions

- Comparing Across Ratios (p. 83) – understand example 3.
- Ratios and Geometry (p. 84) – understand example 4.

Chapter 11: Functions

- Other Function Notations (p. 91) – understand example 6.
- Functions on Graphs (pp. 92-93) – understand examples 8-9.
- Domain and Range (pp. 93-94) – memorize definitions, understand example 10.

Chapter 19: Matrices

- Matrix Dimensions (p. 179)
- Finding the Determinant of a (2 × 2) Matrix (p. 181) – memorize equation.

Chapter 22: Probability

- Probability and Data Tables (p. 213) – understand examples 6-7.
- Expected Value (p. 216) – understand example 11.

Chapter 27: Inequalities

- Algebra with Inequalities (pp. 256-257) – memorize rule, understand examples 1-2.
- Graphing Inequalities (pp. 257-258) – memorize rules, understand example 3.

Chapter 33: Shifting and Transforming Functions

- Rules for Shifting and Transforming Functions (p. 291) – memorize rules.

Chapter 35: Miscellaneous Topics

- Venn Diagrams (pp. 305-306) – understand example 1.
- Mapping (p. 308) – understand example 5.

Rarely Tested

Chapter 10: Ratios and Proportions
- Direct and Indirect Proportions (pp. 84-85) – memorize equations, understand example 5.

Chapter 12: Mean, Median, Mode, and Range
- Finding the Median in a Table (p. 106) – understand example 8.

Chapter 16: Quadratics
- The Vertex (p. 141) – memorize vertex form equation and how to find x-coordinate of the vertex, understand example 9.

Chapter 17: Trigonometry
- Trigonometric Identity To Know (p. 149) – memorize identity, understand example 7.

Chapter 25: Complex Numbers
- The Complex Conjugate (pp. 242-243) – memorize definition.

Chapter 28: Exponential Growth and Decay
- Exponential Growth and Decay Equations (p. 264) – memorize equations.
- Exponential Growth (pp. 264-265) – understand example 1.
- Exponential Decay (p. 265) – understand example 2.
- General Exponential Form (p. 266) – memorize general form and what the constants mean.

Chapter 31: Arcs and Sectors
- Arcs (pp. 280-281) – memorize equation, understand examples 1-2.
- Inscribed Angle Theorem (p. 281) – memorize rule.
- Sectors (pp. 281-282) – memorize equation, understand examples 3-4.

Chapter 34: Statistics
- Description of A Survey (pp. 296-297) – memorize definitions and understand example 1.
- Shapes of Distributions (pp. 297-298) – memorize definitions and understand example 2.
- Stem and Leaf Plot (pp. 299-300) – understand example 5.
- Sample proportion (pp. 300-301) – understand example 6.

Chapter 35: Miscellaneous Topics
- Made-Up Math (p. 306) – understand example 2.
- Logic (p. 307) – memorize contrapositive rule, understand example 3.

Level 3 Study Guide – Advanced Topics

Math Level: Medium, Hard

Best For: Students Scoring 28-32

Prevalence on ACT: Common, Somewhat Common, Less Common, Rarely Tested

If you want to score 30+ on the ACT Math, you need to know how to solve these advanced topics. These advanced topics are the ones that are commonly tested on the difficult and very difficult questions from 45-60. Now, do not let the "advanced" name intimidate you. Yes, some of these topics are very difficult, but many are "advanced" simply because most students do not know them.

If you work through these topics and memorize the equations, you will know how to solve many "advanced" questions at the end of ACT Math Tests from questions 45-60 and will be in the best position to score 30+ on test day!

2 Test-Taking Tricks To Know

Chapter 1: Backsolving (A Powerful Test-Taking Trick)

Chapter 2: Substitution (Another Test-Taking Trick)

Level 1 and 2 Topics to Make Sure You Know

Before starting the advanced topics listed on the following pages, make sure you know the topics listed below from the core fundamentals (Level 1) and advanced fundamentals (Level 2). These topics are ones that we have seen many students, even very strong math students, struggle on. Many of these topics are not taught in school or are taught very briefly. To score 30+, you NEED to know all these fundamental topics.

Chapter 3: Geometry Part 1 – Angles

- Interior Angles of Polygons (pp. 8-9) – memorize equation, understand examples 2-3.
- Drawn to Scale Trick (p. 9)

Chapter 4: Geometry Part 2 – Shapes

- Area and Volume (p. 14) – memorize equations, understand examples 1-3.
- Areas, Volumes, and Units (pp. 15-16) – memorize conversions, understand example 4.
- Special Right Triangles (p. 18) – memorize triangle proportions, understand example 7.

Chapter 5: Lines

- Point-Slope Form (p. 33) – memorize equation, understand example 5.
- Midpoint Formula (p. 34) – memorize equation, understand example 7.
- Distance Formula (p. 35) – memorize equation, understand example 8.
- Solving for Intercepts (p. 36) – memorize rules, understand example 9.

Chapter 6: Fractions

- Combining Fractions (p. 41) – know how to add or subtract fractions with numbers and variables, understand example 1.
- Dividing Fractions (pp. 41-42) – know the flip and multiply trick, understand example 2.
- Use Your Calculator (p. 45) – know how to turn decimals into fractions with your calculator.

ACT Math Study Guide (Level 3)

Chapter 7: Algebra Skills
- Negative Numbers and Exponents (p. 52) – understand how to enter negative numbers and exponents correctly in your calculator, understand example 3.
- Taking Square Roots in Algebraic Equations (p. 56) – memorize when to use the $\pm$ sign, understand example 8.

Chapter 8: Number Theory
- Types of Numbers (pp. 61-62) – memorize definitions, understand examples 1-2.
- Greatest Common Factor (p. 63) – understand examples 4-5.
- Least Common Multiple (p. 64) – understand example 6.
- One Solution vs. Infinite Solutions, vs. No Solution (pp. 66-67) – memorize rules, understand example 8.

Chapter 9: Percentages
- Simple Percentage (pp. 72-73) – understand example 3.
- Percentage Increase and Decrease (pp. 76-77) – memorize equations, understand examples 1-3.
- Percentage Change (p. 77) – memorize equation, understand example 4.

Chapter 10: Ratios and Proportions
- Ratio and a Total (p. 82) – memorize the "x" trick, understand example 1.
- Comparing Across Ratios (p. 83) – understand example 3.
- Ratios and Geometry (p. 84) – understand example 4.
- Direct and Indirect Proportions (pp. 84-85) – memorize the equations, understand examples 5-6.

Chapter 11: Functions
- Composite Functions (pp. 90-91) – understand example 5.
- Other Function Notations (p. 91) – understand example 6.

Chapter 12: Mean, Median, Mode, and Range
- Finding the Average (pp. 102-104) – understand examples 1-5.
- Outliers and Mean, Median, Mode, and Range (p. 105) – understand examples 6-7.
- Finding the Median in a Table (p. 106) – understand example 8.

Chapter 13: Exponents and Roots
- Basic Exponent Rules (pp. 112-113) – memorize rules (especially the fractional exponent rule), understand examples 1-3, understand change of base trick for example 4.
- Simplifying Square Roots (pp. 114-115) – understand examples 5-6.

Chapter 14: Logarithms
- Basics of Logarithms (pp. 123-124) – know how to turn a logarithm to exponential form, understand examples 1-2.
- Memorize Change of Base Rule (pp. 123-124)

Chapter 15: Systems of Equations
- Solving with Elimination and Substitution (p. 129) – understand examples 1-2.
- Word Problems (pp. 130-131) – understand examples 3 and 4.

Chapter 16: Quadratics

- "Easy to Factor" Quadratics (p. 136) – memorize equations, understand example 2.
- Solutions for Quadratic Equations (pp. 137-138) – understand examples 3-4.
- How Solutions Appear on a Graph (pp. 138-139) – memorize rules, understand example 5.
- The Quadratic Formula (p. 139) – memorize equation, understand example 6.

Chapter 17: Trigonometry

- Basic Trigonometry – SOH-CAH-TOA (pp. 146-147) – understand examples 1-3.
- Using Trigonometry to Find Side Lengths in Right Triangles (pp. 147-148) – understand examples 4-5.
- Inverse Trigonometric Functions (pp. 148-149) – understand example 6.
- Trigonometric Identity To Know (p. 149) – memorize identity, understand example 7.
- Amplitude (p. 151) – memorize rule, understand example 8.

Chapter 18: Absolute Value

- Absolute Value and Unknown Variables (pp. 173-174) – understand example 2.

Chapter 19: Matrices

- What is a Matrix? (p. 179)
- Matrix Addition and Subtraction (pp. 179-180) – understand examples 1-2.
- Matrix Dimensions (p. 179)
- Finding the Determinant of a (2×2) Matrix (p. 181) – memorize equation, understand example 3.

Chapter 20: Repeating Patterns

- Repeating Decimals (p. 191) – understand examples 1-2.

Chapter 21: Circles, Ellipses, and Hyperbolas

- Equation of a Circle (p. 198-199) – memorize equation, understand examples 1-2.

Chapter 22: Probability

- 3 Probability Rules to Know (pp. 211-212) – memorize the 3 rules, understand examples 3-5.
- Probability and Data Tables (p. 213) – understand examples 6-7.

Chapter 23: Permutations, Combinations, and Organized Counting

- Factorial (p. 224) – understand example 1 and factorial with numbers, do not worry about example 2.
- Organized Counting (pp. 226-227) – understand examples 5-7.

Chapter 24: Sequences

- Arithmetic Sequences (p. 235) – memorize arithmetic sequence definition, understand example 1.
- Geometric Sequences (p. 236) – memorize geometric sequence definition, understand example 3.

Chapter 25: Complex Numbers

- Multiplying Complex Numbers (pp. 241-242) – understand example 2.
- The Complex Conjugate (pp. 242-243) – memorize rule, understand example 3.
- Use Your Calculator for Complex Numbers (p. 243) – see if your calculator has an i button!

ACT Math Study Guide (Level 3)

Chapter 26: Word Problems
- Understand 4 Tips for Solving Word Problems (p. 250)

Chapter 27: Inequalities
- Graphing Inequalities (pp. 257-258) – memorize rules, understand example 3.

Chapter 28: Exponential Growth and Decay
- Exponential Growth and Decay Equations (p. 264) – memorize equations.
- Exponential Growth (pp. 264-265) – understand example 1.
- Exponential Decay (p. 265) – understand example 2.
- General Exponential Form (p. 266) – memorize general form and what the constants mean.

Chapter 30: Scientific Notation
- How To Write Numbers in Scientific Notation (pp. 277-278) – understand examples 1-2.

Chapter 31: Arcs and Sectors
- Arcs (pp. 280-281) – memorize equation, understand examples 1-2.
- Inscribed Angle Theorem (p. 281) – memorize rule.
- Sectors (pp. 281-282) – memorize equation, understand examples 3-4.

Chapter 32: Vectors
- What is a Vector? (p. 285)
- Vector Addition and Subtraction (p. 286) – understand examples 1-2.

Chapter 34: Statistics
- Description of A Survey (pp. 296-297) – memorize definitions and understand example 1.
- Shapes of Distributions (pp. 297-298) – memorize definitions and understand example 2.
- Stem and Leaf Plot (pp. 299-300) – understand example 5.
- Sample proportion (pp. 300-301) – understand example 6.

Chapter 35: Miscellaneous Topics
- Venn Diagrams (pp. 305-306) – understand example 1.
- Made-Up Math (p. 306)
- Logic (p. 307) – memorize contrapositive rule.
- Mapping (p. 308) – understand example 5.

ACT Math Study Guide (Level 3)

Advanced Topics for Level 3 Students

The advanced topics listed below are the ones that are commonly tested on the difficult and very difficult questions from 45-60 at the end of the ACT Math Test. **We recommend that you work down the list in the order it is presented: start with the topics that you are likely to see on test day and work your way to the rarely tested topics.** If you have limited time preparing for the ACT, do not worry about completing the "Rarely Tested" topics.

Mastering the advanced topics and memorizing the equations listed below will prepare you for the advanced questions at the end of ACT Math Tests and put you in the best position to score 30+ on test day!

Likely to See on Test Day

Chapter 17: Trigonometry

- Law of Sines (pp. 158-159) – memorize equation, understand example 12.
- Law of Cosines (pp. 160) – memorize equation, understand example 14.

Chapter 19: Matrices

- Matrix Multiplication (pp. 182-186) – understand examples 4-5.

Chapter 21: Circles and Ellipses

- Advanced Circle Questions (pp. 199-200) – memorize 2 principles, understand examples 3-4.
- Ellipses (pp. 201-202) – memorize ellipse equation, know how to draw an ellipse given the equation, understand examples 5-6.
- Foci on an Ellipse (p. 203) – know where the foci are located.

Chapter 22: Probability

- Advanced Probability Questions (pp. 214-215) – understand examples 8-10.

Sometimes on the ACT

Chapter 4: Geometry Part 2 – Shapes

- Volume of Other Three-Dimensional Solids (p. 16) – memorize equation, understand example 5.
- Third Side of a Triangle Rule (p. 21) – memorize rule, understand example 11.
- Other Rules You Might Need To Know (p. 22) – memorize all rules and equations.

Chapter 12: Median, Mode, and Range

- Weighted Average (p. 104) – memorize equation, understand examples 3-4.

Chapter 13: Exponents and Roots

- Cube Roots (pp. 115-116) – understand example 7.
- Roots and Variables with Powers (p. 116) – understand example 8.

Chapter 29: Unit Conversion

- Dimensional Analysis (pp. 272-273) – understand examples 3-4.

ACT Math Study Guide (Level 3)

Chapter 32: Vectors

- Vector Addition and Subtraction on A Graph (pp. 286-287) – know "tip-to-tail" method, understand example 3.
- Magnitude of a Vector (p. 288) – memorize definition and equation.

Less Commonly Tested

Chapter 17: Trigonometry

- Graphing Cosine and Sine Functions (p. 150) – know basics about each graph.
- Period (pp. 152-153) – memorize rule, understand example 9.
- Vertical and Horizontal Shifts for Sine and Cosine Functions (pp. 154-155)
- Summary of Transformation Rules for Sine and Cosine Functions (p. 155) – memorize rules.

Chapter 20: Repeating Patterns

- Repeating Patterns with Powers and the Units Digit (pp. 192-193) – understand example 3, recognize commonly tested repeating patterns with powers and the units digit (do not need to memorize)
- Repeating Patterns with Powers of i (p. 194) – memorize pattern, understand example 5.
- How to Solve Repeating Patterns Questions (p. 195)

Chapter 23: Factorial, Permutations, Combinations, and Organized Counting

- Permutations (p. 225) – know how to use your calculator to solve, understand example 3.
- Combinations (p. 226) – know how to use your calculator to solve, understand example 4.

Chapter 27: Inequalities

- Advanced Graphing Inequalities (pp. 259-260) – memorize rules for shading, understand example 4.

Chapter 33: Shifting and Transforming Functions

- Rules for Shifting and Transforming Functions (p. 291) – memorize rules.
- Graphing and Shifting Cubics (p. 292)
- Shifting All Other Functions (p. 293)

Rarely Tested

Chapter 11: Functions

- Domain and Range (pp. 93-95) – memorize rules, understand examples 10-13.
- Inverse Functions (p. 96) – understand example 14.

Chapter 14: Logarithms

- Logarithm Rules (p. 124-125) – memorize rules, understand example 3.
- Natural Logarithms (p. 125) – understand example 5.

Chapter 16: Quadratics

- The Discriminant (p. 140) – memorize rules, understand example 7.
- The Vertex (pp. 141-142) – memorize vertex form equation and how to find x-coordinate of the vertex, understand examples 9-10.

Chapter 17: Trigonometry
- Unit Circle (pp. 161-163) – refamiliarize yourself with the unit circle. You do not need to memorize the entire thing. Memorize 3 basic principles of the unit circle and the "All Students Take Calculus" rule. Understand example 16.

Chapter 18: Absolute Value
- Absolute Value and Inequalities (pp. 174-175) – understand examples 3-4.

Chapter 22: Probability
- Expected Value (pp. 216-217) – memorize equation, understand examples 11-12.

Chapter 24: Sequences
- Recursive Sequences (p. 237) – understand how to use recursive sequences and example 4.

Chapter 25: Complex Numbers
- The Complex Plane (p. 244) – know how to graph complex numbers on the complex plane, understand example 4.

Chapter 34: Statistics
- Standard Deviation (pp. 298-299) – memorize rule, understand examples 3-4

Chapter 35: Miscellaneous Topics
- Pattern Spotting (p. 307-308) – understand example 4.
- Binomial Theorem and Pascal's Triangle (pp. 310-311) – understand example 7. You do not need to know how to draw Pascal's Triangle.
- Vertical Asymptotes (p. 313) – memorize rule, understand example 10.

ACT Math Study Guide (Level 4)

Level 4 Study Guide – Expert Level Topics

Math Level: Hard, Expert

Best For: Students Aiming For 33-36 on ACT Math

Prevalence on ACT: Less Common, Rarely Tested

If your goal is to score 33-36 on the ACT Math, you need to know EVERYTHING tested on the ACT. That means you should understand EVERYTHING in this book. While knowing everything is a challenging task given how many topics the ACT Math includes, Level 4 concepts cover the most common obscure and rarely tested topics that you can see on test day and the additional equations you should memorize. All these topics have appeared on the ACT before, so they are fair game to appear on your ACT.

Before you work on Level 4 concepts, makes sure that you know all the topics in the Level 3 study guide and have all the equations memorized. All topics in this section are very advanced and rarely tested, so you should only move onto these topics once you have mastered everything in the Level 3 study guide.

Important Tips to Achieve 33-36

If you are aiming for 33-36, make sure you know how to solve all level 4 questions at the end of each chapter. These questions are written specifically for students like you and will help you learn how to solve the most advanced questions that appear on the ACT.

The difficult questions at the end of each ACT Math Test (questions 45-60) can include any topic. Most commonly, it is a mix of advanced topics (Ex: matrix multiplication, ellipses, law of sines, etc.) and regular topics (ratios, averages, quadratics, geometry, etc.) presented in a difficult way. Therefore, it is important to make sure you work through the level 2-4 question in all chapters of this book even if the general topic of the chapter seems easy.

To achieve a 33-36, you need to (1) have all the equations and rules memorized for test day and (2) be familiar with all topics on the ACT so you can set up and solve questions quickly and efficiently on test day. Time management can be the difference between a 32 and a 35. Putting in the time and working through all chapters of this book will put you in the best position for achieving your goals on test day!

2 Test-Taking Tricks To Know

Chapter 1: Backsolving (A Powerful Test-Taking Trick)

Chapter 2: Substitution (Another Test-Taking Trick)

ACT Math Study Guide (Level 4)

Expert Level Topics to Know

Before starting these topics, go to the Level 3 Study Guide and make sure you know all Level 3 topics! There are some level 2 and level 3 topics included in the list below. These are topics that we see many strong math students struggle with because the topics are not commonly taught in school or are the ones students commonly forget. All topics listed below are very important ones to master for anyone aiming for 33-36 on the ACT.

Chapter 4: Geometry Part 2 – Shapes

- Volume of Other Three-Dimensional Solids (p. 16) – memorize equation, understand example 5.
- Special Right Triangles (p. 18) – understand example 8.
- Third Side of a Triangle Rule (p. 21) – memorize rule, understand example 11.
- Other Rules You Might Need To Know (p. 22) – memorize all rules and equations

Chapter 7: Algebra Skills

- Negative Numbers and Exponents (p. 52) – understand how to enter negative numbers and exponents correctly in your calculator, understand example 3.
- Taking Square Roots in Algebraic Equations (p. 56) – memorize when to use the $\pm$ sign, understand example 8.

Chapter 8: Number Theory

- Types of Numbers (pp. 61-62) – memorize definitions, understand examples 1-2.
- One Solution vs. Infinite Solutions, vs. No Solution (pp. 66-67) – memorize rules.

Chapter 10: Ratios and Proportions

- Comparing Across Ratios (p. 83) - understand example 3.
- Direct and Indirect Proportions (pp. 84-85) – memorize the equations, understand examples 5-6.

Chapter 11: Functions

- Other Function Notation (pp. 91-92) – understand example 7.
- Domain and Range (pp. 93-95) – memorize rules and understand examples 11-13.
- Inverse Functions (p. 96) – understand example 14.

Chapter 12: Median, Mode, and Range

- Weighted Average (pp. 103-104) – memorize equation, understand examples 3-4.
- Finding the Average (pp. 104-105) – understand example 5.

Chapter 13: Exponents and Roots

- Basic Exponent Rules (pp. 112-113) – memorize rules (especially the fractional exponent rule), understand change of base trick for example 4.
- Cube Roots (pp. 115-116) – understand example 7.
- Roots and Variables with Powers (p. 116) – understand example 8.

Chapter 14: Logarithms

- Memorize Change of Base Rule (pp. 123-124)
- Logarithm Rules (pp. 124-125) – memorize rules, understand examples 3-4.
- Natural Logarithms (p. 125) – understand example 5.

Chapter 15: Systems of Equations

- Word Problems (pp. 130-131) – understand examples 3 and 4.

Chapter 16: Quadratics

- The Quadratic Formula (p. 139) – memorize equation, understand example 6.
- The Discriminant (p. 140) – memorize rules, understand examples 7-8.
- The Vertex (pp. 141-142) – memorize vertex form equation and how to find x-coordinate of the vertex, understand examples 9-10.

Chapter 17: Trigonometry

- Trigonometric Identity To Know (p. 149) – memorize identity, understand example 7.
- Graphing Cosine and Sine Functions (p. 150) – know basics about each graph.
- Period (pp. 152-153) – memorize rules, understand example 9.
- Vertical and Horizontal Shifts for Sine and Cosine Functions (pp. 154-155) – understand example 10.
- Summary of Transformation Rules for Sine and Cosine Functions (p. 155) – memorize rules.
- Graphing Tangent Functions (pp. 156-157) – know basics of graph and period rules, understand example 11.
- Law of Sines (pp. 158-159) – memorize equation, understand examples 12-13.
- Law of Cosines (p. 160) – memorize equation, understand example 14.
- Unit Circle (pp. 161-163) – memorize the unit circle, memorize 3 basic principles of the unit circles and the "All Students Take Calculus" rule, understand examples 15-16.

Chapter 18: Absolute Value

- Absolute Value and Inequalities (pp. 174-175) – know how to set up and solve, understand examples 3-4.

Chapter 19: Matrices

- Matrix Dimensions (p. 179)
- Finding the Determinant of a (2×2) Matrix (p. 181) – memorize equation, understand example 3.
- Matrix Multiplication (pp. 182-186) – understand examples 4-5.

Chapter 20: Repeating Patterns

- Repeating Decimals (p. 191) – understand examples 1-2.
- Repeating Patterns with Powers and the Units Digit (pp. 192-193) – understand examples 3-4, recognize commonly tested repeating patterns with powers and the units digit (do not need to memorize)
- Repeating Patterns with Powers of i (p. 194) – memorize pattern, understand examples 5-6.
- How to Solve Repeating Patterns Questions (p. 195)

Chapter 21: Circles, Ellipses, and Hyperbolas

- Equation of a Circle (p. 198-199) – memorize equation, understand examples 1-2.
- Ellipses (pp. 201-202) – memorize ellipse equation, know how to draw an ellipse given the equation, understand examples 5-6.
- Foci on an Ellipse (p. 203) – understand examples 6-7.
- Hyperbolas (pp. 204-205) – memorize equations for vertical and horizontal hyperbolas, understand example 8.

ACT Math Study Guide (Level 4)

Chapter 22: Probability
- 3 Probability Rules to Know (pp. 211-212) – memorize the 3 rules, understand examples 3-5.
- Advanced Probability Questions (pp. 214-215) – understand examples 8-10
- Expected Value (pp. 216-217) – memorize equation, understand examples 11-12

Chapter 23: Permutations, Combinations, and Organized Counting
- Factorial (p. 224) – understand factorial definition and examples 1-2.
- Permutations (p. 225) – know how to use your calculator to solve, understand example 3.
- Combinations (p. 226) – know how to use your calculator to solve, understand example 4.
- Organized Counting (p. 227) – understand examples 6-7.
- Advanced Combinations, Permutations, and Organized Counting (pp. 228-229) – understand examples 8-9.

Chapter 24: Sequences
- Arithmetic Sequences (p. 235) – memorize equation and understand example 2.
- Geometric Sequences (p. 236) – memorize equation at bottom of page.
- Recursive Sequences (p. 237) – understand how to use recursive sequences and example 4.
- Explicit Formula for Recursive Sequences (p. 238) – understand example 5.

Chapter 25: Complex Numbers
- The Complex Conjugate (pp. 242-243) – memorize rule, understand example 3.
- Use Your Calculator for Complex Numbers (p. 243) – see if your calculator has an *i* button!
- The Complex Plane (p. 244) – know how to graph complex numbers on the complex plane, understand example 4.
- Absolute Value of a Complex Number (pp. 244-245) – memorize equation, understand example 5.
- Distance Between Complex Numbers (p. 245) – memorize equation, understand example 6.

Chapter 26: Word Problems
- Understand 4 Tips for Solving Word Problems (p. 250)

Chapter 27: Inequalities
- Advanced Graphing Inequalities (pp. 259-260) – memorize rules for shading, understand examples 4-5.

Chapter 28: Exponential Growth and Decay
- Exponential Growth and Decay Equations (p. 264) – memorize equations.
- Exponential Growth (pp. 264-265) – understand example 1.
- Exponential Decay (p. 265) – understand example 2.
- General Exponential Form (p. 266) – memorize general form and what the constants mean.
- Graphing General Exponential Form (pp. 266-267)
- Advanced Exponential Growth and Decay Equations (p. 267) – memorize equations, understand example 3.

Chapter 29: Unit Conversion
- Dimensional Analysis (pp. 272-273) – understand examples 3-5.

Chapter 31: Arcs and Sectors

- Arcs (pp. 280-281) – memorize equation, understand examples 1-2.
- Inscribed Angle Theorem (p. 281) – memorize rule.
- Sectors (pp. 281-282) – memorize equation, understand examples 3-4.

Chapter 32: Vectors

- What is a Vector? (p. 285)
- Vector Addition and Subtraction (p. 286) – understand examples 1-2.
- Vector Addition and Subtraction on A Graph (pp. 286-287) – know "tip-to-tail" method, understand example 3.
- Magnitude of a Vector (p. 288) – memorize definition and equation.

Chapter 33: Shifting and Transforming Functions

- Rules for Shifting and Transforming Functions (p. 291) – memorize rules.
- Graphing and Shifting Cubics (p. 292)
- Shifting All Other Functions (p. 293)

Chapter 34: Statistics

- Description of A Survey (pp. 296-297) – memorize definitions and understand example 1.
- Shapes of Distributions (pp. 297-298) – memorize definitions and understand example 2.
- Standard Deviation (pp. 298-299) – memorize rule, understand examples 3-4.
- Stem and Leaf Plot (pp. 299-300) – understand example 5.
- Sample proportion (pp. 300-301) – understand example 6.
- Normal Distribution and The Empirical Rule (p. 301) – memorize rules, understand example 7.

Chapter 35: Miscellaneous Topics

- Logic (p. 307) – memorize contrapositive rule, understand example 3.
- Pattern Spotting (p. 307-308) – understand example 4.
- Puzzles (p. 309) – understand example 6.
- Binomial Theorem and Pascal's Triangle (pp. 310-311) – know how to draw Pascal's Triangle, understand examples 7-8.
- Visual Spatial (p. 312) – understand how to solve example 9.
- Asymptotes (pp. 313-315) – memorize vertical and horizontal asymptote rules, understand examples 10-11.

ACT Math Equation Sheet

Below are the equations that you need to memorize for test day. There are many additional rules, approaches, and strategies that are covered in this book that you need to know as well.

Chapter 3: Geometry Part 1 - Angles

Vertical angles are equal.

Adjacent angles are supplementary ($x + y = 180°$)

Given 2 parallel lines,

$\angle 1 = \angle 4 = \angle 5 = \angle 8$

$\angle 2 = \angle 3 = \angle 6 = \angle 7$

Sum of Interior Angles = $180°(n - 2)$ where n is the number of sides.

Chapter 4: Geometry Part 2 – Shapes

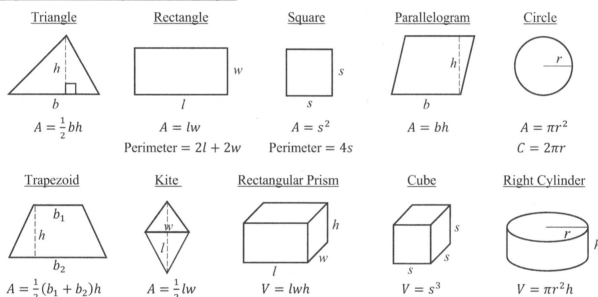

Volumes of Other Three-Dimensional Solids: $V = B \times h$ (where B is the area of the base and h is the height).

Pythagorean Theorem: $a^2 + b^2 = c^2$

Pythagorean Triples: 3, 4, 5 Right Triangle; 5, 12, 13 Right Triangle

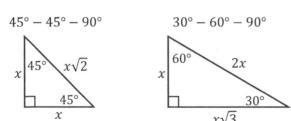

Third Side of a Triangle Rule

The sum of the two shorter sides of a triangle, a and b, must be greater than the longest side of a triangle, c

$$a + b > c$$

Area of Equilateral Triangle: $A = \frac{s^2\sqrt{3}}{4}$

- xxvii -

Chapter 5: Lines

Slope $= \frac{rise}{run} = \frac{y_1-y_2}{x_1-x_2}$

midpoint $= \left(\frac{x_1+x_2}{2}, \frac{y_1+y_2}{2}\right)$

Point-Slope Form: $y - y_1 = m(x - x_1)$

Distance $= \sqrt{(x_1-x_2)^2 + (y_1-y_2)^2}$

Chapter 8: Number Theory

Types of Numbers:

- Integers are whole numbers (Ex: $-4, 3, 102$).
- Prime Numbers are integers that are only divisible by 1 and itself (Ex: 2, 3, 5, 7, 11 ...). Note that 1 is not a prime number and 2 is the only prime even number.
- Rational numbers are any number that can be expressed as a fraction (Ex: $\frac{2}{5}, -\frac{11}{3}$). Any integer is also a rational number (Ex: $-22, 3{,}600, 12$).
- Irrational numbers are any numbers that cannot be expressed as a fraction (Ex: $\pi, \sqrt{5}$).
- Undefined numbers are numbers with a zero in the denominator (Ex: $\frac{6}{0}, -\frac{10}{0}$).
- Imaginary numbers are real numbers multiplied by the imaginary unit i (Ex: $-3i, 8i$).

Greatest Common Factor: The greatest common factor of a set of numbers is the largest positive integer that divides evenly into all numbers in the set with no remainder. For example, for the set of numbers 12, 18, and 30, the greatest common factor is 6.

Least Common Multiple: The least common multiple is the smallest positive integer that is divisible by all numbers in the set. For example, the least common multiple of 2 and 3 is 6.

One Solution	Zero Solutions	Infinite Solutions
• Coefficients for the x-terms are different. • Constants (numbers) can be same or different.	• Coefficients for the x-terms are the same. • Constants (numbers) are different.	• Both sides of the equation must be identical. • Coefficients for the x-terms and constants are the same.

Chapter 9: Percentages

$\frac{is}{of} = \frac{\%}{100}$

Percentage Change $= \frac{\text{Final Value} - \text{Initial Value}}{\text{Initial Value}} \times 100$

Percentage greater than: $\frac{\text{New}}{\text{Original}} = \frac{100 + \%}{100}$

Percentage less than: $\frac{\text{New}}{\text{Original}} = \frac{100 - \%}{100}$

Chapter 10: Ratios and Proportions

Direct Proportion: $y = kx$ (where k is a constant)

Indirect Proportion: $y = \frac{k}{x}$ (where k is a constant)

Chapter 12: Mean, Median, Mode, and Range

Average $= \frac{\text{Sum}}{\text{Number of Items}}$

Weighted Average $= \frac{(\text{average \#1})(\text{weight \#1}) + (\text{average \#2})(\text{weight \#2})}{\text{weight \#1} + \text{weight \#2}}$

ACT Math Equation Sheet

Chapter 13: Exponents and Roots

$a^x \times a^y = a^{x+y}$ $\qquad$ $\frac{a^x}{a^y} = a^{x-y}$ $\qquad$ $(a^x)^y = a^{xy}$ $\qquad$ $a^{\frac{x}{y}} = \sqrt[y]{a^x}$

$a^{-x} = \frac{1}{a^x}$ $\qquad$ $a^0 = 1$ $\qquad$ $\sqrt[n]{xy} = \sqrt[n]{x} \times \sqrt[n]{y}$ $\qquad$ $\sqrt[n]{\frac{x}{y}} = \frac{\sqrt[n]{x}}{\sqrt[n]{y}}$

Chapter 14: Logarithms

$\log_a b = c$ $\quad$ is the same as $\quad$ $a^c = b$ $\qquad$ Change of Base Rule: $\log_b a = \frac{\log(a)}{\log(b)}$

$\log_a(xy) = \log_a x + \log_a y$ $\qquad\qquad$ $\log_a\left(\frac{x}{y}\right) = \log_a x - \log_a y$

$\log_a x^y = y \log_a x$ $\qquad\qquad$ $\log_a 1 = 0$

$\ln b = c$ $\quad$ is same as $\quad$ $e^c = b$

Chapter 16: Quadratics

For $ax^2 + bx + c$: $x = \frac{-b \pm \sqrt{b^2 - 4ac}}{2a}$ $\qquad$ Vertex Form: $y = a(x-h)^2 + k$

Discriminant Rules:

Discriminant Value	Types of Solutions
$b^2 - 4ac > 0$	2 real solutions
$b^2 - 4ac = 0$	1 real solution
$b^2 - 4ac < 0$	0 real solutions, 2 complex solutions

Chapter 17: Trigonometry

$\sin(x°) = \frac{opposite}{hypotenuse}$ $\qquad\qquad$ $\sin^{-1}\left(\frac{opposite}{hypotenuse}\right) = x°$

$\cos(x°) = \frac{adjacent}{hypotenuse}$ $\qquad\qquad$ $\cos^{-1}\left(\frac{adjacent}{hypotenuse}\right) = x°$

$\tan(x°) = \frac{opposite}{adjacent}$ $\qquad\qquad$ $\tan^{-1}\left(\frac{opposite}{adjacent}\right) = x$

$\sin^2\theta + \cos^2\theta = 1$

Period for sine, cosine, secant, and cosecant $= \frac{2\pi}{B}$ $\qquad$ Law of Sines: $\frac{\sin(A)}{a} = \frac{\sin(B)}{b} = \frac{\sin(C)}{c}$

Period for tangent and cotangent $= \frac{\pi}{B}$ $\qquad$ Law of Cosines: $a^2 = b^2 + c^2 - 2bc\cos(A)$

Chapter 19: Matrices

For a (2 × 2) matrix $\begin{bmatrix} a & b \\ c & d \end{bmatrix}$, the determinant $= ad - bc$

Chapter 21: Circles, Ellipses, and Hyperbolas

Circle: $(x - h)^2 + (y - k)^2 = r^2$

Ellipse: $\frac{(x-h)^2}{a^2} + \frac{(y-k)^2}{b^2} = 1$

Horizontal Hyperbola: $\frac{(x-h)^2}{a^2} - \frac{(y-k)^2}{b^2} = 1$

Vertical Hyperbola: $\frac{(y-k)^2}{a^2} - \frac{(x-h)^2}{b^2} = 1$

Chapter 22: Probability

Probability $= \frac{\text{Desired Outcome}}{\text{All Possible Outcomes}}$

Rule #1 To Know: The sum of the probabilities of all possible outcomes is equal to 1.

Rule #2 To Know: $P(A \text{ or } B) = P(A) + P(B)$

Rule #3 To Know: $P(A \text{ and } B) = P(A) \times P(B)$

Expected Value $= P(A) \times A + P(B) \times B + P(C) \times C \dots$

Chapter 23: Factorial, Permutation, Combinations, and Organized Counting

$5! = 5 \times 4 \times 3 \times 2 \times 1$

$n! = n(n-1)(n-2)\dots(2)(1)$

Permutation (Order Matters): $_nP_r = \frac{n!}{(n-r)!}$

Combination (Order Doesn't Matter): $_nC_r = \frac{n!}{r!(n-r)!}$

Chapter 24: Sequences

Arithmetic Sequence: add/subtract common difference between terms.

Geometric Sequence: multiply/divide common ratio between terms.

Arithmetic Sequence to find nth term: $t_n = t_1 + d(n - 1)$

Geometric Sequence to find the nth term: $t_n = t_1 r^{n-1}$

Chapter 25: Complex Numbers

$i = \sqrt{-1}$

$i^2 = -1$

$a + bi$ and $a - bi$ are complex conjugates.

$(a + bi)(a - bi) = a^2 + b^2$

The Powers of i:

$i^1 = i$

$i^2 = -1$

$i^3 = -i$

$i^4 = 1$

Any complex number $a + bi$ is graphed on the complex plane at point (a, b).

$|a + bi| = \sqrt{a^2 + b^2}$

For any two complex numbers $a + bi$ and $c + di$, distance $= \sqrt{(a-c)^2 + (b-d)^2}$

ACT Math Equation Sheet

Chapter 27: Inequalities

When multiplying or dividing by a negative number, switch the direction of the inequality sign.

Graphing inequalities:

- For greater than and less than (> and <), draw a dashed line. For greater than or equal to and less than or equal to (≥ and ≤), draw a solid line.
- For greater than and greater than or equal to (> and ≥), shade above the line. For less than and less than or equal to (< and ≤), shade below the line.
- For circles and ellipses, shade inside for less than and less than or equal to (< and ≤) and shade outside for greater than and greater than or equal to (> and ≥).

Chapter 28: Exponential Growth and Decay

Simple Growth: $A = P(1 + r)^t$

Simple Decay: $A = P(1 - r)^t$

Compound Growth: $A = P(1 + \frac{r}{n})^{nt}$

Compound Decay: $A = P(1 - \frac{r}{n})^{nt}$

P = initial value
A = current value
r = rate of the growth or decay
t = time interval
n = number of times compounded per time interval

General Exponential Form: $y = ab^x$ where a is the y-intercept, b is the rate of change, and x is the time interval.

Chapter 31: Arcs and Sectors

Arc: $\frac{\text{Arc Length}}{\text{Circumference}} = \frac{\text{Angle Measure}}{360°}$ $\frac{L}{2\pi r} = \frac{\theta}{360}$ L = arc length
θ = central angle
r = radius

Sector: $\frac{\text{Sector Area}}{\text{Area of Circle}} = \frac{\text{Angle Measure}}{360°}$ $\frac{S}{\pi r^2} = \frac{\theta}{360}$ S = sector area
θ = central angle
r = radius

Chapter 32: Vectors

Standard form: $v = Ai + Bj$ Component Form: $v = \langle A, B \rangle$

For vector $Ai + Bj$ or $\langle A, B \rangle$, magnitude = $\sqrt{A^2 + B^2}$

Chapter 34: Basic Statistics

Standard Deviation: A set of values that is closer together has a lower standard deviation, and a set of values that is farther apart has a higher standard deviation.

The Empirical Rule for Normal Distribution:

- 68% of the data is within one standard deviation of the mean.
- 95% of the data is within two standard deviations of the mean.
- 99.7% of the data is within three standard deviations of the mean.

Chapter 35: Miscellaneous Topics

Binomial Theorem and Pascal's Triangle

Row	Exponent	Pascal's Triangle
0	$(a+b)^0$	1
1	$(a+b)^1$	1 1
2	$(a+b)^2$	1 2 1
3	$(a+b)^3$	1 3 3 1
4	$(a+b)^4$	1 4 6 4 1
5	$(a+b)^5$	1 5 10 10 5 1

Vertical Asymptote Rule:

- Vertical asymptotes occur when the denominator of a rational function is equal to zero

Horizontal Asymptotes Rules

1. If the degree of the denominator is larger than the degree of the numerator, the horizontal asymptote is always at $y = 0$.
2. If the degree of the denominator is smaller than the degree of the numerator, there is NO horizontal asymptote.
3. If the degree of the numerator and denominator are equal, the horizontal asymptote is found by dividing the leading coefficients of the polynomials.

Introduction to ACT Math

Before we start this book, let's begin by understanding the basic format of the ACT Math Test and general strategies you will need for success.

Format of the Test

The ACT Math Test consists of one section: a 60-minute section with 60 questions. A calculator is allowed in this section, and you should use your calculator a lot! Even for simple mental math, use the calculator. This will help keep your mind fresh and avoid simple mistakes.

Difficulty of the Questions

As you progress through the test, the difficulty of the questions increases. The first 10 questions in general will be much easier. As you move towards the later questions, the difficulty will increase slightly until around question 45, where the questions will quickly get much more difficult. The table below provides a general breakdown of the difficulty of questions based on the question number.

Difficulty	Question Number
Very Easy	1 – 10
Easy	11 – 25
Medium	26 – 44
Hard	45 – 60

By no means are the numbers exact (more advanced question can certainly appear before question 45 and easier questions can appear later in the test), but the trend is pretty consistent across most ACTs. In this book, the practice questions in each chapter will increase in difficulty just as they do on the ACT.

Time Management

On average, you have 1 minute to answer each question. Some questions can be solved very quickly while others can take much longer to solve. In general, you should be solving the earlier questions in less than 60 seconds, as the later, more difficult questions will require more time.

If you get to a question that you do not know how to solve, circle the number, bubble in an answer, and move on. You can always come back to the questions that you circled at the end if you have time left. It is important to answer questions as quickly as possible but not to go so fast that you make simple mistakes. Keep yourself moving through the section and find the questions that you know how to solve. Every question is worth the same amount.

Depending on your math abilities, your precise strategy for managing time on this section will vary. High achieving math students will need to answer all 60 questions. This requires working quickly through the first 45 questions and saving enough time to solve the most difficult questions at the end. On the other hand, if math is not your strength, focusing your time on the first 45 questions and guessing on the questions you do not know how to solve to will help you get your best score. Again, every question is worth the same one point, so it is better to spend your time crushing the easier/medium level questions rather than rushing to get to the hardest questions at the end. Every student is different, so it is up to you to find the best strategy for you to maximize your score!

Guessing

There is no penalty for guessing. Make sure that you bubble in an answer for every single question. On a multiple-choice test, there is no best method for guessing, so look at the answer choices and pick the answer that looks best to you.

6 Test Day Tips to Maximize Your Score

The 6 test-taking tips below will help you maximize your scores on test day.

1. **Keep Moving.** Do not get stuck on any one question for too long. We often see students make this mistake and run out of time before finishing all 60 questions. If you get stuck on a question, mark it, bubble in your best guess, and move on. You can come back to the question at the end if you have time left over. Remember, there is no penalty for guessing.

2. **Look For Questions You Know How To Solve If Time Is Running Out.** For students who are not strong at math, running out of time is not unusual on the ACT Math. If you know that you are running low on time, start to look for questions that you know how to solve and questions that you can solve quickly.

3. **Do Your Best To See All 60 questions.** Remember, questions 45-60 are challenging but the questions do not necessarily keep increasing in difficulty as you get closer and closer to question 60. For example, on one recent ACT, question 51 was the hardest question on the test but questions 58 and 60 were actually much easier. It is best to skip the hardest questions or questions that stump you and save them for last. Many students made the mistake of getting stuck on question 51 and ran out of time before they even saw questions 58 and 60. If they instead skipped question 51 and had time to see questions 58 and 60, they could have answered those questions correctly and achieved a higher score!

4. **Memorize The Equations.** In this book, the equations, formulas, and rules that you need to memorize are in bold lettering. Having all of equations, formulas, and rules memorized for test day are critical to solving questions more quickly and maximizing your score.

5. **Use The Calculator!** Use your calculator as much as possible. Even for simple calculations, avoid mental math as much as possible, as mental math often leads to avoidable errors.

6. **Practice Like Its Test Day.** When working on practice ACT tests, set a timer and strictly follow the timer. The best way to get ready for test day is to treat your practice ACTs like it is the real thing.

Not sure what the circle indicates? Go back to the page i to learn about the 4 levels and how to best use this book.

Chapter 1: Backsolving

Chapter 1: Backsolving

In the first two chapters, you will learn two important test-taking techniques: backsolving and substitution. **As you work through the rest of the book, use these techniques whenever you can to solve questions.**

Backsolving is plugging the answer choices back into the question. On the ACT, you are given 5 answer choices for multiple choice questions, and one of those 5 choices must be correct. Rather than solving the question algebraically and determining whether your answer matches one of the answer choices, you can guess-and-check with the answer choices to find which one is correct. Backsolving is often the fastest and easiest way to solve ACT questions, especially if you get stuck and cannot solve a question algebraically, so use it to your advantage.

Backsolving can be done using five steps:

1. **Start with C.** Plug the value back into the question. The answer choices are always in order of smallest to largest or largest to smallest so starting in the middle will save you time.

2. **Solve the question using this value.** Find any other unknowns if necessary.

3. **If this answer choice works correctly, you're done!** Bubble it in and move on.

4. **If this answer choice does not work, cross it off.** If you know the correct answer needs to be smaller or larger than the value you just tried, cross off any other incorrect answers.

5. **Pick one of the remaining answer choices and plug it back into the question.** Repeat this until you find the correct answer. Remember, one of the 5 answer choices must work!

> **Example 1:** If $\sqrt{x+10} - 2\sqrt{x-2} = 0$, what is the value of x?
> A. 2   B. 6   C. 14   D. 18   E. 21

Solution: The quickest and easiest way to solve this question is backsolving. Finding the correct answer is just a process of guess-and-check. Below, you can see how the correct answer B, when $x = 6$, makes the equation be true.

$$\sqrt{6+10} - 2\sqrt{6-2} = 0$$
$$\sqrt{16} - 2\sqrt{4} = 0$$
$$4 - 2(2) = 0$$
$$4 - 4 = 0$$
$$0 = 0$$

The answer is B. If we plug in any of the other answer choices, we will get an equation that is not equal on both sides and is incorrect.

> **Example 2:** If $\frac{3}{x+1} = \frac{2}{x}$, what is the value of x?
> A. −2   B. 0   C. 1   D. 2   E. 3

Solution: The quickest way to solve this question is backsolving. Plug the answer choices back into the question. Below, you can see how the correct answer D, when $x = 2$, makes the equation true.

$$\frac{3}{2+1} = \frac{2}{2}$$
$$\frac{3}{3} = \frac{2}{2}$$
$$1 = 1$$

The answer is D

Backsolving Practice: Answers on page 323.

1. If $3^x + 4^x = 91$, what is the value of x?

    A. 1.5
    B. 2
    C. 2.5
    D. 3
    E. 4

2. The sum of 2 numbers is 85. If the smaller number is 45 less than the larger number, what is the larger number?

    A. 20
    B. 40
    C. 55
    D. 65
    E. 70

3. For what value of x is the equation $3.25x + 6 = 5x - 8$ true?

    A. 4
    B. 6
    C. 8
    D. 12
    E. 14

4. The length of a rectangle is 8 inches longer than its width. If the perimeter of the rectangle is 52 inches. What is the width of the rectangle?

    A. 4
    B. 9
    C. 11
    D. 18
    E. 26

5. The product of 2 integers is 52. The larger integer is 1 more than 3 times the smaller integer. What is the value of the larger integer?

    A. 4
    B. 9
    C. 12
    D. 13
    E. 17

6. 150 tickets were sold to a concert. VIP tickets were sold for $10 and normal tickets were sold for $5. If total sales were $1,100. How many of the VIP tickets were sold?

    A. 40
    B. 65
    C. 70
    D. 80
    E. 90

7. If $3^x = 2187$, what is the value of x?

    A. 3
    B. 5
    C. 6
    D. 7
    E. 9

8. James withdrew one fifth of his savings last week. This week James withdrew one quarter of the remaining amount. He is left with $150. How much did he originally have?

    A. $195
    B. $220
    C. $250
    D. $280
    E. $300

9. If $\sqrt{3x} = 9$, what is the value of x?

    A. 3
    B. 9
    C. 27
    D. 81
    E. 243

Chapter 1: Backsolving

10. $\frac{12x}{5} + 2 = \frac{4}{10}x$

What is the value of x in the equation above?

A. -2
B. -1
C. 2
D. 5
E. 10

11. If the area of a rectangle is 16 and one side has a length of 20, what is the width of the rectangle?

A. $\frac{2}{5}$
B. $\frac{1}{2}$
C. $\frac{4}{5}$
D. 1
E. $\frac{6}{5}$

12. In a triangle, angle Y is twice the measure of angle X, and angle Z is three times the measure of angle X. What is the measure of angle X?

A. 20
B. 30
C. 45
D. 60
E. 90

13. Which of the following values of x satisfies the equation below?

$$\left|\frac{1}{2}x + 6\right| = 8$$

I. -28
II. -4
III. 4

A. I only
B. II only
C. III only
D. I and III only
E. I, II, and III

14. The sum of integers l and m is 200. When l is divided by 7, it is equal to m. What is the value of m?

A. 15
B. 20
C. 25
D. 30
E. 35

15. $\sqrt{x} = x - 2$

For the equation above, what value(s) of x make the equation true?

A. 4
B. 2
C. 1
D. 0
E. 1, 4

Chapter 2: Substitution

Do you prefer working with numbers or variables? We would guess your answer is numbers! On the ACT, some questions have many unknown variables and few or no numbers at all. Most students hate these questions. If you prefer to work with numbers, let's work with numbers! With substitution, we substitute simple numbers in for variables and solve the question using numbers instead of relying on more complex algebra with variables.

Substitution can be done with these four steps:

1. **Pick a number for the variable(s) in the question.**
    a. **Pick easy numbers...avoid using 0 and 1. Use 2, 3, 4 or other easy numbers.** Use 10 for percent problems, 10 or 20 for group size, etc.
    b. **Select different numbers for each variable.** For example, if a question has an x and a y, pick $x = 2$ and $y = 3$.
    c. **Follow any rules in the question.** For example, if a question says x is a number that is negative and even, pick $x = -2$.
2. **Write down the number(s) that you have picked.**
3. **Use your number(s) to work your way through the question and find your answer.**
4. **Plug your number(s) into the answer choices. The correct answer will be the one that matches your answer.**

Substitution may seem a bit confusing just reading the steps, so let's take a look at some example questions to see how useful this technique can be.

Example 1: Jeremy has n boxes of candy bars. Each box contains m bars of candy. Jeremy has to sell 70% of his candy bars to make enough money for rent. Which of the following expresses the number of candy bars Jeremy must sell in terms of m and n?

A. $0.7(m + n)$ B. $70nm$ C. $nm + m$ D. $0.7nm$ E. $mn - 0.7$

Solution: This question may at first seem intimidating with all the variables. To make this question easier, let's plug in numbers. We can say that Jeremy has 2 boxes of candy, so $n = 2$, and that each box contains 5 bars of candy, so $m = 5$. With our numbers, Jeremy has a total of 10 candy bars. He needs to sell 70% to make enough money for rent, so we can find the total candy bars that he must sell by finding 70% of 10.

$$0.7(10) = 7$$

With our numbers, Jeremy must sell 7 candy bars, so our answer is 7. Now, we can plug in the values we selected for n and m into the answer choices and see which one is equal to 7. Here, we find that D works.

$$0.7nm = 0.7(2)(5) = 7$$

None of the other answer choices are equal to 7 when we plug in our values for n and m. No matter what numbers you pick for n and m, you will find that **D is the answer**.

Example 2: If $\cos(2x) = a$, which of the following must be true for all values of x?

A. $\sin(2x) = a$ B. $\cos(x) = a$ C. $\sin(x + 90) = a$ D. $\cos(90 - 2x) = a$ E. $\sin(90 - 2x) = a$

Solution: The easiest way to solve this question is to pick a value for x and use your calculator. Let's pick $x = 10$. First, we need to find out what a equals if $x = 10$.

$$\cos(20) = 0.9397$$

Now that we know what a equals, we can plug in $x = 10$ for the x-values in the answer choices to see which is equal to 0.9397. Here, we can see how the correct answer choice of E works.

$$\text{Sin}(90 - 20) = \sin(70) = 0.9397$$

This trick will work for any value of x that we pick. **The answer is E.**

> **Example 3:** If the length of a rectangle is tripled and the width is halved, how many times larger is the area of the new rectangle than the area of the original rectangle?
>
> A. 1.5   B. 2   C. 3   D. 4   E. 6

Solution: To make this question easier, we can pick values for the length and width of the rectangle. Let's make the length 3 and the width 2. Now, we just follow the steps in the questions.

Original

The length is tripled: $3(3) = 9$ The new length is 9.

The width is halved: $2(\frac{1}{2}) = 1$ The new width is 1.

New

Next, we find the areas of the rectangles and compare. The new rectangle has an area of 9. The original rectangle has an area of 6, so we find that the new rectangle is 1.5 times as large. **The answer is A**

Substitution Practice: Answers on page 323.

1. When the positive integer n is divided by 8, the remainder is 4. What is the remainder of $2n$ when divided by 8?

    A. 0
    B. 1
    C. 2
    D. 3
    E. 4

2. If the sides of a rectangle are all quadrupled, what multiple of the original area is the new rectangle's area?

    A. 2
    B. 4
    C. 8
    D. 10
    E. 16

3. When each side of a square with side length s is lengthened by 4 inches, which of the following expresses the new area of the square?

    A. $s^2 + 4$
    B. $s^2 + 16$
    C. $(s^2 + 4)^2$
    D. $(s + 4)^2$
    E. $4s + 16$

4. For variables a, b, and c, the expression $0 < a < b < c$ is true. Which of the following expressions has the smallest value?

    A. $\frac{b}{c}$
    B. $\frac{c}{b}$
    C. $\frac{a}{c}$
    D. $\frac{c}{a}$
    E. $\frac{a}{b}$

5. If x and y are positive integers such that $x + y = 11$, what is the value of $\frac{x-11}{3y}$?

    A. $-\frac{1}{3}$
    B. $\frac{1}{3}$
    C. $\frac{4}{5}$
    D. 1
    E. 3

PrepPros

6. If $\frac{x}{5} = \frac{y}{2}$, which of the following is equal to $\frac{y}{3}$?

  A. $\frac{4x}{15}$
  B. $\frac{2x}{15}$
  C. x
  D. $\frac{2x}{3}$
  E. $\frac{x}{8}$

7. Money raised by m school clubs is to be divided equally among the clubs. Based on school records, n people each gave p dollars? How much will each club receive?

  A. mpn
  B. $\frac{mp}{n}$
  C. $\frac{np}{m}$
  D. $pn + m$
  E. $(m - n)p$

8. If x is an odd integer and y is an even integer, which of the following must be an odd integer?

  A. $2x^2 + y$
  B. $3x + y$
  C. $2x + 6$
  D. $xy - y$
  E. $x - \frac{y}{2}$

9. If $\cos(x + y) = p$, which of the following must be true for all values of x?

  A. $\cos(2x + 2y) = 2p$
  B. $\cos(x - y) = p$
  C. $\sin(90 - x - y) = p$
  D. $\cos(90 + x + y) = p$
  E. $\sin(-x - y) = p$

10. For all real numbers x and z such that the product of x and 5 is z, which of the following represents the sum of z and 3 in terms of x?

  A. $x + 3$
  B. $5x + 3$
  C. $5(x + 3)$
  D. $\frac{x+3}{5}$
  E. $\frac{x}{5} + 3$

11. If $3x = 4y = 6z$, which of the following expresses the average of x and y in terms of z?

  A. $\frac{7z}{4}$
  B. $\frac{5z}{3}$
  C. $\frac{10}{4z}$
  D. $z + 2$
  E. $\frac{13z}{9}$

12. The distance between Albert's front door and the end of his driveway is d miles. If he can run at c miles per hour, how long will it take him to run from his front door to the end of the driveway in minutes?

  A. $\frac{d}{c}$
  B. $60c$
  C. $\frac{60d}{c}$
  D. $\frac{60c}{d}$
  E. $\frac{cd}{60}$

13. If x is an even integer and $3^{2x} + 3^{2x} + 9^x = z$, which of the following expresses z in terms of x?

  A. 3^{2x+1}
  B. 3^{3x}
  C. 9^{2x}
  E. $9^x + 27$

> Want video explanations for every chapter in the book and 1,250+ practice questions? Go to page i to learn how to sign up.

Chapter 3: Geometry Part 1 – Angles

In this chapter, we will cover all the rules you need to know for angles questions on the ACT. For angles questions, **put your pencil to work by finding and labeling unknown angles**. The more angles you label, the easier it will be to find the angle you need to know to answer the question.

Intersecting Lines

If two lines intersect, what do we know about the relationships between the angles?

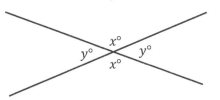

1. **Vertical angles are equal.**
2. **Adjacent angles are supplementary (x and y add to 180°).**

Parallel Lines

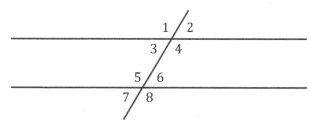

Given two parallel lines, we know the following are true:
1. **Vertical angles are equal** (ex: ∠1 = ∠4).
2. **Alternate interior angles are equal** (ex: ∠3 = ∠6).
3. **Opposite interior angles are supplementary** (ex: ∠3 + ∠5 = 180° and ∠4 + ∠6 = 180°).
4. **Corresponding angles are equal** (ex: ∠2 = ∠6).

All those rules and fancy terms are nice, but all you really need to know is that whenever two parallel lines are intersected by another line, there are two sets of identical angles.

$$\angle 1 = \angle 4 = \angle 5 = \angle 8$$

$$\angle 2 = \angle 3 = \angle 6 = \angle 7$$

Any of the angles from the first list will be supplementary with any of the angles from the second list. For example, ∠1 + ∠6 = 180° and ∠4 + ∠7 = 180°. As long as you memorize which angles are identical, you will be able to handle parallel lines questions.

Example 1:

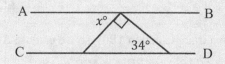

In the figure above, $\overline{AB}$ is parallel with $\overline{CD}$. What is the value of x?

    A. 34   B. 40   C. 48   D. 53   E. 56

Solution: We know that all angles in a triangle add up to 180°, so we can find the unknown third angle in the triangle above.

$$\text{Third angle} = 180° - 34° - 90° = 56°$$

The third angle we just found and $x°$ are alternate interior angles, so they must be equal. **The answer is E.**

TIP – Extend Parallel Lines

Sometimes questions with parallel lines will not always look like the parallel lines in the figure. If the lines just hit and stop (ex: the corner of a parallelogram), take your pencil and extend the lines yourself to make the question look like the figure above. Then, it will be much easier to tell which angles are identical.

Interior Angles in Polygons

You need to know the sum of the interior angles of a…

Triangle	Quadrilateral	Pentagon	Hexagon
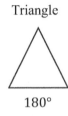	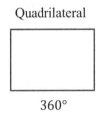		
180°	360°	540°	720°

For any polygon,

Sum of Interior Angles = $180°(n - 2)$ where n is the number of sides.

It does not matter what the shape looks like. All that matters for the sum of the interior angles is the number of sides. You can see how this works with the examples below:

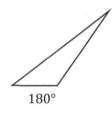 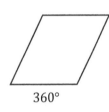 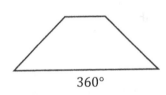 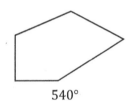

180°   360°   360°   540°

Example 2: In $\triangle ABC$ below, the measure of $\angle ABD$ is 68°, the measure of $\angle ACD$ is 40°, D is on $\overline{BC}$, and $\overline{AD}$ is a bisector of $\angle CAB$. What is the measure of $\angle ADC$?

A. 72
B. 92
C. 100
D. 104
E. 108

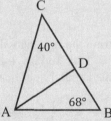

Solution: We know that all angles in a triangle add to 180°, so we can use $\triangle ABC$ to find $\angle CAB$.

$$\angle CAB + \angle ABD + \angle ACD = 180°$$

Since we are given $\angle ABD = 68°$ and $\angle ACD = 40°$, we can solve for $\angle CAB$.

$$\angle CAB + 68° + 40° = 180°$$

$$\angle CAB = 180° - 68° - 40°$$

$$\angle CAB = 72°$$

The question tells us that $\overline{AD}$ is a bisector of $\angle CAB$. A bisector cuts an angle in half, so we know that
$$\angle CAD = \angle BAD$$
Since the entire angle $\angle CAB = 72°$, we now know that $\angle CAD$ and $\angle BAD$ are half of $\angle CAB$ and
$$\angle CAD = \angle BAD = 36°$$
Now that we know these angles, we can use $\triangle ADC$ to find $\angle ADC$. Again, we know all the angles in the triangle must add to $180°$ so
$$\angle ADC + \angle ACD + \angle CAD = 180°$$
We are given that $\angle ACD = 40°$ and just found that $\angle CAD = 36°$. Now we can solve for $\angle ADC$.
$$\angle ADC + 40° + 36° = 180°$$
$$\angle ADC = 180° - 40° - 36°$$
$$\angle ADC = 104°$$

The answer is D.

Example 3: For the given figure, what is the value of x?

A. 60
B. 72
C. 88
D. 90
E. 105

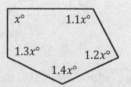

Solution: The figure above has 5 sides, so the total interior angles are equal to $180°(5-2) = 540°$.
$$x° + 1.3x° + 1.4x° + 1.2x° + 1.1x° = 540°$$
$$6x° = 540°$$
$$x = 90$$

The answer is D.

TIP – All figures are drawn to scale

All figures on the ACT are drawn to scale! You can trust the angles and side lengths in the figure. If you are given a figure and do not know how to solve the question, look at the answer choices to see if you can make an educated guess on which answer looks correct. Quite often, you can rule out certain answer choices that clearly do not match the figure.

The only exception is if you see, "Note: Figure not drawn to scale." This almost never occurs on the ACT anymore. Just in case you do see it, do not trust the figure.

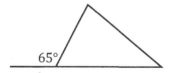
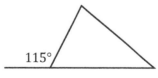

Note: Figure not drawn to scale.

In the figures above, we see that the angle labelled as $65°$ in the figure on the left is clearly incorrect. On the other hand, the figure on the right has no note, so we know the $115°$ is correct and can trust how the figure is drawn to scale.

Geometry Part 1 – Angles Practice: Answers on page 323.

1. In the figure below, two parallel lines are intersected by $\overline{AB}$. What is the value of x?

   A. 30
   B. 40
   C. 50
   D. 80
   E. 140

   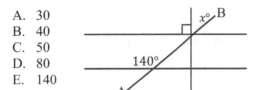

2. What is the value of x in the figure below?

   A. 25
   B. 30
   C. 35
   D. 40
   E. 45

3. In the figure below, $AE = DE$, $BE = CE$, and $\overline{BC}$ is parallel to $\overline{AD}$. If $x = 32$, what is the measure of $\angle BCE$?

   A. 26
   B. 28
   C. 32
   D. 48
   E. 64

4. In the figure below, $\overline{LN}$ intersects $\overline{KM}$ at point P. What is the measure of $\angle LPM$?

   A. 12
   B. 37
   C. 61
   D. 129
   E. 143

   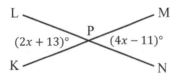

5. In the figure below, lines h and k are parallel. What is the value of x?

   A. 150
   B. 126
   C. 102
   D. 96
   E. 84

   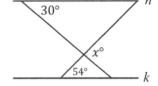

6.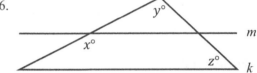

   In the figure above, lines k and m are parallel. If $x = 148$ and $y = 70$, what is the value of z?

   A. 102
   B. 78
   C. 58
   D. 44
   E. 32

7. In the figure below, if $y = 54$, what is the value of x?

   A. 102
   B. 108
   C. 112
   D. 120
   E. 126

   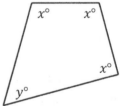

8.

   Note: Figure not drawn to scale.

   In the figure above, lines m and n are parallel. What is the value of b?

   A. 43
   B. 89
   C. 112
   D. 137
   E. 155

- 10 -

9. In the figure below, $\overline{AD} = \overline{AB}$, $\overline{CD} = \overline{BC}$, $\angle ABD = 65°$, and $\angle ABC = 135°$. What is the measure of $\angle BCD$?

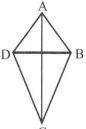

A. 35
B. 40
C. 45
D. 50
E. 55

10.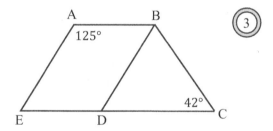

In the figure above, $\overline{AB}$ is parallel to $\overline{CD}$. What is the value of x?

A. 51
B. 78
C. 108
D. 117
E. 129

11.

In the figure above, $\overline{AB}$ and $\overline{EC}$ are parallel, $\overline{AE}$ and $\overline{BD}$ are parallel. What is the measure of $\angle ABC$?

A. 138
B. 125
C. 105
D. 97
E. 83

12. The sum of the interior angle measures of a certain polygon is 1080°. How many sides does this polygon have?

A. 6
B. 7
C. 8
D. 9
E. 10

13.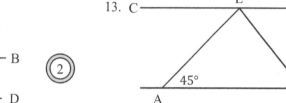

In the figure above, $\overline{AB}$ is parallel to $\overline{CD}$. What is the measure, in degrees, of $\angle AED$?

A. 165
B. 150
C. 145
D. 140
E. 135

14.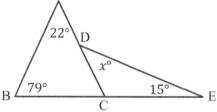

Note: Figure not drawn to scale.

In the figure above, what is the value of x ?

A. 101
B. 86
C. 79
D. 64
E. 52

15. Triangle LMN and the collinear points L, N, and P are shown below. What is the measure of ∠M ?

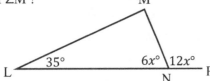

A. 55
B. 65
C. 75
D. 85
E. 95

16.

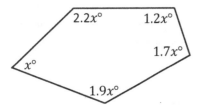

In the figure above, what is the value of x ?

A. 57.6
B. 58.5
C. 60
D. 62.25
E. 67.5

17.

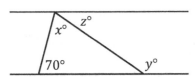

Which of the following expressions is correct for the figure above?

A. $x + y + z = 180$
B. $x + 70 = y$
C. $x + 70 + z = 180 - y$
D. $z - 70 = x$
E. $z - y + 70 = x$

18. The measures of four of the interior angles of a hexagon are 65°, 70°, 95°, and 110°. What is the sum of the last two interior angles?

A. 180
B. 270
C. 340
D. 380
E. 440

19.

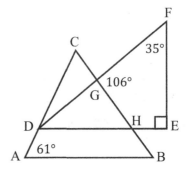

Note: Figure not drawn to scale.

In the figure above, $\overline{AB}$ is parallel to $\overline{DE}$. What is the measure of ∠ACB?

A. 51
B. 55
C. 68
D. 74
E. 81

20. The intersection of lines m and n forms the 4 angles ∠X, ∠W, ∠Y, and ∠Z. The measure of ∠X is 9 times the measure of ∠Z. Which of the following is equal to ∠Z?

A. 12
B. 18
C. 20
D. 28
E. 36

21. Ray $\overrightarrow{BD}$ bisects $\angle ABC$, ray $\overrightarrow{BE}$ bisects $\angle ABD$, the measure of $\angle CBD = (4x-8)°$ and $\angle ABE = (x+9)°$. What is the measure of $\angle ABC$ in degrees?

    A. 13
    B. 22
    C. 60
    D. 88
    E. 122

22.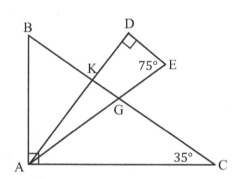

    In the figure above, $AG = CG$. What is the measure of $\angle AKB$?

    A. 67
    B. 70
    C. 75
    D. 80
    E. 85

Chapter 4: Geometry Part 2 — Shapes

The ACT loves to ask geometry questions, and you will see them throughout the math test. Most commonly, you will need to know how to find the area and volume of various shapes or apply the rules for various types of triangles. However, you will not be given any equations, so **you need to memorize all of the equations and rules that are bolded in this chapter**. As long as you have the equations memorized, you will be ready to solve any geometry questions with shapes.

Area and Volume

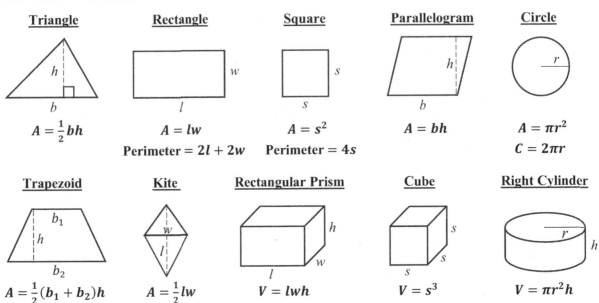

Example 1: One side of rectangle $ABCD$ has a length of 9 inches. A square whose area is equal to the area of rectangle $ABCD$ has a side length of 12 inches. What is the width, in inches, of rectangle $ABCD$?

A. 9   B. 12   C. 16   D. 18   E. 21

Solution: Since the area of rectangle $ABCD$ and the square are equal, we first find the area of the square.

$$A = 12^2 = 144$$

Now, we know the area of rectangle $ABCD$ is 144 square inches and that one side length is 9 inches, so we can solve for the width using $A = lw$.

$$144 = (9)(w)$$
$$w = 16$$

The answer is C.

Example 2: Amanda is freezing ice cream in a circular cake pan to make an ice cream cake. The cake pan has a diameter of 25 cm. If Amanda uses 2,000 cm^3 of ice cream to make the ice cream cake, which of the following is closest to the height, in centimeters, of the ice cream cake?

A. 12   B. 8   C. 6   D. 4   E. 2

Solution: To solve, we will use the equation for the volume right cylinder. We know the volume is equal to 2,000 cm^3. The radius of a circle is equal to half of the diameter, so the radius is equal to 12.5 cm. Now, we can solve for the height.

$$V = \pi r^2 h$$
$$2000 = \pi(12.5)^2 h$$

$$\frac{2000}{\pi(12.5)^2} = h$$

$$4.07 = h$$

The height is equal to 4.07 cm, which is closest to 4. **The answer is D.**

Example 3: Morgan is making a poster for her room. Her original poster did not fit on her wall, so she is changing the dimensions by tripling the width and halving the length. If the original area of the poster was $4A$, what is the area of the new poster in terms of A?

A. $\frac{3}{2}A$ B. $2A$ C. $4A$ D. $6A$ E. $9A$

Solution: Method #1 – The Math Teacher Way: We know the area of the original poster is $4A$, so

$$4A = lw$$

Now, we just need to see how the area changes with the new length and width:

$$\text{New Area} = (0.5l)(3w) = 1.5lw$$

The new area is 1.5 times as large as the old area. From the first equation, we know that $4A = lw$, so plugging in the $4A$, we can find the new area in terms of A.

$$\text{New Area} = 1.5(4A) = 6A$$

The answer is D.

Method #2 – Substitution: If solving this question algebraically seems confusing, well that's because it is! To make this question easier, use the substitution we learned in Chapter 2 and pick values for the length and width of the original poster. Let's say the length is 2 and the width is 3, so the original poster has an area of 6. Now, use the numbers we picked to solve the rest of the question.

$$\text{New Width} = 3(3) = 9$$

$$\text{New Length} = 2(0.5) = 1$$

$$\text{New Area} = lw = (9)(1) = 9$$

The original area was 6 and the new area is 9. The new area is 1.5 times larger than the original area, so we can apply that same change to the poster's original area of $4A$.

$$\text{New Area} = 1.5(\text{Original Area}) = 1.5(4A) = 6A$$

The answer is D.

Areas, Volumes, and Units

The ACT loves to ask area or volume questions with various units. The most common are yards and feet or feet and inches. Students often answer these questions incorrectly because they make mistakes with unit conversion, even though the math is very simple. For example, let's consider the following example:

Example 4: A professional soccer field is 136 yards long and 93 yards wide. What is the area of a professional soccer field in *square feet*?

A. 113,832   B. 37,944   C. 12,648   D. 4,216   E. 1,405

Solution: The key to solving these questions properly is **convert the units BEFORE solving for the area or volume.** For Example 4, we should convert the length and width of the soccer field from yards to feet and then solve for the area. 1 yard is 3 feet, so we can use that conversion to find the length and width in feet.

Length: 136 yards × 3 = 408 feet   Width: 93 yards × 3 = 279 feet

To find the area of the soccer field, we use the area of a rectangle equation and solve.

$$A = lw = (408\ ft)(279\ ft) = 113{,}832\ ft^2$$

The answer is A.

You should memorize the unit conversions in bold below:

Yards and Feet	Feet and Inches
1 yard = 3 feet	**1 foot = 12 inches**
1 square yard = 9 square feet	1 square foot = 144 square inches
1 cubic yard = 27 cubic feet	1 cubic foot = 1,728 inches

The ACT has commonly tested unit conversion questions on recent tests. **When solving these questions, always convert units BEFORE solving for any area or volume.** For more advanced questions, knowing the other conversion above can also be useful. The square yard, square feet, and square inches are used when finding area while the cubic yard, cubic feet, and cubic inches are for volume.

Volumes of Other Three-Dimensional Solids

We already know how to find the volume of a rectangular prism (a box), a cube, and a right cylinder, but how do we find the volumes of other three-dimensional solids? The volume of any three-dimensional shape can be calculating using the equation

$$V = B \times h$$

where B is the area of the base and h is the height. This equation is helpful for calculating the volume of a shape that is not one of the ones that we have already covered or is an odd shape that does not have a simple volume equation.

Example 5: Ming is building a sculpture out of wood. The base of the sculpture is shown below. If Ming plans to make the sculpture 7 feet tall, what is the volume, in cubic feet, of the entire sculpture?

A. 70
B. 140
C. 210
D. 280
E. 350

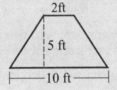

Solution: First, we need to find the area of the base, which here is a trapezoid. Using the trapezoid area formula, we find the area:

$$A = \frac{1}{2}(b_1 + b_2)h = \frac{1}{2}(2 + 10)\,5 = 30$$

The area of the base is 30 ft². Now, we can use the volume equation and the height, which is 7 feet, to solve.

$$V = B \times h = (30)(7) = 210$$

The answer is C.

Right Triangles

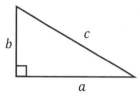

All right triangles follow the Pythagorean Theorem:

$$a^2 + b^2 = c^2$$

where a and b are the lengths of the legs and c is the hypotenuse. You can only use this equation for right triangles.

Example 6: In the triangle ABC, point D is the midpoint of $\overline{AB}$, $AC = 12$ m, and $BC = 15$ m. To the closest meter, what is the length of CD?

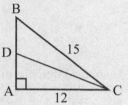

- A. 14
- B. 13
- C. 11
- D. 9
- E. 4

Solution: To find the length of CD, we need to find the length of AD and use the Pythagorean theorem. To find AD, we need to first find AB using the Pythagorean theorem.

$$12^2 + b^2 = 15^2 \rightarrow 144 + b^2 = 225 \rightarrow b^2 = 81$$

$$b = 9$$

$AB = 9$. Point D is the midpoint of AB, so we know that AD is half of AB. $AD = 4.5$. Now that we know AD, we can use the Pythagorean theorem again to solve for CD.

$$12^2 + 4.5^2 = c^2 \rightarrow 144 + 20.25 = c^2 \rightarrow 164.25 = c^2$$

$$c = 12.82$$

$CD = 12.82$, which is closest to 13. **The answer is B.**

TIP – Pythagorean Triples

Pythagorean triples are sets of whole numbers that work in the Pythagorean theorem. On the ACT, you should look out for the two common Pythagorean triples.

3, 4, 5 Right Triangle

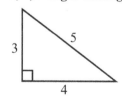

5, 12, 13 Right Triangle

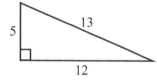

These triangles can also be scaled up by multiplying all of the side lengths by the same number to create more Pythagorean triples. For example, a 3, 4, 5 right triangle can be doubled to become a 6, 8, 10 right triangle, tripled to become 9, 12, 15, and so on.

Special Right Triangles

You will need to be familiar with two special right triangles: 45° − 45° − 90° and 30° − 60° − 90°. The side lengths of these triangles are always in a particular ratio.

45° − 45° − 90°

30° − 60° − 90°

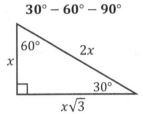

Example 7: In the triangle below, $y = 10$. What is the value of x ?

A. 3
B. 5
C. 8
D. 10
E. It cannot be determined from the information given.

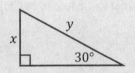

Solution: This is a 30° − 60° − 90° right triangle, so we just need to use the ratio of side lengths to solve. The shortest side, x, is always half the length of the hypotenuse, y. We know that $y = 10$, so $x = \frac{1}{2}(10) = 5$.
The answer is B.

Example 8: Triangle ABC below is a right isosceles triangle. What is the area of triangle ABC?

A. 128
B. $128\sqrt{2}$
C. 64
D. $64\sqrt{2}$
E. 32

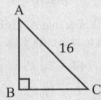

Solution: A right isosceles triangle is the same as a 45° − 45° − 90° right triangle. To find the area of triangle ABC, we need to know side lengths AB and BC. To find these side lengths, we can use the ratio from the 45° − 45° − 90° right triangle. We are looking for the legs of the triangle, which are the x's, and we are given that the hypotenuse, which is the $x\sqrt{2}$. Since we know the hypotenuse is equal to 16, we can solve for x.

$$x\sqrt{2} = 16$$

$$x = \frac{16}{\sqrt{2}} = \frac{16}{\sqrt{2}} \times \frac{\sqrt{2}}{\sqrt{2}} = \frac{16\sqrt{2}}{2} = 8\sqrt{2}$$

We know that $AB = BC = 8\sqrt{2}$. Now that we know the base and height, we can solve for the area of triangle ABC.

$$\text{Area of ABC} = \frac{1}{2}(8\sqrt{2})(8\sqrt{2}) = \frac{1}{2}(128) = 64$$

The answer is C.

Similar Triangles

Similar triangles are triangles with the same shape but different sizes. **The angles are identical, and the side lengths are proportional.**

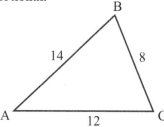
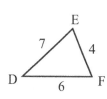

For similar triangles, the ratio of the side lengths is always the same:

$$\frac{AB}{DE} = \frac{BC}{EF} = \frac{AC}{DF}$$

Example 9: In triangle ABC, $\overline{DE}$ is parallel to $\overline{BC}$, $AE = 8$, $AC = 20$, and $AB = 18$. What is the length of AD?

A. 4.1
B. 7.2
C. 8.8
D. 12.2
E. 15.4

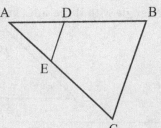

Solution: Triangles ADE and ABC are similar triangles. Anytime a line drawn parallel to one of the bases makes a smaller triangle, the smaller triangle will be similar to the larger triangle. Here, $\overline{DE}$ creates the smaller similar triangle. Since the triangles are similar, we know the side lengths must be proportional.

$$\frac{AD}{AB} = \frac{AE}{AC}$$

$$\frac{AD}{18} = \frac{8}{20}$$

$$20\,AD = 144$$

$$AD = \frac{144}{20} = 7.2$$

The answer is B.

Backup Method – Educated Guess: Remember that the figures on the ACT are drawn to scale. Even if we have no idea how to solve this question, we can look at the figure and see that AD is almost the same length as AE, which is 8. Answer choice A is way too small and answer choices D and E are way too large. We know the answer needs to be B or C, so you have a 50:50 chance of guessing this correctly.

This method works almost all the time on figures questions the ACT, especially on the most difficult shapes questions at the end of the test. **Be sure to always look at the answer choices before guessing randomly to see if you can make an educated guess.** On some questions, you can even find the correct answer by just using the figure and the answer choices.

More Triangles

An equilateral triangle is a triangle in which all three sides are equal and all angles are equal to 60°.

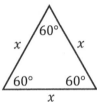

An isosceles triangle is a triangle in which two sides are equal and two angles are equal.

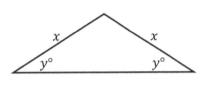

A scalene triangle is a triangle with three sides and three angles that are all different.

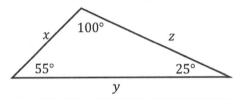

Example 10:

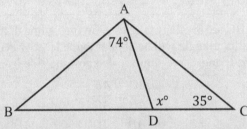

Triangle ABC is an isosceles triangle in which BC is the longest side. What is the value of x?

   A. 82   B. 99   C. 109   D. 111   E. 137

Solution: Since ABC is an isosceles triangle and BC is the longest side, we know $AB = AC$. That means we can find $\angle B$:

$$\angle B = \angle C = 35°$$

Once we know $\angle B = 35°$, we can find $\angle ADB$ because we know the other two angles in triangle ADB.

$$\angle ADB = 180° - 35° - 74° = 71°$$

The angle $x°$ that we are looking for is adjacent to $\angle ADB$, so we can solve:

$$x° = 180° - 71° = 109°$$

The answer is C.

Backup Method – Educated Guess: Remember that the figures on the ACT are drawn to scale. If you just look at the figure and the angle, you can eliminate answer choices A, which is too small, and E, which is too large. From there, you can estimate the angle on your own and take your best guess between answer choices B, C, and D.

Third Side of a Triangle

Can you make a triangle with side lengths of 4, 5, and 10? What about with side lengths of 4, 5, and 9? Or with side lengths of 4, 5, and 8? While this may at first seem confusing, there is a simple rule:

The sum of the two shorter sides of a triangle, a and b, must be greater than the longest side of a triangle, c.

$$a + b > c$$

Let's use this rule to review the three potential triangles introduced above. We will start with a triangle with side lengths of 4, 5, and 9.

$$4 + 5 \not> 9$$

Since the sum of the shorter side lengths are equal to the longest side, we cannot make a triangle.

Let's try side lengths of 4, 5, and 10.

$$4 + 5 \not> 10$$

The two shorter sides cannot even reach the end of the longest side, so again we cannot make a triangle.

What about side lengths of 4, 5, and 8?

$$4 + 5 > 8$$

Since the sum of the smaller side lengths are greater than the longest side, we can make a triangle!

> **Example 11:** Triangle ABC has two sides of lengths 10 and 15. Which of the following could NOT be the third side of triangle ABC?
> A. 5   B. 8   C. 13   D. 19   E. 23

Solution: To solve, we just need to test each answer choice to find which one does not work with our third side of the triangle rule. For answer choices A, B, and C, the longest side would be 15. For answer choices D and E, the number in the answer choice would be the longest side.

Let's start with answer choice A.

$$5 + 10 \not> 15$$

The sides of 5 and 10 are equal to 15, so no triangle can be formed.

If we test the rest of the answer choices, we see that each of them works.

For B: $8 + 10 > 15$

For C: $13 + 10 > 15$

For D: $10 + 15 > 19$

For E: $10 + 15 > 23$

The answer is A.

Other Rules You Might Need to Know

Since there is so much geometry tested on the ACT, there is still more geometry that we will not fully cover in this book! Below are some additional geometry rules that you may need to know for test day. Any students aiming for very high math scores should memorize all the rules below.

1. **Side Lengths and Angles in a Triangle**

   The smallest side in a triangle is opposite from the smallest angle. The largest side in a triangle is opposite from the largest angle.

2. **Other Triangle Definitions**
   - A **acute triangle** has angles that are all less than 90°.
   - An **obtuse triangle** has 1 angle that is greater than 90°.
   - A **right triangle** has 1 angle that is equal to 90°.

3. **Area of an Equilateral Triangle**

   Find the area of an equilateral triangle with side lengths s with the equation. $A = \frac{s^2\sqrt{3}}{4}$

   Memorize this equation. It can be extremely helpful for advanced triangles questions.

4. **Half of an Equilateral Triangle is a 30° – 60° – 90° right triangle.**

   Cutting an equilateral triangle in half vertically creates two 30° – 60° – 90° right triangles.

5. **Tangent Lines and Circles**

   A tangent line to a circle is a straight line that just touches the circle at one point. The angle between the radius of the circle and the tangent line is always 90°. Two tangent lines to a circle from a single point are congruent.

   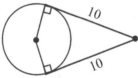

6. **Perimeters and Maximizing the Enclosed Area**

   Given a certain perimeter, a circle always maximizes the enclosed area. If you must make a rectangular shape (more common in question on the ACT), a square maximizes the enclosed area. For example, if you have 40 feet of fence to enclose a yard and are not given an answer choice that is a circle, a square with side lengths of 10 feet gives you the largest possible enclosed area (100 square feet).

7. **Pythagorean Theorem and Types of Triangles**

   If $a^2 + b^2 = c^2$, it is a right triangle.

   If $a^2 + b^2 > c^2$, it is an acute triangle.

   If $a^2 + b^2 < c^2$, it is an obtuse triangle.

Geometry Part 2 – Shapes Practice: Answers on pages 323-324.

1. If the area of rectangle ABCD below is 48, what is the area of the shaded region?

   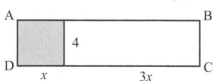

   A. 4
   B. 8
   C. 12
   D. 16
   E. 24

2. The circumference of a circle is 16π inches. What is the area of half of the circle, in square inches?

   A. 8π
   B. 18π
   C. 32π
   D. 36π
   E. 64π

3. James is going to build a triangular bed for roses on the side of his house. He is going to put a fence around the rose bed. Two sides of the rose bed will be up against his house. A diagram of the rose bed is shown below. To the closest foot, how many feet of fencing will James need to enclose the roses?

   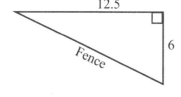

   A. 3
   B. 11
   C. 14
   D. 16
   E. 23

4. In the shape below, all angles are right angles. What of the following is closest to the area of the shape?

   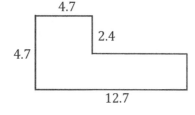

   A. 20.8
   B. 40.5
   C. 42.5
   D. 53.5
   E. 59.7

5. The perimeter of a parallelogram is 60 inches, and 1 of its side measures 20 inches. What are the sides lengths, in inches, of the other 3 sides?

   A. 20, 20, 20
   B. 20, 10, 10
   C. 20, 15, 15
   D. 20, 14, 14
   E. It cannot be determined

6. Each side of a square ABCD has a length of 40 meters. A certain rectangle whose area is equal to the area of square ABCD has a width of 25 meters. What is the length, in meters, of the rectangle?

   A. 15
   B. 30
   C. 40
   D. 64
   E. 100

7. The perimeter of a certain rectangle is 56 yards. The longer sides of the rectangle are 4 yards longer than each of the shorter sides of the rectangle. What is the length, in yards, of one of the longer sides of the rectangle?

   A. 10
   B. 12
   C. 13
   D. 16
   E. 24

8. The diameter of a circle is 22 centimeters. What is the circumference of the circle?

   A. 11π
   B. 22π
   C. 33π
   D. 44π
   E. 484π

9. The length and width of rectangle ABCD are 16 and 9 respectively. A certain square has an area equal to the area of rectangle ABCD. What is the perimeter of the square?

   A. 12
   B. 24
   C. 48
   D. 50
   E. 144

10. What are the maximum number of square pieces of cloth, each 4 inches on a side, that can be cut from a piece of fabric that is 3 feet long and 5 feet wide?

A. 16
B. 45
C. 60
D. 96
E. 135

11. In the figure below, $\overline{BE}$ is parallel with $\overline{CD}$. Which of the following statements is true?

A. $\dfrac{AB}{BC} = \dfrac{BE}{CD}$
B. $\dfrac{AB}{AC} = \dfrac{AE}{CD}$
C. $\dfrac{BE}{AE} = \dfrac{AE}{CD}$
D. $\dfrac{BC}{ED} = \dfrac{BE}{AB}$
E. $\dfrac{BE}{CD} = \dfrac{AE}{AD}$

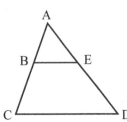

12. Penelope is decorating a picture to hang on her wall and wants to wrap string around the border. The picture is in the shape of a right triangle, as shown below. Penelope only has 42 inches of string, so she will not be able to wrap the entire border. To decorate, she will start at point A, go to point C, go to point B, and then go until the string ends. How far from point B will the string end?

A. 4
B. 6
C. 8
D. 10
E. 12

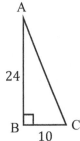

13. If a triangle has two sides with lengths 6 and 8, what is the length of the third side?

A. 2
B. 4
C. 6
D. 8
E. It cannot be determined

14. The larger shaded circle has a radius of 10. The smaller circles each have a radius of 2. What is the area of the shaded region below?

A. 36π
B. 64π
C. 81π
D. 92π
E. 100π

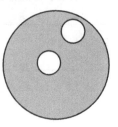

15. Triangle ABC has two sides of length 7 and 12. Which of the following could NOT be the length of the third side of the triangle?

A. 5
B. 7
C. 12
D. 15
E. 18

16. In the graph below, what is the area of quadrilateral ABCD?

A. 13.5
B. 19
C. 22
D. 24.5
E. 28

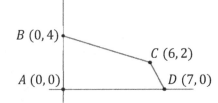

17. Leucadia has a park that is 180 feet by 90 feet. What is the area of the park in square *yards*?

A. 1,800
B. 3,600
C. 5,400
D. 16,200
E. 48,600

18. Shown below is a regular hexagon inscribed in a circle whose radius is 6 inches. What is the perimeter, in inches, of the hexagon?

A. 12π
B. 18
C. 24
D. 30
E. 36

19. A rectangular swimming pool has a volume of 2,880 cubic feet. If the pool is 15 feet deep and 16 feet long, how wide, in feet, is the pool?

   A. 12
   B. 14
   C. 15
   D. 16
   E. 18

20. What is the area of the trapezoid below?

   A. 288
   B. 368
   C. 416
   D. 448
   E. 504

   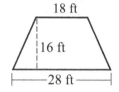

21. Mary has a 120-inch piece of wire. She will use all the wire to make a rectangle and a circle. If the rectangle has a width of 7 inches and a length of 15 inches, which of the following is approximately the radius of the circle?

   A. 12
   B. 14
   C. 16
   D. 21
   E. 25

22. The area of a rectangle is 500 square inches, and its width is 5 times its length. What is the perimeter of the rectangle?

   A. 20
   B. 50
   C. 120
   D. 250
   E. 500

23. Equilateral triangle ABC is shown below. What is the value of k?

   A. -2
   B. 0
   C. 2
   D. 4
   E. 6

   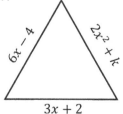

24. What is the area of the triangle below?

   A. $36\sqrt{3}$
   B. 36
   C. 24
   D. $18\sqrt{3}$
   E. 18

   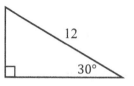

25. A right triangle that is w feet by x feet is inside of a rectangle that is y feet by z feet. The area of the shaded region is what fraction of the large rectangle, in terms of $w, x, y,$ and z?

   A. $\dfrac{yz-wx}{yz}$
   B. $\dfrac{yz+\frac{1}{2}wx}{yz}$
   C. $\dfrac{\frac{1}{2}(y-x)(z-w)}{wx}$
   D. $\dfrac{\frac{1}{2}(y-x)(z-w)}{yz}$
   E. $\dfrac{yz-\frac{1}{2}wx}{yz}$

   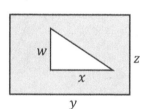

26.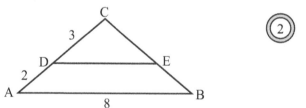

   Note: The figure is not drawn to scale.

   In the figure above, $\overline{AB}$ is parallel to $\overline{DE}$. Which of the following is equal to the length of DE?

   A. 5
   B. $\dfrac{16}{3}$
   C. $\dfrac{13}{2}$
   D. $\dfrac{24}{5}$
   E. $\dfrac{40}{3}$

27.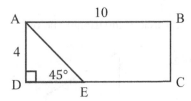

For the figure above, what is the perimeter of quadrilateral AECB?

A. $20 + 4\sqrt{2}$
B. $28 + 4\sqrt{3}$
C. $24 + 4\sqrt{2}$
D. 24
E. 28

28.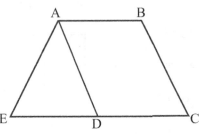

In the figure above, $\overline{AB}$ and $\overline{EC}$ are parallel, $\overline{AD}$ and $\overline{BC}$ are parallel, $AD = AE$, and the measure of $\angle ABC$ is 110°. What is the measure of $\angle EAD$?

A. 110
B. 80
C. 65
D. 50
E. 40

29. Ayesha is making a flowerpot for her mom for Mother's Day. Her mom's current favorite flowerpot, which is in the shape of a right cylinder, holds 6 liters of water. Ayesha is going to make a new flowerpot in the shape of a right cylinder with the twice the width and twice the height. How many liters of water will the new flowerpot hold?

A. 12
B. 18
C. 24
D. 36
E. 48

30. Which of the following sets of integers could be the lengths of the three sides of a triangle?

A. 1, 2, 3
B. 2, 3, 5
C. 4, 6, 11
D. 8, 9, 15
E. 10, 15, 25

31. A triangle has interior angles with measures in the ratio of 4:8:12. If the shortest side of the triangle is 6, what is the length of the second longest side?

A. $6\sqrt{3}$
B. 9
C. 12
D. 18
E. $18\sqrt{2}$

32. In the figure below, lines $\overline{AD}$ and $\overline{EC}$ intersect at F, which is at the center of rectangle ACDE, and $\overline{BF} \perp \overline{AC}$. What fraction of the area of ACDE does the shaded region represent?

A. $\frac{1}{16}$
B. $\frac{1}{12}$
C. $\frac{1}{10}$
D. $\frac{1}{8}$
E. $\frac{1}{6}$

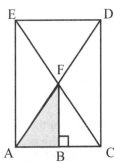

33.

In the figure above, $\overline{BC}$ is parallel to $\overline{DE}$. What is the length of AC?

A. 10
B. 20
C. 25
D. 27.5
E. 30

34. Simone is building a box to store all of her textbooks. She has a spot in the corner of her room to put the box that is 20 inches wide and 24 inches long. If the box must have a total volume of 7,200 cubic inches, what is the height, in inches, of the box?

   A. 12
   B. 15
   C. 18
   D. 20
   E. 24

38. In the figure below, the diameter of the circle is 10 inches. What is the area of the square inside of the circle?

   A. 25
   B. 50
   C. 80
   D. 100
   E. 150

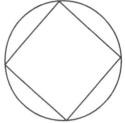

35. The length of the rectangular prism shown below is 3 times the width. The height and the width are the same. The volume of the prism is 81 cubic inches? What is the length, in inches, of the prism?

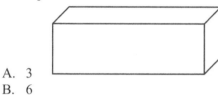

   A. 3
   B. 6
   C. 9
   D. 12
   E. 15

39. What fraction of an 8-inch diameter pie is equivalent to the area of one slice of a 16-inch diameter pie if the larger pie is cut into 8 equal slices?

   A. $\frac{1}{8}$
   B. $\frac{1}{6}$
   C. $\frac{1}{4}$
   D. $\frac{1}{2}$
   E. $\frac{3}{4}$

36. How many cubes with a side length of 5 inches can fit into a cube with a side length of 15 inches?

   A. 3
   B. 5
   C. 10
   D. 25
   E. 27

40. A soda can with a diameter of 4 inches and a height of 4.5 inches is going to be poured into a glass with a diameter of 3 inches and a height of 12 inches. How many inches from the top will the soda fill the glass up to?

   A. 2.5
   B. 4
   C. 4.5
   D. 7.5
   E. 8

37. Christina's yard is 120 feet long and 45 feet wide. What is the area, in square *yards*, of her yard?

   A. 165
   B. 600
   C. 1,000
   D. 1,800
   E. 5,400

41. Rodrigo will pour concrete to make a patio with the dimensions, in feet, shown in the figure below. He will pour the concrete to a depth of 6 inches. How many cubic feet of concrete will Rodrigo need to make the patio?

   A. 80
   B. 114
   C. 156
   D. 228
   E. 312

42. In isosceles trapezoid ABCD below, $\overline{AB}$ is 10 inches long, $\overline{DC}$ is 15 inches long, and triangle AED has an area of 10 square inches. What is the area of the trapezoid in square inches?

 A. 80
 B. 90
 C. 100
 D. 120
 E. 150

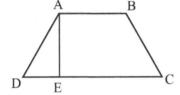

43. Diego has 100 feet of fencing that he will use to build a rectangular pen for his chickens. What is the maximum area, in square feet, that he can make using only the 100 feet of fencing for the perimeter?

 A. 250
 B. 400
 C. 600
 D. 624
 E. 625

44.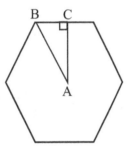

In the regular hexagon above, $AB = 12$. What is the area of $\triangle ABC$?

 A. 12
 B. $12\sqrt{2}$
 C. $12\sqrt{3}$
 D. $18\sqrt{3}$
 E. 18

45. Donovan is shipping lunch boxes in a large cubic box with side lengths of 3 feet. If the lunch boxes have dimensions of 9 inches long, 6 inches wide, and 3 inches tall, how many lunch boxes can fit in each cubic box?

 A. 24
 B. 162
 C. 288
 D. 864
 E. 3,888

46. The dimensions shown below are in feet. What is the area, in square feet, of the shaded region in terms of x?

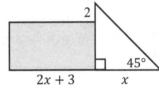

 A. $4x^2 + 3x$
 B. $4x^2 + 1$
 C. $2x^2 + 3x$
 D. $2x^2 - x - 6$
 E. $2x^2 + 3x - 2$

47. The formula for the volume, V, of a sphere is $V = \frac{4}{3}\pi r^3$, where r is the radius. Michelle is filling up a ball with water as part of a science fair project. If the ball can hold a total of 950 cubic inches of water when it is completely filled, approximately what is the radius of the ball?

 A. 6.1
 B. 8.9
 C. 14.2
 D. 20.1
 E. 26.7

48. Tom stored his leftover tomato soup in a container that is 4 inches wide, 6 inches long and 6 inches high. In the container, the tomato soup is 4 inches deep. Tom is going to pour his soup into a new container with dimension of 5 inches wide, 8 inches long, and 5 inches high. How many inches will the height of the tomato soup be in the new container?

    A. 2.0
    B. 2.4
    C. 3.8
    D. 5.0
    E. 6.6

49. As shown below, $\overline{BE}$ divides rectangle ACDF into 2 trapezoids. The measure of $\angle ABE$ is 60°. The lengths of $\overline{EF}$, $\overline{BE}$ and $\overline{BC}$ are given in inches. What is the area, in square inches, of rectangle ACDF?

    A. 125
    B. $100\sqrt{2}$
    C. $125\sqrt{3}$
    D. $160\sqrt{3}$
    E. 192

    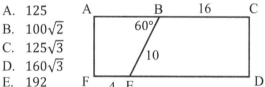

50. A standard Rubik's cube consists miniature cubes called "cubies." One Rubik's cube has 3 layers, and each layer has 9 "cubies" arranged in a 3 × 3 square. If the side length of a "cubie" is 0.8 inches, which of the following is closest to the total volume, in cubic inches, of a 6 Rubik's cubes?

    A. 83
    B. 103
    C. 162
    D. 389
    E. 512

51. If the circle below has an area of 16π, what is the area of the equilateral triangle below?

    A. 128
    B. $64\sqrt{3}$
    C. $\frac{64\sqrt{3}}{3}$
    D. $\frac{128\sqrt{3}}{3}$
    E. $128\sqrt{3}$

52. A box is going to be constructed from a rectangular piece of plastic 40 inches by 20 inches by cutting a square piece of equal size from each of the corners and bending up the sides to make a 90° angle with the base. If the base of the finished box is 300 square inches, what will the volume of the box be?

    A. 450
    B. 800
    C. 900
    D. 1,200
    E. 1,500

53. The figure below shows a ramp made out of solid wood. The length is 24 inches, the width is 8 inches, and the height is 7 inches. The angle where the width and height meet is 90°. Which of the following values is closest to the volume, in cubic inches, of the wood used to construct the ramp?

    A. 576
    B. 672
    C. 857
    D. 1,203
    E. 1,344

54.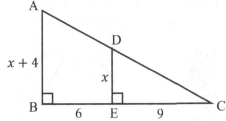

In the figure above, what is the length of AC ?

A. $2\sqrt{59}$
B. $3\sqrt{34}$
C. $5\sqrt{13}$
D. $8\sqrt{6}$
E. $2\sqrt{119}$

55. What is the area of triangle MNP below?

A. $\frac{25}{2}$
B. $\frac{25\sqrt{2}}{2}$
C. $\frac{25\sqrt{3}}{2}$
D. 25
E. $25\sqrt{2}$

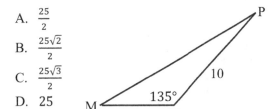

56. Which of the following expressions represents the area, in square coordinate units, of trapezoid PQRS in the standard (x, y) coordinate plane below?

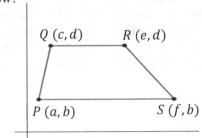

A. $\frac{(e-c)+(f-a)}{2}(d-b)$
B. $\frac{(d+b)}{2}(c-a)$
C. $\frac{1}{2}(e+d+a+f)(d-b)$
D. $\frac{1}{2}(a-c)(b-d)$
E. $\frac{(e+d)-(f+b)}{2}(c-a)$

Chapter 5: Lines

ACT questions commonly ask you how to use and solve linear functions, which is just a fancy term for lines. Linear functions appear in the form $y = mx + b$. In this chapter, we will cover all the equations and common types of questions that appear on the ACT involving lines in the xy-plane.

Slope

Given any two points on a line (x_1, y_1) and (x_2, y_2),

$$\text{Slope} = \frac{rise}{run} = \frac{y_1 - y_2}{x_1 - x_2}$$

The slope measures how steep a line is. A line with a higher slope is steeper while a line with a lower slope is flatter. The rise is the change in the y-coordinates, and the run is the change in the x-coordinates. For example, if a line has a slope of $\frac{1}{2}$, the line will go up 1 unit for every 2 units we move to the right, or it will go down 1 unit for every 2 units we move to the left. Lines with a positive slope go up and to the right, and lines with a negative slope go down and to the right.

> **Example 1:** In the standard (x, y) coordinate plane, what is the slope of the line that passes through $(-7, 6)$ and $(2, 3)$?
>
> A. $-\frac{9}{5}$ B. $-\frac{3}{5}$ C. $-\frac{1}{3}$ D. $\frac{1}{3}$ E. $\frac{3}{5}$

Solution: $\text{Slope} = \frac{6-3}{-7-2} = \frac{3}{-9} = -\frac{1}{3}$

The answer is C.

> **Example 2:** In the standard (x, y) coordinate plane, a line passes through points $(9, r)$ and $(-1, 3)$ and has a slope of 3. What is the value of r?
>
> A. 33   B. 27   C. 21   D. 15   E. 13

Solution:
$$\text{Slope} = \frac{r-3}{9-(-1)} = 3$$
$$\frac{r-3}{10} = 3$$
$$r - 3 = 30$$
$$r = 33$$

The answer is A.

Slopes of Parallel and Perpendicular Lines

If two lines are parallel, the lines have the same slope. For example, if lines A and B are parallel and line A has a slope of 3, line B also has a slope of 3.

If two lines are perpendicular, the slopes of the lines are the negative reciprocals of one another. To find the negative reciprocal, take the slope of the initial line, flip the fraction, and make it negative. For example, if lines A and B are perpendicular and line A has a slope of $\frac{3}{2}$, the slope of line B is $-\frac{2}{3}$.

Example 3: Points $(4, 10)$ and $(1, 31)$ are located on line q. If line p is perpendicular to line q, which of the following equations could be the equation of line p?

A. $y = 7x + 28$ B. $y = \frac{1}{7}x - \frac{5}{2}$ C. $y = -7x + 10$ D. $y = -\frac{1}{7}x + 2$ E. $y = 5x + 3$

Solution: To start, we need to find the slope of line q.

$$\text{Slope} = \frac{10 - 31}{4 - 1} = \frac{-21}{3}$$

$$\text{Slope} = -7$$

Line q has a slope of -7. Since line p is perpendicular to line q, line p must have a slope of $\frac{1}{7}$. **The answer is B.**

Slope-Intercept Form

Slope-intercept form is the simplest form of a line and the one that you are likely most comfortable with.

$$y = mx + b$$

where **m is the slope** and **b is the y-intercept**.

As an example, consider the graph of $y = 2x - 2$ below:

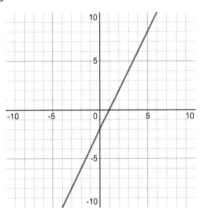

We can see both the slope and the y-intercept on the graph. The y-intercept is where the line crosses the y-axis, which we can clearly see at $y = -2$. We can also see the slope is 2 by tracing how the line moves: for every 2 units we move up, the graph moves one unit to the right. Make sure you are comfortable identifying the y-intercept and slope of a line from the graph.

Example 4: The graph in the standard (x, y) coordinate plane below is represented by one of the following equations. Which one?

A. $y = -\frac{1}{2}x + 3$
B. $y = -2x - 3$
C. $y = 2x + 3$
D. $y = \frac{1}{2}x - 3$
E. $y = \frac{1}{2}x + 3$

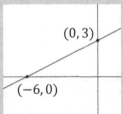

Solution: To solve, we need to find the y-intercept and the slope. The y-intercept is at $y = 3$. To find the slope, we need two points on the line. Here, we can use $(-6, 0)$ and $(0, 3)$.

$$\text{Slope} = \frac{0 - 3}{-6 - 0} = \frac{-3}{-6} = \frac{1}{2}$$

The slope is $\frac{1}{2}$ and the y-intercept is $y = 3$, so the equation of the line is $y = \frac{1}{2}x + 3$. **The answer is E.**

Point-Slope Form

If we only know the slope of a line and a point on the line, we need to use point-slope form:

$$y - y_1 = m(x - x_1)$$

where (x_1, y_1) **is a point on the line and m is the slope.** Once we plug in the slope and point to point-slope form, we can turn the equation back into slope-intercept form by solving for y.

> **Example 5:** Line w passes through points $(2, 10)$ and $(5, -2)$. What is the y-intercept of line w?
> A. -4 B. 7   C. 12   D. 18   E. 25

Solution: To start, we need to find the slope of line w.

$$\text{Slope} = \frac{10 - (-2)}{2 - 5} = \frac{12}{-3} = -4$$

Now that we know the slope, we can use point-slope form. We can plug in either point and then solve for y. For this example, we will use the point $(2, 10)$.

$$y - 10 = -4(x - 2)$$
$$y - 10 = -4x + 8$$
$$y = -4x + 18$$

Once we have the equation in slope-intercept form, we see that the y-intercept is 18. **The answer is D.**

> **Alternate Method – Plug a point into $y = mx + b$ form.**
>
> When dealing with lines in $y = mx + b$ form, you can also plug the (x, y) coordinates of a point on the line into the equation and then solve for the y-intercept. To see how this works, let's go back to example 5. Once we found the slope was -4, we could have set the equation up like this:
>
> $$y = -4x + b$$
>
> To find b-value, we can plug in one of the points from the line for x and y and solve for b. Here, we will use $(2, 10)$.
>
> $$10 = -4(2) + b$$
> $$b = 18$$
>
> Now that we know the b-value, we can write the equation in slope-intercept form:
>
> $$y = -4x + 18$$
>
> Note that this "Plug a point into $y = mx + b$ form" approach and the point-slope form method we used in the solution to Example 5 both find slope-intercept form. You can use whichever one you feel more comfortable with on test day.

Standard Form

Lines can also appear in standard form:

$$Ax + By = C$$

The coefficients in this form do not show the slope or the y-intercept. They actually show nothing, so standard form is not particularly useful. To turn standard form into slope-intercept form, solve for y. Once we have the equation in slope-intercept form, we can find the slope and the y-intercept for the line.

Example 6: In the standard (x, y) coordinate plane, what is the slope of the line $-4x + 3y = 15$?

A. -4 B. $-\frac{4}{3}$ C. $\frac{3}{4}$ D. $\frac{4}{3}$ E. 4

Solution: Convert the line from standard form to slope-intercept form. To do this, we need to solve for y.

$$-4x + 3y = 15$$
$$3y = 4x + 15$$
$$y = \frac{4}{3}x + 5$$

After putting the line in slope-intercept form, we can see the slope is $\frac{4}{3}$. **The answer is D.**

Midpoint Formula

Given any two points on a line (x_1, y_1) and (x_2, y_2),

$$\text{midpoint} = \left(\frac{x_1 + x_2}{2}, \frac{y_1 + y_2}{2}\right)$$

Example 7: C is the midpoint of AB. If point A is at $(3, 6)$ and point C is at $(5, 2)$, which of the following is point B?

A. $(4, 4)$ B. $(1, 2)$ C. $(7, -2)$ D. $(1, 10)$ E. $(7, 8)$

Solution: We are given the midpoint, point C, and one of the endpoints, point A. We can plug the values into the midpoint formula to solve for the coordinates of point B.

To solve for the x-coordinate, plug in the x-coordinates for the midpoint and the endpoint that we are given.

$$5 = \frac{3+x}{2}$$
$$10 = 3 + x$$
$$x = 7$$

The x-coordinate is $x = 7$.

To solve for the y-coordinate, plug in the y-coordinates for the midpoint and the endpoint that we are given.

$$2 = \frac{6+y}{2}$$
$$4 = 6 + y$$
$$y = -2$$

The y-coordinate is -2. Point B is at $(7, -2)$. **The answer is C.**

Distance Formula

Given any two points (x_1, y_1) and (x_2, y_2),

$$\text{Distance} = \sqrt{(x_1 - x_2)^2 + (y_1 - y_2)^2}$$

The distance formula can be used to solve for the distance between any two points in the (x, y) coordinate plane.

If you do not like the distance formula, you also use the Pythagorean Theorem to find the distance between two points. To do so, sketch a coordinate plane and draw a triangle, and solve for the hypotenuse. You can see how this works in the example below.

> **Example 8:** What is the distance, in coordinate units, between the points $(-2, 1)$ and $(5, 4)$ in the standard (x, y) coordinate plane?
>
> A. $3\sqrt{2}$ B. $\sqrt{34}$ C. $\sqrt{58}$ D. $\sqrt{74}$ E. 9

Solution: We can solve for distance between the two points with the distance formula or by sketching a triangle.

Method #1 – Distance formula: Solve with the distance formula using $(-2, 1)$ as (x_1, y_1) and $(5, 4)$ as (x_2, y_2).

$$\text{Distance} = \sqrt{(-2 - 5)^2 + (1 - 4)^2}$$

$$\text{Distance} = \sqrt{(-7)^2 + (-3)^2}$$

$$\text{Distance} = \sqrt{58}$$

The answer is C.

Method #2 – Sketch a triangle: Draw a coordinate plane and make a triangle.

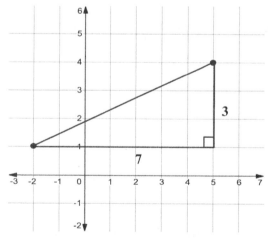

Using the triangle, we see that the base has a length of 7 and the height has a length of 3. To find the distance between the 2 points, use the Pythagorean Theorem:

$$7^2 + 3^2 = c^2$$

$$58 = c^2$$

$$c = \sqrt{58}$$

The answer is C.

Solving for Intercepts

The x-intercept is the point where a line crosses the x-axis. **To solve for the x-intercept, set $y = 0$ and solve for x.**

The y-intercept is the point where the line crosses the y-axis. **To solve for the y-intercept, set $x = 0$ and solve for y.**

> **Example 9:** For the line $10 - 2y = 5x$, what is the sum of the x-intercept and the y-intercept?
> A. 2   B. 3   C. 5   D. 7   E. 9

Solution: To find the x-intercept, set $y = 0$ and solve for x.

$$10 - 2(0) = 5x$$
$$10 = 5x$$
$$x = 2$$

The x-intercept is at $x = 2$.

To find the y-intercept, set $x = 0$ and solve for y.

$$10 - 2y = 5(0)$$
$$10 - 2y = 0$$
$$2y = 10$$
$$y = 5$$

The y-intercept is at $y = 5$.

The sum of the x-intercept and y-intercept is $2 + 5$, so the **answer is D.**

Lines Practice: Answers on page 324.

1. In the standard (x, y) coordinate plane, a line intersects the x-axis at $(-1, 0)$ and contains the point $(7, 2)$. What is the slope of the line?

   A. $\frac{1}{4}$
   B. $\frac{1}{3}$
   C. $\frac{7}{3}$
   D. 3
   E. 4

3. A line in the standard (x, y) coordinate plane passes through the points $(-7, 5)$ and $(1, -4)$. The slope of the line is:

   A. $-\frac{9}{8}$
   B. $-\frac{1}{6}$
   C. $\frac{1}{6}$
   D. $\frac{9}{8}$
   E. 6

2. In the standard (x, y) coordinate plane, what is the midpoint of the line segment with endpoints $(2, 6)$ and $(6, 10)$?

   A. $(3, 6)$
   B. $(4, -4)$
   C. $(-4, -4)$
   D. $(4, 8)$
   E. $(8, 16)$

4. The point $(5, m)$ lies on the graph of the line $y = -\frac{2}{5}x + 11$ in the standard (x, y) coordinate plane. What is the value of m ?

   A. 6
   B. 9
   C. 11
   D. 13
   E. 16

5. Which of the following statements is true about the graph of the equation $3y - 4x = -6$ in the xy-plane?

   A. The line has a negative slope and a negative y-intercept.
   B. The line has a negative slope and a positive y-intercept.
   C. The line has a positive slope and a negative y-intercept.
   D. The line has a positive slope and a positive y-intercept.
   E. The line has a positive slope and no y-intercept.

6. When graphed in the standard (x, y) coordinate plane, the line with equation $\frac{1}{3}x - 3y = \frac{1}{2}$ has a slope of:

   A. $\frac{1}{9}$
   B. $\frac{1}{6}$
   C. $\frac{2}{3}$
   D. 1
   E. 9

7. When the point Y $(2, 4)$ is graphed in the standard (x, y) coordinate plane, the midpoint of line XY is at $(-2, 3)$. What are the coordinates of point X?

   A. $(0, 3.5)$
   B. $(4, 0)$
   C. $(6, 5)$
   D. $(-6, 2)$
   E. $(0, 1)$

8. Which of the following is the correct equation for the graph below?

   A. $y = 4x + 2$
   B. $y = -\frac{1}{2}x + 4$
   C. $y = -2x + 4$
   D. $y = 2x + 4$
   E. $y = 2x + 2$

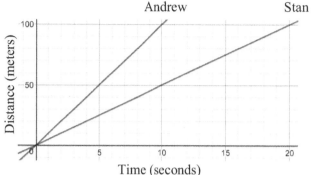

Questions 8 and 9 refer to the graph below.

The graph above shows the positions of Andrew and Stan during a 100m rowing race.

9. According to the graph, what is the rate that Stan rowed at during the race in meters per second?

   A. 2
   B. 5
   C. 10
   D. 15
   E. 20

10. If Andrew and Stan wanted cross the finish line at the exact same time, how many meters of a head start would Stan need to be given before Andrew and Stan begin rowing?

    A. 10
    B. 25
    C. 40
    D. 50
    E. 100

11. In the standard (x, y) coordinate plane, a line with a slope of -3 passes through the points $(-2, -6)$ and $(5, b)$. What is b equal to?

    A. 27
    B. 15
    C. -15
    D. -23
    E. -27

12. The equation $p = 1.04t + 101.5$ models the price of a stock, p, in dollars t minutes after 3pm on a certain day. According to this equation, what would the stock price be in dollars at 3pm?

    A. 0
    B. 1.04
    C. 100.46
    D. 101.50
    E. 102.54

13. What is the length, in coordinate units, of a line with endpoints at $(-9, -2)$ and $(3, 7)$?

    A. $\sqrt{117}$
    B. 12
    C. 13
    D. 15
    E. $2\sqrt{61}$

14. In the standard xy-plane, what is the slope of a line perpendicular to $6x = 4y + 10$?

    A. -1
    B. $\frac{2}{3}$
    C. $\frac{3}{2}$
    D. $-\frac{2}{3}$
    E. $-\frac{3}{2}$

15. A doctor uses the model $w = 9a + 19.5$ to estimate the weight, w, of a boy in terms of the boy's age, a, in years. Based on the model, what is the expected increase in the boy's weight, in pounds, from his 3rd to 7th birthday?

    A. 9
    B. 18
    C. 19.5
    D. 27
    E. 36

16. When a roadmap is drawn in the (x, y) coordinate plane, one rest stop is drawn at $(-2, 6)$ and a second is drawn at $(8, 14)$. If 1 coordinate unit represents 10 miles, which of the following is the closest to the straight-line distance in miles between the two rest stops?

    A. 55
    B. 80
    C. 100
    D. 130
    E. 160

17. Line k passes through the points $(-2, 10)$ and $(4, 28)$. Which of the following is the equation for line k?

    A. $y = \frac{2}{3}x$
    B. $y = 3x + 16$
    C. $y = 3x + 4$
    D. $y = \frac{1}{3}x + 12$
    E. $y = \frac{1}{3}x + 15$

18. The graph below shows the function $f(x)$. $f(x)$ and $g(x)$ (not shown) are perpendicular lines. Which of the following could define $g(x)$?

    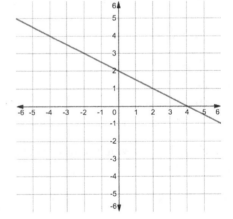

    A. $g(x) = -2x - 2$
    B. $g(x) = -\frac{1}{2}x + 4$
    C. $g(x) = \frac{1}{2}x + 2$
    D. $g(x) = 2x - 3$
    E. $g(x) = -\frac{1}{2} - 4$

19. The points $(3,7)$, $(0,5)$ and $(-6,1)$ lie on a line in the standard (x,y) coordinate plane. Which of the following points also lies on that line?

   A. $(-5,2)$
   B. $(-3,5)$
   C. $(-2,4)$
   D. $(5,10)$
   E. $(9,11)$

20. The line with the equation $\frac{5}{4}x + \frac{1}{2}y = 3$ is graphed in the (x,y) coordinate plane. What is the x-intercept of the line?

   A. $-\frac{15}{8}$
   B. $\frac{1}{2}$
   C. $\frac{5}{12}$
   D. 3
   E. $\frac{12}{5}$

21. In the xy-plane below, line a (shown below) is parallel to line b (not shown). What is the slope of line b?

   A. 1
   B. $\frac{1}{2}$
   C. 2
   D. -1
   E. -2

22. In the standard (x,y) coordinate plane, the point $(1,7)$ is 13 coordinate units away from which of the following points?

   A. $(6,-5)$
   B. $(4,-8)$
   C. $(-7,-2)$
   D. $(-4,18)$
   E. $(13,20)$

23. The graph of the line $y = kx - 2$ is graphed in the xy-plane and k is a constant. If the line contains the point (a,b) and $a \neq 0$ and $b \neq 0$, what is the slope of the line in terms of a and b?

   A. $\frac{a+2}{b}$
   B. $\frac{b+2}{a}$
   C. $\frac{2-a}{b}$
   D. $\frac{b-2}{a}$
   E. $\frac{a-2}{b}$

24. A line in the xy-plane has a slope of 3 and passes through the point $(2a, 6a)$, where a is a nonzero constant. What is the y-intercept of this line in terms of a?

   A. $0a$
   B. $3a$
   C. $\frac{16}{3}a$
   D. $12a$
   E. Cannot be determined

25. Lines p, q, and r are shown in the standard (x,y) coordinate plane below. All three lines intersect at $(0,5)$. The slope of line q is equal to the average of the slopes of lines p and r. What is the x-intercept of line q?

   A. 3
   B. $\frac{10}{3}$
   C. $\frac{7}{2}$
   D. $\frac{18}{5}$
   E. $\frac{15}{4}$

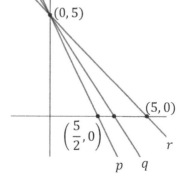

26. In the standard (x, y) coordinate plane, lines m and n are perpendicular and intersect at point $(3, 5)$. If the slope of line m is $-\frac{2}{3}$, what is the y-intercept of line n?

   A. $\left(0, \frac{1}{2}\right)$
   B. $(0, 3)$
   C. $\left(0, \frac{13}{3}\right)$
   D. $(0, 7)$
   E. $\left(0, \frac{19}{2}\right)$

27. In the standard (x, y) coordinate plane, line a contains the points $(2, 11)$ and $(5, 2)$, and line b contains the points $(-5, 0)$ and $(-1, 4)$. At what point does line a intersect line b?

   A. $(9, 14)$
   B. $\left(\frac{9}{2}, \frac{19}{2}\right)$
   C. $(3, 8)$
   D. $\left(\frac{18}{5}, \frac{31}{4}\right)$
   E. $\left(0, \frac{87}{6}\right)$

Chapter 6: Fractions

For success on the ACT, you will need to be comfortable with fractions. Fractions are one of those topics that many students hate. If you are one of those students, fear not! In this chapter, we will cover all the fundamental techniques that will allow you to answer any question involving fractions quickly and efficiently.

1. Combining Fractions

To add or subtract fractions, we must make the denominators the same by finding the least common multiple of the numbers or expressions in the denominators. For example, consider adding the fractions below:

$$\frac{1}{2} + \frac{2}{5}$$

Here, the least common denominator is 10. An easy trick to find a common denominator is to multiply the numbers in the denominator together. For the fractions above, $2 \times 5 = 10$. Once we find the least common denominator, we can convert all fractions to have the same common denominator and then combine.

$$\frac{1}{2} \times \frac{5}{5} + \frac{2}{5} \times \frac{2}{2} = \frac{5}{10} + \frac{4}{10} = \frac{9}{10}$$

On the ACT, you will often see questions with expressions in the denominators instead of just numbers. These are more difficult, but the concept and approach are the exact same.

> **Example 1:** $\frac{1}{x} + \frac{3}{x-4}$
>
> Which of the following is equivalent to the equation above for $x \neq 0$ and $x \neq 4$?
>
> A. $\frac{4x-4}{x(x-4)}$ B. $\frac{4}{2x-4}$ C. $\frac{4x-12}{x-4}$ D. $\frac{x-1}{x(x-4)}$ E. $\frac{4}{x(x-4)}$

Solution: To start, we need to find the common denominator. Here, the common denominator is the product of the two denominators: $x(x-4)$. We need to multiply the top and bottom of each fraction by the term they are missing in the denominator.

$$\frac{1}{x} \times \frac{x-4}{x-4} + \frac{3}{x-4} \times \frac{x}{x} = \frac{x-4}{x(x-4)} + \frac{3x}{x(x-4)} = \frac{x-4+3x}{x(x-4)} = \frac{4x-4}{x(x-4)}$$

The answer is A.

Shortcut Solution – Substitution: For any "equivalent" questions like this one, we can also use the method we discussed in Chapter 2 and plug in a value for x.

2. Dividing Fractions

Let's say that you are solving a question and get

$$\frac{2}{3}x = \frac{1}{5}$$

To solve for x, we divide both sides by $\frac{2}{3}$. **How do we divide a fraction by a fraction? Take the fraction on the bottom, flip it to get the reciprocal, and then multiply the top and bottom fractions together.** It's as easy as that!

$$x = \frac{\frac{1}{5}}{\frac{2}{3}} = \frac{1}{5} \times \frac{3}{2} = \frac{3}{10}$$

- 41 -

We can use this method any time we are dividing by a fraction even if the right side is a whole number. For example, if we have

$$\frac{2}{7}x = 3$$

To solve, we need to divide both sides by $\frac{2}{7}$, so we use the same trick of flipping the fraction and multiplying by the reciprocal.

$$x = \frac{3}{\frac{2}{7}} = 3 \times \frac{7}{2} = \frac{21}{2}$$

Example 2: $\quad \frac{3}{4}x + \frac{1}{5} = \frac{1}{3}$

For the equation above, what is the value of x?

A. $\frac{2}{30}$ B. $\frac{8}{45}$ C. $\frac{1}{3}$ D. $\frac{2}{3}$ E. $\frac{3}{4}$

Solution: First, we need to combine like terms by subtracting $\frac{1}{5}$ from both sides.

$$\frac{3}{4}x = \frac{1}{3} - \frac{1}{5}$$

Next, we need to combine the numbers on the right side by finding the common denominator. For 3 and 5, the least common denominator is 15.

$$\frac{1}{3} \times \frac{5}{5} - \frac{1}{5} \times \frac{3}{3} = \frac{5}{15} - \frac{3}{15} = \frac{2}{15}$$

Now, substitute this back into the equation.

$$\frac{3}{4}x = \frac{2}{15}$$

To isolate x, we divide both sides by $\frac{3}{4}$, so we flip the fraction and multiply by the reciprocal.

$$x = \frac{2}{15} \times \frac{4}{3} = \frac{8}{45}$$

The answer is B.

3. Simplifying Fractions

When simplifying fractions, you must be able to divide all terms in the numerator and denominator by the same number. Simplifying fractions with only numbers is easy.

$$\frac{6}{15} \div \frac{3}{3} = \frac{2}{5}$$

Many students struggle when there are multiple terms in the numerator or denominator. Let's start with a variable in the numerator.

$$\frac{2x + 10}{4}$$

Can we simplify this fraction? Yes, but only if we can divide all terms by the same number. Here, we can divide every term by 2, so we can simplify the fraction.

$$\frac{2x+10}{4} \div \frac{2}{2} = \frac{x+5}{2}$$

Many students will make a mistake and only divide the first term by 2 and not the 10 like this:

$$\frac{2x+10}{4} \neq \frac{x+10}{2}$$

WRONG! You must divide all terms by the same number to simplify. If you cannot divide all terms by the same number, you cannot simplify the fraction. For example, if we instead had

$$\frac{8x+3}{4}$$

we can no longer simplify this fraction, but we can split this fraction into two:

$$\frac{8x+3}{4} = \frac{8x}{4} + \frac{3}{4} = 2x + \frac{3}{4}$$

If you cannot simplify a fraction by dividing all terms by the same number, you should look to split and simplify the fraction this way.

The same concept applies for simplifying fractions when we have variables in the denominator.

$$\frac{3}{6x+30}$$

Can we simplify this fraction? Yes, all terms can be divided by 3, so we can simplify the fraction.

$$\frac{3}{6x+30} \div \frac{3}{3} = \frac{1}{2x+10}$$

Again, make sure that you divide all terms by the same number. If you cannot divide all terms by the same number, the fraction cannot be simplified. For example, if we had

$$\frac{3}{6x+10}$$

we cannot simplify the fraction. While we just saw that you can split up the numerators of a fraction, you cannot split up the denominators.

$$\frac{3}{6x+10} \neq \frac{3}{6x} + \frac{3}{10}$$

We cannot simplify a fraction like this one at all.

Example 3:

$$\frac{12x+2}{6} + \frac{1}{3}$$

Which of the following is equivalent to the equation above?

A. $2x + \frac{1}{2}$ B. $2x + \frac{2}{3}$ C. $\frac{7}{3}x + \frac{1}{3}$ D. $4x + \frac{7}{3}$ E. $4x + \frac{2}{3}$

②

Solution: First, we need to make the denominators the same, so we can combine the fractions. The least common denominator of 3 and 6 is 6.

$$\frac{12x+2}{6} + \frac{1}{3} \times \frac{2}{2} = \frac{12x+2}{6} + \frac{2}{6} = \frac{12x+4}{6}$$

Next, we simplify the fraction. All the terms can be divided by 2.

$$\frac{12x+4}{6} \div \frac{2}{2} = \frac{6x+2}{3}$$

PrepPros

Finally, we can split the numerator and simplify to solve.

$$\frac{6x+2}{3} = \frac{6x}{3} + \frac{2}{3} = 2x + \frac{2}{3}$$

The answer is B.

Shortcut Solution – Substitution: For any "equivalent" questions like this one, we can also use the method we discussed in Chapter 2 and just plug in a value for x.

4. Getting Rid of Fractions

For questions with only numbers in the denominator, it is usually easiest to get rid of the fractions. **We can get rid of the fractions by multiplying both sides by the least common multiple of the numbers in the denominator.** The least common multiple is the same as the least common denominator we discussed earlier in this chapter.

$$\frac{1}{4}x + \frac{1}{2} = \frac{3}{8}x$$

The least common multiple of 4, 2, and 8 is 8, so we can multiply all terms by 8 to eliminate the fractions.

$$\frac{1}{4}x \times 8 + \frac{1}{2} \times 8 = \frac{3}{8}x \times 8$$

The equation becomes

$$2x + 4 = 3x$$

Now, solving is easy!

$$x = 4$$

If you struggle with fractions, always use this method to turn fractions into whole numbers.

Example 4: If $\frac{3x}{5} - \frac{2x}{6} - \frac{1}{2} = \frac{x}{10}$, what is the value of x?

A. 10   B. 6   C. 5   D. 3   E. 2

Solution: Since all the terms in denominator are numbers, we can get rid of the fractions. The least common multiple of 5, 6, 2, and 10 is 30, so we can multiply all of the terms by 30.

$$\frac{3x}{5} \times 30 - \frac{2x}{6} \times 30 - \frac{1}{2} \times 30 = \frac{x}{10} \times 30$$

$$18x - 10x - 15 = 3x$$

$$8x - 15 = 3x$$

$$8x = 3x + 15$$

$$5x = 15$$

$$x = 3$$

The answer is D.

Shortcut Solution – Backsolve: Rather than doing all of the math, plug the answer choices back into the original equation to see which one makes the equation true.

Chapter 6: Fractions

5. Turn Fractions into Decimals

If you really hate fractions, another trick is to turn fractions into decimals. You can always turn fractions into decimals using your calculator.

Example 5:
$$\frac{3}{4}x - \frac{4}{10} = \frac{1}{2}x$$

For the equation above, what is the value of x?

A. $\frac{3}{8}$ B. $\frac{8}{25}$ C. $\frac{2}{5}$ D. $\frac{3}{2}$ E. $\frac{8}{5}$

Solution: We can change the fractions to decimals.

$$0.75x - 0.4 = 0.5x$$

Now, we solve for x algebraically.

$$0.75x = 0.5x + 0.4$$
$$0.25x = 0.4$$
$$x = \frac{0.4}{0.25}$$

Using your calculator, we can find the value for x.

$$x = 1.6$$

To tell which answer choice is equivalent to 1.6, you can plug the answer choices into your calculator to see which one is equal to 1.6. **The correct answer is E.**

6. Use Your Calculator

Did you know that your calculator can solve most fractions questions for you? **Almost all calculators have the capability to turn a decimal into a fraction and vice versa.** This can make fractions questions on the ACT far easier and faster to solve.

The steps below outline how to use the fractions function in two of the most popular types of calculators.

<u>TI-83/84 Graphing Calculator</u>

1. Enter the decimal you want to change into a fraction.
2. Press the MATH button.
3. Select Frac.
4. The calculator will display the decimal as a fraction.

<u>TI30XS Scientific Calculator</u>

1. Enter the decimal you want to change into a fraction.
2. Press 2nd then PRB to select F↔D.
3. Press Enter (=).
4. The calculator will display the decimal as a fraction.

If you have any other type of calculator than the 2 listed above, go to YouTube and look up a tutorial for how to turn fractions into decimals for your calculator.

If your calculator cannot turn fractions into decimals and you solve for the correct answer in decimal form, you can enter fractions in the answer choices into your calculator to convert them to decimals to find which one matches the answer you found.

Fractions Practice: Answers on page 324.

1. $\frac{4}{3} + \frac{3}{2} =$

2. $\frac{3}{5} - \frac{1}{4} =$

3. $\frac{7}{8} + \frac{1}{2} =$

4. $\frac{2}{3} - \frac{5}{2} =$

5. $\frac{6}{7} - \frac{1}{3} =$

6. $\frac{21}{5} + \frac{3}{2} =$

7. $\frac{16}{3} - \frac{7}{2} =$

8. $\frac{\frac{3}{5}}{\frac{4}{3}} =$

9. $\frac{\frac{1}{2}}{\frac{1}{3}} =$

10. $\frac{\frac{2}{5}}{\frac{3}{2}} =$

11. $\frac{\frac{4}{3}}{\frac{1}{3}} =$

12. If $\frac{2}{7}x + 8 = 15$, then $x = ?$

    A. $-\frac{49}{2}$
    B. $\frac{7}{2}$
    C. $\frac{22}{7}$
    D. $\frac{49}{2}$
    E. 55

13. If $\frac{2a}{3} = \frac{4}{3}$, what is the value of a?

    A. $\frac{1}{6}$
    B. $\frac{1}{4}$
    C. $\frac{1}{2}$
    D. 2
    E. 4

14. Which of the following is equal to $\frac{1}{3} + \frac{1}{2} + \frac{3}{5}$?

    A. $\frac{9}{30}$
    B. $\frac{2}{3}$
    C. $\frac{9}{10}$
    D. $\frac{33}{30}$
    E. $\frac{43}{30}$

15. In a class of sixth graders, every student participates in no more than one sport. $\frac{1}{10}$ play lacrosse, $\frac{1}{6}$ play field hockey, $\frac{1}{4}$ play soccer, and $\frac{7}{60}$ play football. What fraction of the class does not play any of these 4 sports?

    A. 0
    B. $\frac{1}{240}$
    C. $\frac{11}{30}$
    D. $\frac{38}{60}$
    E. $\frac{73}{80}$

16. If $\frac{7}{5}x = \frac{9}{8}$, what is the value of x?

    A. $\frac{5}{8}$
    B. $\frac{8}{9}$
    C. $\frac{9}{7}$
    D. $\frac{45}{56}$
    E. $\frac{56}{45}$

17. What is the least common denominator for the fractions $\frac{1}{12}, \frac{4}{5},$ and $\frac{3}{8}$?

    A. 40
    B. 60
    C. 96
    D. 240
    E. 480

18. Jiang and Kris are painting the walls in the gym. They started with 8 gallons of paint. On the first day, Jiang used $1\frac{3}{4}$ gallons of paint and Kris used $3\frac{1}{8}$ gallons of paint. How many gallons of paint were left after the first day?

    A. $2\frac{7}{8}$
    B. $3\frac{1}{8}$
    C. $3\frac{5}{8}$
    D. $3\frac{7}{8}$
    E. $4\frac{7}{8}$

19. San Clarita High School has 150 students, and $\frac{1}{5}$ of the students are taking Biology. Of the students NOT taking Biology, $\frac{1}{3}$ are taking Chemistry. No students are taking both Biology and Chemistry. How many students are taking Chemistry?

    A. 20
    B. 30
    C. 40
    D. 60
    E. 120

20. Monique, Cassandra, and Maria decorated a cake together. Cassandra decorated $\frac{2}{7}$ of the cake and Monique decorated $\frac{1}{3}$ of the cake. How much of the cake did Maria decorate?

    A. $\frac{1}{5}$
    B. $\frac{1}{3}$
    C. $\frac{8}{21}$
    D. $\frac{13}{21}$
    E. $\frac{7}{10}$

21. Which of the following numbers is halfway between $\frac{1}{6}$ and $\frac{3}{10}$?

    A. $\frac{7}{30}$
    B. $\frac{13}{60}$
    C. $\frac{3}{16}$
    D. $\frac{4}{15}$
    E. $\frac{1}{4}$

22. A gas tank has a capacity of 270 gallons and is $\frac{7}{9}$ full of gas. Anissa then removes $\frac{1}{5}$ of the gas in the tank. How many gallons of gas are left in the tank?

    A. 42
    B. 84
    C. 168
    D. 210
    E. 252

23. If $x > 0$, which of the following is equivalent to $\frac{2}{x} + \frac{1}{3}$?

    A. $\frac{6x+3}{3x}$
    B. $\frac{3}{x+3}$
    C. $\frac{6+x}{3x}$
    D. $\frac{6+x}{x}$
    E. $\frac{2x}{x+3}$

24. A group of 200 students are selecting shirts to wear for the homecoming game. For the game, students were given a choice of 1 of 3 shirts. Of the 200 students, $\frac{1}{5}$ chose a blue shirt, $\frac{1}{4}$ chose a black shirt, and $\frac{3}{10}$ chose a white shirt. The remaining students expressed no choice. How many of the students expressed no choice?

    A. 10
    B. 30
    C. 50
    D. 80
    E. 150

25. What is the least common denominator of the fractions $\frac{6}{33}, \frac{2}{22}$, and $\frac{17}{65}$?

A. 120
B. 726
C. 4,290
D. 12,870
E. 47,190

26. The difference $\frac{1}{4} - \frac{-2}{3}$ lies in which of the following intervals?

A. $0 < x \leq \frac{1}{4}$
B. $\frac{1}{4} < x \leq \frac{1}{2}$
C. $\frac{1}{2} < x \leq \frac{3}{4}$
D. $\frac{3}{4} < x \leq 1$
E. $1 < x \leq \frac{5}{4}$

27. Given consecutive negative integers a, b, c, and d, such that $a < b < c < d$, which of the following has the smallest value?

A. $\frac{a}{d}$
B. $\frac{a}{b}$
C. $\frac{c}{a}$
D. $\frac{ab}{d}$
E. $\frac{c+d}{a}$

28. Which of the following numbers is halfway between $\frac{3}{4}$ and $\frac{12}{5}$?

A. $\frac{63}{20}$
B. $\frac{63}{40}$
C. $\frac{27}{20}$
D. $\frac{15}{18}$
E. $\frac{15}{20}$

29. Given consecutive negative integers a, b, c, and d such that $a > b > c > d$, which of the following expressions has the greatest value?

A. a
B. $a - b$
C. $\frac{a}{d}$
D. $\frac{d}{a}$
E. $\frac{d-c}{b-a}$

30. Which of the following is equal to $\frac{3+9x}{15}$?

A. $\frac{3+3x}{5}$
B. $\frac{1+9x}{5}$
C. $\frac{1+3x}{5}$
D. $\frac{1}{5} + 3x$
E. $3 + \frac{3x}{5}$

31. Which of the following is equal to $\frac{2}{x-1} + \frac{3}{x}$, for all $x \neq 0$ and $x \neq 1$?

A. $\frac{5x-3}{x^2-x}$
B. $\frac{3x-3}{x^2-x}$
C. $\frac{5x+3}{x^2-x}$
D. $\frac{-1}{x-1}$
E. $\frac{5}{x^2-x}$

32. Given consecutive positive integers a, b, c, and d, such that $a > b > c > d$, which of the following has the largest value?

A. $\frac{d}{c}$
B. $\frac{a+b}{d}$
C. $\frac{a}{b}$
D. $\frac{a+c}{b+d}$
E. $\frac{a+b}{c+d}$

Chapter 6: Fractions

33. Which of the following is equivalent to $\frac{x}{x+1} - \frac{3}{x-1}$?

   A. $\frac{x^2-4x-3}{x^2-1}$
   B. $\frac{x^2+2x-3}{x^2-1}$
   C. $\frac{x^2+4x+3}{x^2-1}$
   D. $\frac{x-3}{x^2-1}$
   E. $\frac{x^2-x-3}{x^2-1}$

34. Which of the following is equivalent to $\frac{x^2+5x}{x}$?

   A. $\frac{x+5}{x}$
   B. $\frac{x^2+5}{x}$
   C. $x + 5$
   D. $x^2 + 5$
   E. $6x$

35. Which of the following is equivalent to the equation below where $x \neq 2$?

   $$\frac{4}{x-2} + \frac{6}{3(x-2)}$$

   A. $\frac{12}{3x-6}$
   B. $\frac{22}{3x-2}$
   C. $\frac{16}{3x-2}$
   D. $\frac{28}{3x-2}$
   E. $\frac{6}{x-2}$

36. For $\frac{1}{3}x + \frac{2}{7} = \frac{4}{7}x$, what does x equal?

   A. $\frac{6}{5}$
   B. $\frac{5}{6}$
   C. $\frac{6}{7}$
   D. $\frac{7}{6}$
   E. $\frac{6}{19}$

37. A box contains combination of blue, red, pink, and yellow jellybeans. $\frac{1}{5}$ of the jellybeans are blue, $\frac{1}{4}$ are red, $\frac{3}{10}$ are pink, and the remaining 25 jellybeans are yellow. How many more red jellybeans are there than blue?

   A. 30
   B. 25
   C. 20
   D. 10
   E. 5

38. For $x - \frac{4}{5} = 2 + \frac{1}{3}x$, $x = ?$

   A. $\frac{34}{21}$
   B. $\frac{21}{10}$
   C. $\frac{21}{5}$
   D. $\frac{34}{5}$
   E. $\frac{10}{3}$

39. A container is $\frac{1}{6}$ full of water. After adding 22 cups of water, the container is $\frac{5}{8}$ full. What is the volume of the container in cups?

   A. 16
   B. $35\frac{1}{5}$
   C. 38
   D. 48
   E. $58\frac{2}{3}$

40. Which of the following expressions is equivalent to $\frac{\frac{x+1}{x}}{\frac{2}{x+3}}$?

   A. $\frac{2x}{x^2+4x+3}$
   B. $\frac{x^2+4x+3}{2x}$
   C. $\frac{x^2+3x+3}{2x}$
   D. $\frac{2x+2}{x^2+3x}$
   E. $\frac{2x+4}{2x}$

41. Which of the following lists those integer values of a for which the fraction $\frac{2}{a}$ lies between $\frac{1}{7}$ and $\frac{1}{4}$?

A. 7 only
B. 7 and 8
C. 9 only
D. 9, 10, 11, 12, and 13
E. 12, 13, 14, and 15

42. Which of the following expressions is equivalent to $\frac{\frac{x-2}{x+3}}{\frac{x+2}{x+1}}$?

A. $\frac{x^2-4}{x^2+4x+3}$
B. $\frac{x^2-x-2}{x^2+5x+6}$
C. $\frac{x^2+x-6}{x^2+3x+2}$
D. $\frac{x^2+5x+6}{x^2-x-2}$
E. $\frac{x^2+4x+3}{x^2-4}$

43. Which of the following expressions is equivalent to $\frac{\frac{x}{3}+\frac{2}{3}}{\frac{2}{3}-\frac{1}{5}}$?

A. $\frac{x+2}{5}$
B. $\frac{5x+5}{7}$
C. $\frac{5x+10}{7}$
D. $\frac{15x+30}{7}$
E. $5x+10$

44. What value of x satisfies the equation below?

$$\frac{5x^2+2x}{x^2-4} - \frac{3x}{x-2} = \frac{3}{x+2}$$

A. -2
B. $-\frac{3}{2}$
C. 1
D. $\frac{3}{2}$
E. 2

Chapter 7: Algebra Skills

Many ACT questions will test your core algebra skills. To answer these questions correctly, you will need to be able to isolate an unknown such as x or y or solve an equation. For any algebra question, be sure to take your time, write out each step of the question, and use the calculator to avoid silly mistakes like making a mental math error or forgetting a negative sign.

In this section, we will cover the algebra skills that you will need in your toolbox for test day.

1. PEMDAS

In algebra, order of operations is critical to solving math questions correctly. PEMDAS is an acronym to help you remember the order of operations in algebra. The rules of PEMDAS are below:

1. **P – Parentheses:** Complete any calculations inside parentheses first.
2. **E – Exponents:** Next, complete any exponents or square roots.
3. **MD – Multiplication and Division:** Complete any multiplication and division (left-to-right)
4. **AS – Addition and Subtraction:** Complete any addition and subtraction (left-to-right)

Make sure you do the multiplication and division step left-to right! This is where the ACT most often tries to trick students. For example, if we are given

$$16 \div 4 \times 2 - 3$$

We need to work left-to-right when completing multiplication and division. If solved correctly, we will start by dividing 16 by 4 and then multiply by 2. Once we complete the multiplication and division, we will subtract 3.

Correct: $16 \div 4 \times 2 - 3 = 4 \times 2 - 3 = 8 - 3 = 5$

Many students make the mistake of doing the multiplication first and then dividing.

Incorrect: $16 \div 4 \times 2 - 3 = 16 \div 8 - 3 = 2 - 3 = -1$

Example 1: What is the value of the expression $22 + (-4)^2 \div 2 \times (5 + 10)$?
  A. 40   B. 72   C. 120   D. 142   E. 285

Solution: First, complete any calculations in parentheses.

$$22 + (-4)^2 \div 2 \times 15$$

Next, complete the exponents.

$$22 + 16 \div 2 \times 15$$

Complete any multiplication and division from left-to-right.

$$22 + 16 \div 2 \times 15 = 22 + 8 \times 15 = 22 + 120$$

Finally, complete the addition.

$$22 + 120 = 142$$

The answer is D. As long as you follow the PEMDAS steps correctly and work left-to-right correctly, these questions should be easy!

Shortcut Solution – Use Your Calculator: You can also enter these questions directly into your calculator. Your calculator is programed to do PEMDAS correctly, so as long as you enter the equation correctly, the calculator will just tell you the answer. It's that easy!

PrepPros

2. Negative Numbers

The ACT really really really loves questions with negative numbers. These questions are a prime place where students make simple mistakes by not knowing how to properly do algebra with negative numbers. Let's review where students most often make mistakes to make sure that you ace these questions on test day.

Subtracting Negative Numbers

You likely already know that when subtracting a negative number, the negative signs turn into a positive sign and you add the numbers together. For example

$$2 - (-4) = 2 + 4 = 6$$

That's easy! The mistake students more often make is forgetting to distribute a negative sign to multiple terms. For example, if you are solving

$$5x - (2x - 5)$$

make sure to distribute the negative sign to both the $2x$ and the -5. Many students forget to distribute the negative sign.

Incorrect: $5x - (2x - 5) = 5x - 2x - 5 = 3x - 5$

Correct: $5x - (2x - 5) = 5x - 2x - (-5) = 3x + 5$

Example 2: Which of the following expressions is equivalent to $2(a + b) - 3(a - 4b)$?
  A. $-a - 11b$ B. $-a - 9b$ C. $-a - 3b$ D. $-a + 6b$ E. $-a + 14b$

Solution: Distribute the -3 to both the a and $-4b$ and combine like terms.

$$2(a + b) - 3(a - 4b) = 2a + 2b - 3a - 3(-4b) = 2a + 2b - 3a + 12b = -a + 14b$$

The answer is E.

Negative Numbers and Exponents

The second common mistake occurs when negative numbers are raised to a power. The important thing to understand is

$$-2^2 \text{ is not the same as } (-2)^2$$

For -2^2, you first square the 2 and then multiply by the negative sign. For $(-2)^2$, you just square -2. As a result, we see

$$-2^2 = -4$$
$$(-2)^2 = 4$$

This principle is very important to understand and can be tested on more difficult ACT questions. **Make sure you always put negative numbers in parentheses when you enter them into your calculator!** If you do not use the parentheses, you will get the wrong answer.

Example 3: If x is a real number such that $-x^3 < 0$, which of the following *must* be true?
  A. $x \neq 0$ B. $x > 0$ C. $x < 0$ D. $x \geq 0$ E. $x \leq 0$

Solution – "Math Teacher Way": The negative sign is not in parentheses, so we need to do the exponent first and then multiply by the negative sign. In order for $-x^3$ to be negative, x^3 must be positive. For x^3 to be positive, x must be positive. x cannot equal 0 since $-0^3 = 0$. **The answer is B.**

Shortcut Solution – Substitution: For conceptual math questions like this, it is easiest to pick test numbers, plug them into the equation, and see if they work or not. Here, let's try $x = -2$, $x = 0$, and $x = 2$.

$$\text{For } x = -2, -(-2)^3 = -(-8) = 8$$
$$\text{For } x = 0, -(0)^3 = 0$$
$$\text{For } x = 2, -(2)^3 = -(8) = -8$$

The only value that gave a number less than 0 is $x = 2$, so **the answer is B**.

3. Combining Like Terms

Whenever you have the chance, you should combine like terms. Doing so will help you simplify the equation and get to the correct answer more quickly.

> **Example 4:** If $2(3x - 6) + 3y = 6x - y + 8$, what is the value of y?
>
> A. 5   B. 3   C. 1   D. −1   E. −5

Solution: First, distribute the 2 on the left side of the equation.

$$6x - 12 + 3y = 6x - y + 8$$

We have x and y terms on both sides of the equation, so we need to combine like terms. Here, the $6x$ terms on both sides cancel, so we get

$$-12 + 3y = -y + 8$$

Now, combine the y-terms and the numbers and solve. Add y and 12 to both sides to get.

$$4y = 20$$
$$y = 5$$

The answer is A.

4. Cross Multiply Fractions

Whenever you have two fractions equal to one another, we can cross multiply to get rid of the fractions.

$$\frac{x}{z} = \frac{y}{w}$$

Cross multiplying, we get

$$xw = yz$$

> **Example 5:** If $\frac{3x}{4} = \frac{6}{7}$, what is the value of x?
>
> A. $\frac{9}{14}$ B. $\frac{7}{8}$ C. $\frac{8}{7}$ D. $\frac{4}{3}$ E. $\frac{14}{9}$

Solution:
$$\frac{3x}{4} = \frac{6}{7}$$
$$21x = 24$$
$$x = \frac{24}{21} = \frac{8}{7}$$

The answer is C.

5. Square Both Sides of an Equation Correctly

In algebra questions with square roots, you often need to square both sides to get rid of the square root. It is important to remember that you need to square both sides and not just each individual term. Students will often make a mistake on a question like the example below.

Example 6: $\sqrt{x} = x - 2$

What value(s) of x solve the equation above?

A. 1 B. 4 C. 2 D. 1, 4 E. 1, 2

Solution: When we see the x under the square root in this question, we start by squaring both sides of the equation. Most students will properly get rid of the square root on the left side of the equation, but they make a mistake on the right side by doing this:

$$x = x^2 - 4$$

WRONG! We cannot just square each individual term. We must square the entire equation on each side, so it should look like this:

$$(\sqrt{x})^2 = (x - 2)^2$$

If you prefer, you can also write out the right side of the equation like this to help make sure you remember to properly expand the expression.

$$(\sqrt{x})^2 = (x - 2)(x - 2)$$

If we properly square both sides of the equation, we get

$$x = x^2 - 4x + 4$$

From here, we can combine like terms, set the equation equal to zero, and factor. Moving all of the terms to the right side, we get

$$0 = x^2 - 5x + 4$$
$$0 = (x - 4)(x - 1)$$
$$x = 1, 4$$

It looks like there are two answers to this question, but that is not the case! **Anytime you square both sides of an equation, you NEED to plug the answers back into the original equation to look for extraneous solutions.** Sometimes when you square both sides of an equation, you get fake answers that look correct but do not actually work. Let's start by checking $x = 1$.

$$\sqrt{1} = 1 - 2$$
$$1 \neq -1$$

We see that $x = 1$ does not work in the original equation, so it is an extraneous solution. Now, we can check $x = 4$.

$$\sqrt{4} = 4 - 2$$
$$2 = 2$$

We find that $x = 4$ works in the original equation, so **the answer is B.**

Shortcut solution – Backsolve: We can backsolve this question using the answer choices. By plugging the answer choices in of 1, 2, and 4 in for x, we can test each answer choice. Only 4 works, so the answer is B.

Whenever you see a question like this, you should just plug the answer choices back in. It is much faster and easier than solving out algebraically!

6. Algebra with Inequality Signs

To solve inequalities on the ACT, treat the inequality signs ($<$, $>$, $\leq$, $\geq$) like an $=$ sign and solve using algebra. Inequalities can be solved as normal algebraic expressions with the exception of one very important rule:

When multiplying or dividing by a negative number, switch the direction of the inequality sign.

This rule is the most important thing to remember from this section and where students most commonly make mistakes on inequalities questions. As a quick example, let's see how to solve the equation below.

$$-5x - 3 > 11$$
$$-5x > 14$$

When dividing by -5, we switch the direction inequality sign, so

$$x < -\frac{14}{5}$$

Let's see a second example:

$$5x + 10 \leq 2x - 44$$

The first step is combining like terms. We subtract $2x$ from both sides to get the x-terms on the left side. We then subtract 10 from both sides to get the numbers on the right side.

$$5x - 2x \leq -44 - 10$$
$$3x \leq -54$$
$$x \leq -\frac{54}{3}$$
$$x \leq -18$$

In this example, we never multiply or divide by a negative number, so the inequality sign stays the same. Just because we are working with a negative number does not mean we need to flip the inequality sign. Some students flip the sign whenever they divide and see a negative sign. Don't make that mistake! Only flip the inequality when you multiply or divide both sides by a negative number.

> **Example 7:** Which of the following inequalities is equivalent to $2x - 6y < 4x - 14$?
> A. $x > 6y - 14$ B. $x < 3y - 7$ C. $x > 3y - 7$ D. $x < -3y + 7$ E. $x > -3y + 7$

Solution: To solve, we need to isolate x. We need to do this because all the answer choices have x isolated on the left side of the equation. To isolate x, we need to move the x-terms to the left side and all other terms to the right side. To do this, we need to subtract $4x$ from both sides and add $6y$ to both sides.

$$2x - 6y < 4x - 14$$
$$2x - 4x < 6y - 14$$
$$-2x < 6y - 14$$

To get x by itself, we need to divide both sides by -2. Since we are dividing by a negative, we also need to switch the direction of the inequality sign.

$$x > \frac{6y - 14}{-2}$$

Now, we can simplify the terms on the right side of the equation and solve.

$$x > -3y + 7$$

The answer is E.

7. Taking Square Roots in Algebraic Equations

When solving an algebra question, you may need to find the value of a variable that is squared. For example, if we have the equation

$$x^2 = 9$$

we need to take the square root of both sides to solve. Many students take the square root and get $x = 3$, which is WRONG! To take the square root properly, we need to use the following rule

When taking the square root of a squared variable (x^2), add a $\pm$ in front of the number.

For the example equation above, we should solve using the following steps to solve properly.

$$x^2 = 9$$
$$\sqrt{x^2} = \pm\sqrt{9}$$
$$x = \pm 3$$
$$x = -3, 3$$

1. Take square root of both sides.
2. Add a $\pm$ sign in front of the number.
3. Simplify

Notice that we get 2 answers! This makes sense because both $(-3)^2$ and 3^2 equal 9.

Now, it is important to clarify that this only applies to taking the square root of algebraic equations with squared terms, like x^2. **You do not add a $\pm$ sign when taking the square root of only a number.**

Correct: $\sqrt{9} = 3$ **Incorrect:** $\sqrt{9} = \pm 3$

The square root of 9 is only 3, not ± 3. Square roots are always positive. Understanding this difference is important for solving questions involving square roots and variables correctly.

Example 8: What value(s) of x are solutions to the equation $x^2 + 10 = 46$?

A. -6 B. 6 C. $2\sqrt{14}$ D. $0, 6$ E. $-6, 6$

Solution: When solving an equation with an x^2 term and numbers, start by getting the x^2 term on one side by itself. To do that, we need to subtract 10 from both sides.

$$x^2 + 10 = 46$$
$$x^2 = 36$$

Now, we can take the square root of both sides. Since we are taking the square root with an x^2 term, we need to add a $\pm$ sign in front of the number.

$$\sqrt{x^2} = \pm\sqrt{36}$$
$$x = \pm 6$$
$$x = -6, 6$$

The correct answer is E.

Chapter 7: Algebra Skills

Algebra Skills Practice: Answers on page 325.

1. Which of the following expressions is equivalent to $(x^4 + x) + (x^3 - x)$?

    A. x^7
    B. $x^4 + x^3 - x^2$
    C. $x^4 + x^3$
    D. x^{12}
    E. $x^{12} + 2x$

2. Given $g = -5, r = 3$, and $m = 2$, $(g - m)(r - g + m) = ?$

    A. -70
    B. -56
    C. -20
    D. 0
    E. 30

3. If $4x - 18 = 14$, $x = ?$

    A. -1
    B. 4
    C. 8
    D. 12
    E. 32

4. If $x = -1$ and $y = 3$, what is the value of $x^3 + 2x^2y - 5xy^2 + 3y$?

    A. -43
    B. -1
    C. 47
    D. 59
    E. 61

5. Which expression is equivalent to $(3x^2 - 2x + 5) - (-2x^2 + 3x - 2)$?

    A. $x^2 - x + 7$
    B. $x^2 + x + 3$
    C. $x^2 - 5x + 7$
    D. $5x^2 + x + 3$
    E. $5x^2 - 5x + 7$

6. The solution set of $3 - 5x \geq -22$ is the set of all real values of x such that:

    A. $x \geq -5$
    B. $x \leq -5$
    C. $x \geq 2$
    D. $x \geq 5$
    E. $x \leq 5$

7. Which expression is equivalent to $(x^2 + 5) - (2x^2 - 2)$?

    A. $-x^2 + 3$
    B. $-x^2 + 7$
    C. $3x^2 + 3$
    D. $3x^2 + 7$
    E. $3x^2 - 3$

8. Given $z = \sqrt{25} + 3 - 4 \div 2$, what does z equal?

    A. -4
    B. -3
    C. 2
    D. 6
    E. $-4, 6$

9. If $x = -2$, what is the value of b in the equation $x - \frac{1}{4}b = 2$?

    A. -16
    B. -4
    C. 0
    D. 4
    E. 16

10. Which of the following is equivalent to the expression below?

    $(x^2y^2 - 4x^3 + 2xy^2) - (2x^2y^2 + 2x^3 - 3xy^2)$

    A. $3xy^2 - 6x^3 - 5xy^2$
    B. $3xy^2 + 6x^3 - xy^2$
    C. $-x^2y^2 + 2x^3 - 5xy^2$
    D. $-x^2y^2 - 6x^3 + 5xy^2$
    E. $x^2y^2 + 6x^3 - 3xy^2$

11. What is the greatest integer solution to $-8x + 3 > -14.4$?

   A. -2
   B. -1
   C. 1
   D. 2
   E. 3

12. If $5(3x - 3) - 2(2x - 4) = 5(2x + 2)$, what is the value of x?

   A. -13
   B. 3
   C. 9
   D. 17
   E. 33

13. Which of the following inequalities describes the solution set for $6x - 7 > 2x + 4$?

   A. $x > -\frac{3}{4}$
   B. $x < -\frac{3}{8}$
   C. $x > \frac{11}{8}$
   D. $x < \frac{11}{4}$
   E. $x > \frac{11}{4}$

14. What value of x makes the expression $3(5x - 20) - (5x - 60) = 80$ true?

   A. 4
   B. 8
   C. 10
   D. 12
   E. 20

15. For the equation $3x^2 + 15 = 18$, what value(s) of x make the equation true?

   A. $\frac{\sqrt{3}}{3}$
   B. 1
   C. $\sqrt{11}$
   D. $-\sqrt{11}, \sqrt{11}$
   E. $-1, 1$

16. Which of the following inequalities is equivalent to $-2a - 8b > 30a - 48$?

   A. $b > 4a + 48$
   B. $b > 4a - 6$
   C. $b < 4a + 6$
   D. $b < -4a + 6$
   E. $b > -4a + 6$

17. Which of the following expressions is equivalent to $\frac{2a}{3b} = \frac{5}{a+1}$?

   A. $3a + 1 = 15b$
   B. $2a^2 + 1 = 15b$
   C. $2a^2 + 2a = 3b + 5$
   D. $2a^2 + 2a = 15b$
   E. $2a^2 + 2a = 8b$

18. If $\frac{x+4}{4} = \frac{k+1}{2}$ and $k = 2$, what is the value of x?

   A. 2
   B. 4
   C. 6
   D. 8
   E. 10

19. For what value of x is the equation $x - 3 = \sqrt{x + 17}$ true?

   A. -5
   B. -1
   C. 1
   D. 5
   E. 8

20. If $\sqrt{3x + 10} = x + 2$, what is the value of x?

   A. 6
   B. 2
   C. 0
   D. -2
   E. -3

Chapter 7: Algebra Skills

21. For what value of x is the expression $\frac{8x+24}{x+3} = x$ true?

    A. 3
    B. 5
    C. 8
    D. 12
    E. 15

22. What is the value of the expression $12 \div 2 - 5 + (-3)^3 \times 2$?

    A. -58
    B. -53
    C. -52
    D. 50
    E. 55

23. What is the solution set of the equation $\sqrt{x-3} = x - 3$?

    A. $\{1\}$
    B. $\{3\}$
    C. $\{4\}$
    D. $\{3, 4\}$
    E. The set of all real numbers

24. Given that $\frac{5}{x} = \frac{2}{3}$ and $\frac{8}{y} = x$, what is the value of y?

    A. $\frac{8}{15}$
    B. $\frac{16}{15}$
    C. 2
    D. $\frac{52}{3}$
    E. 60

25. What is the value of the expression $\frac{12 \div 3 \times (-2)^2 + 11}{(2-5)^3 \times 10 \div 5}$?

    A. -2
    B. $-\frac{1}{2}$
    C. $\frac{1}{5}$
    D. $\frac{1}{2}$
    E. 2

26. Let x and y represent real numbers with the property $x^2 - y = 0$. Which of the following statements MUST be true?

    A. $x > 0$ and $y > 0$
    B. $x > 0$ and $y < 0$
    C. $x = \pm\sqrt{y}$ and $y > 0$
    D. $x = 0$ and $y \neq 0$
    E. $x = \pm\sqrt{y}$ and $y < 0$

27. Which of the following operations will produce the largest result when substituted in for the blank in the expression $101 \_\_\_ (-\frac{1}{41})$?

    A. Averaged with
    B. Divided by
    C. Minus
    D. Plus
    E. Multiplied by

28. Given that the equation $\frac{8k}{4b} = \frac{1}{3}$ is true, what is the value of $\frac{b}{k}$?

    A. $\frac{1}{6}$
    B. $\frac{1}{2}$
    C. 2
    D. 6
    E. Cannot be determined

29. Let a and b represent real numbers with the property $a - b - 2 > 0$. Which of the following statements MUST be true?

    A. $a - b = 2$
    B. $a - b > 2$
    C. $a < 0$ and $b > 0$
    D. $a > 2$ and $b < 0$
    E. $a < 2$ and $b > 0$

30. The inequality $3x^3y > 0$ is true for real numbers x and y, where $y < 0$. If it can be determined, which of the following statements must be true?

A. x is a positive even integer.
B. x is a positive odd integer.
C. $x < 0$
D. $x > 0$
E. Cannot be determined from the given information.

31. If $\frac{4x+y}{2x+y} = \frac{8}{5}$, what is the value of $\frac{y}{x}$?

A. $\frac{3}{4}$
B. $\frac{4}{3}$
C. $\frac{5}{8}$
D. $\frac{8}{13}$
E. $\frac{13}{36}$

32. If the positive integers x and y are relatively prime (their greatest common factor is 1) and $\frac{1}{6} + \frac{1}{3} \times \frac{1}{2} \div \frac{4}{5} = \frac{x}{y}$, then $x + y = ?$

A. 4
B. 7
C. 9
D. 11
E. 59

33. For every negative value of a, all the following statements are true except:

A. $3a < 0$
B. $a^7 < 0$
C. $|a| + 2a < 0$
D. $|a| - a = 0$
E. $a - 2a^2 < 0$

Chapter 8: Number Theory

Number theory is the study of sets of positive whole numbers and related topics. In this chapter, we will review a variety of concepts related to numbers that appear on the ACT.

Types of Numbers

To start, let's review the types of numbers that you need to know for test day. **You need to memorize all the definitions below.**

- **Integers** are whole numbers (Ex: $-4, 3, 102$).
- **Positive numbers** are numbers that are greater than 0 (Ex: $1, 2, 3, 4 \ldots$).
- **Negative numbers** are numbers that are less than 0 (Ex: $-1, -2, -3, -4 \ldots$).
- **Even numbers** are numbers that are divisible by 2 (Ex: $2, 4, 6, 8 \ldots$).
- **Odd numbers** are numbers that are not divisible by 2 (Ex: $1, 3, 5, 7 \ldots$).
- **Prime Numbers** are integers that are only divisible by 1 and itself (Ex: $2, 3, 5, 7, 11 \ldots$). Note that 1 is not a prime number and 2 is the only prime even number.
- **Rational numbers** are any number that can be expressed as a fraction (Ex: $\frac{2}{5}, -\frac{11}{3}$). Any integer is also a rational number (Ex: $-22, 3{,}600, 12$).
- **Irrational numbers** are any numbers that cannot be expressed as a fraction (Ex: $\pi, \sqrt{5}$).
- **Undefined numbers** are numbers with a zero in the denominator (Ex: $\frac{6}{0}, -\frac{10}{0}$).
- **Imaginary numbers** are real numbers multiplied by the imaginary unit i (Ex: $-3i, 8i$).

> **Example 1:** The solution to the equation $124 + 9x = -3x + 328$ is a number that is
> A. Irrational B. Negative and odd C. Positive and prime D. Positive and even E. Undefined

Solution: To solve for x, we need to combine like terms. We can move all the x-terms to the left side by adding $3x$ to both sides, and we can move the numbers to the right side by subtracting 124 from both sides.

$$124 + 9x = -3x + 328$$
$$9x + 3x = 328 - 124$$
$$12x = 204$$
$$x = \frac{204}{12} = 17$$

The solution to the equation is 17. 17 is a positive, odd integer and a prime number. **The answer is C.**

> **Example 2:** Let a be a positive integer and let $x = \sqrt{a}$. Which of the following expressions represents a rational number for all values of a?
> A. $\frac{x}{3}$ B. $x - 1$ C. $3x$ D. x^2 E. $\sqrt{x}$

Solution: A rational number must be able to be expressed as a fraction or be an integer. To tell which of the answer choices is a rational number, we can plug in $\sqrt{a}$ for x in each answer choice.

- For A, we get $\frac{\sqrt{a}}{3}$. Expressions with square roots are irrational numbers, so A is incorrect.

- 61 -

- For B, we get $\sqrt{a} - 1$. Expressions with square roots are irrational, so B is incorrect.
- For C, we get $3\sqrt{a}$. Again, square roots are irrational, so C is incorrect.
- For D, we get $(\sqrt{a})^2 = a$. When you square a square root, the square root disappears. a is an integer, which is a rational number, so **D is correct.**
- For E, we get $\sqrt{\sqrt{x}}$, which can be rewritten as $\sqrt[4]{x}$. Roots are irrational, so E is incorrect.

D is correct. All other answer choices have roots in the expression and are irrational.

Properties of Even and Odd Numbers

You should know the properties of even and odd numbers in the table below.

Number Types	Addition/Subtraction	Multiplication
Even and Even	Even	Even
Even and Odd	Odd	Even
Odd and Odd	Even	Odd

While these may seem simple, knowing these properties can help with questions that ask about even and odd numbers.

> **Example 3:** For the equation $mn^2 + 3m = p$, if m is a positive, even number and n is a negative, odd number, p must be
>
> A. Negative and even B. Negative and odd C. Positive and even D. Positive and odd E. Zero

Solution: Method #1 – Substitution. The easiest way to solve this question is to use substitution and pick numbers for m and n. As long as we follow the rules in the question (m is positive and even, n is negative and odd), we can pick any numbers. It is best to pick small numbers to make the algebra easier. Let's pick $m = 2$ and $n = -3$. Now, we can plug our values for m and n into the equation and solve for p.

$$mn^2 + 3m = p$$
$$2(-3)^2 + 3(2) = p$$
$$2(9) + 6 = p$$
$$18 + 6 = p$$
$$24 = p$$

With our values, we got $p = 24$, which is a positive, even number, so we can see that **C is correct.** No matter what numbers we select, as long as we follow the rules outlined in the question, p will always be positive and even.

Method #2 – Rules of Even and Odd Numbers. We can also solve this question conceptually by using our rules for odd and even numbers in the table above.

Let's start by figuring out if p will be positive or negative. For the mn^2 term, $m > 0$ and $n^2 > 0$ (since squared terms are always positive). A positive number multiplied by a positive number is always positive, so $mn^2 > 0$. Since $m > 0$, $3m > 0$. Since both mn^2 and $3m$ are positive, the sum of those terms will be positive. p is positive.

Next, let's find out if p is odd or even. Let's start with the mn^2 term. We know that m is even, but what about n^2? n is odd, so n^2 is odd × odd, which is odd. So, mn^2 is even × odd, which is even. $3m$ is also going to be even, since $3m$ is odd × even, which is even. As a result, we see that $mn^2 + 3m$ is even + even, which is even. p is even.

Using our rules for even and odd numbers, we find that p is positive and even. **C is the correct answer.**

*Note: Solving questions like Example 3 conceptually is often much more difficult and time-consuming, so we always recommend using substitution for questions like this if you can.

Greatest Common Factor

The greatest common factor of a set of numbers is the largest positive integer that divides evenly into all numbers in the set with no remainder. For example, for the set of numbers 12, 18, and 30, the greatest common factor is 6. 6 is the largest number that divides evenly into 12, 18, and 30.

> **Example 4:** What is the greatest common factor for the set of numbers 56, 112, 182?
> A. 2   B. 8   C. 14   D. 28   E. 56

Solution: The easiest way to solve any greatest common factor question with numbers is to backsolve using the answer choices. We are looking for the largest number that divides evenly into 56, 112, and 182. To solve, all we need to do is grab a calculator and start with the largest value in the answer choices, which is 56. 56 divides evenly into 56 and 112 but does not divide evenly into 182, so 56 is incorrect. 28 divides evenly into 56 and 112 but again does not divide evenly into 182, so 28 is incorrect. 14 divides evenly into 56, 112, and 182, as we can see below:

$$56 \div 14 = 4$$
$$112 \div 14 = 8$$
$$182 \div 14 = 13$$

The correct answer is C. 8 does not divide evenly into 182. 2 divides evenly into all 3 numbers but 2 is smaller than 14, so 2 is not the greatest common factor.

For more advanced greatest common factor questions, the ACT can ask you to find the greatest common factor for an expression with variables. For these questions, we are looking for the largest term that we can factor out from all other terms. For a simple example to start, let's consider the expression

$$3x^2 + 6x$$

The greatest factor is $3x$, because we can factor our $3x$ from both the $3x^2$ term and the $6x$ term. If we factor $3x$ from $3x^2$, we have x left over. If we factor $3x$ from $6x$, we have 2 left over. We can rewrite the expression above as

$$3x(x + 2)$$

to show the greatest common factor, $3x$, factored out from the original expression.

PrepPros

Example 5: What is the greatest monomial factor for the expression $3x^3y - 12x^2$?

A. $3x^3$ B. $3x^2$ C. $12x^2y$ D. x E. xy

Solution: To find the greatest monomial factor (monomial factor is just a fancy algebra word for an algebraic expression with only one term), we need to find the largest number and variable(s) that we can factor out from both terms.

Let's start with the number. What is the largest number that we can factor out from both terms? The answer is 3 because both 3 and 12 are divisible by 3.

What about the variables? To factor out a variable, the variable must appear in all terms in the expression. Since y only appears in the $3x^2y$ term and not in the $-12x$ term, we cannot factor y out from both terms. Okay, so what about x? If a variable appears in all terms in the expression, we can factor out the lowest power. The first term, $3x^3y$, has x^3 while the second term, $-12x^2$, has x^2. The lowest power is x^2, so we can factor out an x^2.

Combining the number, 3, and variable, x^2, that we factored out, we find the greatest monomial factor is $3x^2$. We can rewrite the original expression as
$$3x^2(xy - 4)$$
to show the greatest monomial factor factored out from the original expression. **The correct answer is B.**

Least Common Multiple

The least common multiple is the smallest positive integer that is divisible by all numbers in the set. For example, the least common multiple of 2 and 3 is 6 because 6 is the smallest number that is divisible by both 2 and 3.

A multiple of a number is when we multiply that number by another number. For example, the multiples of 4 are 4, 8, 12, 16, 20, 24, and so on. Any positive number that is divisible by 4 is a multiple of 4.

Example 6: What is the least common multiple for 5, 6, and 20?

A. 20   B. 30   C. 60   D. 120   E. 3,000

Solution: To find the least common multiple, we can list the multiples of 5, 6, and 20 and look for the smallest number that appears on all 3 lists.

Multiples of 5: 5, 10, 15, 20, 25, 30, 35, 40, 45, 50, 55, **60**, 65, 70 ...

Multiples of 6: 6, 12, 18, 24, 30, 36, 42, 48, 54, **60**, 66 ...

Multiples of 20: 20, 40, **60**, 80 ...

We see the least common multiple is 60. While 120 and 3,000 are divisible by 5, 6, and 20, they are not the smallest number that is a multiple of all 3 and therefore not the least common multiple. **The answer is C.**

Shortcut Solution: The fastest and easiest way to solve is to backsolve using the answer choices. We do not recommend using the method above. However, it is important to understand the method above, as you may need to use that method for other types of least common multiple questions.

To solve, grab your calculator, start with answer choice A, and see if the number is divisible by 5, 6, and 8. Here, 20 is not divisible by 6, so we would next try 30. 30 is not divisible by 20, so we would move on to 60. 60 is divisible by all 5, 6, and 20, so we know we found the answer. We are looking for the least common multiple, so there is no need to even check any large numbers once you find an answer choice that works.

Prime Factorization

Prime factorization is a method of expressing a number as a product of its prime factors. The most common approach to prime factorization is making a factor tree. In the factor tree, we keep dividing numbers and creating more branches until we are left with only prime numbers. Let's start by finding the prime factorization of 20.

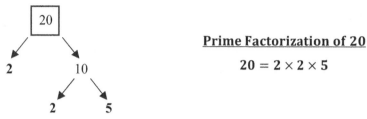

The prime factors (2, 2, and 5) are shown in bold. To show the prime factorization of 20, we multiply all the prime factors together, so the prime factorization of 20 is $2 \times 2 \times 5$.

Example 7: Which of the following is the correct prime factorization of 6,006?
  A. $2 \cdot 3 \cdot 7 \cdot 11 \cdot 13$ B. $6 \cdot 7 \cdot 11 \cdot 13$ C. $6 \cdot 7 \cdot 143$ D. $7 \cdot 11 \cdot 13$ E. $2 \cdot 3 \cdot 1{,}001$

Solution: To solve, we can set up a factor tree for 6,006.

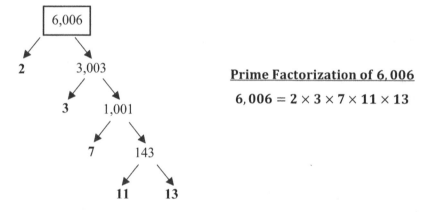

The dots in the answer choices are another way in math to show multiplication. From our factor tree, we see the prime factors (shown in bold on the factor tree) are 2, 3, 7, 11, and 13. **The answer is A.**

All the other answer choices are incompletely factored or do not multiply to 6,006. In B and C, 6 is not a prime number. In E, 1001 is not prime. In D, $7 \cdot 11 \cdot 13$ does not multiply to 6,006.

The prime factorization shown above is only one example of a correct factor tree. Depending on the numbers you divide by to start, you factor tree may look a bit different than the one above. For example, the first branches from 6,006 could be 6 and 1,001. No matter how you start the tree, you will get the same prime factorization as long as you do the math correctly and continue to divide the branches of the tree until you get only prime numbers.

One Solution vs. Infinite Solutions vs. No Solution

We need to know how to tell when an algebraic expression will have one solution, infinite solutions, and no solution. To start, let's see how a question testing you on this topic might appear on the ACT.

> **Example 8:** For the equation $3x - 8 = ax - 12$, under which condition will there be no solution?
> A. $a = 0$ B. $a = 3$ C. $a \neq 3$ D. $a > 0$ E. There is no such condition.

Before we come back to solve Example 8, let's learn the rules for one solution, infinite solutions, and no solution.

One Solution

Any algebraic expression that can be solved for a single value of x will have one solution. For example, if we have the expression.

$$9x - 2 = 5x + 10$$

we can solve for x. Subtract $5x$ from both sides and add 2 to both sides to get:

$$4x = 12$$
$$x = 3$$

We get 1 solution for x. Memorize the rules below to know how to spot this quickly.

> **Rule for 1 Solution**
>
> **The coefficients of the x-terms are different. The constants (numbers) can be the same or different.** Anytime the expression has x-terms with different coefficients and no higher powers of x, such as x^2, there is always 1 solution.

In the example we just solved, the x-terms, $9x$ and $5x$ have different coefficients, so, using the rule for 1 solution, we know there will be 1 solution without having to solve the equation.

Infinite Solutions

An algebraic expression with infinite solutions must be true for any value of x. **For an equation to have infinite solutions, both sides of the equation must be identical.** Some examples of equations with infinite solutions are below:

$$6x - 12 = 6x - 12 \qquad 7x^2 = 7x^2 \qquad x^3 - 4x + 5 = x^3 - 4x + 5$$

For the expressions above, we can plug any value for x and the expression will be true.

> **Rule for Infinite Solutions**
>
> **Both sides of the equation must be identical. The coefficients of the x-terms and the constants (numbers) must be the same.** Anytime both sides of the expression are identical, any value of x makes the expression true, so there are infinite solutions.

Chapter 8: Number Theory

No Solution

An algebraic expression with no solution cannot be solved for any value of x. **For this to occur, the expression must have the same coefficients for the variable(s) on both sides and the constants (numbers) must be different.** Some examples of equations with no solution are below:

$$x - 2 = x + 5 \qquad 6x - 12 = 6x + 1 \qquad 7x^2 = 7x^2 + 10$$

No matter what value we plug in for x, we can never make any of the equations above true. Notice that the terms with variables (the terms with x or x^2 in the above examples) are equal but the numbers are not. Anytime an equation looks like this, there is no solution.

> **Rule for No Solution**
>
> **The coefficients of the x-terms are the same. The constants (numbers) are different.** Anytime we see these characteristics in an algebraic expression, there is no solution.

Now that we know the rules, let's go back to Example 8.

> **Example 8:** For the expression $3x - 8 = ax - 12$, under which condition will there be no solution?
>   A. $a = 0$ B. $a = 3$ C. $a \neq 3$ D. $a > 0$ E. There is no such condition.

Solution: For there to be no solution, we need the coefficients of the x-terms to be the same and the constants (numbers) to be different. In the equation above, the number are already different, so we just need to make the coefficients of x-terms the same. For this to occur, we need $a = 3$ so the expression becomes

$$3x - 8 = 3x - 12$$

which has no solution. **The answer is B.**

> # Two Solutions for Algebraic Expressions
>
> For a challenge question, the ACT can also include an algebraic expression that has two solutions. For an algebraic expression to have 2 solutions, the equation must either (1) have an x^2-term or (2) have an x-term inside absolute value bars.
>
> ### Two Solutions with an x^2-term
>
> Let's say we are given the algebraic expression $x^2 - 6 = -2$. To solve, we could add 6 to both sides and get
>
> $$x^2 = 4$$
>
> Taking the square root of both sides we get.
>
> $$x = \pm 2$$
>
> **So, we get 2 solutions!** Remember that in Chapter 7 (pg. 56) we learned that when we take the square root of both sides with x^2, we must put a $\pm$ in front of the number.
>
> ### Two Solutions with Absolute Value
>
> Let's say we are given the expression $|x| + 3 = 10$. To solve, we subtract 3 from both sides and get
>
> $$|x| = 7 \quad \rightarrow \quad x = 7 \text{ and } x = -7$$
>
> **When we have a variable inside the absolute value bars, there will be 2 solutions.** If you are not familiar with this topic, we will learn more about algebra with absolute values bars in Chapter 18.

Number Theory Practice: Answers on page 325.

1. The least common multiple of 6, 9, and 12 is:

   A. 18
   B. 24
   C. 36
   D. 72
   E. 108

2. If $7 < \sqrt{a} < 8$, which of the following could be a?

   A. 2.8
   B. 7.3
   C. 15.5
   D. 51.8
   E. 66.8

3. The solution to the equation $4a + 12 = 36$ is which of the following types of numbers listed below?

   I. Integer
   II. Rational
   III. Irrational
   IV. Negative
   V. Positive

   A. II and V only
   B. II and IV only
   C. I and III only
   D. I and II only
   E. I, II, and V only

4. What is the greatest common factor of 48, 84, and 138?

   A. 12
   B. 6
   C. 3
   D. 2
   E. 1

5. What is the greatest integer solution to the equation $7x + 3 \leq 36.4$?

   A. 3
   B. 4
   C. 5
   D. 6
   E. 7

6. Which of the following arranges the numbers $\frac{7}{4}$, $1.\overline{75}$, 1.17, and $1.\overline{17}$ into ascending order?

   A. $\frac{7}{4} < 1.\overline{75} < 1.\overline{17} < 1.17$
   B. $\frac{7}{4} < 1.17 < 1.\overline{17} < 1.\overline{75}$
   C. $1.17 < 1.\overline{17} < 1.\overline{75} < \frac{7}{4}$
   D. $1.17 < 1.\overline{17} < \frac{7}{4} < 1.\overline{75}$
   E. $1.\overline{17} < 1.17 < \frac{7}{4} < 1.\overline{75}$

7. If x is an integer less than -1, which of the following correctly orders $x^2, \frac{1}{x}$, and $|x|$ from greatest to smallest?

   A. $x^2 > |x| > \frac{1}{x}$
   B. $\frac{1}{x} > |x| > x^2$
   C. $|x| > x^2 > \frac{1}{x}$
   D. $\frac{1}{x} > x^2 > |x|$
   E. $x^2 > \frac{1}{x} > |x|$

8. Let x be a positive odd integer and y be a negative even integer. The expression $x^2 y^2$ is a:

   A. Positive odd integer.
   B. Positive even integer.
   C. Negative odd integer.
   D. Negative even integer.
   E. None of the above.

9. The statement $5x - (2x - 1) + 4 = 3x + 2$ is true for:

   A. $x = 0$ only
   B. $x = 1$ only
   C. $x = 2$ only
   D. all values of x.
   E. no values of x.

10. The prime factorization of 558 is:

    A. 6×93
    B. 2×279
    C. $3 \times 3 \times 31$
    D. $2 \times 3 \times 31$
    E. $2 \times 3 \times 3 \times 31$

Chapter 8: Number Theory

11. Which of the following values is a rational number?

    A. $\sqrt{16} - 3$
    B. $\sqrt{3} + 4$
    C. 4.5π
    D. $\sqrt{25} - \sqrt{24}$
    E. $5\sqrt{5}$

12. The graph of the function shown below will be undefined at what value(s) of x?

    $$f(x) = \frac{3}{x^2 - 4x}$$

    A. -4 only
    B. 0 only
    C. 4 only
    D. 0 and 4 only
    E. $-4, 0,$ and 4 only

13. Two lights are turned on at the same time and begin flashing. The first light flashes every 28 seconds. The second light flashes every 12 seconds. How many seconds after the lights are turned on will both lights flash at the same time?

    A. 56
    B. 84
    C. 112
    D. 168
    E. 336

14. What is the greatest monomial factor for the expression $16ab^3 - 24b^5$?

    A. b^3
    B. $4ab^2$
    C. $4b^3$
    D. $8ab^3$
    E. $8b^3$

15. The statement $x - 2(3x - 2) + 11 = -5x + 15$ is true for:

    A. $x = -4$ only
    B. $x = -2$ only
    C. $x = 0$ only
    D. all values of x.
    E. no values of x.

16. The expression $\frac{4a - 3b}{3b - a}$ is undefined whenever b is equal to:

    A. $\frac{1}{3}a$
    B. $\frac{3}{4}a$
    C. $\frac{4}{3}a$
    D. $3a$
    E. $4a$

17. The expression $10 - 4z = -6.5z + 10$ has how many solutions?

    A. 0
    B. 1
    C. 2
    D. 3
    E. Infinitely many

18. When $6 \leq x \leq 10$ and $13 \leq y \leq 18$, the smallest possible value for $\frac{2}{y - x}$ is:

    A. $\frac{1}{6}$
    B. $\frac{1}{4}$
    C. $\frac{2}{7}$
    D. $\frac{2}{3}$
    E. $\frac{18}{13}$

19. Which of the following expressions, when evaluated, equals an irrational number?

    A. $\frac{\sqrt{20}}{\sqrt{5}}$
    B. $\frac{\sqrt{5}}{\sqrt{20}}$
    C. $\left(\sqrt{5}\right)^2$
    D. $\sqrt{5} \times \sqrt{20}$
    E. $\sqrt{5} + \sqrt{20}$

20. If a and b are real numbers such that $b - a > b + a$, which of the following MUST be true?

    A. $a > b$
    B. $b > a$
    C. $b > 0$
    D. $a < 0$
    E. $b > 0$ and $a < 0$

21. Which of the following must be true for each set of 5 consecutive positive integers greater than 10?

   I. At least 1 of the integers is a multiple of 3.
   II. At least 2 of the integers have a common prime factor.
   III. At least 1 of the integers is prime.

   A. I only
   B. II only
   C. I and III only
   D. I and II only
   E. I, II, and III

22. The equation below has no solution, and a is a constant. What is the value of a?

   $$8x + 6 = a(-3x + 2) - x$$

   A. -3
   B. $-\frac{8}{3}$
   C. 0
   D. $\frac{7}{3}$
   E. 3

23. Which of the following inequalities is true for all positive integers m?

   A. $m \geq m^2$
   B. $\sqrt{m} + 3 \geq m^2$
   C. $m \geq \frac{m}{2} + 2$
   D. $m \leq \frac{1}{m}$
   E. $m \leq \sqrt{m^2 + 1}$

24. The least common multiple of 2 numbers is 192. The greater of the 2 numbers is 96. What is the maximum value of the other number?

   A. 2
   B. 6
   C. 16
   D. 48
   E. 64

25. If $a < b$ and $a > 12$, what is the least possible integer value of $a + b$?

   A. 23
   B. 24
   C. 25
   D. 26
   E. 27

26. For some real number a, $\sqrt{a^2} \neq a$. Therefore a must be:

   A. Zero
   B. Positive
   C. Odd
   D. Negative
   E. Even

27. Given the equation $4x = \sqrt{3} - x$, which of the following expressions is rational number?

   A. $\sqrt{x}$
   B. $x + 2$
   C. $2x$
   D. $x^2 + 3$
   E. x^3

28. $$ax^2 + 4(3x^2 + 2b) = 15x^2 + 24$$

   In the equation above, a and b are constants. If the equation has no real solution, what is the value of a?

   A. 2
   B. 3
   C. 5
   D. 12
   E. 16

29. Which of the following expressions is the greatest monomial factor of $105x^3y + 45x^2y^2$?

   A. $15x^2y$
   B. $15x^2y^2$
   C. $15x^3y^2$
   D. $415x^2y$
   E. $415x^3y^2$

30. The greatest common factor of 2 whole numbers is 5. The least common multiple of these same 2 numbers is 60. What are the 2 numbers?

    A. 4 and 15
    B. 5 and 10
    C. 5 and 15
    D. 15 and 20
    E. 20 and 60

31. Which of the following numbers has exactly 5 distinct positive integer factors?

    A. 12
    B. 14
    C. 16
    D. 25
    E. 30

32. For all real values of x such that $0 < x < 1$, which of the following expressions has the smallest value?

    A. $2 - x$
    B. x^2
    C. $\sqrt{x}$
    D. $-\sqrt{x}$
    E. $-\frac{1}{x}$

33. Let a and b represent real numbers. If the solution to the equation $\sqrt{7 - (a + b)}$ is imaginary. Which of the following statements about a and b must be true?

    A. $a > b$
    B. $a < b$
    C. $b + a < 7$
    D. $b + a = 7$
    E. $b + a > 7$

34. For all real numbers, $a, b,$ and c such that $c > b > a$ and $a < 0$, which of the following inequalities must be true?

    A. $ca < ba$
    B. $ca > ba$
    C. $\frac{a}{c} < \frac{a}{b}$
    D. $a - c > c - b$
    E. $c - b > b - a$

35. For an upcoming event, Zaire oversees organizing the seating for dinner. After finding out the total number of guests, he does some calculations and discovers that if each table has 9 guests, there will be no leftover seats. The day before the event, 5 guests cancel and will no longer attend, so Zaire now must reorganize. He decides to add one table and now there will be 8 guest per table and no leftover seats. How many tables did Zaire end up using for the event?

    A. 9
    B. 13
    C. 14
    D. 16
    E. 20

Chapter 9: Percentages

On the ACT, you will need to know how to solve questions with simple percentages and with percentage increases and decreases. While percentages may seem simple, they can often stump students who do not know how to set them up correctly. This chapter will show you all the skills you need to know to handle percentage questions quickly and easily on test day.

Simple Percentages

Simple percentage questions can be solved by properly setting up a proportion:

$$\frac{is}{of} = \frac{\%}{100}$$

You can think of the "of" as the starting value (the 100%) and the "is" as the percentage of the starting value. If you are given a percentage value, you always put it where the % is.

Example 1: Joey buys a new set of golf clubs for $720 when the clubs are on sale for 80% of the original price. What was the original price, in dollars, of the set of golf clubs?
   A. 576   B. 648   C. 864   D. 900   E. 1296

Solution: Method #1 – Proportion: To solve, we can set up a proportion:

$$\frac{720}{x} = \frac{80}{100}$$

$$80x = 72{,}000$$

$$x = \frac{72{,}000}{80} = 900$$

The answer is D.

Method #2 – Decimal Shortcut:

You can also turn percentages into decimals by dividing the percentage value by 100. 120% is the same as 1.2. 85% is the same as 0.85. For this question, we can turn 80% in 0.8 and solve:

$$0.8x = 720$$

$$x = \frac{720}{0.8} = 900$$

The answer is D. We recommend the decimal shortcut, as it is faster for solving percentage questions.

Example 2: Isaiah purchased a new watch for 72% of the original price. Isaiah paid no sales tax. If the original price was $160, which of the following is closest to the price Isaiah paid for the watch?
   A. 45   B. 88   C. 115   D. 138   E. 222

Solution: Here, we can turn the 72% into 0.72. Let the price Isaiah paid for the watch be p. We know that Isaiah paid 72% of the original price of $160 so

$$p = 0.72(160)$$

$$p = 115.2$$

Isaiah paid $115.20 for the watch, which is closest to 115. **The answer is C.**

The ACT can also ask you to deal with multiple percent changes in the same question. To solve these questions the fastest, you should do all the percent changes together in one step.

> **Example 3:** Fred is trying to sell his bicycle, but he is having a hard time finding someone interested in buying it. To sell the bicycle quickly, Fred decides to sell the bicycle for 95% of the original price to Dave. Dave sells the bicycle 6 months later for 80% of the price that he purchased the bicycle for from Fred. The price that Dave sells the bicycle for is what percent of the original price of the bicycle?
>
> A. 90   B. 87.5   C. 80   D. 76   E. 65

Solution: Method 1 – "Math Teacher Way": Let the original price of the bicycle be p. When Fred sells the bicycle to Dave for 95% of the original price, you multiply by 0.95. When Dave later sells the bicycle for 80% of the purchase price, you multiply by 0.8. The final price that Dave sold the bicycle for is then:

$$p(0.95)(0.8) = 0.76p$$

The final price is 76% of the original price. **The answer is D.**

Method 2 – Plug In Numbers: The part about this question that confuses most students is that we are never given any actual price for the bicycle. To make this question easier, pick an original price for the bicycle and use that price to solve. Let's say the original price of Fred's bicycle $100. 100 is always a good number to pick for percentage problems because it is easy to calculate percent changes from 100. Since Dave buys the bicycle for 95% of the original price, Dave pays $95 for the bicycle. Dave then sells the bicycle for 80% of the $95, so you can solve for the final price:

$$\text{Final Price} = 0.8(95) = 76$$

The final price is $76. Since the original price was $100, the final price is 76% of the original price. **The answer is D.**

Simple Percentages Practice: Answers on page 325.

1. What is 80% of 50?

   A. 10
   B. 20
   C. 40
   D. 42
   E. 45

2. On his English test, Justin missed 8 of the 50 questions. What percentage did Justin answer correctly?

   A. 20%
   B. 40%
   C. 60%
   D. 75%
   E. 84%

3. Jim is a farmer. Last year he planted 280 acres of corn and 420 acres of soybeans. What percent of the acres Jim planted was corn?

   A. 28%
   B. 40%
   C. 66%
   D. 75%
   E. 150%

4. 48 is 150% of what number?

   A. 24
   B. 30
   C. 32
   D. 40
   E. 72

5. If $y = 200$ and x is 40% of y, what is 125% of x?

   A. 60
   B. 80
   C. 100
   D. 120
   E. 150

6. When a black bear hibernates, its heart rate drops by 15 beats per minute. This drop is 25% of its normal heart rate. What is the black bear's normal heart rate?

   A. 20
   B. 30
   C. 45
   D. 60
   E. 75

7. Christina has 10 hours of free time each week. If she spends 18% of her free time reading, how many <u>minutes</u> a week will she spend reading?

   A. 1.8
   B. 18
   C. 64
   D. 96
   E. 108

8. Cardiff Market is selling their famous tri-tip steak sandwiches at a local music and arts festival. As a special promotion, they promise to donate 27% of the sandwich sales to charity. If they sold $870 dollars in sandwiches, how much will they be donating to charity?

   A. $234.90
   B. $247.00
   C. $469.80
   D. $525.50
   E. $722.10

9. Last month, Amanda spent a total of $800. She spent $240 on food, $90 on gas, $400 on rent, and $70 on clothing. The category that Amanda spent the second most on is closest to what percentage of her total spending?

   A. 12%
   B. 20%
   C. 30%
   D. 50%
   E. 60%

10. A survey at the local high school of 25 students from the senior class revealed that only 20% of the students liked the school's lunches. If the other 275 seniors have the same percentage of students who like the school's lunch as those surveyed, how many students in the entire senior class like the school's lunch?

    A. 55
    B. 60
    C. 80
    D. 220
    E. 240

11. How Did Attendees First Hear About Coachella?

Source	Percent of those surveyed
Social Media	35%
Friend Attended	12%
TV	5%
Internet	38%
Other	10%

    The table above shows a summary of 1,500 responses from attendees at Coachella when asked how they first learned about the festival. Based on the table, how many people learned from a friend who attended or from social media?

    A. 525
    B. 675
    C. 705
    D. 720
    E. 815

Chapter 9: Percentages

12. At the Palm Coast Country Club, approximately 12 percent of junior members and 26 percent of premium members have a golfing membership. If there are 252 junior members and 780 premium members, which of the following is closest to the total number of junior and premium members who have a golfing membership?

   A. 467
   B. 350
   C. 233
   D. 203
   E. 30

14. Big Storage is offering a new storage shed. The original storage shed was 6 feet wide, 10 feet long, and 8 feet tall. The new storage shed's dimensions will be 80% of the original width, 75% of the original length, and 90% of the original height. To the nearest 1%, what percent will the volume of the new storage shed be when compared to the volume of the original storage shed?

   A. 54
   B. 66
   C. 78
   D. 81
   E. 85

13. Rebecca sells her pickup truck to Jeremy for 76% of the original price. Jeremy does some work on the car and then sells it for 110% of the price that he purchased the car for. Which of the following is closest to percent of the original price that Jeremy sold the car for?

   A. 70
   B. 84
   C. 86
   D. 93
   E. 110

15. The groups of students who are graduating with honors from the university have a variety of different majors. 30% are science majors, 15% are history majors, 25% are humanities majors, and the remaining 24 students are all business majors. Of the students graduating with honors, how many more science majors were there than history majors?

   A. 6
   B. 12
   C. 15
   D. 25
   E. 30

Percentage Increase and Decrease

Percentage questions are more difficult when there is an increase or a decrease to the percentage, but you can still set them up as a proportion.

$$\text{Percentage greater than: } \frac{\text{New}}{\text{Original}} = \frac{100 + \%}{100} \qquad \text{Percentage less than: } \frac{\text{New}}{\text{Original}} = \frac{100 - \%}{100}$$

The "original" is the starting value (the 100%), and the "new" is the percentage increase or decrease from the starting value. If you are given a percentage value, you always put it in where the % sign is.

Example 1: Jarvis construction company is building a new exit ramp for the local highway. The company initially said that the project would take 250 days, but a forecast for bad winter weather led the company to estimate that the project would take 12% longer to finish. How many days does Jarvis now estimate that the new exit ramp will take to complete?

A. 260   B. 262   C. 276   D. 280   E. 284

Solution:

$$\frac{x}{250} = \frac{100 + 12}{100}$$

$$100x = (250)(112)$$

$$x = \frac{(250)(112)}{100} = 280$$

The answer is D.

It is also important to know the shortcut for solving percentage increase and decrease questions. Let's say you want to increase x by 30%. Normally if we want to increase x by 30%, you will find 30% of the value and then add it to x:

$$x + 0.3x$$

This is the same as

$$x + 0.3x = x(1 + 0.3) = 1.3x$$

Instead of finding 30% of x and adding it to the original value, you can simply multiply x by 1.3. This trick will work for any percent value. To increase a value by 4%, multiply by 1.04. To decrease a value by 10%, multiply by 0.9. This technique will help you solve percentage increase and decrease questions more quickly and effectively on the ACT.

Both this decimal shortcut technique and the proportion technique work, so you should use the one that you are most comfortable with.

Example 2: Tim grew 15% more tons of tomatoes in 2019 than in 2018. If Tim's grew 23 tons of tomatoes in 2019, approximately how many tons of tomatoes did Tim grow in 2018?

A. 26.5   B. 24.5   C. 21.5   D. 20   E. 19.5

Solution: Here, let's use the decimal shortcut technique. To increase by 15%, we multiply by 1.15.

$$(1.15)(\text{tons in 2018}) = \text{tons 2019}$$

$$(1.15)(\text{tons in 2018}) = 23$$

$$\text{tons in 2018} = \frac{23}{1.15}$$
$$\text{tons in 2018} = 20$$

The answer is D.

Example 3: The price of a painting decreased by 8% in 2017, increased by 25% in 2018, and increased by 40% in 2019. What percentage greater is the price of the painting in 2019 than the original price at the beginning of 2017?

    A. 73   B. 61   C. 57   D. 48   E. 25

Solution: Let the original price of the painting be p. When the price is decreased by 8% in 2017, we multiply by $(1 - 0.08)$ because it is the original price minus 8%. When the price is increased by 25% in 2018, we multiply by $(1 + 0.25)$ because we are adding 25% onto the price from 2017. When the price is increased by 40% in 2019, we multiply by $(1 + 0.40)$ because we are adding 40% onto the price from 2018. The final price is then:

$$p(1 - 0.08)(1 + 0.25)(1 + 0.40) = p(0.92)(1.25)(1.40) = 1.61p$$

The $1.61p$ shows that the price in 2019 is 61% higher than the price in 2017. **The answer is B.**

For other percentage questions, you need to know how to calculate what percent a value increases or decrease by. To solve these questions, you can use the equation below:

$$\text{Percentage Change} = \frac{\text{Final Value} - \text{Initial Value}}{\text{Initial Value}} \times 100$$

If the percent change is a positive number, it is a percentage increase. If the percent change is a negative number, it is a percentage decrease.

Example 4: In 2017, the average price of an avocado in California was $1.43. In 2018, the average price of an avocado in California was $1.54. Which of the following is closest to the percentage increase of the price of an avocado from 2017 to 2018?

    A. 7.1%   B. 7.7%   C. 8.2%   D. 8.4%   E. 8.7%

Solution:

$$\text{Percentage Change} = \frac{1.54 - 1.43}{1.43} \times 100 = 7.7\%$$

The answer is B.

Percentage Increase and Decrease Practice: Answers on pages 325-326.

1. What number is 60% greater than 50?

   A. 20
   B. 30
   B. 60
   C. 70
   D. 80

2. What number is 30% less than 30?

   A. 9
   B. 15
   C. 21
   D. 24
   E. 27

3. Bob bought a house at a 20% discount. If the house was initially priced at 600,000, what was the price, in dollars, Bob paid?

   A. 120,000
   B. 480,000
   C. 560,000
   D. 720,000
   E. 750,000

4. Last year, 700 students graduated from Eastlake High. This year, 8% fewer students graduated than last year. How many students graduated this year?

   A. 620
   B. 644
   C. 648
   D. 756
   E. 760

5. In 2017, Jimmy's Surfboard Shapers made 1,231 surfboards. In 2018, Jimmy's Surfboard Shapers made 1,391 surfboards. Which of the following is closest to the percentage increase in surfboards shaped from 2017 to 2018?

   A. 11%
   B. 13%
   C. 16%
   D. 18%
   E. 21%

6. Julie drives an average of 50 miles per hour during her 30-mile commute to work. Today, Julie is in a rush, so she drives 20% faster. How many minutes does it take her to drive to work today?

   A. 24
   B. 28
   C. 30
   D. 32
   E. 36

7. James bought three shirts during a 30% off sale for $168. How much would the three shirts cost without the sale?

   A. $118
   B. $138
   C. $200
   D. $218
   E. $240

8. The price of two sandwiches was $20 before tax. If a sales tax of 8% is added, how much were the two sandwiches with the sales tax?

   A. $18.40
   B. $20.08
   C. $20.80
   D. $21.60
   E. $23.20

9. John's average weekly grocery bill for 2016 was $176.45. His average weekly grocery bill for 2017 was $190.56. Which of the following is the closest to the percent increase on John's average grocery bill from 2016 to 2017?

   A. 7.1%
   B. 7.4%
   C. 7.7%
   D. 8.0%
   E. 8.6%

10. Amy paid $76.00 for dinner after an 8% tax was paid. What was the price of her dinner before tax?

    A. $69.92
    B. $70.37
    C. $71.44
    D. $73.90
    E. $75.20

Chapter 9: Percentages

11. Bob's Woodshop buys 2 tons of wood from The Wood Depot. 1 ton of wood costs $2500. Bob gets a 15% discount for being a frequent customer. After the discount is applied, Bob has to pay a 10% sales tax. How much does Bob pay for the 2 tons of wood?

    A. $2,125
    B. $2,750
    C. $4,250
    D. $4,675
    E. $5,500

15. Julie's bakery sold 1,200 cookies in September and 1,403 cookies in October. If the percent increase from September to October was the same as the percent increase from August to September, which of the following is closest to the number of cookies Julie's bakery sold in August?

    A. 997
    B. 1,026
    C. 1,061
    D. 1,425
    E. 1,613

12. The price of the new PowerBros external phone charger is 30% more than that of the old version. If the old version costs $85.00, which of the following best approximates the cost, in dollars, of the new external phone charger?

    A. $25.50
    B. $59.50
    C. $110.50
    D. $126.20
    E. $283.35

16. When dining out, Dave spends an additional 32% on top of the listed price of the items he purchases after tax and tip are included. If Dave spends a total of $386 on a dinner for his family, what was the total listed price of the items purchased at the dinner before tax and tip were added?

    A. $117.76
    B. $262.48
    C. $292.42
    D. $509.52
    E. $567.65

13. Andrew and Cole both work on a farm picking apples. Andrew picks apples 30% faster than Cole. If Andrew picked 325 apples yesterday, how many apples did Cole pick?

    A. 200
    B. 250
    C. 290
    D. 425
    E. 500

17. Holly started the semester with $600 on her meal plan. Each meal costs $8. After eating three meals, what percent of her total dining dollars remaining was her fourth meal?

    A. 1.33%
    B. 1.38%
    C. 13.33%
    D. 13.88%
    E. 14.03%

14. Max bought a new pair of hiking shoes for $118.00 dollars after an 8% sales tax. What was the price of the hiking shoes before the sales tax was added?

    A. $108.56
    B. $109.26
    C. $110.92
    D. $111.20
    E. $112.00

18. John negotiated a 13% decrease from the initial listed price for the SUV he purchased. If he purchased the car for $34,000, which of the following is closest to the initial listed price of the SUV?

    A. $4,420
    B. $29,600
    C. $38,500
    D. $39,080
    E. $47,000

19. This month, Stella decided to try to be more energy efficient by turning off the lights in her house when she was not in the rooms and by using her air conditioning less. If her energy bill last month was $85.95 and her energy bill this month is $76.24, to the nearest tenth of a percent, what percent did her energy bill decrease?

A. 12.7%
B. 12.4%
C. 11.8%
D. 11.3%
E. 10.9%

 20. Thomas recently purchased a new computer for college. Thomas had a coupon for a 20% discount from the original price. All items sold from the computer store also include an 8% sales tax added at the register. If Thomas paid a final price $850.76, which included the discount and sales tax, what was the original price of the computer?

A. $1148.52
B. $1063.45
C. $984.68
D. $898.45
E. $780.64

 21. In 2021, 275 biology majors and cognitive science majors make up 2.5% of the undergraduate students at Washington University. In 2022, 450 biology majors make up 3.6% of the undergraduate students at Washington University. Which of the following statements about the undergraduate students at Washington University is correct?

A. There are 13.6% more students in 2022 than in 2021.
B. There are 12.0% more students in 2022 than in 2021.
C. There are 1.1% more students in 2022 than in 2021.
D. There are 1.1% fewer students in 2022 than in 2021.
E. There are 12.0% fewer students in 2022 than in 2021.

 22. Julie spent 2 hours and 20 minutes a day studying for her ACT over the first three weeks of her test prep. During the last week before her first ACT, she studied an extra 30% a day. How much time did Julie spend studying during the last week?

A. 3 hours and 2 minutes
B. 2 hours and 51 minutes
C. 15 hours and 20 minutes
D. 20 hours and 2 minutes
E. 21 hours and 14 minutes

 23. Dave is currently producing 250 pies per week. His boss wants him to increase the number of pies he is making by 12% each week. In two weeks, approximately how many pies will Dave be making?

A. 262
B. 274
C. 280
D. 308
E. 314

 24. The product of three numbers is 2160. One of the numbers, z, is 25% greater than the other two numbers, which are the same. What is the value of z?

A. 6
B. 8
C. 9
D. 12
E. 15

25. A pair of vintage sneakers has been owned by three different people. The first owner sold the sneakers and made a 30% profit. The second owner resold the sneakers and made a 25% profit. The third owner resold the sneakers for a 40% profit. The final resale price is approximately what percentage more than the original price?

   A. 82%
   B. 95%
   C. 128%
   D. 150%
   E. 228%

27. A rectangle is changed by decreasing its length by 20% and increasing its width by $q\%$. If these alterations increased the area of the rectangle by 8%, what is the value of q?

   A. 8
   B. 10
   C. 20
   D. 25
   E. 35

26. John's business made p dollars in profit in 2015. In 2016, he made 30% more in profit than in 2015. In 2017, he made 6% less in profit than in 2016. About what percent was the increase in John's profit over the 2 years?

   A. 22%
   B. 24%
   C. 38%
   D. 65%
   E. 74%

28. A sculpture was originally purchased for p dollars. The first owner sold the sculpture and made a 130% profit. The second owner resold the sculpture and made a 65% profit. Which of the following correctly solves for the final price the sculpture was sold for in terms of p?

   A. $(1.95)p$
   B. $(1.3)(0.65)p$
   C. $(1.3)(1.65)p$
   D. $(2.3)(0.65)p$
   E. $(2.3)(1.65)p$

Chapter 10: Ratios and Proportions

Ratios

We use ratios to make comparisons between two things. Ratios do not give the exact number of items but instead allow us to concisely compare the relationship between two things at the same time.

As an example, if we have oranges and apples in a basket in the ratio of $2:3$, it does not necessarily mean that we have 2 oranges and 3 apples. Instead, the ratio tells us that for every 2 oranges, there are 3 apples. As a result, **you can think of this ratio as $2x:3x$** because we must multiply 2 and 3 by the same value to keep the $2:3$ ratio. Using this "x" trick will help you on many ratio questions where you are given a ratio but not any exact numbers.

On the ACT, you will need to solve ratio questions in four different ways. We will review the four types of ratio questions below along with the methods you should use to solve them:

#1 - Ratio and a Total

Example 1: The ratio of red marbles to green marbles in a bag is $4:6$. If there are a total of 80 marbles in the bag and all of the marbles in the bag are red or green, how many of the marbles are red?

A. 8   B. 20   C. 32   D. 36   E. 52

Solution: Method #1: The "x" trick. We can think of the ratio $4:6$ as $4x:6x$, where the $4x$ represents the red marbles and the $6x$ represents the green marbles.

$$\text{Red Marbles} + \text{Green Marbles} = 80$$

$$4x + 6x = 80$$

$$10x = 80$$

$$x = 8$$

To solve for the red marbles, we plug $x = 8$ back into the $4x$.

$$\text{Red Marbles} = 4x = 4(8) = 32$$

The answer is C.

Method #2: Set up a Proportion. We can set up a proportion from the ratio. Since the ratio or red marbles to green marbles is $4:6$, we know that

$$\frac{\text{Red Marbles}}{\text{Total Marbles}} = \frac{4}{10}$$

We know there are 80 total marbles, so we can set up an equation to solve for the unknown number of red marbles.

$$\frac{x}{80} = \frac{4}{10}$$

$$10x = 320$$

$$x = 32$$

The answer is C.

#2 – Ratios as Proportions

Example 2: Beth is baking her famous chocolate cupcakes for her mother's birthday party. For every 3 cupcakes, Beth uses 10 pieces of chocolate. If Beth needs to make 42 cupcakes for the party, how many pieces of chocolate will she need to buy?
  A. 13   B. 42   C. 70   D. 126   E. 140

Solution: Set up the values from the ratio as a proportion. Here, we set up the proportion as

$$\frac{\text{cupcakes}}{\text{pieces of choclate}} = \frac{\text{cupcakes}}{\text{pieces of choclate}}$$

Now, we can plug in the values from the question and solve.

$$\frac{3 \text{ cupcakes}}{10 \text{ pieces of chocolate}} = \frac{42 \text{ cupcakes}}{x \text{ pieces of chocolate}}$$

$$3x = 420$$

$$x = \frac{420}{3} = 140$$

The answer is E.

#3 – Comparing Across Ratios

Example 3: The ratio of x to y is 3:4. The ratio of y to z is 2:10. What is the ratio of $x:z$?
  A. 3:10   B. 3:20   C. 15:4   D. 4:15   E. 2:10

Solution: We need to make the variable that appears in both ratios, y, have the same numerical value. To do that, we multiply the second ratio by 2, so

$$\begin{array}{cc} x:y & y:z \\ 3:4 & 2:10 \end{array}$$

becomes

$$\begin{array}{cc} x:y & y:z \\ 3:4 & 4:20 \end{array}$$

Now that the y-values are the same (both are equal to 4), we can compare across the ratios to find $x:z$.

$$x:z = 3:20$$

The answer is B.

#4 – Ratios and Geometry

Example 4: In rectangle ABCD, the ratio of the lengths of side AB to side BC is 8:5. If the total perimeter of the rectangle is 156 feet, what is the length of the longer side of the rectangle?

    A. 6   B. 12   C. 30   D. 48   E. 96

Solution: To start, sketch out rectangle ABCD. We can think of the ratio as $8x:5x$ instead of $8:5$. We can label the sides of our rectangles using $8x$ and $5x$ as the side lengths.

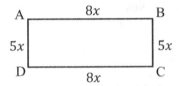

The perimeter of the rectangle is

$$8x + 8x + 5x + 5x = 156$$
$$26x = 156$$
$$x = \frac{156}{26} = 6$$

Now that we have solved for x, we can solve for the longer sides of the rectangle.

$$\text{Longer Sides} = 8x = 8(6) = 48$$

The answer is D.

Proportions

On the ACT, you need to know the equations for two types of proportions: direct proportions and indirect proportions.

Direct Proportion

In a direct proportion, y varies directly with x. In simpler terms, x and y will move together. As x increases, y increases, and as x decreases, y decreases. The equation for direct proportions is

$$y = kx \quad \text{(where } k \text{ is a constant)}$$

Example 5: If y varies directly with x and $y = 27$ when $x = 3$, what is the value of x when $y = 90$?

    A. 30   B. 27   C. 20   D. 13   E. 10

Solution: When solving proportions, we always start by solving for the constant k. We can solve for k using the pair of x and y-values the question gives us.

$$27 = k(3)$$
$$k = 9$$

Now, we know the equation for the proportion is $y = 9x$. To solve, plug $y = 90$ and solve for x.

$$90 = 9(x)$$
$$x = 10$$

The answer is E.

Indirect Proportion

In an indirect proportion, y varies inversely with x. In simpler terms, x and y will move opposite to one another. As x increases, y decreases, and as x decreases, y increases. The equation for indirect proportions is:

$$y = \frac{k}{x}$$

> **Example 6:** If y varies inversely with the square of x and $y = 45$ when $x = 2$, what is the value of y when $x = 6$?
>
>   A. 5   B. 15   C. 78   D. 112   E. 405

Solution: Since y varies directly with the square of x, the indirect proportion equation looks like

$$y = \frac{k}{x^2}$$

Be careful of changes like this, as it is a common way the ACT can make proportions questions more difficult. We start by solving for k using the x and y-values the question gives us.

$$45 = \frac{k}{2^2}$$

$$k = 180$$

We now know the indirect proportion equation for this question is $y = \frac{180}{x^2}$. To solve, we plug in $x = 6$ and solve for y.

$$y = \frac{180}{6^2} = \frac{180}{36} = 5$$

The answer is A.

Ratios and Proportions Practice: Answers on page 326.

1. If a dodgeball team has 6 girls and 11 total team members, what is the ratio of boys to girls?

   A. 5:6
   B. 6:5
   C. 6:11
   D. 12:10
   E. 15:6

2. On a map, $\frac{1}{2}$ inch represents 15 miles. How many miles apart are two gas stations that are $3\frac{1}{2}$ inches apart on the map?

   A. 15
   B. 25
   C. 55
   D. 105
   E. 120

3. The ratio of Joey's age to his brother's age is 4:3. The sum of their ages is 49. How old is Joey?

   A. 21
   B. 24
   C. 28
   D. 30
   E. 33

4. The combined length of 3 pieces of fabric is 105 inches. The lengths of the pieces are in a 4:5:6 ratio. What is the length, in inches, of the longest piece of fabric?

   A. 7
   B. 24
   C. 28
   D. 35
   E. 42

5. A state lottery has 2 out of every 9 tickets as a winner. Yesterday, 120 people bought a winning ticket. How many total tickets were purchased yesterday?

   A. 150
   B. 240
   C. 540
   D. 780
   E. 1080

6. A factory that produces fidget spinners can make 2,000 fidget spinners each hour. Of those 2,000 fidget spinners, 17 are randomly selected and inspected. If the factory produces 30,000 fidget spinner this week, how many will be selected for inspection?

   A. 145
   B. 170
   C. 205
   D. 225
   E. 255

7. In a triangle, the lengths of the three sides are in the ratio of 3: 6: 7. If the perimeter is 64, what is the length of the shortest side?

   A. 4
   B. 12
   C. 16
   D. 24
   E. 28

8. Atrazine, a weed killer commonly used by farmers, is such a concentrated substance that only 1L can be used to spray up to 4 hectares of farm fields. If one hectare is equal to approximately $2\frac{1}{2}$ acres, how many acres of farm fields could 25 L of atrazine be used to spray?

   A. 100
   B. 150
   C. 250
   D. 625
   E. 1,750

9. In a parking lot, 3 out of every 8 spaces are for compact cars. If there are 675 spaces for compact cars, how many spaces in the parking lot are NOT for compact cars?

   A. 1,800
   B. 1,575
   C. 1,350
   D. 1,265
   E. 1,125

10. In a drawer full of buttons, the ratio of tan to silver to gold buttons is 2:3:4. If all buttons in the draw are tan, silver, or gold, how many total buttons could be in the drawer?

    A. 8
    B. 14
    C. 24
    D. 27
    E. 30

11. Samantha rows 30 meters in 6.8 seconds. If she rows at the same rate for 2 minutes, which of the following is the closest to the number of meters she will row?

    A. 200
    B. 410
    C. 530
    D. 720
    E. 850

12. If x varies directly with y and $x = 15$ when $y = 3$, what is the value of x when $y = 15$?

    A. 3
    B. 5
    C. 15
    D. 75
    E. 225

13. Four friends buy a winning lottery ticket worth $25,000. They agree to give four times as much to charity as they will spend for fun. How much do they give to charity?

    A. $5,000
    B. $8,000
    C. $12,500
    D. $18,000
    E. $20,000

Chapter 10: Ratios and Proportions

14. At Mount Laguna High School, 6 out of every 10 students take biology, and 3 out of every 8 students who take biology are juniors. If there are 5,000 students at Mount Laguna, how many of the students are juniors who take biology?

    A. 1,125
    B. 1,214
    C. 1,270
    D. 1,596
    E. 1,625

15. Bailey is baking bread, and the recipe calls for $\frac{3}{4}$ of a teaspoon of yeast and $3\frac{1}{2}$ cups of flour. She decides to use an entire 3 teaspoon pack of yeast and will keep the same ratio. How many cups of flour will she need?

    A. $3\frac{1}{2}$
    B. 7
    C. 8
    D. $10\frac{1}{2}$
    E. 14

16. Julie knows that 30 miles per hour is 44 feet per second. If a cheetah is running 70 miles per hour, approximately how fast is it running in feet per second?

    A. 36
    B. 48
    C. 86
    D. 103
    E. 127

17. The number of snails in the Sanders family pond varies inversely with the number of fish. Last summer, there were 150 fish and 1200 snails. If this summer there are 250 fish, how many snails are in the pond?

    A. 100
    B. 150
    C. 720
    D. 1200
    E. 2000

18. The ratio of the total amount of money raised by three different clubs is $6:8:9$. If the total amount of money raised by all three clubs is $322, what is the difference in money raised between the club that raised the most and the least money?

    A. 23
    B. 42
    C. 69
    D. 138
    E. 184

19. The weight of an object on Mars is approximately $\frac{6}{10}$ of its weight on Earth. The weight of an object on the Saturn is approximately $\frac{21}{10}$ of its weight on Earth. If an object weights 150kg on Earth, approximately how many more kilograms does it weight on Saturn than on Mars?

    A. 60
    B. 150
    C. 210
    D. 225
    E. 250

20. If $x:y = 7:2$ and $y:z = 3:2$, what is the ratio of $x:z$?

    A. $3:1$
    B. $2:7$
    C. $7:2$
    D. $14:4$
    E. $21:4$

21. The ratio of four sides of a quadrilateral is $2:3:5:7$. If the perimeter of the quadrilateral is 68, what is the length of the second longest side?

    A. 4
    B. 12
    C. 13.6
    D. 20
    E. 28

22. A recent study examined how the amount of sunlight (S), pesticides (P), and organic matter (M) affected the height of corn plants (H). It was discovered that sunlight and organic matter varied directly with plant height while pesticides varied inversely. Which of the following formulas is correct?

A. $H = kSMP$
B. $H = \frac{kSM}{P}$
C. $H = \frac{kP}{SM}$
D. $H = \frac{k}{SMP}$
E. $H = \frac{kSP}{M}$

23. In a certain rectangle, the ratio of the lengths of the 2 sides is 7:4. If the area of the rectangle is 252 square inches, what is the length of the shorter side?

A. 12
B. 14
C. 18
D. 21
E. 24

24. If m is directly proportional with the square root of n and $m = 40$ when $n = 25$, what is the value of m when $n = 13$?

A. 20.8
B. $2\sqrt{13}$
C. $8\sqrt{13}$
D. $8\sqrt{21}$
E. 65.4

25. The degree measures of the interior angles in a hexagon are in the ratio of $1:2:2:3:5:7$. What is the measure of the largest interior angle of the hexagon?

A. 48
B. 96
C. 144
D. 252
E. 336

26. The ratio of a to b is 4 to 1. The ratio of b to c is 3 to 10. What is the value of $\frac{2a-c}{3b}$?

A. -2
B. $-\frac{2}{3}$
C. $\frac{7}{9}$
D. $\frac{14}{9}$
E. $\frac{27}{7}$

27. Javon is constructing a box. The ratio of the length to the width to the height of the box must be 5 to 4 to 2. If the volume of the box is 2,560 in^3, what is the height, in inches, of the box?

A. 4
B. 8
C. 20
D. 32
E. 128

28. The high school football team is raising money to upgrade the turf on the field. The team has only sophomore, junior, and senior members. The ratio of sophomores to juniors to seniors on the football team is 2:4:5. Sophomores on average raised $40 per person, juniors on average raised $55 per person, and seniors on average raised $72 per person. What is the average amount raised per team member?

A. 55
B. 57
C. 59
D. 60
E. 62

Chapter 11: Functions

A function is defined as a mathematical relationship between a variable x and the function $f(x)$. For every value of x, there is exactly one value of $f(x)$. For any function, there will be an input, which appears as the term in the parentheses of a function, and an output, which will be the value that $f(x)$ equals.

Function Basics

In order to solve functions questions on the ACT, we first need to know where to properly plug in the input to a function. For the function
$$f(x) = 5x - 2$$
we plug in the input for x. You are likely used to the input being a number, but the input can include variables as well. No matter what the input is, we plug it in for the x in the equation:
$$f(3) = 5(3) - 2 = 13$$
$$f(-2x) = 5(-2x) - 2 = -10x - 2$$
$$f(a - 11) = 5(a - 11) - 2 = 5a - 57$$

Example 1: If $f(x) = 3\sqrt{x} + 11$, what is the value for $f(25)$?
   A. 15   B. 26   C. 34   D. 64   E. 86

Solution: To solve, plug in the input to the function.
$$f(25) = 3\sqrt{25} + 11 = 3(5) + 11 = 15 + 11 = 26$$
The answer is B.

Example 2: A function, f, is defined by $f(x, y) = 4x - y^2$. What is the value of $f(5, 2)$?
   A. -17 B. 9   C. 16   D. 24   E. 48

Solution: This function sure looks weird, but we solve it in the exact same way as we just did except that now we are given a value for x and y. To solve, plug in 5 for x and 2 for y.
$$f(5, 2) = 4(5) - 2^2 = 20 - 4 = 16$$
The answer is C.

Example 3: If $f(x) = \frac{10x}{x+4}$, for what value of x does $f(x) = 5$?
   A. 1   B. 2   C. 4   D. 5   E. 10

Solution: If we are given the output, which is 5 in this question, and are asked to find the input, we plug in the output for $f(x)$ and solve for the input x.
$$5 = \frac{10x}{x + 4}$$
$$5(x + 4) = 10x$$
$$5x + 20 = 10x$$
$$20 = 5x$$
$$4 = x$$
The answer is C.

Composite Functions

Quite often, the ACT will ask you to solve composite functions. A composite function is a function that is written inside of another function. We will use the examples below to learn how to solve composite functions questions correctly.

Example 4: If $f(x) = 3x + 10$ and $g(x) = x - 5$, what is the value of $f(g(8))$?

A. 3   B. 9   C. 19   D. 29   E. 43

Solution: If you are asked to solve a composite function, there are two methods to solve: (1) solve for the composite function or (2) work inside out. Both methods are shown below.

Method #1 - Solve for the composite function: In this question, we want to solve for the function $f(g(x))$. To do so, we plug the entire $g(x)$ function in for the x in the $f(x)$ function.

$$f(g(x)) = 3(x - 5) + 10 = 3x - 15 + 10 = 3x - 5$$

Now that we know the composite function $f(g(x)) = 3x - 5$, we can plug in 8 for x and solve.

$$f(g(8)) = 3(8) - 5 = 24 - 5 = 19$$

The answer is C.

Method #2 - Work inside out: Rather than solve for the composite function, we can also work from the inside out to solve for $f(g(8))$. To start, we can solve for $g(8)$.

$$g(8) = 8 - 5 = 3$$

We now know that $g(8) = 3$, so we can simplify the function we are solving for.

$$f(g(8)) = f(3)$$

Now, we just solve for $f(3)$.

$$f(3) = 3(3) + 10 = 19$$

The answer is C.

Both of these methods work for any composite function questions on the ACT, so you should use the one that you are more comfortable with.

Example 5: If $f(x) = 2x^2 - 7$ and $g(x) = x + 3$, what is $f(g(x - 1))$?

A. $2x^2 + 2$ B. $2x^2 + 8x + 1$ C. $2x^2 + 12x + 11$ D. $2x^2 - 3$ E. $2x^2 - 4$

Solution: This question looks more difficult since we now have $x - 1$ as the input, but we should still treat this as a composite function. Both of the methods outlined in Example 4 will work to solve. Below, we will use the inside out method. First, we can solve for $g(x - 1)$:

$$g(x - 1) = (x - 1) + 3 = x + 2$$

We now know that $g(x - 1) = x + 2$, so we can simplify what we are solving for.

$$f(g(x - 1)) = f(x + 2)$$

Now, we solve for $f(x + 2)$.

$$f(x + 2) = 2(x + 2)^2 - 7 = 2(x^2 + 4x + 4) - 7 = 2x^2 + 8x + 8 - 7 = 2x^2 + 8x + 1$$

$$f(g(x-1)) = 2x^2 + 8x + 1$$

The answer is B.

Common Mistake to Avoid: Remember that $(x+2)^2 \neq x^2 + 4$. You need to multiply out the term because $(x+2)^2$ is the same as $(x+2)(x+2)$.

Other Function Notations

Do you know what $(f \circ g)(x)$ or $(fg)(x)$ means? If not, you are not alone. Most students we work with see these other function notations and are confused about what to do. No need to worry though! All of the other function notations that can come up on test day are in the table below. If you memorize what these notations mean, you will be prepared to solve any questions with them on test day.

Operation	Function Notation
Composite	$(f \circ g)(x) = f(g(x))$
Sum	$(f+g)(x) = f(x) + g(x)$
Difference	$(f-g)(x) = f(x) - g(x)$
Product	$(fg)(x) = (f \cdot g)(x) = f(x) \times g(x)$
Quotient	$\left(\dfrac{f}{g}\right)(x) = \dfrac{f(x)}{g(x)}$

Example 6: If $f(x) = 2x^2 + 1$ and $g(x) = x^2 - 1$, which of the following expressions represents $(fg)(x)$?

    A. $3x^2$ B. $2x^2 - 1$ C. $2x^4 - 1$ D. $2x^4 + 2x^2$ E. $2x^4 - x^2 - 1$

Solution: $(fg)(x)$ is the same as $f(x) \times g(x)$, so we need to multiply the functions together.

$$(fg)(x) = (2x^2 + 1)(x^2 - 1)$$

To solve, we need to multiply these quadratics together by FOIL (First, Outer, Inner, Last). If you need to review how this works, you can go to Chapter 16.

$$(fg)(x) = (2x^2 + 1)(x^2 - 1) = 2x^4 - 2x^2 + x^2 - 1 = 2x^4 - x^2 - 1$$

The answer is E.

Example 7: Let $(f \circ g)(x) = (2x+1)^2 - 3$ and $g(x) = 2x + 1$. Which of the following expressions defines $(g \circ f)(x)$?

    A. $2x^2 - 2$ B. $2x^2 - 5$ C. $2x^2 - 7$ D. $\sqrt{2x+1} + 3$ E. $\sqrt{2x+1} - 1$

Solution: On more difficult questions, the ACT will give you a puzzle question with functions. These are challenging to solve and normally appear in the last 15 questions of the test.

To solve this question, we first need to remember that $(f \circ g)(x) = f(g(x))$. We also know that $g(x) = 2x + 1$, so we can plug in $2x + 1$ for $g(x)$ and get

$$(f \circ g)(x) = f(g(x)) = f(2x+1)$$

The input of $2x + 1$ is plugged in for x in the function $f(x)$ we are trying to find. Since we know that $(f \circ g)(x) = (2x + 1)^2 - 3$, we can replace $2x + 1$ with x to work backwards and find $f(x)$. We get

$$f(x) = x^2 - 3.$$

Now that we know $f(x)$, we can find $(g \circ f)(x)$. Again, remember that $(g \circ f)(x)$ is the same as $g(f(x))$. To solve, we need to plug $f(x)$, which is $x^2 - 3$, into $g(x)$

$$(g \circ f)(x) = g(f(x)) = g(x^2 - 3) = 2(x^2 - 3) + 1 = 2x^2 - 5$$

The answer is B.

Functions on Graphs

When a function is graphed, the input, x, is on the x-axis and the output, $f(x)$, is on the y-axis. Another way to better understand how functions appear on a graph is to remember that for any linear function

$$f(x) = mx + b \quad \text{is the same as} \quad y = mx + b$$

When graphing a function $f(x)$, you can think of $f(x)$ as the y-coordinate and x as the x-coordinate. Using the input as x and the output as y, we can find points in the standard (x, y) plane and graph any function.

Example 8:

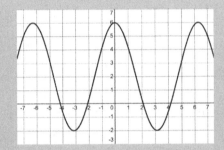

The function $f(x)$ is shown in the standard (x, y) coordinate plane above. What is the minimum value of this function?

A. -2 B. -1 C. 6 D. π E. 2π

Solution: The minimum value of the function is the point(s) on the graph where y-coordinate is smallest. In the function above, the minimum value is where $y = -2$, so **the answer is A.**

What if this question instead asked for the maximum value of the function? Well, now we just look for the highest point on the graph, which is at $y = 6$.

Easy right? For any questions asking for the minimum or maximum value of a function, you just need to look at the graph and find the smallest or largest y-value.

Example 9:

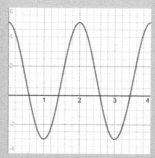

The function $f(x) = 4\cos(\pi x) + 1$ is graphed in the standard (x, y) coordinate plane above. How many x-intercepts does the graph of the function have on the interval $0 < x < 4$?

A. 1 B. 2 C. 3 D. 4 E. 5

Solution: To find the number of x-intercepts on the graph of the function, we count the number of times the function crosses the x-axis. We see the function crossing the x-axis 4 times, so **the answer is D**.

Domain and Range

Another common type of common functions question will ask you about the domain or range of a function.

- **Domain**: The set of all possible input, x, values to a function.
- **Range**: The set of all output, y, values to a function.

If you are looking at the graph of a function, **the domain is all the x-values that appear on the graph** and **the range is all the y-values that appear on the graph**.

To see how this works, let's find the domain and range of the graph below.

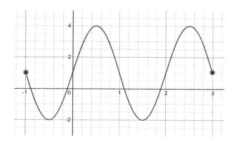

We see x-values on the graph from $x = -1$ to $x = 3$, so for the graph above the domain is $\{-1 \leq x \leq 3\}$. Since the dots on the graph are solid, we include -1 and 3 in the domain and use the less than or equal to and greater than or equal to signs. If the dots were open, the domain would instead use the greater than and less than signs and would be $\{-1 < x < 3\}$. .

We see y-values on the graph from $y = -2$ to $y = 4$, so for the graph above the range is $\{-2 \leq y \leq 4\}$.

Example 10:

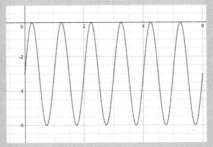

The graph of $f(x) = 3\sin(2\pi x) - 3$ is shown above. What is the range of $f(x)$?

A. $-6 \leq y \leq 0$ B. $-3 \leq y \leq 0$ C. $-3 \leq y \leq 3$ D. $0 \leq y \leq 3$ E. $0 \leq y \leq 6$

Solution: To solve, look for the y-values on the graph. We see y-values from $y = -6$ to $y = 0$, so the range of $f(x)$ is $-6 \leq y \leq 0$. **The answer is A.**

Example 11:

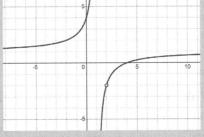

The graph $f(x) = \frac{(x-4)(x-2)}{(x-1)(x-2)}$ is shown above. What is the range of $f(x)$?

A. $\{y|y \neq 0\}$ B. $\{y|y \neq 1\}$ C. $\{y|y \neq 4\}$ D. $\{y|y \neq -2 \text{ and } y \neq 1\}$ E. $\{y| \neq 0 \text{ and } y \neq 1\}$

Solution: Looking at this graph, you might notice there is a horizontal invisible line at $y = 1$ the graph approaches but never crosses. We call this a **horizontal asymptote** at $y = 1$. Because there are no points on the graph where $y = 1$, the range of the function will not include $y = 1$. All points above the horizontal asymptotes $y = 1$ appear on the graph, but what about below?

Do you see that open dot at the point $(2, -2)$? We call this point a **hole** in the graph. Holes occur when the numerator and denominator of a function both equal 0. If we plug in $x = 2$ to $f(x)$, we will get $f(2) = \frac{0}{0}$. We can also spot that there is going to be a hole at $x = 2$ because we see $(x - 2)$ in the numerator and denominator. When the same term appears in the numerator and denominator, it always creates a hole. Holes in the graph are undefined and are never included in the domain.

But a hole does not automatically mean the value is not included in the range, as there could be another point with the y-value elsewhere on the graph. In the graph above, however, there is no point where $y = 2$, so it is also not included in the range.

As a result, we see that the function includes all y-values except at $y = 1$ (the horizontal asymptote) and $y = -2$ (the hole). In fancy math terms, this would appear as $\{y|y \neq -2 \text{ and } y \neq 1\}$, which means all values of y except $y = -2$ and $y = 1$. **The answer is D.**

Horizontal asymptotes are rarely tested on the ACT, but you should still know how to solve for them just in case. If you need to review asymptotes, the rules for solving them are covered in Chapter 35.

Continuing to look at the graph in Example 11, you can see there is a vertical invisible line at $x = 1$ that the graph approaches but never crosses. There is no point on the graph when $x = 1$. We call this a **vertical asymptote** at $x = 1$. Because there is no point on the graph where $x = 1$, the domain of the function will not include $x = 1$.

There is also an open dot at $x = 2$. We call this point a **hole** in the graph. Holes are not included in the domain since there is no point where $x = 2$ on the graph. All other values for x appear on the graph, so the domain is all values of x except $x \neq 1$ and $x \neq 2$. Mathematically, the domain could be written as $\{x | x \neq 1 \text{ and } x \neq 2\}$.

Vertical asymptotes occur when the denominator of a function is equal to 0. If we plug in $x = 1$ to $f(x)$, we get $f(1) = \frac{3}{0}$, which is undefined. Again, since vertical asymptotes are points where the function is undefined, they are never included in the domain.

What if you are not given a picture graph in the question? To solve for vertical asymptotes, you set the denominator equal to zero and solve. If there is a hole in the graph, such as the one at $x = 2$ in example 11, we cancel those terms. So for the graph in example 11, the only term left in the denominator is $x - 1$. To find the vertical asymptote, we set $x - 1$ equal to 0 and solve.

$$x - 1 = 0$$
$$x = 1$$

We see there is a vertical asymptote at $x = 1$. Even if we were not given the graph, we could easily solve for any vertical asymptotes. Remember vertical asymptotes are points where the graph is undefined and are not included in the domain.

> **Example 12:** The domain of $f(x) = \frac{5}{x^2 - 5x + 6}$ is the set of all real numbers EXCEPT:
>
>   A. $\frac{5}{6}$ B. 2   C. -3 D. 2 and 3   E. -2 and 3

Solution: Whenever you are asked about the domain and see a fraction in a function, look for where the function is undefined. To make the function undefined, set the denominator equal to 0 and solve for x.

$$x^2 - 5x + 6 = 0$$
$$(x - 2)(x - 3) = 0$$
$$x = 2, 3$$

$f(x)$ is undefined when $x = 2$ and $x = 3$, so these points are not included in the domain of the function. If we graphed $f(x)$, we would see vertical asymptotes at $x = 2$ and $x = 3$. **The answer is D.**

> **Example 13:** Two real-valued functions are defined as $f(x) = \sqrt{x} + 1$ and $g(x) = x - 3$. What is the domain of $f(g(x))$?
>
>   A. $[0, \infty)$ B. $[1, \infty)$ C. $[3, \infty)$ D. $[5, \infty)$ E. $[-\infty, \infty)$

Solution: First, we need to solve for $f(g(x))$ by plugging $g(x)$ into $f(x)$.

$$f(g(x)) = \sqrt{x - 3} + 1$$

Now, we need to learn how the domain is restricted with a square root. Values underneath a square root must be greater than or equal to 0. Any value of x that makes the term underneath the square root negative cannot be included in the domain. **To find the domain with a square root, set the term underneath the square root greater than or equal to zero and solve for x.**

$$x - 3 \geq 0$$
$$x \geq 3$$

The domain of $f(g(x))$ is $x \geq 3$. Written in interval notation, this is $[\,3, \infty)$. **The answer is C.**

To illustrate why the domain is restricted, let's plug in $x = 1$, which is not part of the domain, to $f(g(x))$ and see what happens.

$$f(g(1)) = \sqrt{1-3} + 1 = \sqrt{-2} + 1$$

You cannot have a negative term underneath the square root, so $x = 1$ has no real number output and therefore cannot be included in the domain.

If you need to review vertical asymptotes or just want more practice, go to Chapter 35.

Inverse Functions

Inverse functions, written as $f^{-1}(x)$, are rarely tested on the ACT, but they are pretty easy to solve, so let's go over them just in case you see an inverse functions question on test day. To find the inverse of any function, switch the input x and the output $f(x)$ and solve for $f(x)$. Let's see how this works in the example below.

Example 14: Given the function $f(x) = \frac{10x-7}{2}$, what is the value for $f^{-1}(6.5)$?

A. -7 B. $-\frac{13}{2}$ C. $\frac{3}{2}$ D. 2   E. $\frac{9}{2}$

Solution: To find the inverse, we switch the input x and the output $f(x)$. Most students find it easiest to start by replacing $f(x)$ with y, so our function becomes

$$y = \frac{10x - 7}{2}$$

To find the inverse, switch the x and y and then solve for y.

$$x = \frac{10y - 7}{2}$$
$$2x = 10y - 7$$
$$2x + 7 = 10y$$
$$\frac{2x + 7}{10} = y$$

Once we have solved for y, we have found the inverse function. So, we can replace y with $f^{-1}(x)$.

$$f^{-1}(x) = \frac{2x + 7}{10}$$

Now that we know the inverse, we can find $f^{-1}(6.5)$ by plugging in 6.5

$$f^{-1}(6.5) = \frac{2(6.5) + 7}{10} = \frac{20}{10} = 2$$
$$f^{-1}(6.5) = 2$$

The answer is D.

Chapter 11: Functions

Functions Practice: Answers on pages 326-327.

For questions 1-24, use the functions below.

$$f(x) = 2x^2 - 7$$
$$g(x) = -3x + 10$$
$$h(x) = x - 3$$

1. What is the value of $f(4)$?

2. What is the value of $g(-31)$?

3. What is the value of $f(-10)$?

4. What is the value of $h(-19)$?

5. What is the value of $f(3x)$?

6. What is the value of $g(x-3)$?

7. What is the value of $f(8) - g(2)$?

8. What is the value of $(g - h)(-4)$?

9. What is the value of $(f + g - h)(5)$?

10. What it the value of $(g - f)(-3x)$?

11. For what value of x does $h(x) = -5$?

12. For what value of x does $g(x) = 31$?

13. For what value of x does $f(x) = 43$?

14. For what value of x does $g(x) = -11$?

15. What is the value of $g(h(-11))$?

16. What is the value of $f(h(2x))$?

17. What is the value of $(f \circ h)(-4)$?

18. What is the value of $(fg)(x)$?

19. What is the value of $(hg)(11)$?

20. What is the value of $(gh)(x+1)$?

21. What is the value of the value of $(\frac{f}{g})(3)$?

22. What is the value of $(\frac{h}{f})(3 - 2x)$?

23. For what value of x does $g(h(x)) = 18$?

24. What is the value of $(g \circ f)(3x)$?

25. Given $f(x) = x^2 - 4(2x - 1)$, what is the value of $f(-2)$?

    A. -20
    B. 0
    C. 11
    D. 16
    E. 24

26. A function, f, is defined by $f(x, y) = 5x^2 - 2y$. What is the value of $f(3,7)$?

    A. 3
    B. 21
    C. 31
    D. 39
    E. 337

27. What is the value of $f(-3)$ given the function $f(x) = 3x^2 + 3x + 10$?

    A. -46
    B. -26
    C. -4
    D. 28
    E. 36

28. Given $f(x, y, z) = 2y^2 - 4xz + z^3$, what is the value of $f(5, -2, -3)$?

    A. 41
    B. 29
    C. -37
    D. -83
    E. -91

29. Given the functions $f(x) = 2x^2 + x$ and $g(x) = 2x - 1$, what is the value of $g(f(2))$?

    A. 3
    B. 10
    C. 15
    D. 19
    E. 22

30. The fluctuation of the water depth at a wetland is shown in the figure below. One of the values gives the positive difference, in inches, between the greatest water depth and least water depth shown in the graph. Which value is it?

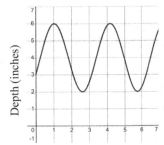

Number of hours after 1pm

A. 2
B. 3
C. 4
D. 6
E. 7

31. For the function $f(x) = \frac{x+1}{3}$, what is the value of $f^{-1}(x)$?

A. $\frac{3x-1}{3}$
B. $3x - 1$
C. $\frac{x+1}{3}$
D. $\frac{-x-1}{3}$
E. $\frac{x-1}{3}$

32. Given $f(x) = -6x^3 + 2x^2$, what is $f(-3)$ equal to?

A. -180
B. -144
C. 12
D. 144
E. 180

33. If $f(x) = -3x^2 - x$ and $g(x) = -7x + 1$, $(f+g)(2)$ is equal to:

A. 1
B. -3
C. -3
D. -10
E. -27

34. For the functions $f(x) = 3x + 7$ and $g(x) = 2x - 3$, $(f \circ g)(5)$ is equal to:

A. 7
B. 11
C. 22
D. 28
E. 41

35. If $f(x) = x + \frac{1}{2x}$ and $g(x) = \frac{1}{x}$ what is the value of $f(g(\frac{1}{4}))$?

A. -6
B. -4
C. 4
D. $4\frac{1}{8}$
E. 6

36. Functions f and g are defined as $f(x) = -5x + 2$ and $g(x) = 10 - f(x)$. The value of $g(3)$ is:

A. -13
B. -3
C. 7
D. 23
E. 30

37. The graph of $f(x) = 4\cos(3x) + 3$ is shown below. What is the range for this function?

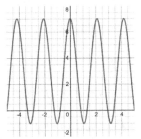

A. $-1 < y < 7$
B. $-5 < y < 5$
C. $-1 \leq y \leq 7$
D. $-1 \leq y \leq 4$
E. $-5 \leq y \leq 5$

38. The domain of $f(x) = \frac{27-x}{x^2-6x+9}$ is all real numbers EXCEPT:

   A. 27 only
   B. 9 only
   C. 3 only
   D. −3 and 3 only
   E. 3 and 9 only

39. Given $h(x) = 4x - 7$, which of the following expressions is equal to $h(-2x + 1)$ for all x in its domain?

   A. $8x + 1$
   B. $8x - 13$
   C. $-8x + 8$
   D. $-8x - 3$
   E. $-8x - 6$

40. A function g satisfies $g(5) = 11$ and $g(6) = 8$. A function h satisfies $h(8) = -3$ and $h(6) = 5$. What is the value of $g(h(6))$?

   A. −3
   B. 5
   C. 6
   D. 8
   E. 11

41.

x	$t(x)$	$p(x)$
1	−3	4
2	0	3
3	2	−1
4	9	−7

The table above shows some values for the functions t and p. For what value of x does $t(x) + p(x) = 2$?

   A. 1
   B. 2
   C. 3
   D. 4
   E. 5

42. Given the function below, what is $f(2)$?

$$f(x) = \begin{cases} 3x - 4; x < 2 \\ \frac{1}{3} \cdot 2^x; x \geq 2 \end{cases}$$

   A. 2
   B. $\frac{4}{3}$
   C. $\frac{1}{3}$
   D. $\frac{1}{2}$
   E. 0

43. The graph of $f(x) = \frac{x}{x^2+8x+16}$ is shown below. What is the domain of $f(x)$?

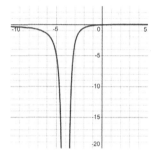

   A. $\{x | x \neq -4\}$
   B. $\{x | x \neq -1\}$
   C. $\{x | x \neq 0\}$
   D. $\{x | x \neq 4\}$
   E. $\{x | x \neq -4 \text{ and } x \neq 0\}$

44. The domain of $f(x) = \frac{5}{x^3-16x}$ is the set of all real numbers EXCEPT:

   A. $\frac{5}{16}$
   B. 4
   C. −4 and 4
   D. 0 and −4
   E. 4, 0, and −4

45. Two functions are defined as $f(x) = x^2 - 2$ and $g(x) = 2x - 3$. Which of the following expressions represents $(f \circ g)(x)$?

   A. $2x^2 - 5$
   B. $2x^2 - 11$
   C. $4x^2 - 12x + 7$
   D. $4x^2 - 12x - 11$
   E. $4x^2 + 11$

46. $p(x) = x^2 + 2x - b$

For the function p defined above, b is a constant and $p(2) = 5$. What is the value of $p(-3)$?

A. -18
B. 0
C. 3
D. 5
E. 12

47.

x	$g(x)$
2	11
4	23
6	35

Some values of a linear function g are shown above. Which of the following defines $g(x)$?

A. $g(x) = 4x + 3$
B. $g(x) = 6x - 1$
C. $g(x) = 4x + 7$
D. $g(x) = 5x + 5$
E. $g(x) = x + 9$

48. The graph of $f(x) = \dfrac{-x^2 - x + 12}{5x^2 - 25x + 30}$ is shown below. The domain of $f(x)$ is all value of x EXCEPT:

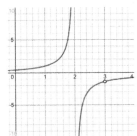

A. 0
B. 2
C. 3
D. 0 and 2
E. 2 and 3

49. $f(x) = x^2 + 10x - 24$
$g(x) = x^2 - 4$

Which of the following expressions is equivalent to $\left(\dfrac{f}{g}\right)(x)$ for $x > 2$?

A. $\dfrac{x+12}{x+2}$
B. $\dfrac{1}{x-2}$
C. $\dfrac{x+12}{x-2}$
D. $\dfrac{x(x+2)}{x-2}$
E. $10x + 6$

50. The domain of $f(x) = \dfrac{x-2}{x^3 - 7x^2 - 18x}$ is the set of all real numbers EXCEPT:

A. $-\dfrac{1}{9}$
B. 0
C. -2 and 9
D. 0 and -2
E. -2, 0, and 9

51. A function is defined as $f(z) = 3z - 13$, and its domain is the set of integers from $1 - 20$ including 1 and 20. For how many values of z is $f(z)$ negative?

A. 0
B. 4
C. 5
D. 12
E. 20

52. Consider the functions $f(x) = \sqrt{x}$ and $g(x) = 4x + 5$. What is the domain of $f(g(x))$?

A. $x \geq \dfrac{-5}{4}$
B. $x > \dfrac{-5}{4}$
C. $x \leq \dfrac{4}{5}$
D. $x \geq \dfrac{5}{4}$
E. $x \geq -5$

53. If $f(x) = 3x^2 - 5x + 2$ and $g(x) = x^2 + 3$, which of the following expressions represents $(fg)(x)$?

    A. $4x^2 - 5x + 4$
    B. $3x^4 + 6x^2 - 15$
    C. $3x^4 + 11x^2 - 6x - 9$
    D. $3x^4 - 5x^3 + 11x^2 - 15x + 6$
    E. $9x^4 - 30x^3 + 37x^2 - 20x + 4$

54. The domain of the function $f(x) = \frac{3}{15-|3x|}$ is all real values of x EXCEPT:

    A. 0
    B. 0 and 3
    C. 0 and 5
    D. -5 and 5
    E. $-\frac{1}{5}$ and 5

55. The function f is defined by $f(x) = 3x^2 - 5x + 10$. If the function $f(x-2)$ is written in the form $ax^2 + bx + c$, what is the value of $a + b + c$?

    A. 30
    B. 18
    C. 10
    D. 8
    E. 5

56. $f(x) = \frac{(x-2)^4 - 3}{(x-3)^2 - 4(x-2) + 8}$

    For what value x is the function above undefined?

    A. 1
    B. 2
    C. 3
    D. 4
    E. 5

57. If $g(f(x)) = \sqrt{x+3} - 4$ and $f(x) = x + 3$, what is the domain of $f(g(x))$?

    A. $[-3, \infty)$
    B. $[0, \infty)$
    C. $[3, \infty)$
    D. $[-3, 3]$
    E. $(-\infty, 0]$

58. Given functions $f(x) = x^2 + 6x - 7$ and $g(x) = 3^x$, for what values of x does $g(f(x)) = 1$?

    A. 0 only
    B. 1 only
    C. -1 and 7 only
    D. 0 and -1 only
    E. -7 and 1 only

59. For all values of x there is a function g such that $3g(x) = g(5x)$. If $g(20) = 18$, what is the value of $g(4)$?

    A. 90
    B. 72
    C. 60
    D. 18
    E. 6

60. The 2 functions f and g are defined as $f(x) = 6x - a$ and $g(x) = 4x + 4$, where a is a real number. If $f(g(x)) = g(f(x))$, then what is the value of a?

    A. 0
    B. $-\frac{20}{3}$
    C. $\frac{3}{2}$
    D. $\frac{28}{5}$
    E. $\frac{24}{3}$

Chapter 12: Mean, Median, Mode, and Range

To start, let's review the basic definitions of mean, median, mode, and range:

Mean (average): The sum divided by the number of items.

Median: The middle number in a list of numbers when ordered from smallest to largest.

Mode: The number that appears most often.

Range: The difference between the smallest and the largest numbers.

On the ACT, you need to know how to solve mean (average) questions. For these questions, remember that:

$$\text{Average} = \frac{\text{Sum}}{\text{Number of Items}}$$

Example 1: The five students who sit in the front row of Ms. Rashard's class averaged 24 points on last Friday's quiz. If the first four students received scores of 22, 28, 17, and 25, what was the score of the fifth student?

    A. 24   B. 26   C. 28   D. 29.   E. 31

Solution: Let's call the fifth student's score x and set up the question using the average equation.

$$24 = \frac{22+28+17+25+x}{5}$$

$$24 = \frac{92+x}{5}$$

$$120 = 92 + x$$

$$x = 28$$

The answer is C.

Example 2: The AP Biology final is out of 100 points. The first period class of 6 students gets an average score of 85. The second period class of 9 students gets an average score of 90. What is the average score for all the students combined?

    A. 86   B. 87   C. 87.5   D. 88   E. 89

Solution: To solve this question, we need to find out the total number of points scored by all students from both classes and then divide by the total number of students (15).

In the equations below, x represents the sum of the test scores for all 6 students in the 1st period class and y represents the sum of the test scores for all 9 students in the 2nd period class. To start, we can find the total number of points the 6 students in the 1st period class received.

$$85 = \frac{x}{6}$$

$$x = 510$$

The first period students received a total of 510 points. Even though we do not know the individual scores of each student's tests, we know the total. We can repeat this same calculation for the 2nd period class.

$$90 = \frac{y}{9}$$

$$y = 810$$

Notice that to find the total points for each class, we multiplied the class average by the number of students. In general terms, **we multiply the average by the number of items to find the sum. This is commonly the first step in many average questions, so make sure that you remember this simple step to find the sum whenever you are given an average.**

Now, we can solve for the average score for all students combined.

$$\text{Average Score} = \frac{\text{Total Points}}{\text{Total Students}} = \frac{510+810}{15} = \frac{1320}{15} = 88$$

The answer is D.

> **Example 3:** Erica's golden retriever gave birth twice in the last two years. Her first litter had 7 puppies with an average weight of p lbs. Her second litter had 5 puppies with an average weight of m pounds. Which of the following expressions correctly calculates the average weight w, in pounds, of all of the puppies that Erica's golden retriever gave birth to over the last two years?
>
> A. $w = \frac{p+m}{12}$ B. $w = \frac{p}{7} + \frac{m}{5}$ C. $w = \frac{7p+5m}{12}$ D. $w = \frac{7m+5p}{12}$ E. $w = \frac{mp}{12}$

Solution: Method 1 – "Math Teacher Way": To find the average puppy weight, we need to find the total weight of all the puppies and divide it by the total number of puppies. First, we can find the total weight of her first litter:

$$p = \frac{\text{sum}}{7}$$

$$7p = \text{total weight of puppies in 1st litter}$$

We can repeat this to find the total weight of the second litter:

$$m = \frac{\text{sum}}{5}$$

$$5m = \text{total weight of puppies in 2nd litter}$$

We know that there are 12 puppies total, so now we can calculate the average weight.

$$w = \frac{7p+5m}{12}$$

The answer is C.

Method 2 – Pick Numbers. For many students, this question is difficult because we are not given any values for the average weights of the litters. To make this question easier, we can use substitution and pick numbers. Let's say the first litter has an average weight of 1 pound ($p = 1$) and the second litter has an average weight of 3 pounds ($m = 3$). We can use our numbers to solve for the average weight of the puppies in both litters.

$$\text{Total Weight of 1st Litter} = 7 \times 1 = 7$$

The first litter had 7 puppies with an average weight of 1 pound, so the total weight of the litter is 7 pounds.

$$\text{Total Weight of 2nd Litter} = 5 \times 3 = 15$$

The second litter had 5 puppies with an average weight of 3 pounds, so the total weight is 15 pounds. Now, we can find the average weight of each puppy from these two litters.

$$w = \frac{7+15}{12} = \frac{22}{12} = \frac{11}{6}$$

With our values of $p = 1$ and $m = 3$, we found that $w = \frac{11}{6}$. To find the correct answer choice, plug in our values of $p = 1$ and $m = 3$ to the answer choices and see which one gives you $w = \frac{11}{6}$. Below, you can see how the correct answer choice C gives us the correct value for w.

$$w = \frac{7(1)+5(3)}{12} = \frac{22}{12} = \frac{11}{6}$$

The answer is C.

Example 4: During the first 30 minutes of work at Birkee's Bakery, Vaivani decorated 23 cookies per minute for the first 10 minutes and then at 14 cookies per minute for the next 20 minutes. Which of the following gives the average number of cookies that Vaivani decorated per minute for her first 30 minutes at work?

    A. 15   B. 16   C. 16.5   D. 17   E. 18.5

Solution: In this question, we are given two averages that do not equally affect the final result. Since the first average of 23 cookies per minute is for 10 minutes and the second average of 14 cookies per minute is for 20 minutes, these averages cannot be treated equally. In math, this is called a **weighted average**. To solve weighted average questions with two items, we can use the equation below:

$$\text{Weighted Average} = \frac{(\text{average \#1})(\text{weight \#1}) + (\text{average \#2})(\text{weight \#2})}{\text{weight \#1} + \text{weight \#2}}$$

In this equation, the two averages are the given averages, so we plug in 23 for average #1 and 14 for average #2. The weight refers to the significance of the data point. Exactly what the weight is will depend on the question. For Example 4, the weight is the number of minutes, with 10 being weight #1 and 20 being weight #2. If there was a question where we were trying to calculate your final grade and 70% of your grade was from homework and 30% was from tests, the percentages of 70 and 30 would be the weights. The weights are used to reflect that certain averages have more "weight," or more significance, than others.

Now, let's get back to Example 4 and use the weighted average formula to solve:

$$\text{Average Number of Cookies} = \frac{(23)(10)+(14)(20)}{10+20} = 17$$

The answer is D.

The weighted average formula is a very important one and can be used to solve many ACT average questions. Looking back to Example 2, we can use a weighted average to solve. In that question, the averages are given as 85 for the first class and 90 for the second class. The weight is the number of students in each class, which is 6 and 9.

$$\text{Average Score} = \frac{(85)(6)+(90)(9)}{6+9} = 88$$

We even could use the weighted average formula for Example 3. The averages are given to be p and m. The weight is the number of puppies in each litter, which is 7 and 5.

$$\text{Average Puppy Weight} = \frac{(p)(7)+(m)(5)}{7+5} = \frac{7p+5m}{12}$$

Make sure that you understand how the weighted average formula works. As you can see, knowing how to properly find a weighted average can allow you to solve many difficult-looking average questions in one quick step.

Example 5: Patricia's average score on her first 4 chemistry tests is 88. How many points higher than her current average score must Patricia score on her 5th test for her new average on all 5 tests to increase by 2 points?

    A. 10   B. 8   C. 6   D. 5   E. 4

Solution: Patricia's new average score will be 90. Since we know Patricia's current average is 88, we can find the total number of points Patricia must have scored on her first 4 tests.

$$88 = \frac{\text{total points on 4 tests}}{4}$$

$$\text{total points on 4 tests} = 352$$

Since we know the final average must be 90, we can now solve for the 5th test score, x.

$$90 = \frac{352+x}{5}$$
$$x = 98$$

Patricia's 5th test score is 98, which is 10 points higher than the original average of 88. **The answer is A.**

Mathematically, this works because the additional 10 points above the average are equally divided over 5 tests, so the overall score will increase by $\frac{10}{5}$, or 2 points. If that shortcut method is confusing to you, just stick with the normal method we used to solve questions like this.

> **Example 6:** The mean household income in a neighborhood with 80 residents is $90,250 per year. If a new family moves in with a household income of $1,859,000, which of the following values for the neighborhood will most likely change the least?
>
>   A. Mean   B. Median   C. Maximum   D. Range   E. Standard Deviation

Solution: The new family has a much higher household income than the mean household income for the rest of the neighborhood. In statistics, we call values that are far higher or lower than any other numbers in the data set outliers. **Any outlier will greatly increase the range and maximum value**. The new family's income is also so large that it will increase the mean household income for the neighborhood. The standard deviation, which is a measure of how close or far apart numbers in a data set are from the average and will be covered in Chapter 34, will also increase from an outlier. We have not learned about standard deviation yet in this book, but we will cover it more in the statistics chapter.

The median will change the least. Since the median is the middle value in a data set, **any outliers always have a minimal effect on the median. The answer is B.**

> **Example 7:** For her science fair experiment, Monica wanted to find out if her tree frog or bullfrog has the bigger jump. She placed each frog on a starting spot and then measured how far the frogs jumped, in inches. The results for each frog, in inches, are below:
>
> Tree Frog: 41, 18, 30, 8, 14, 33
> Bullfrog: 38, 19, 66, 48, 45, 33, 10
>
> If f is the median jump length for the tree frog and h is the median jump length for the bullfrog, what is the value of $h - f$?
>
>   A. 14   B. 20   C. 24   C. 29   D. 38

Solution: To start, we need to reorder the numbers in each data from smallest to largest.

Tree Frog: 8, 14, 18, 30, 33, 41
Bullfrog: 10, 19, 33, 38, 45, 48, 66

Next, we cross out numbers from both sides to find the median. For data sets with an odd number of numbers, such as the bullfrog data in this question, the median is just the middle value. For data sets with an even number of numbers, such as the tree frog data in this question, you need to take the average of the two middle numbers to find the median.

Tree Frog: ~~8, 14,~~ 18, 30, ~~33, 41~~   Bullfrog: ~~10, 19, 33,~~ 38, ~~45, 48, 66~~

Tree Frog median = $f = \frac{18+30}{2} = 24$ Bullfrog median = $h = 38$

$$h - f = 38 - 24 = 14$$

The answer is A.

Finding the Median in a Table

The ACT also sometimes asks you to find the median value in a frequency table. For these questions, we will need to use a more efficient method than listing all the values and crossing off to find the median value.

Example 8: The school newspaper recently surveyed 51 students about their monthly consumption of cheeseburgers. The results of the survey are summarized in the table below. What was the median number of cheeseburgers eaten each month by the students in the survey?

Number of Burgers Eaten	Number of Students
0	7
1	19
2 - 3	8
4 - 5	13
6 +	4

A. 0   B. 1   C. 2 - 3   D. 4 - 5   E. 6 +

Solution: The trick to solving these questions is to identify what term the median in the data set is. To find the median term, there are three quick steps:

1. **Add 1 to the total number of items in the data set.**

2. **Divide that number by 2.**

    - If we have a data set with an odd number of items, the number we get is the term that is the median.

    - If we have a data set with an even number of items, we will get an answer that ends in 0.5. In this case, the median is the average of the two middle terms. The two middle terms are the integers right above and below the value that we get from our first two steps. For example, if we have a group of 20, we would get 10.5 in step 2. This tell us that two middle terms will be the 10th and 11th terms. We find the median by finding the average of the 10th and 11th terms.

3. **Find where the term is in the table.**

In this question, we have 51 students who were surveyed, so following Step 1 above

$$\frac{51+1}{2} = 26$$

we find the 26th student will be the median data point in the set. To find where the 26th student is in the table, start at the top of the table and simply add up the students until you find the 26th student. Here, there are 7 students who ate 0 burgers and 19 who ate 1 burger. If we add 7 and 19 together, we get 26, so we can tell that the 26th student ate 1 burger. As a result, the median is 1 and **the answer is B**.

Chapter 12: Mean, Median, Mode, and Range

Mean, Median, Mode and Range Practice: Answers on page 327.

1. A certain group consists of 7 girls, 5 of whom are 15 and 2 of whom are 8. What is the mean age of the girls in the group?

   A. 8
   B. 10
   C. 11.5
   D. 13
   E. 15

2. The tips that a barista earned for 1 week were $25 on Monday, $45 on Tuesday, and $30 on Wednesday, Thursday, and Friday. What was the barista's average daily tips for these 5 days?

   A. $31
   B. $32
   C. $33
   D. $35
   E. $36

3. The average of 6 numbers is 93. What is the 6th number if the first 5 are 99, 86, 93, 89, 92 ?

   A. 88
   B. 93
   C. 95
   D. 99
   E. 100

4. What is the difference between the mean and the median of the data set $\{4, 8, 9, 7, 12\}$?

   A. 0
   B. 1
   C. 2
   D. 3
   E. 4

5. If James scored 10 touchdowns in the first 7 games of the year, how many touchdowns does he need to score in the 8th game to average 2 touchdowns per game after 8 games?

   A. 2
   B. 6
   C. 8
   D. 10
   E. 16

6. What is the sum of three consecutive even integers whose mean is 44 ?

   A. 88
   B. 120
   C. 126
   D. 132
   E. 138

7. John and Karen work at the bakery. John works 7 hours per day, and Karen works 6 hours per day. John produces x brownies per hour and Karen produced y brownies per hour. Which of the following expressions gives the average number of brownies John and Karen produce per hour?

   A. $\frac{x+y}{13}$
   B. $\frac{7x+6y}{13}$
   C. $\frac{xy}{13}$
   D. $\frac{6x+7y}{13}$
   E. $\frac{x}{7}+\frac{y}{6}$

8. The mean age of 6 people at a graduation dinner is 40. When the oldest person, who is 95 years old, leaves the table, what is the mean age of the 5 people remaining at the table?

   A. 29
   B. 32
   C. 33
   D. 35
   E. 36

9. John and Aaron tracked their 400-meter race times, which are listed below in seconds. The median for John's race times is x and median for Aaron's race times is y. What is the value of $x - y$?

   John: 76, 68, 62, 68, 79, 70
   Aaron: 63, 58, 68, 61, 67, 66

   A. 0.5
   B. 1
   C. 2.5
   D. 4
   E. 4.5

Questions 10-11 refer to the table below.

Points	Frequency
0	3
10	0
20	1
30	2
50	3
100	1

A student playing Skee-Ball tracked the points he received from each of his 10 throws.

10. Which of the following is the mean score of the student's 10 throws?

    A. 20
    B. 28
    C. 33
    D. 35
    E. 38

11. What was the median value of the points scored from the 10 throws?

    A. 20
    B. 25
    C. 30
    D. 40
    E. 50

12. If x represents the larger of 2 numbers that have a difference of 39, which of the following expressions represents the average of the 2 numbers?

    A. $x + 19.5$
    B. $x - 19.5$
    C. $\frac{x+39}{2}$
    D. $\frac{x-39}{2}$
    E. $\frac{39}{2}$

13. The scores for the 43 students in AP Biology were reported, and the mean, median, range, and standard deviation were found. The teacher made an error in grading, and the student with the highest score actually scored 8 points higher. Which of the following will not change after the student's score is corrected?

    A. Range
    B. Mean
    C. Standard Deviation
    D. Median
    E. Both Range and Median.

14. Number of iPhones per Household

iPhones	Frequency
0	6
1	3
2	1
3	5
4	4
5	2

A recent survey asked 21 households how many iPhones they owned. Based on the table above, what was the median number of iPhones?

    A. 1
    B. 2
    C. 3
    D. 4
    E. 5

15. If x is equal to $k + 8$ and y is equal to $3k + 12$, which of the following expresses the average of x and y in terms of k?

    A. $k + 10$
    B. $2k + 10$
    C. $4k$
    D. $4k + 10$
    E. $4k + 20$

16. Production Run A of axles results in 35 axles with an average weight of a pounds. Production run B of axles results in 15 axles with an average weight of b pounds. Which of the following expressions gives the average weight w of all the axles that are be produced during two runs of Production run A and one run of Production Run B?

   A. $w = \frac{35b+15a}{50}$
   B. $w = \frac{2a+b}{3}$
   C. $w = \frac{70a+15b}{85}$
   D. $w = \frac{35a+15b}{85}$
   E. $w = \frac{a}{35} + \frac{b}{15}$

17. There is a list of 29 numbers, all of which are unique. Which of the following would definitely NOT affect the median?

   A. Increasing the largest number in the data set.
   B. Increasing all numbers in the data set by 10.
   C. Making the smallest value in the data set the largest value in the data set.
   D. Increasing the smallest value in the data set by 5.
   E. Multiplying all numbers in the data set by 2.

18. Ashley wanted to save an average of $20 per week over the past 15 weeks. For the first 5 weeks, she saved an average of $15 per week. For the next 5 weeks, she saved an average of $19 per week. For the last 5 weeks, she saved an average of $23 per week. How much more should she have saved each week to hit her goal?

   A. $0.50
   B. $0.75
   C. $0.80
   D. $1.00
   E. $1.50

19. The mean score of 10 students on a 36-point test is 23.8 points. If the student with the highest score is removed, the mean score for the other 9 students is 23 points. How many points did the student with the highest score have?

   A. 28
   B. 31
   C. 33
   D. 36
   E. 38

20. As part of a social studies project, Tommy surveyed 50 of his friends about their daily use of a social media app. The results are shown in the table below.

Number of Videos Viewed	Number of Students
0 – 5	4
6 – 20	11
21 – 40	8
41 – 60	9
> 60	18

Based on the survey above, which of the following could be the median number of pictures viewed?

   A. 19
   B. 24
   C. 35
   D. 49
   E. 81

21. Set A and Set B each consist of 6 numbers. The 2 sets contain identical numbers except for the largest value in each set. The largest value in Set A is greater than the largest value in Set B. The value of which of the following must be less for Set B than for Set A?

   A. Mean only
   B. Median only
   C. Mode only
   D. Mean and median only
   E. Mean and mode only

PrepPros

22. John drove 40 miles per hour for 15 minutes and then drove 20 miles per hour for 10 minutes. Which of the following gives the average rate, in miles per hour, that he drove during the 25 minutes?

A. 28
B. 30
C. 32
D. 34
E. 36

23. James is running in a 50-mile ultramarathon. For the first 15 miles, James runs at an average pace of 8 minutes per mile. For the next 25 miles, James runs at an average pace of 6.5 minutes per mile. For the last 10 miles, James runs at an average pace of 5 minutes per mile. What was James' average pace over the entire race?

A. 6
B. 6.50
C. 6.65
D. 7
E. 8.15

24. Which of the following is equivalent to the average of 5 consecutive even integers $a, b, c, d,$ and e such that $a < b < c < d < e$?

A. $\frac{a+d}{2}$
B. $\frac{bc}{2}$
C. $\frac{abc}{3}$
D. $\frac{bd}{2}$
E. c

25.   11, 18, 20, X, Y, Z, 35, 36, 44

The list of numbers above is ordered from least to greatest. If the mode is 35, the median is 30, and the mean is 28, what is the value of X?

A. 22
B. 23
C. 25
D. 26
E. 28

26. The average score of a team of 4 golfers is 86. A second team has the same first three scores but the fourth score is 16 points higher than the fourth score of the first team. What is the average score of the second team?

A. 68.5
B. 90
C. 92
D. 94
E. 102

27. Ben has an average score of 72 points on 7 equally weighted tests. How many points higher than his average must Ben score on his 8th equally weighted test be to raise his average on all 8 tests by 3 points?

A. 3
B. 6
C. 18
D. 21
E. 24

28. To increase the mean of 6 numbers by 5, by how much would the sum of the 6 numbers have to increase?

A. $\frac{5}{6}$
B. $\frac{6}{5}$
C. 5
D. 25
E. 30

29. The median of a set of 4 numbers $\{29, 4, 101, x\}$ is 51, and the mean of a set of 6 numbers $\{14, 61, 17, y, 28, z\}$ is 35. Which of the following values is equal to $y + z - x$?

A. -3
B. 17
C. 39
D. 73
E. 90

- 110 -

30. There are 2 basketball teams playing in the championship game. The first team has 15 players with an average height of 76 inches. The second team has 11 players with an average height of 69 inches. Which of the following is the closest to the average height, in inches, of the players on both teams?

    A. 70
    B. 71
    C. 72
    D. 73
    E. 74

31. Shandra's math class has 12 tests in total. Shandra has an average of 82 on her first 8 tests. What does she need to average on the last 4 tests to increase her average to 87?

    A. 92
    B. 93
    C. 95
    D. 96
    E. 97

32. Melissa's grade in history class is determined by 4 100-point tests and a 200-point final. Her average score on the tests is x and her score in the final is y. Which of the following is an expression for Melissa's final grade?

    A. $\frac{4x+y}{6}$
    B. $\frac{2x+y}{3}$
    C. $\frac{4x+y}{2}$
    D. $2x + y$
    E. $4x + 2y$

33. The average weight of 2 groups of seals at the zoo is 136 pounds. The first group of 18 seals has an average weight of 126 pounds. The second group has 10 seals. What is the average weight of the second group of seals?

    A. 136
    B. 144
    C. 150
    D. 154
    E. 158

34. The mean of 7 integers is 18. The median of these 7 integers is 11. Five of the integers are 2, 5, 9, 11, and 70. Which of the following could be one of the other integers?

    A. 9
    B. 10
    C. 18
    D. 20
    E. 23

35. Sven collects baseball cards. The average price of Sven's 12 most expensive baseball cards is x. After Sven sells the two most expensive baseball cards, the average price of the remaining cards is y. Which of the following expressions represents the total price of Sven's two most expensive baseball cards?

    A. $12x - 10y$
    B. $12(x - y)$
    C. $12y - 10x$
    D. $\frac{12x - 10y}{2}$
    E. $\frac{12x + 10y}{22}$

36. In order for Mr. Walsh's class to get a pizza party, the class average on the final must be at least 85%. The first fifteen students received an average of 82%. What is the lowest possible score that the 16th student can receive and still allow the class of 20 students to get a pizza party?

    A. 55
    B. 60
    C. 70
    D. 80
    E. 85

Chapter 13: Exponents and Roots

Exponents

Let's start by reviewing the common exponent rules that you need to know on the ACT.

Rule Name	Rule	Example
Product Rule	$a^x \times a^y = a^{x+y}$	$3^3 \times 3^4 = 3^7$
Quotient Rule	$\dfrac{a^x}{a^y} = a^{x-y}$	$\dfrac{5^9}{5^4} = 5^5$
Power Rule	$(a^x)^y = a^{xy}$	$(2^4)^3 = 2^{12}$
Fraction Power Rule	$a^{\frac{x}{y}} = \sqrt[y]{a^x}$	$6^{\frac{2}{3}} = \sqrt[3]{6^2}$
Negative Exponent Rule	$a^{-x} = \dfrac{1}{a^x}$	$11^{-4} = \dfrac{1}{11^4}$
One Power Rule	$a^1 = a$	$(-4)^1 = -4$
Zero Power Rule	$a^0 = 1$	$13^0 = 1$

Make sure that you memorize all of these rules for test day. The product, quotient, and power rules will be tested most often, but you also need to know the fraction power rule and negative exponent rule for more difficult questions. To successfully solve exponent questions, you will need to use multiple of these rules together.

Example 1: For all nonzero x and y, the expression $\dfrac{2x^6y^7}{16x^2y^{14}}$ is equivalent to:

A. $\dfrac{x^3y^7}{8}$ B. $\dfrac{x^4}{8y^7}$ C. $\dfrac{x^3y^2}{8}$ D. $\dfrac{y^7}{14x^4}$ E. $\dfrac{x^8y^{21}}{8}$

Solution: To solve, we use the quotient rule for the exponents. For the numbers, we follow normal algebra rules to simplify, so $\dfrac{2}{16}$ simplifies to $\dfrac{1}{8}$.

$$\dfrac{x^{6-2}\, y^{7-14}}{8}$$

$$\dfrac{x^4 y^{-7}}{8}$$

Using the negative exponent rule, we get

$$\dfrac{x^4}{8y^7}$$

The answer is B. A good trick with negative exponents is that if we switch the term from a numerator to the denominator or vice versa, the negative power turns into a positive power. In the last step of the solution to Example 1, the y^{-7} term in the denominator switches to y^7 when we move the term from the numerator to the denominator.

Example 2: For all nonzero x and y, which of the following is equal to $\frac{(-2xy^3)^2}{x}$?

A. $-2xy^6$ B. $-2x^2y^5$ C. $4xy^6$ D. $4x^2y^5$ E. $4y^6$

Solution: Here, it is easiest to start with the power rule and simplify the numerator. Make sure that you remember to distribute the power to all the terms including the -2 at the front.

$$\frac{4x^2y^6}{x}$$

Now, we use the quotient rule to simplify the x-terms.

$$4xy^6$$

The answer is C.

Example 3: If $4^{3x+1} = 4^{-x+7}$, what is the value of x?

A. $\frac{1}{2}$ B. 1   C. $\frac{3}{2}$ D. 2   E. 3

Solution: In this question, the bases are the same, so the exponents must be equal.

$$3x + 1 = -x + 7$$
$$4x = 6$$
$$x = \frac{3}{2}$$

The answer is C.

Example 4: For what value of x is $9^{2x} = 27^{x+4}$ true?

A. 2   B. 3   C. 4   D. 8   E. 12

Solution: Method #1 – "Math Teacher Way": To use any of our exponent rules, we need the bases of our exponents to be equal. The trick to this question is to recognize that 9 is the same as 3^2 and 27 is the same as 3^3, so we can make the bases of both terms 3. Plugging in 3^2 for 9 and 3^3 for 27, we get

$$(3^2)^{2x} = (3^3)^{x+4}$$
$$3^{4x} = 3^{3x+12}$$

Since the terms are equal, we can set the exponents equal and solve.

$$4x = 3x + 12$$
$$x = 12$$

The answer is E.

Method #2 – Backsolve with your Calculator: Since we are given an equation and possible values of x, we can plug the answer choices in for x and use a calculator to see which one makes the equation true. Only one answer will work, so we can find which answer choice is correct without doing any actual math!

For this question, if we plug in $x = 12$ to the original equation, 9^{24} and 27^{16} will give us the same answer on your calculator. The numbers are very large, but you should still be able to tell that they are equal. **The answer is E.**

Exponents Exercise: For questions 1-12, simplify the expressions until you only have positive exponents. For questions 13-20, solve for x. Answers on page 327.

1. $(x^4y)(x^2y^2) =$
2. $(3x^3)(2x^4)\left(\frac{1}{2}x^{-2}\right) =$
3. $(8x^{-3}y^4)(3x^6y^3) =$
4. $(2xy^3)^2 =$
5. $3x^{-2}y^5 =$
6. $\frac{18x^8}{2x^4} =$
7. $9x^{-3}yz^{-2} =$
8. $(x^{-2}y^2)(xy^{-2}) =$
9. $\frac{x^{-3}yz^2}{xyz} =$
10. $(3x^5y^{-2}z)^2 =$
11. $\frac{(4xy^2)^2}{xy} =$
12. $\frac{(5x^4y^{-2})^2}{(2x^{-3}y)^3} =$
13. $12^{-3} \times 12^5 = 144^x$
14. $\frac{7^2 \times 7^x}{49} = 7^8$
15. $\frac{x^7}{x^5} = 25$
16. $7^{-2x+3} = 7^{2-x}$
17. $(2^x)^3 = 2^4 \times 2^{\frac{3}{2}}$
18. $9^{\frac{3}{2}} = 3^{\frac{x}{2}}$
19. $16^{\frac{3}{2}} = 2^x$
20. $\frac{8}{8^{-3}} = 2^{2x-4}$

Roots

On the ACT, you will need to often simplify and solve equations with roots. Let's begin by reviewing the common root rules:

$$\sqrt{xy} = \sqrt{x} \times \sqrt{y} \qquad \sqrt{18} = \sqrt{9} \times \sqrt{2} = 3\sqrt{2}$$

$$\sqrt{\frac{x}{y}} = \frac{\sqrt{x}}{\sqrt{y}} \qquad \frac{\sqrt{24}}{\sqrt{6}} = \sqrt{\frac{24}{6}} = \sqrt{4} = 2$$

To simplify a square root, factor the number underneath the radical and take out any pairs.

$$\sqrt{50} = \sqrt{5 \times 5 \times 2} = 5\sqrt{2}$$

In the example above, there is a pair of 5's underneath the radical, so we can take the 5 out. The 2 is not part of a pair, so it stays underneath the radical. Here's one more example:

$$\sqrt{108} = \sqrt{2 \times 2 \times 3 \times 3 \times 3} = (2 \times 3)\sqrt{3} = 6\sqrt{3}$$

Here, we have a pair of 2's and a pair of 3's, so we take both out and move them to the front. The third 3 is not part of a pair, so it says underneath the radical.

For some questions, you might need to go backwards and put a number outside back underneath the radical. To do this, take the number outside and put it back under the radical as a pair.

$$6\sqrt{3} = \sqrt{6 \times 6 \times 3} = \sqrt{108}$$

Example 5: If $\sqrt{45} + \sqrt{20} = x\sqrt{5}$, then $x = ?$

   A. 5   B. 6   C. 9   D. 13   E. 36

Solution: We need to simplify the radicals on the left side of the equation.

$$\sqrt{45} = \sqrt{3 \times 3 \times 5} = 3\sqrt{5}$$

$$\sqrt{20} = \sqrt{2 \times 2 \times 5} = 2\sqrt{5}$$

Plugging those values in to the left side of the equation, we get

$$3\sqrt{5} + 2\sqrt{5} = x\sqrt{5}$$
$$5\sqrt{5} = x\sqrt{5}$$
$$x = 5$$

The answer is A.

"Cheat Method" – Use Your Calculator and Backsolve: You can also plug in $\sqrt{45} + \sqrt{20}$ to find out what it equals. We can then backsolve with the answer choices to find which answer choice, when multiplied by $\sqrt{5}$ gives us the same value in the calculator. You can also use this method for Example 6.

> **Example 6:** If $\sqrt{2x} = 5\sqrt{6}$, then $x = ?$
> A. 900   B. 450   C. 150   D. 75   E. 30

Solution – Method #1: To solve for x, move the 5 back underneath the radical.

$$\sqrt{2x} = \sqrt{6 \times 5 \times 5}$$
$$\sqrt{2x} = \sqrt{150}$$

For these to be equal, the terms under the radical must be equal, so

$$2x = 150$$
$$x = 75$$

The answer is D.

Method #2: We can also solve this question by squaring both sides.

$$(\sqrt{2x})^2 = (5\sqrt{6})^2$$
$$2x = 25 \times 6$$
$$2x = 150$$
$$x = 75$$

The answer is D.

Remember, these same rules still apply to roots other than just square roots.

$$\sqrt[3]{xy} = \sqrt[3]{x} \times \sqrt[3]{y} \qquad\qquad \sqrt[3]{16} = \sqrt[3]{8} \times \sqrt[3]{2} = 2\sqrt[3]{2}$$

$$\sqrt[5]{\frac{x}{y}} = \frac{\sqrt[5]{x}}{\sqrt[5]{y}} \qquad\qquad \sqrt[5]{\frac{5}{32}} = \frac{\sqrt[5]{5}}{\sqrt[5]{32}} = \frac{\sqrt[5]{5}}{2}$$

To simplify a cube root, factor underneath the radical and take out triples of the same number.

$$\sqrt[3]{24} = \sqrt[3]{2 \times 2 \times 2 \times 3} = 2\sqrt[3]{3}$$

To simplify a 4th root, factor underneath the radical and take out four of the same number.

$$\sqrt[4]{80} = \sqrt[4]{2 \times 2 \times 2 \times 2 \times 5} = 2\sqrt[4]{5}$$

You are unlikely to see any higher roots on the ACT, but if you do just follow this same pattern to simplify any root.

PrepPros

Example 7: If $a = \sqrt[3]{162}$ and $b = \sqrt[3]{40}$, then $a + b = ?$

A. $3\sqrt[3]{18} + 2\sqrt[3]{10}$ B. $2\sqrt[3]{20} + 2\sqrt[3]{5}$ C. $6\sqrt[3]{2} + 5\sqrt[3]{2}$ D. $3\sqrt[3]{6} + 2\sqrt[3]{5}$ E. $6\sqrt[3]{30}$

Solution: To start, let's simplify to find the value of a.

$$a = \sqrt[3]{162} = \sqrt[3]{3 \times 3 \times 3 \times 6} = 3\sqrt[3]{6}$$

Now, simplify b.

$$b = \sqrt[3]{40} = \sqrt[3]{2 \times 2 \times 2 \times 5} = 2\sqrt[3]{5}$$

We can solve

$$a + b = 3\sqrt[3]{6} + 2\sqrt[3]{5}$$

The answer is D.

Roots and Variables with Powers

When you have exponent questions with roots and variables with powers underneath the root, it is easiest to turn the root into a power and then use the exponent rules to solve. For example,

$$\sqrt[3]{x^5 y} = (x^5 y)^{\frac{1}{3}} = (x^5)^{\frac{1}{3}} y^{\frac{1}{3}} = x^{\frac{5}{3}} y^{\frac{1}{3}}$$

The example above can also be solved using our fraction power rule, but this same trick will help make more complicated questions much easier.

Example 8: Which of the following is equivalent to $\sqrt[3]{5x^6 y^{18}}$?

A. $\sqrt[3]{5}\, x^2 y^6$ B. $\sqrt[3]{5 x^3 y^{15}}$ C. $\sqrt[3]{5 x^3 y^{15}}$ D. $5 x^2 y^6$ E. $xy^9 \sqrt{5x}$

Solution: To start, turn the root into an exponent.

$$(5x^6 y^{18})^{\frac{1}{3}}$$

Next, distribute the exponent to all terms.

$$(5x^6 y^{18})^{\frac{1}{3}} = 5^{\frac{1}{3}} (x^6)^{\frac{1}{3}} (y^{18})^{\frac{1}{3}}$$

Use the exponent rules to solve.

$$5^{\frac{1}{3}} (x^6)^{\frac{1}{3}} (y^{18})^{\frac{1}{3}} = \sqrt[3]{5}\, x^2 y^6$$

The answer is A.

Chapter 13: Exponents and Roots

Roots Exercise: For questions 1-12, simplify the radical. For questions 13-20, solve for x. Answers on page 327.

1. $\sqrt{60} =$
2. $\sqrt{150} + \sqrt{24} =$
3. $6\sqrt{5} - \sqrt{80} =$
4. $\sqrt{32} - \sqrt{18} + \sqrt{72} =$
5. $\sqrt[3]{48} + \sqrt[3]{162} =$
6. $\dfrac{\sqrt{45}}{\sqrt{15}} =$
7. $\dfrac{5\sqrt{12}}{10\sqrt{3}} =$
8. $\sqrt{8ab^4} =$
9. $\sqrt{16x^2 y} =$
10. $\sqrt[4]{a^{12} b^2} =$
11. $\sqrt[3]{24x^6 y^4} =$
12. $\sqrt{16x^{10}} =$
13. $\sqrt{3x-2} = \sqrt{18}$
14. $\sqrt{15} = \dfrac{\sqrt{x}}{\sqrt{3}}$
15. $\sqrt{18} \times \sqrt{3} = x\sqrt{6}$
16. $\sqrt{x} - \sqrt{40} = \sqrt{10}$
17. $\sqrt{3x} + \sqrt{8} = \sqrt{50}$
18. $(3\sqrt{5})^2 = 2x$
19. $\sqrt{6x} = 2\sqrt{6}$
20. $\sqrt[3]{54} + \sqrt[3]{16} = x\sqrt[3]{2}$

Exponents and Roots Practice: Answers on page 328.

1. $(2x^4)(9x^9)$ is equivalent to:

   A. $11x^{13}$
   B. $11x^{36}$
   C. $18x^{13}$
   D. $18x^{36}$
   E. $144x^{36}$

2. Joe's spaceship can travel 2.5×10^6 feet per second. How many seconds would it take his spaceship to travel 10×10^{13} feet?

   A. 7.5×10^{-7}
   B. 2.5×10^{20}
   C. 4.0×10^7
   D. 7.5×10^7
   E. 4.0×10^{20}

3. Which of the following is equal to $x^{\frac{3}{4}}$, for all values of x?

   A. $\sqrt{x^{\frac{1}{4}}}$
   B. $\sqrt[3]{x^4}$
   C. $\sqrt[4]{x^3}$
   D. $\sqrt{x^3}$
   E. $\dfrac{x^3}{4}$

4. Let a be any real number such that $25 < a^2 < 49$, which of the following is a possible value of a?

   A. 4.62
   B. 6.49
   C. 7
   D. 26.4
   E. 250.8

5. For all nonzero values of x and y, which of the following expressions is equivalent to $-\dfrac{24x^3 y^6}{6x^2 y}$?

   A. $-30xy^5$
   B. $-18xy^5$
   C. $-4x^5 y^7$
   D. $-4x^3 y^6$
   E. $-4xy^5$

6. Which of the following expressions is equivalent to $(a^3 b^4 c^2)(a^5 b^3 c^6)$ for all real values of a, b, and c?

   A. $a^{15} b^{12} c^8$
   B. $a^{15} b^7 c^{12}$
   C. $a^9 b^7 c^{10}$
   D. $a^8 b^{12} c^{12}$
   E. $a^8 b^7 c^8$

PrepPros

7. What is the smallest integer greater than $\sqrt{52}$?

A. 6
B. 7
C. 8
D. 9
E. 10

8. What value of x makes the equation below true?

$$\frac{16^x}{4^3} = 4^7$$

A. 3
B. 5
C. 10
D. 16
E. 256

9. Given that $5x - \sqrt{2} = 10$, what is the value of x?

A. $2 - \frac{\sqrt{2}}{5}$
B. $2 - \sqrt{2}$
C. $2 + \frac{\sqrt{2}}{5}$
D. $2 + \sqrt{2}$
E. $5 - \sqrt{2}$

10. If x is a positive number, which of the following is equivalent to $\sqrt{16x^2}$?

A. $4x$
B. $4x^2$
C. $16x$
D. $64x$
E. $256x^4$

11. Let a be any real number such that $3 < \sqrt{a} < 7$. which of the following is a possible value of a?

A. 1.80
B. 5.30
C. 8.50
D. 46.2
E. 59.4

12. For all nonzero numbers $a, b,$ and c, the expression $\frac{3a^7b^2c^5}{6a^2b^5c}$ is equivalent to:

A. $\frac{a^5c^5}{2b^3}$
B. $\frac{a^5c^4}{2b^3}$
C. $\frac{a^5bc^5}{2b^3c^2}$
D. $\frac{(3abc)^{14}}{(6abc)^6}$
E. $2a^5b^3c^4$

13. What is the value of $(25^{\frac{1}{2}} - 8^{\frac{1}{3}})^3$?

A. 1
B. 2
C. 8
D. 27
E. 343

14. For all positive real numbers x, which of the following expressions is equivalent to $\frac{\left(\frac{x^{17}}{x^6}\right)}{\left(\frac{1}{x^4}\right)}$?

A. x^7
B. x^{11}
C. x^{15}
D. x^{19}
E. x^{27}

15. Which of the following expressions is equivalent to $\sqrt[y]{x^z}$?

A. $x^{\frac{z}{y}}$
B. $x^{\frac{y}{z}}$
C. x^{y+z}
D. x^{z-y}
E. x^{yz}

16. For all nonzero values of x, $\frac{(2x)^3}{(4x)^3}$ is equal to:

A. $\frac{1}{32}$
B. $\frac{1}{16}$
C. $\frac{1}{8}$
D. $\frac{1}{4}$
E. $\frac{1}{2}$

Chapter 13: Exponents and Roots

17. The expression $(x^{\frac{1}{3}})^6 (x^{\frac{4}{3}})^5$ is equivalent to:

    A. x^4
    B. $x^{\frac{16}{3}}$
    C. $x^{\frac{26}{3}}$
    D. $x^{\frac{55}{9}}$
    E. $x^{\frac{59}{3}}$

18. For $3x\sqrt{7} + 3 = 15$, what is the value of x?

    A. $\frac{6\sqrt{7}}{7}$
    B. $\frac{4\sqrt{7}}{7}$
    C. $12 - 3\sqrt{7}$
    D. $6\sqrt{7}$
    E. $4\sqrt{7}$

19. For what value is $4^{x+4} = 2^{3x}$ true?

    A. 2
    B. 4
    C. 8
    D. 12
    E. 16

20. Which of the following expressions is equivalent to $(x^2 - 3)^{-5}$?

    A. $\frac{1}{x^{10}} - \frac{1}{3^5}$
    B. $\frac{1}{x^{10}} + 15$
    C. $-x^5 + 3^5$
    D. $\frac{1}{(x^2-3)^5}$
    E. $\frac{1}{(3x^2)^5}$

21. If a is a positive even integer and b is a positive odd integer, $(5x)^a \times (-5x)^b > 0$ is true for all values of x such that:

    A. $x > 0$
    B. $x < 0$
    C. $x \geq 0$
    D. $x \leq 0$
    E. All real numbers

22. Given m and n such that $x^{2m-10} = x^6$ and $(x^n)^3 = x^{15}$, what is the value of $x^m x^n$?

    A. x^7
    B. x^{11}
    C. x^{13}
    D. x^{21}
    E. x^{40}

23. If x and y are positive rational numbers such that $x^{5y} = 10$, then $x^{10y} = ?$

    A. 20
    B. 30
    C. 50
    D. 80
    E. 100

24. For how many integers x is the equation $\frac{(4x^4)^2}{(2x^2)^4} = 1$ true?

    A. 0
    B. 1
    C. 2
    D. 3
    E. An infinite number

25. If a and b are positive real numbers, which of the following is equivalent to $\frac{(4a^{-3}b^2)^3}{16ab^{-4}}$?

    A. $\frac{b}{4a^{10}}$
    B. $\frac{b^9}{4a^{10}}$
    C. $\frac{4b^9}{a}$
    D. $\frac{4b^{10}}{a^{10}}$
    E. $4a^{10}b^{10}$

26. Which of the following expressions is equal to $\frac{5}{3-\sqrt{5}}$?

   A. $-\frac{2}{5}$
   B. $\frac{5}{4}$
   C. 5
   D. $\frac{15-5\sqrt{5}}{4}$
   E. $\frac{15+5\sqrt{5}}{4}$

27. If x and y are positive real numbers, which of the following is equivalent to $\frac{x^{-3}y^{\frac{1}{3}}}{x^2 y^{-2}}$?

   A. $\frac{y^{\frac{2}{3}}}{x^5}$
   B. $\frac{y^{\frac{7}{3}}}{x^5}$
   C. $\frac{y^{\frac{7}{3}}}{x^{-5}}$
   D. $\frac{\sqrt[3]{y}}{x^5}$
   E. $\frac{\sqrt[3]{y^2}}{x^{-5}}$

28. The expression $\sqrt[4]{g^8 m^2}$ is equivalent to:

   A. $\sqrt{g}\, m^{-2}$
   B. $g^2 \sqrt{m}$
   C. $g^{\frac{1}{2}} m^{\frac{1}{2}}$
   D. $g^{-\frac{1}{2}} m^{-2}$
   E. $g^2 m^{-\frac{1}{2}}$

29. $\left(\frac{2}{7}\right)^{-\frac{3}{2}} = ?$

   A. $\frac{7\sqrt{7}}{2\sqrt{2}}$
   B. $\frac{3\sqrt{7}}{2}$
   C. $\frac{2\sqrt{3}}{7}$
   D. $\frac{7}{5}$
   E. $-\frac{8}{5}$

30. Which of the following is an equivalent form of $\sqrt[2]{16a^2 b^6 c}$?

   A. $16ab^4 \sqrt{c}$
   B. $16ab^3 \sqrt{c}$
   C. $4ab\sqrt{b^3 c}$
   D. $4ab^4 \sqrt{c}$
   E. $4ab^3 \sqrt{c}$

31. For a positive real number y, where $y^{20} = 16$, what is the value of y^5 ?

   A. 2
   B. $2\sqrt{4}$
   C. 4
   D. $4\sqrt{2}$
   E. 8

32. Which of the following expressions is equivalent to $(27x^3)^{\frac{1}{3}}$?

   A. $3x$
   B. $9x$
   C. $27x$
   D. $\sqrt[3]{27x}$
   E. $3\sqrt[3]{3}$

33. $\frac{5}{\sqrt{2}} + \frac{3}{2} = ?$

   A. $\frac{3\sqrt{2}+10}{2}$
   B. $\frac{5\sqrt{2}+3}{2}$
   C. $4\sqrt{2}$
   D. $5 + 3\sqrt{2}$
   E. 2

Chapter 13: Exponents and Roots

34. For all positive values of x, $(\sqrt[3]{x^5})(\sqrt[4]{x^{-3}})$ is equal to:

    A. $x^{\frac{2}{7}}$
    B. $x^{\frac{1}{2}}$
    C. $x^{\frac{11}{12}}$
    D. x^2
    E. $x^{\frac{8}{3}}$

35. If x is a positive even integer and y is a negative odd integer, then $(y)^x(-y^3)$ is:

    A. Positive and even
    B. Positive and odd
    C. Zero
    D. Negative and even
    E. Negative and odd

36. If $27^{a-1} = 3$ and $4^{a+b} = 64$, then $b = ?$

    A. $\frac{1}{2}$
    B. $\frac{5}{3}$
    C. $\frac{8}{3}$
    D. 3
    E. $\frac{11}{3}$

37. Which of the following is an equivalent form of $\sqrt[3]{16x^5y}$?

    A. $16x^2 \sqrt[3]{y}$
    B. $16x \sqrt[3]{xy}$
    C. $2x^2 \sqrt[3]{2y}$
    D. $2x \sqrt[3]{2x^2y}$
    E. $2x \sqrt[3]{y}$

38. For all $x < 0$, which of the following is NOT equivalent to $\sqrt[4]{\sqrt[3]{x^2}}$?

    A. $x^{\frac{1}{6}}$
    B. $\sqrt[2]{x^{12}}$
    C. $\sqrt[2]{\sqrt[6]{x^2}}$
    D. $\sqrt[6]{x}$
    E. $\sqrt[2]{\sqrt[3]{x}}$

39. Which of the following is an equivalent form of $\sqrt[3]{24x^4y^2z^3}$?

    A. $2xz\sqrt{3xy^2}$
    B. $8xz\sqrt[3]{3xy^2}$
    C. $2xz\sqrt[3]{3xy^2}$
    D. $8xz\sqrt{xy^2}$
    E. $2xz\sqrt[3]{xy^2}$

40. If p and q are positive integers such that $(\sqrt[3]{4})^p = 16^{3q}$, what is the value of $\frac{q}{p}$?

    A. 18
    B. 6
    C. 3
    D. $\frac{1}{6}$
    E. $\frac{1}{18}$

41. The equation $-x^3 = \sqrt[2]{x^6}$ is true for all values of x such that:

    A. $x > 0$
    B. $x < 0$
    C. $x \geq 0$
    D. $x \leq 0$
    E. All real numbers

42. For all positive values of a and b, $a^{\frac{1}{5}}b^{\frac{3}{2}}$ can be written in which of the following radical forms?

A. $\sqrt[10]{ab^3}$
B. $\sqrt[10]{a^2b^3}$
C. $\sqrt[10]{a^3b^6}$
D. $b\sqrt[10]{a^2b^5}$
E. $ab\sqrt[10]{ab^6}$

44. Let a and b be nonzero numbers such that $3^{a-2} = 5b$. Which of the following is an expression for 3^a in terms of b?

A. $\frac{1}{4b^2}$
B. $\frac{1}{9b}$
C. $5b^3$
D. $15b^2$
E. $45b$

43. For all positive values of x and y, $\sqrt{\frac{4x}{y}} - \sqrt{\frac{y}{x}}$ is equivalent to which of the following?

A. 4
B. $\frac{4\sqrt{xy}}{y-x}$
C. $\frac{4x-y}{y-x}$
D. $\frac{2x-y}{\sqrt{xy}}$
E. $2\sqrt{xy}$

45. $\frac{5}{\sqrt{2}} + \frac{3}{\sqrt{6}} = ?$

A. $\frac{5\sqrt{2}+3\sqrt{6}}{3}$
B. $\frac{5\sqrt{2}+\sqrt{6}}{2}$
C. $\frac{15\sqrt{3}+3\sqrt{6}}{8}$
D. $3\sqrt{6}$
E. $2\sqrt{6} - 2\sqrt{2}$

Chapter 14: Logarithms

On the ACT, you need to be familiar with how logarithms and natural logarithms work, the basic rules for logarithms, and how to convert a logarithm to exponential form.

Basics of Logarithms

Let's begin with the basics of how logarithms work:

$$\log_a b = c \quad \text{is the same as} \quad a^c = b$$

Logarithms are just a different form of exponents. Both equations describe the same relationship between the values a, b, and c, where a is the base and c is the exponent. To make this a bit easier, let's use some numbers.

$$\log_3 3 = 1 \quad \text{is the same as} \quad 3^1 = 3$$
$$\log_3 9 = 2 \quad \text{is the same as} \quad 3^2 = 9$$
$$\log_3 27 = 3 \quad \text{is the same as} \quad 3^3 = 27$$

The majority of logarithms questions on the ACT ask you to understand how the basics of logarithms work. To solve, you will almost always switch from logarithmic form to exponential form.

> **Example 1:** When $\log_4 x = 3$, what is x?
> A. 12   B. 16   C. 48   D. 64   E. 81

Solution: To solve, we need to turn the logarithm into exponential form. The base is 4 and the exponent is 3, so the exponential form is

$$x = 4^3 = 64$$

The answer is D.

> **Example 2:** What integer does $5(\log_3 9 + \log_2 8)$ equal?
> A. 5   B. 10   C. 15   D. 20   E. 25

Solution: First, let's find the value of $\log_3 9$ by converting the logarithm to exponential form.

$$\log_3 9 = x \quad \text{is the same as} \quad 3^x = 9$$

We know that $3^2 = 9$, so $x = 2$, which means that $\log_3 9 = 2$. We can repeat this for $\log_2 8$.

$$\log_2 8 = x \quad \text{is the same as} \quad 2^x = 8$$

We know that $2^3 = 8$, so $x = 3$, which means that $\log_2 8 = 3$.

Now, we can plug in our values for $\log_3 9$ and $\log_2 8$ to the equation and solve.

$$5(\log_3 9 + \log_2 8) = 5(2 + 3) = 25$$

The answer is E.

Shortcut solution – Use Your Calculator: We can solve this entire question using your calculator! To do so, we will use the logarithm change of base rule.

$$\log_b a = \frac{\log(a)}{\log(b)}$$

Now that we know the change of base rule, we can use the calculator to solve for $\log_3 9$ and $\log_2 8$:

$$\log_3 9 = \frac{\log(9)}{\log(3)} = 2 \qquad \log_2 8 = \frac{\log(8)}{\log(2)} = 3$$

To solve, plug in the values to the original equation.

$$5(\log_3 9 + \log_2 8) = 5(2 + 3) = 25$$

The answer is E.

Some of you may have the change of base formula in your calculators. For those of you with a TI-83 or TI-84 calculator, you click MATH and then scroll down until you see LOGBASE. If you click on that, your calculator will show you

$$\log_\square \square$$

and you can just type in the exact values for any question like example 2. Many other calculators have this programmed in as well, so you should check if yours does! If not, you can just use the change of base rule we used above.

Logarithm Rules

You should also know the following basic rules for logarithms. You very rarely need to use these rules to solve questions on the ACT, but they have appeared on the test before and are fair game to appear again.

Rules	Formulas
Product	$\log_a(xy) = \log_a x + \log_a y$
Quotient	$\log_a\left(\dfrac{x}{y}\right) = \log_a x - \log_a y$
Log of a Power	$\log_a x^y = y \log_a x$
Log of 1	$\log_a 1 = 0$

You will only need to use these rules for questions where the change of base rule is not enough to solve. Most likely, these will be difficult questions towards the end of the ACT Math Test.

Example 3: If $\log_9 3^x = \dfrac{3}{2}$, what is the value of x?

   A. $\dfrac{3}{2}$ B. 3   C. $\dfrac{7}{2}$ D. 4   E. 5

Solution: We can use the log of a power rule to simplify the left side of the equation to get

$$x \log_9 3 = \dfrac{3}{2}$$

Next, we can use our change of base equation to solve for $\log_9 3$.

$$\log_9 3 = \dfrac{\log(3)}{\log(9)} = \dfrac{1}{2}$$

Now, we can plug in $\dfrac{1}{2}$ for $\log_9 3$ and solve for x.

$$x\left(\dfrac{1}{2}\right) = \dfrac{3}{2} \rightarrow x = 3$$

The answer is B.

Shortcut Solution – Backsolve: The easiest way to solve this question is to backsolve. Plug in the answer choices for x and use the change of base rule to see which one equals $\dfrac{3}{2}$. Try it with your calculator and the correct answer of $x = 3$.

Example 4: If $\log_b x = p$ and $\log_b y = q$, then $\log_b \frac{x^2}{y} = ?$

A. $p^2 - q$ B. $2p + q$ C. $2p - q$ D. $\frac{2p}{q}$ E. $2(p - q)$

Solution: For a question like this, we need to use the logarithm rules. First, we need to use the quotient rule.

$$\log_b \frac{x^2}{y} = \log_b x^2 - \log_b y$$

Next, we use the power rule.

$$\log_b x^2 - \log_b y = 2\log_b x - \log_b y$$

Since $\log_b x = p$ and $\log_b y = q$, we can plug in p and q to solve.

$$2\log_b x - \log_b y = 2p - q$$

The answer is C.

Questions like example 4 are very rare on the ACT, so this is definitely not a need-to-know topic for all students. With that being said, any students aiming for a high math score should still make sure that you memorize all of the logarithm rules just in case!

Natural Logarithms

On rare occasions, the ACT may also ask you questions with natural logarithms. **Natural logarithm questions are very uncommon, so this is a topic that anyone rushing through this book can skip.** Any natural logarithms questions are almost guaranteed to appear in the difficult questions at the end of the math test.

The same rules that we have covered so far in this chapter all apply for natural logarithms, except than the base is always "e," which is an irrational number approximately equal to 2.71828. The base is not actually written in natural logarithms, so the "e" is invisible.

$$\ln b = c \quad \text{is same as} \quad e^c = b$$

Whenever there is a natural logarithm question on the ACT, it most commonly asks you to solve for a variable. To do so, you will need to go from logarithmic form to exponential form and then solve for the variable using basic algebra.

Example 5: If $\ln(x - 1) = 3$, then $x = ?$

A. $e^3 + 1$ B. $1 - e^3$ C. $\ln 2$ D. $\ln 3 + 1$ E. 4

Solution: First, we need to go from logarithmic form to exponential form. The base is e and the exponent is 3, so we get

$$e^3 = x - 1$$

To solve, we add 1 to both sides to isolate x.

$$e^3 + 1 = x$$

The answer is A.

Logarithms Practice: Answers on page 328.

1. When $\log_5 x = 2$, what is x?

   A. 1
   B. 2.5
   C. 5
   D. 15
   E. 25

2. When $\log_2 x = -4$, what is x?

   A. -16
   B. -8
   C. -4
   D. $\frac{1}{8}$
   E. $\frac{1}{16}$

3. What is $4(\log_4 16)$ equal to?

   A. $\frac{1}{2}$
   B. 1
   C. 2
   D. 4
   E. 8

4. When $\log_x\left(\frac{1}{125}\right) = -3$, what is x?

   A. $\frac{1}{25}$
   B. $\frac{1}{5}$
   C. 3
   D. 5
   E. 25

5. What is the value of $\log_3 \sqrt{27}$?

   A. $\frac{1}{2}$
   B. $\frac{3}{2}$
   C. $\sqrt{2}$
   D. 1
   E. 3

6. What is the value of $5\log_2 8 - 2\log_3 9$?

   A. 3
   B. 5
   C. 11
   D. 19
   E. 28

7. What is the value of the positive real number x such that $\log_x\left(\frac{1}{9}\right) = -2$?

   A. 3
   B. 9
   C. $\frac{1}{3}$
   D. $\frac{1}{9}$
   E. $\frac{1}{81}$

8. For positive real numbers A and B, $\log\frac{B}{A} = ?$

   A. $\frac{\log B}{\log A}$
   B. $\log(B - A)$
   C. $\log(A - B)$
   D. $\log B - \log A$
   E. $\log A - \log B$

9. When $\log_{11} 121^{3x} = 2$, what is x?

   A. $\frac{1}{11}$
   B. $\frac{1}{3}$
   C. $\frac{1}{2}$
   D. 1
   E. 3

10. $\log_3 \sqrt[3]{9} = ?$

    A. 0
    B. $\frac{2}{3}$
    C. 1
    D. $\sqrt[3]{3}$
    E. 9

11. If $\ln(x + 4) = 2$, then $x = ?$

    A. $\sqrt{e - 4}$
    B. $\sqrt{x^2 - 4}$
    C. $2e - 4$
    D. $e^2 - 4$
    E. $4e^2$

Chapter 14: Logarithms

12. What real value of x satisfies the equation $\log_3 27^4 = 6x$?

    A. 2
    B. 3
    C. 6
    D. 27
    E. 81

13. The value of $\log_8 8^{\frac{10}{3}}$ is between which of the following pairs of integers?

    A. 0 and 1
    B. 2 and 3
    C. 3 and 4
    D. 5 and 6
    E. 7 and 8

14. When $\log_8 1 = x^2 - 6x + 9$, what is x?

    A. 0
    B. 2
    C. 3
    D. 6
    E. 9

15. If $\log_8 x = -\frac{2}{3}$, then $x = ?$

    A. -4
    B. $-\frac{1}{4}$
    C. $\frac{1}{12}$
    D. $\frac{1}{4}$
    E. 4

16. $f(x) = \ln(0.5x - 2) + 3$
    $g(x) = 6$

    If the graphs of the two functions above intersect at the point (a, b), what is the value of a?

    A. 6
    B. $2e^3 + 4$
    C. $e^3 - 2$
    D. $\ln(3) + 2$
    E. $\ln(1) - 3$

17. If $\ln(2x - 3) = 2$, then $x = ?$

    A. $\ln(2) - 1$
    B. $\ln(5)$
    C. 5
    D. $2e^2 - 3$
    E. $\frac{e^2 + 3}{2}$

18. If $\log_{(x+2)}(x^2 + 8) = 2$, then $x = ?$

    A. -1
    B. 0
    C. 1
    D. 2
    E. 4

19. If $\ln(x^2 + 10) = 4$, what is x?

    A. $e^4 - 10$
    B. $\sqrt{e^4 - 10}$
    C. $e^2 - \sqrt{10}$
    D. $\ln(e^2 - 10)$
    E. $\ln(e^4 + 10)$

20. For positive integers a and b where $a < 9$, $\log_a 9 = b$. What is the value of $\frac{a}{b}$?

    A. 1
    B. $\frac{2}{3}$
    C. $\frac{3}{2}$
    D. 2
    E. 3

21. Let x be an even integer greater than 3 and let $a = x - 2$. The equation $\log_a b = x$ is true. Which of the following describes every value of b?

    A. Positive and odd
    B. Positive and even
    C. Negative and odd
    D. Negative and even
    E. Even and nonzero only

22. The value of log (x), to the nearest 0.1, is given in the table below for 4 different values of x. To the nearest 0.1, what is the value of $\log(5 \times 10^{400})$?

x	$\log(x)$
5	0.7
50	1.7
500	2.7
5,000	3.7

A. 0.7
B. 280
C. 400.7
D. 403.7
E. 1,360

23. If x is a positive even integer, $a = x + 3$, and $\log_a b = x$, which of the following describes every value of b?

A. Positive and even.
B. Positive and odd.
C. Negative and even.
D. Negative and odd.
E. None of the above.

24. The noise rating, r of a water pump is modeled by the equation $r = 20\log\left(\frac{P}{K}\right)$, where P is the water pressure and K is a constant. What is the noise rating of a water pump whose pressure is 100 times the value of K?

A. 2
B. 20
C. 40
D. 400
E. 2,000

25. What is the solution of the equation $\log_4 \frac{\sqrt{x+31}}{\frac{1}{2}x-1} = 1$?

A. -31
B. 0
C. $\frac{3}{4}$
D. 2
E. 5

26. If $\log_a x = v$ and $\log_a y = w$, then $\log_a xy^3 = ?$

A. $3(v + w)$
B. $v + 3w$
C. $v + w$
D. $3vw$
E. vw

27. The total amount of money in a saving account at Bing's Bank is given by the formula $A = A_0(2^{\frac{t}{3}})$, where A is the total amount of money t years after an initial amount of A_0 was invested. Which of the following expressions gives the total number of years it will take for an initial investment of $50 to increase to $200?

A. 3
B. 9
C. $\log_2 25$
D. $3\log_{50} 200$
E. $3\log_2 4$

28. If x is a positive integer, y is a negative integer, and $\log_{5x} z = y$, what are the range of possible values of z?

A. $z > 1$ and $z < -1$
B. $0 < z < 1$
C. $0 < z < 0.2$
D. $0 < z < 5$
E. $z > 5$

29. If $\log_a x^2 = p$ and $\log_a(2y)^3 = m$, then $\log_a(2xy) = ?$

A. $2p + 3m$
B. $5pm$
C. $\frac{p}{2} + \frac{m}{3}$
D. $\frac{pm}{6}$
E. $\frac{3p}{2} + \frac{2m}{3}$

Chapter 15: Systems of Equations

A system of equations is a set of two equations with the same set of unknowns. The ACT most commonly hides systems of equations questions in word problems. You will need to turn the word problem into two equations and then solve for one or both unknowns.

Before we tackle the word problems, let's start with how to solve a system of equations when we are given the equations. The easiest methods are elimination and substitution. You will need to be familiar with both of these methods to solve systems of equations questions correctly.

Elimination

We cannot solve an equation with two variables, so elimination is all about trying to eliminate one variable and get an equation with only one unknown that can be solved. To do this, we need to make the coefficients for one variable have the same value and opposite signs in the two equations. With addition, one of the variables will cancel out, leaving us an equation with just one unknown that can be solved.

Example 1: If $10x - 4y = 16$ and $2x + 4y = 8$, what is the value of y?
    A. 1   B. 2   C. 4   D. 8   E. 10

Solution: Whenever we have a system of equation where none of the variables are already isolated, "elimination" is the fastest way to get to the answer. Since we are asked to solve for y, we want to cancel the x-terms. To do so, we multiply the second equation by -5.

$$10x - 4y = 16$$
$$-5\,(2x + 4y = 8)$$

$$10x - 4y = 16$$
$$-10x - 20y = -40$$

Next, add the equations together and solve for y. Notice that the x-terms cancel out.

$$-24y = -24$$
$$y = 1$$

The answer is A.

Substitution

In substitution, we want to isolate one variable in the fastest and easiest way possible. Once we have an isolated variable, we can substitute that value into the other equation and have an equation with one variable that we can solve.

Example 2: If $12x + 8y = 8$ and $y = 6x - 14$, what does x equal?
    A. -2 B. 1   C. 2   D. 7   E. 12

Solution: If we are given a question where one of the variables is already isolated, use the "substitution" method. In this question, y is already isolated. We know that $y = 6x - 14$ from the second equation, so we can substitute $6x - 14$ for the y in the first equation.

$$12x + 8(6x - 14) = 8$$
$$12x + 48x - 112 = 8$$
$$60x - 112 = 8$$

PrepPros

$$60x = 120$$
$$x = 2$$

The answer is C.

Word Problems

Many word problems are systems of equations questions in disguise. For these questions, the biggest challenge is turning the words into equations. If you can do that successfully, you then just need to solve the system of equations. Systems of equations questions on the ACT most commonly look something like this:

> **Example 3:** For her garden, Mary buys 42 plants for a total of $108. Mary is only going to plant tomatoes and peppers. If a tomato plant costs $3.00 and pepper plant costs $2.00, how many pepper plants did Mary buy?
>
> A. 10   B. 12   C. 16   D. 18   E. 24

Solution: Let x be the number of tomato plants and y be the number of pepper plants. We can write two equations. The first equation comes from the fact that we know Mary bought a total of 42 plants.

$$x + y = 42$$

The second equation includes the prices of each plant to add to the total amount of money Mary spent buying the 42 plants.

$$3x + 2y = 108$$

Once we have these two equations, we can use elimination to solve. We are solving for the number of pepper plants, y, so we can eliminate the tomato plants, x, by multiplying the first equation by -3.

$$-3(x + y = 42)$$
$$3x + 2y = 108$$

$$-3x - 3y = -126$$
$$3x + 2y = 108$$

Next, add the equations together and solve for y. Notice that the x-terms cancel out.

$$-y = -18$$
$$y = 18$$

The answer is D.

On more challenging questions, there can be more than two unknowns, and we will need to write more than 2 equations.

> **Example 4:** Malik made $738 selling his artwork this month and is counting his cash. Malik only has $1, $5, and $20 bills. He counts and notices that he has 5 more $5 bills than $20 bills and 6 more $1 bills than $5 bills. How many $1 bills does Malik have?
>
> A. 33   B. 38   C. 48   D. 53   E. 68

Solution: Method #1 – "Math Teacher Way": Let x be the number of $1 bills, y be the number of $5 bills, and z be the number of $20 bills. We can write three equations. First, we are told that Malik has $738. To find the total amount of money Malik has, we multiply the number of bills by the dollar amount of each bill. Those must add up to a total of $738.

$$1x + 5y + 20z = 738$$

We have one equation with three unknowns. Well, that looks no fun! We cannot solve an equation with three unknowns, so we need to write a few more equations with the rest of the information from the question.

We are told Malik has 5 more $5 bills than $20 bills and 6 more $1 bills than $5 bills, so the other equations are
$$z + 5 = y$$
$$y + 6 = x$$

We are asked to solve for $1 bills, which is x, so we want to put y and z in terms of x. First, let's use the equation $y + 6 = x$ above to solve for y in terms of x. Subtracting 6 from both sides we get
$$y = x - 6$$

Next, we need to solve for z in terms of x. To do so, we can plug in $x - 6$ for y in the equation $z + 5 = y$.
$$z + 5 = x - 6$$
$$z = x - 11$$

Now that we have y and z in terms of x, we can plug these values into our first equations and solve for x.

$$1x + 5(x - 6) + 20(x - 11) = 738$$
$$1x + 5x - 30 + 20x - 220 = 738$$
$$26x = 988$$
$$x = 38$$

The answer is B. Okay…that was not easy. Good news! There is an easier way to solve questions like this.

Method 2 – Backsolve: The answer choices tell us the possible number of $1 bills. We can use the answer choices and play guess-and-check to see which one is correct. Let's say we are going to check if answer choice B works or not.

Answer choice B says there are 38 $1 bills. If there are 6 more $1 bills than $5 bills, there would be 32 $5 bills. If there are 5 more $5 bills than $20 bills, there would be 27 $20 bills. Now, we just need to see if the total is equal to $738.

$$38(1) + 32(5) + 27(20) = 738$$

38 $1 bills worked to get a total of $738, so **the answer is B.**

None of the other answer choices would give you $738. That's much easier than doing all that fancy algebra, right? **For questions with more than 2 unknown values, always backsolve using the answer choices.**

<u>System of Equations Practice:</u> Answers on pages 328-329.

1.
$$x - 3y = 3$$
$$x + y = 7$$

   The solution to the system of equations above is (x, y). What is the value of x?

   A. 2
   B. 4
   C. 5
   D. 6
   E. 7

2.
$$x - y = 3$$
$$y = 3 - 2x$$

   For the system of equations above, what is the value of x?

   A. 6
   B. 2
   C. 0
   D. −1
   E. −3

3. $0.25x - 2y = -4$
$x + y = 2$

What is the value of y in the system of equation above?

A. -2
B. 0
C. 2
D. 4
E. 6

4. The drama club is selling two types of tickets for the play: student tickets for $7 each and regular tickets for $12 each. If the drama club sold a total of 200 tickets and the ticket sales were $2,025, how many student tickets were sold?

A. 60
B. 75
C. 90
D. 100
E. 125

5. Monique, a manager at a local bakery, is taking all of the $10 and $20 bills in the cash register to the bank at the end of her shift. On her way back to work, she lost the deposit slip, but she remembers that there were 19 bills totaling $260. How many $10 bills were in the cash register at the end of her shift?

A. 6
B. 9
C. 11
D. 12
E. 14

6. At Franky's Surf Shop, the price of a t-shirt is $20, and the price of a hat is $17. Javaun spent $282 on 15 items and only bought t-shirts and hats. How many hats did he buy?

A. 5
B. 6
C. 7
D. 9
E. 10

Use the following information to answer questions 7-9.

Max is bringing desserts to the family picnic. He is going to bring only cookies and brownies. The table below gives the number of brownies and cookies in each box and the price per box.

Foot Item	Number per box	Price
Cookies	18	$6.00
Brownies	12	$8.00

7. If Max spends $150.00 on 20 boxes of cookies and brownies, how many boxes of cookies did he bring to the picnic?

A. 5
B. 8
C. 10
D. 13
E. 15

8. If Max brings 14 boxes that have a total of 222 cookies and brownies, how many boxes of brownies did he bring to the picnic?

A. 3
B. 4
C. 5
D. 7
E. 9

9. If Max brings a total of 210 cookies and brownies and spends $110.00, how many boxes of brownies did he bring?

A. 5
B. 7
C. 8
D. 9
E. 10

10. $3x + 5y = 26$
$x + y = 34$

In the system of equations above, what is the value of x?

A. 18
B. 26
C. 36
D. 72
E. 144

11. Kiki's teacher wrote the following riddle on the board: "There are two integers I am thinking of. The difference between the two integers is 21, and the sum of the larger integer and twice the smaller integer is -15. What is the value of the larger integer?" The answer is:

A. -12
B. -9
C. 6
D. 9
E. 12

Use the following information to answer questions 12-13.

Dale's Donuts sells donut boxes in two sizes: a 6-donut box for $5.25 and a 12-donut box for $10.75. The table below shows the sales for Dale's Donuts on Saturday and Sunday.

	Number of Boxes	Total Sales
Saturday	120	$795.00
Sunday	95	$839.75

12. How many 6-donut boxes did Dale's Donuts sell on Saturday?

A. 90
B. 85
C. 77
D. 63
E. 52

13. How many total donuts did Dale's Donuts sell on Sunday?

A. 768
B. 882
C. 909
D. 942
E. 1050

14. If (x, y) is the solution to the system of equations below, what is the value of y?

$$4x + 3y = 10$$
$$6y + 2x = -4$$

A. -4
B. -2
C. 2
D. 4
E. 8

15. If (x, y) is the solution to the system of equations below, what is the value of x?

$$\frac{y}{x} = 3$$
$$2(y + 12) = 8x$$

A. 2
B. 4
C. 8
D. 12
E. 15

16. Jimmy's Deli sells Reuben sandwiches for $7.35 and Brisket sandwiches for $8.10. Yesterday, the deli made $759.90 from selling a total of 99 Reuben and Brisket sandwiches. How many Reuben sandwiches were sold yesterday?

A. 39
B. 43
C. 56
D. 74
E. 80

17. The product of 2 integers is 96. The greater integer is 2 less than triple the lesser integer. What is the greater integer?

A. 4
B. 6
C. 8
D. 12
E. 16

PrepPros

18. Doug has 25 coins that add up to a total of $2.25. If Doug only has dimes and nickels, how many nickels does Doug have?

A. 1
B. 5
C. 10
D. 20
E. 25

19. A group of 150 people went whitewater rafting. They took 20 total rafts. The rafts could carry either 6 or 8 people. How many 8-person rafts did the group take?

A. 4
B. 6
C. 8
D. 10
E. 15

20. At the Pacific Beach boardwalk, there is a taco stand that sells carnitas and fish tacos. Carnitas tacos have 50 more calories than fish tacos. If 3 carnitas tacos and 2 fish tacos have a total of 650 calories, how many calories does each fish taco have?

A. 100
B. 125
C. 150
D. 175
E. 200

21. Palm Springs Short Film Festival is planning to show three movies tonight that total 277 minutes. The first movie is 5 minutes longer than the second movie, and the second movie is 43 minutes longer than the third movie. How long, in minutes, is the first movie?

A. 62
B. 97
C. 105
D. 110
E. 140

22. James took a trip from Maryland to Boston by car and train. When travelling by car, he averaged 40 miles per hour. When traveling by train, he averaged 60 miles per hour. The trip took him 7 hours and was 400 miles. How far did he travel by train?

A. 120
B. 200
C. 240
D. 310
E. 360

23. Alanna ordered 95 water bottles to give as gifts to the nurses at the hospital. She got three colors: purple, black, and blue. She ordered seven fewer black water bottles than blue water bottles and 11 fewer purple water bottles than black water bottles. How many purple water bottles did she order?

A. 22
B. 25
C. 29
D. 33
E. 40

24. A kayaking company made $5,100 in 1 day by selling three types of tours: Tour A for $50 per person, Tour B for $75 per person, and Tour C for $125 per person. They sold twice as many tour C tickets as tour B. If there were a total of 60 tickets sold, how many tickets were sold for tour B?

A. 7
B. 10
C. 12
D. 20
E. 24

25. The difference of 2 positive integers is 5. The square of the greater number is 95 more than the square of the lesser number. What is the value of the sum of the two integers?

A. 13
B. 19
C. 23
D. 27
E. 35

- 134 -

Chapter 16: Quadratics

Quadratics are mathematical expressions containing a term to the second degree with a standard form of

$$y = ax^2 + bx + c$$

For quadratics on the ACT, you need to be able to multiply binomials (FOIL), factor, interpret quadratics on a graph, use the quadratic formula, and find the vertex.

Multiplying Binomials

In order to multiply binomials, you will need to FOIL, which stands for First, Outer, Inner, Last. You are likely very familiar with how to multiply binomials by now, but just in case you can use the example below to review.

To multiply $(2x + 3)(x + 6)$ ...

$$\text{First terms: } (2x)(x) = 2x^2$$
$$\text{Outer terms: } (2x)(6) = 12x$$
$$\text{Inner terms: } (3)(x) = 3x$$
$$\text{Last terms: } (3)(6) = 18$$

so we get: $(2x + 3)(x + 6) = 2x^2 + 12x + 3x + 18 = \mathbf{2x^2 + 15x + 18}$

Multiplying Perfect Squares – Don't Forget to FOIL

When multiplying perfect squares, make sure to avoid the common mistake of forgetting to FOIL.

$$(x + 5)^2 \neq x^2 + 25$$

To help avoid this mistake, you can write the perfect square as two expressions and then FOIL.

$$(x + 5)^2 = (x + 5)(x + 5) = x^2 + 5x + 5x + 25$$

So

$$(x + 5)^2 = x^2 + 10x + 25$$

Example 1: Which of the following is equivalent to $(2x + 3)^2 + 4x$?

A. $4x^2 + 16x + 9$ B. $4x^2 + 4x + 9$ C. $2x^2 + 4x + 3$ D. $6x^2 + 9$ E. $4x^2 + 12x + 9$

Solution: To solve, multiply out the squared expression and then combine like terms.

$$(2x + 3)^2 + 4x$$
$$(2x + 3)(2x + 3) + 4x$$
$$4x^2 + 12x + 9 + 4x$$
$$4x^2 + 16x + 9$$

The answer is A.

Shortcut Method – Substitution: In Chapter 2, we discussed using substitution (plug in a number for x) to solve a question like this. Solving simpler questions like Example 1 algebraically works but using substitution is a good backup method. This trick is particularly useful if you ever get stuck trying to solve algebraically, as you will still be able to find which answer choice is correct.

Factoring Quadratics

On the ACT, you often need to factor quadratics. Factoring can help you simplify expressions or identify the solutions of a quadratic equation.

The "Box" Method

We can use the "box" method to find the factors for a quadratic equation. The factors will appear on the outside of the box and the quadratic will appear in the box.

To see how this works, let's factor the quadratic below:

$$f(x) = 3x^2 - x - 2$$

1. Place the x^2 term in the top left of the box. Place the number in the bottom right.

2. Write down the two terms that must multiply to the top left term ($3x$ and x) outside the box.

3. Identify which number(s) can multiply to the number in the bottom right of the box (1 and -2, 2 and -1).

4. Place the pairs of number outside the box. You have the correct setup when the top right and bottom left boxes (the x-terms) add up to the middle term in our quadratic, which in this example is $-x$. The factors appear on the outside of the box.

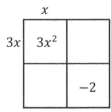

5. Write down the quadratic in factored form. $3x^2 - x - 2 = (3x + 2)(x - 1)$

There are other ways to factor quadratics. If you have a different method that works for you, use that method. We will not review factoring any more beyond this example in this book. If you need to review factoring, look up some lessons and practice problems online and in your textbooks.

"Easy to Factor" Quadratics

Keep an eye out for perfect squares and difference of squares on the ACT. These are very common in quadratics questions, and they can be factored quickly and easily as long as you spot the pattern. The table below shows the three common "easy to factor" quadratics you should know.

Equation	Formula	Example
Perfect Square (Addition)	$(x + y)^2 = x^2 + 2xy + y^2$	$(x + 2)^2 = x^2 + 4x + 4$
Perfect Square (Subtraction)	$(x - y)^2 = x^2 - 2xy + y^2$	$(x - 3)^2 = x^2 - 6x + 9$
Difference of Squares	$(x + y)(x - y) = x^2 - y^2$	$(x + 6)(x - 6) = x^2 - 36$

Example 2: For $\{x | x \neq 3\}$, which of the following expressions is equal to $\frac{x^2-7x+12}{x-3} + 3x + 1$?

A. $\frac{x^2-4x-11}{x-3}$ B. $\frac{-2x+3}{x-3}$ C. $x^2 + 3x + 9$ D. $x - 4$ E. $4x - 3$

Solution: To simplify, we need to factor the numerator of the fraction and see if any expressions cancel.

$$\frac{x^2-7x+12}{x-3} + 3x + 1 = \frac{(x-3)(x-4)}{x-3} + 3x + 1$$

Since there is an $x - 3$ in the numerator and the denominator, we can cancel these and then combine like terms.

$$\frac{\cancel{(x-3)}(x-4)}{\cancel{x-3}} + 3x + 1 = x - 4 + 3x + 1 = 4x - 3$$

The answer is E.

Shortcut Method – Substitution: Pick a value for x and plug that value into the original equation. Here, we pick $x = 2$, the original equation is equal to 5. Then, plug in $x = 2$ to the answer choices and look for which one is equal to 5.

Solutions, Roots, x-intercepts, and Zeros for Quadratic Equations

The ACT may ask you to find the "solutions," "roots," x-intercepts," or "zeros" of a quadratic equation. All these terms refer to the values of x that make $f(x) = 0$. Remember, all these terms mean the same thing. We will refer to these as the "solutions" in the rest of this chapter.

To find the solution(s), set the quadratic equation equal to zero and factor. Let's pick up with the example we are currently working on.

$$3x^2 - x - 2 = 0$$

We just showed how we can factor this quadratic to get

$$(3x + 2)(x - 1) = 0$$

To find the solutions, set each factor equal to zero and solve.

$$3x + 2 = 0 \qquad\qquad x - 1 = 0$$
$$x = -\frac{2}{3} \qquad \text{and} \qquad x = 1$$

The solutions are $x = -\frac{2}{3}$ and $x = 1$.

Remember that the solutions are also the x-intercepts if the quadratic is graphed (more on this on the next page).

Example 3: What is the sum of the roots of the polynomial $f(x) = x^2 - 11x + 18$?

A. -11 B. -7 C. -2 D. 7 E. 11

Solution: To solve, we need to find the values of x that make $f(x) = 0$.

$$x^2 - 11x + 18 = 0$$

We factor the quadratic and then set each factor equal to zero.

$$(x - 2)(x - 9) = 0$$
$$x = 2, 9$$

The solutions are 2 and 9. The sum of the roots is $2 + 9 = 11$. **The answer is E.**

Example 4: Given that $x = 3$ is a solution to $x^2 - bx + 12 = 0$, which of the following polynomials is a factor of $x^2 - bx + 12$?

A. $x - 4$ B. $x - 2$ C. $x - 1$ D. $x + 3$ E. $x + 4$

Solution: Since $x = 3$ is a solution, we know that $(x - 3)$ is one polynomial factor of $x^2 - bx + 12$. We will call the other unknown polynomial $(x + a)$ and solve.

$$(x - 3)(x + a) = x^2 - bx + 12$$

So, how can we figure out what a is? Think about our FOIL and how we get the $+12$ on the right side: we must multiply -3 by a. So $a = -4$. The other factor must be $(x - 4)$.

$$(x - 3)(x - 4) = x^2 - bx + 12$$

The answer is A.

How Solutions Appear on a Graph

Roots or solutions appear as the x-intercepts when graphed. When you have a quadratic or other polynomial in factored form, you can see where the x-intercepts will be. We will review the rules for multiplicity (the power to which a factor is raised) and zeros for polynomial functions below:

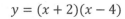
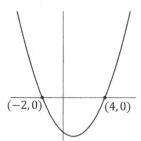

Multiplicity = 1

Zeros: The function has 2 solutions at $x = -2$ and $x = 4$.

Behavior: The function passes straight through the x-axis at the solutions.

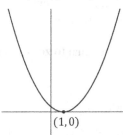

Multiplicity = 2

Zeros: The function has 1 solution at $x = 1$.

Behavior: The function bounces at the solution and does not cross the x-axis.

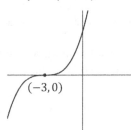

Multiplicity = 3

Zeros: The function has 1 solution at $x = -3$.

Behavior: The function flattens and passes through the x-axis at the solution.

TIP – Functions With No Solution

If a function never crosses the x-axis, that function has no real solutions. In other words, the function does not have any x-intercepts.

As an example, the function $f(x)$ to the right has no real solutions. This function cannot be factored to solve for any real values of x. If you used the quadratic equation, the solutions are complex numbers.

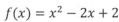
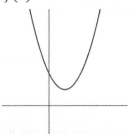

Example 5: Which of the following equations correctly describes the function in the graph below?

A. $y = (x + 2)^2(x - 1)^2(x - 3)$
B. $y = (x + 2)(x - 1)(x - 3)$
C. $y = (x - 2)^2(x + 1)(x + 3)$
D. $y = (x + 2)(x - 1)^2(x - 3)^2$
E. $y = (x - 2)(x + 1)^2(x + 3)^2$

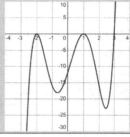

Solution: To solve this question, we need to look at the behavior of the function at each of the x-intercepts. There are x-intercepts at $x = -2$, $x = 1$, and $x = 3$, so we need to see the factors $(x + 2)$, $(x - 1)$, and $(x - 3)$ in the correct answer. Now, we need to find out what power each term should be raised to. At $x = -2$ and $x = 1$, the function bounces, so the $(x + 2)$ and $(x - 1)$ terms are squared. At $x = 3$, the function goes straight through, so the $(x - 3)$ should be to the first power. **The answer is A.**

Shortcut Solution – Use Your Graphing Calculator (if you have one): For those of you with a graphing calculator who know how to use it, you can just graph the answer choices and see which one matches the graph! Sure, it may take some time, but you will be able to guarantee that you get the correct answer.

In general, remember you can always use your graphing calculator to find the zeros for any quadratic functions or to see what the graph of any equation looks like. Many students forget to use their calculators for questions like this.

The Quadratic Formula

If a quadratic is not easily factorable, you will need to use the quadratic formula to solve for the solutions of a quadratic function. You will need to have the quadratic formula memorized.

For $ax^2 + bx + c = 0$, the solution(s) are given by: $x = \frac{-b \pm \sqrt{b^2 - 4ac}}{2a}$

Example 6: Which of the following is a zero for the function $f(x) = x^2 - 8x + 4$?

A. $8 + 4\sqrt{2}$ B. $4 - 2\sqrt{3}$ C. $-4 + 2\sqrt{3}$ D. $-8 + 4\sqrt{3}$ E. $8 - 4\sqrt{3}$

Solution: Since this quadratic cannot be factored, we must use the quadratic formula.

$x = \frac{-(-8) \pm \sqrt{(-8)^2 - 4(1)(4)}}{2(1)}$ 1. Plug in the values for a, b, and c.

$x = \frac{8 \pm \sqrt{64 - 16}}{2}$ 2. Begin to simplify terms.

$x = \frac{8 \pm \sqrt{48}}{2}$ 3. Combine terms under the radical.

$x = \frac{8 \pm 4\sqrt{3}}{2}$ 4. Simplify radical (if possible).

$x = 4 \pm 2\sqrt{3}$ 5. Simplify terms further (if possible).

$x = 4 + 2\sqrt{3}$ and $x = 4 - 2\sqrt{3}$ 6. Identify the value(s) of x.

The answer is B.

Using the quadratic formula is not too common on the ACT, but you should still memorize the equation just in case. If you do need to use the quadratic formula, it will be on the hardest questions from 45-60.

The Discriminant

In the quadratic formula, the discriminant is the $b^2 - 4ac$ term under the radical. This term is very important because it can quickly tell us how many real or complex solutions there will be for any quadratic function. The exact value of the discriminant is not important, but whether it's positive, negative, or zero is!

Discriminant Value	Types of Solutions
$b^2 - 4ac > 0$	2 real solutions
$b^2 - 4ac = 0$	1 real solution
$b^2 - 4ac < 0$	0 real solutions, 2 complex solutions

You should memorize these rules. If you ever see a question about the number of solutions to a quadratic function, use the discriminant to solve.

Example 7: How many rational roots are there to the equation $2x^2 - 7x + 9$?
    A. 0   B. 1   C. 2   D. 3   E. Cannot be determined.

Solution:
$$\text{Discriminant} = b^2 - 4ac = (-7)^2 - 4(2)(9)$$
$$\text{Discriminant} = -23$$

The discriminant is negative, so there are no real solutions. **The answer is A.**

Example 8: In the system of equations below, m is a constant. For which of the following values of m does the system of equations have exactly 1 real solution?
$$y = x^2 - 8x + 10$$
$$y = m - 2x$$
    A. −2   B. −1   C. 0   D. 1   E. 2

Solution: To start, we set the equations equal.
$$x^2 - 8x + 10 = m - 2x$$
$$x^2 - 6x + (10 - m) = 0$$

If the system of equations has one real solution, the equation above should have one real solution and the discriminant should be equal to 0.
$$\text{Discriminant} = b^2 - 4ac = (-6)^2 - 4(1)(10 - m) = 0$$

At this point, we can either test each of the answer choices to see which one makes the discriminant equal 0 or solve algebraically for m. Below shows how to solve algebraically.
$$(-6)^2 - 4(1)(10 - m) = 0$$
$$36 - 40 + 4m = 0$$
$$-4 + 4m = 0$$
$$4m = 4$$
$$m = 1$$

The answer is D.

Just to be clear, Example 9 is an extremely difficult question and would be one of the "who gets a 36" questions on the test. Do not expect to see any questions like this on test day. That being said, this is absolutely fair game, and questions of similar difficulty have been on the test before.

The Vertex

The vertex is the highest or lowest point of a parabola. For the parabola shown below, the vertex is at $(1, -4)$. You should memorize the vertex form equation shown below.

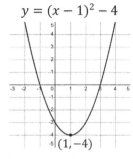

Vertex Form: $y = a(x - h)^2 + k$

- vertex at (h, k)
- when $a > 0$, parabola opens up
- when $a < 0$, parabola opens down

When a quadratic is written in vertex form, we can tell what the vertex is without graphing. As you can see in the example above, we can tell the vertex is at $(1, -4)$. We can think of the vertex as the midpoint of a parabola because the x-coordinate of the vertex is always the midpoint of the two solutions, or x-intercepts. The x-coordinate of the vertex is equal to the average of the solutions. Using the parabola above as an example, we can see how this works. Since the solutions to the parabola are located at $x = -1$ and $x = 3$, the x-coordinate of the vertex is at $x = \frac{-1+3}{2} = 1$, which matches the graph.

Remember, the vertex is always the maximum or minimum of a quadratic. For the example above, the minimum is at $y = -4$.

> **Example 9:** For the equation $f(x) = (x - 6)(x + 2)$, what is the value of x at the minimum value of the function?
>
> A. −2.   B. −1   C. 0   D. 1   E. 2

Solution: The minimum value of a parabola is at the vertex, so we need to find the coordinates of the vertex. Since the function is already in factored form, we see the solutions are at $x = 6$ and $x = -2$. The x-coordinate of the vertex is the average of the solutions, so we can find

$$x = \frac{6 + (-2)}{2} = 2$$

The x-coordinate of the vertex is at $x = 2$, so **the answer is 2.**

Shortcut Method – Backsolve: To find which answer choice minimizes the function, plug the answer choices in for x and see which one gives you the smallest value for $f(x)$.

The average method works perfectly if you are given a quadratic that is already factored. But what if you are not given a quadratic in factored form or vertex form? Good news! There is a second way to quickly find the vertex.

For any quadratic in the form of $ax^2 + bx + c$, you can find the x-coordinate of the vertex using

$$x = -\frac{b}{2a}$$

Make sure you memorize this equation! It can really help you quickly and easily solve any questions where you need to find the vertex of a parabola.

Example 10: Andre runs a business that sells used cameras. To get the cameras ready to sell, Andre must spend x hours repairing and cleaning each camera. The equation $P(x) = -0.05x^2 + 0.4x + 0.9$ models the percentage of profit, P, that Andre gets from selling a camera. Which of the following shows the number of repair hours that maximizes Andre's percentage of profit for selling a camera?

    A. 3   B. 4   C. 6   D. 8   E. 10

Solution: Here, we need to find where Andre's percentage of profit is maximized, so we need to find the vertex of the equation. Since the leading value in the parabola is negative, the parabola is downward facing, so the vertex will be the maximum of the graph. The number of hours will be on the x-axis, so we just need to find the x-coordinate of the vertex to solve.

To find the x-coordinate of the vertex, we can use the equation we just introduced above:

$$x = -\frac{b}{2a} = -\frac{0.4}{2(-0.05)} = 4$$

The answer is B.

Shortcut Method #1 – Backsolve: The question asks which value of x maximizes the function. To solve, plug the answer choices back into the function and see which one gives the biggest value for $P(x)$.

Shortcut Method #2 – Graph the Function: If you have a graphing calculator, you can also graph the equation and find the maximum value. Make sure to use your calculator as much as possible on test day, as it can often shortcut many questions that are difficult to solve algebraically.

Quadratics Practice: Answers on page 329.

1. What are the solutions to the quadratic equation $(4x + 1)(2x - 3) = 0$?

    A. -1 and 3
    B. $-\frac{1}{4}$ and $-\frac{3}{2}$
    C. $-\frac{1}{4}$ and $\frac{3}{2}$
    D. $\frac{1}{4}$ and $-\frac{3}{2}$
    E. $-\frac{1}{4}$ and $-\frac{3}{2}$

2. What is the sum of the solutions of the polynomial $f(x) = x^2 - 7x + 12$?

    A. -7
    B. -4
    C. 3
    D. 4
    E. 7

3. What are the roots of the quadratic equation $3x^2 + 9x - 12 = 0$?

    A. $x = 1$ and $x = 4$
    B. $x = -1$ and $x = 4$
    C. $x = -1$ and $x = -4$
    D. $x = 1$ and $x = -4$
    E. $x = 1$ and $x = -1$

4. What is the sum of the solutions of the equation $x^2 - 4x - 21 = 0$?

    A. -10
    B. -4
    C. 3
    D. 4
    E. 10

5. The lengths of 2 adjacent sides of a rectangle are represented $x + 4$ and $3x - 1$ inches. What expression below represents the area of the rectangle in square inches?

    A. $3x^2 + 12x - 4$
    B. $3x^2 + 11x - 4$
    C. $3x^2 + 7 - 3$
    D. $3x^2 - 12$
    E. $4x + 3$

6. For what value of m does the quadratic $x^2 - 13x + m = 0$ have solutions of $x = 5$ and $x = 8$?

   A. -40
   B. -13
   C. 3
   D. 13
   E. 40

7. The function $f(x)$ is graphed below. Which of the following could define the function $f(x)$?

   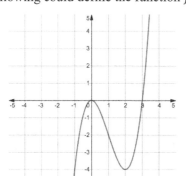

   A. $f(x) = x(x-3)$
   B. $f(x) = x(x+3)$
   C. $f(x) = x^2(x-3)$
   D. $f(x) = x(x+3)^2$
   E. $f(x) = x^2(x+3)$

8. What is the solution set for $5x^2 + 6x = 8$?

   A. $\{\frac{1}{5}, \frac{1}{2}\}$
   B. $\{-\frac{1}{5}, -\frac{1}{2}\}$
   C. $\{\frac{4}{5}, 2\}$
   D. $\{\frac{4}{5}, -2\}$
   E. $\{-\frac{1}{5}, -2\}$

9. For $x^2 \neq 25$, which of the following expressions is equal to $\frac{(x-5)^2}{x^2-25}$?

   A. $\frac{x-5}{x+5}$
   B. $\frac{1}{x+5}$
   C. $\frac{1}{x-5}$
   D. 1
   E. $-\frac{1}{5}$

10. Which of the following are the factors of $abx^2 + (ac - bd)x - cd$?

    A. $(ax - b)(cx - d)$
    B. $(ax + b)(cx - d)$
    C. $(ax + c)(bx - d)$
    D. $(ax - d)(bx + c)$
    E. $(ax + d)(bx + c)$

11. In the equation below, a and b are constants. Which of the following could be the value of a?

    $$9x^2 - 16 = (ax - b)(ax + b)$$

    A. 3
    B. 4
    C. 9
    D. 16
    E. 25

12.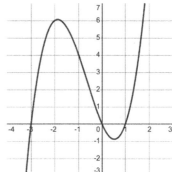

    The function $f(x)$ is graphed above. Which of the following could define the function $f(x)$?

    A. $f(x) = (x-3)(x+1)$
    B. $f(x) = x(x-3)(x+1)$
    C. $f(x) = (x+3)(x-1)$
    D. $f(x) = x(x+3)(x-1)$
    E. $f(x) = x^2(x+3)(x-1)$

13. In the equation below, $j, l, k,$ and m are constants. If the equation has roots of $-4, 3,$ and -5. Which of the following could be a factor of the equation below?

    $$jx^3 + lx^2 - kx - m = 0$$

    A. $x - 4$
    B. $x - 5$
    C. $x - 3$
    D. $x + 3$
    E. Cannot be determined.

14. In the standard (x, y) coordinate plane, the graph of the equation $y = 3(x-2)^2 - 5$ intersects the x-axis at points $(r, 0)$ and $(7, 0)$ and has its vertex at point $(2, -5)$. What is the value of r?

A. $-\frac{7}{2}$
B. -3
C. $-\frac{5}{2}$
D. -2
E. $-\frac{3}{2}$

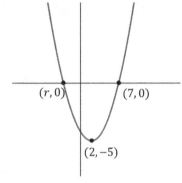

15. Given that $(x+4)$ and $(x+3)$ are factors of $x^2 + cx + d$ and $x = -3$ is the only solution of the quadratic $x^2 + mx + n$, what is dm?

A. 18
B. 24
C. 72
D. 144
E. 300

16. $h(x) = x^4 + 2x^3 - 8x^2 - 18x - 9$

The polynomial above can be written as $(x^2 - 9)(x+1)^2$. What are all the real roots of the equation?

A. $3, -3$
B. $9, 1$
C. $9, 1,$ and -1
D. $3, -3,$ and -1
E. $3, -3, 1,$ and -1

17. The side lengths of a box are represented by x feet, $2x - 3$ feet, and $x + 5$ feet. In terms of x, what is the volume, in square feet, of the box?

A. $4x + 2$
B. $2x^2 - 15x$
C. $2x^2 + 7x - 15$
D. $2x^3 - 15x$
E. $2x^3 + 7x^2 - 15x$

18. Given that $(2x + 3)$ and $(x - 4)$ are the factors of the quadratic $2x^2 + (z-1)x + 2z - 4 = 0$, what is the value of z?

A. -2
B. -4
C. 2
D. 4
E. 8

19. What is the solution set to the equation $x^4 + 7x^2 - 144 = 0$?

A. $\{-4, -3, 3, 4\}$
B. $\{-4, 4, -3i, 3i\}$
C. $\{-3, 3, -4i, 4i\}$
D. $\{-16, -9\}$
E. $\{-3, 3, 25\}$

20. Which of the following most precisely describes the solutions to the equation $3x^2 + 5x + 7 = 0$?

A. 1 rational (double) root
B. 1 irrational (double) root
C. 2 rational roots
D. 3 rational roots
E. 2 complex roots (with nonzero imaginary parts)

21. Which of the following is a solution to the equation below?

$$x^2 + 6x + 3 = 0$$

A. $-3 + \sqrt{6}$
B. $-3 + \sqrt{13}$
C. $-6 - 2\sqrt{6}$
D. $3 - \sqrt{6}$
E. $3 - \sqrt{13}$

22. Which of the following is a solution to the equation below?

$$x^2 - 4x + 1 = 0$$

A. $2 - \sqrt{6}$
B. $-2 + \sqrt{6}$
C. $2 + \sqrt{3}$
D. $-2 - \sqrt{3}$
E. $-2 + 2\sqrt{3}$

23. The height of a rocket in feet is modeled by the function $H(x) = -x^2 + 30x$, where x is the number of seconds after launch. What is the maximum height of the rocket?

    A. 10 feet
    B. 15 feet
    C. 125 feet
    D. 200 feet
    E. 225 feet

24. In the equation $x^3 + mx^2 + nx = 0$, m and n are integers. One possible value of x is 0. The other possible value of x is 5. What is the value of n?

    A. -10
    B. -5
    C. 5
    D. 10
    E. 25

25. Ben is throwing a ball from the top of his building. The ball's height is modeled by the function $H(x) = -x^2 + 10x + 56$, where x is the number of seconds after he throws the ball. At what time in seconds does the ball hit the ground?

    A. 4
    B. 5
    C. 14
    D. 28
    E. 56

26. In the quadratic equation $zx^2 + 6x = 3$, z is a constant. For what value of z, will the equation have one real value?

    A. -3
    B. -1
    C. 1
    D. 3
    E. 6

27. Which of the following is a solution to the equation $2x^2 + 4x + 1 = 0$?

    A. $\frac{-2+\sqrt{2}}{2}$
    B. $2\sqrt{2}$
    C. $-2 + \sqrt{2}$
    D. $-1 - \sqrt{2}$
    E. $\frac{2-\sqrt{2}}{2}$

28. $x = 2$ is one solution to the quadratic $3x^3 - x^2 - 14x + 8 = 0$. Which of the following describes the other two solutions?

    A. Both are complex numbers that are not real.
    B. Both are positive real numbers.
    C. One is a positive real number, and the other is a complex number that is not real.
    D. One is a positive real number, and one is a negative real number.
    E. One is a negative real number, and the other is a complex number that is not real.

29. For the system of equations below, $g, h,$ and j are integers.

    $$y = gx^2$$
    $$2y + j = hx$$

    For which of the following will there be exactly one real (x, y) solution for the system?

    A. $g^2 - 4hj = 0$
    B. $h^2 - 4gj = 0$
    C. $h^2 - 8gj = 0$
    D. $g^2 + 4hj = 0$
    E. $h^2 + 8gj = 0$

30. The equation below is graphed in the xy-plane. If a and b are positive constants and $a \neq b$, how many distinct x-intercepts does the graph have?

    $$x^2 + ax + bx + ab = 0$$

    A. 0
    B. 1
    C. 2
    D. 3
    E. Cannot be determined.

Chapter 17: Trigonometry

Basic Trigonometry

For the easier trigonometry questions on the ACT, just remember **SOH-CAH-TOA**! The majority of trigonometry questions that appear in the first half of the ACT Math test you on the basic trigonometry functions.

If you have not heard of **SOH-CAH-TOA**, it is an acronym to memorize the sine, cosine, and tangent functions. **SOH** stands for Sine equals Opposite over Hypotenuse, **CAH** stands for Cosine equals Adjacent over Hypotenuse, and **TOA** stands for Tangent equals Opposite over Adjacent.

$$\sin(x) = \frac{\text{opposite}}{\text{hypotenuse}} = \frac{9}{15}$$

$$\cos(x) = \frac{\text{adjacent}}{\text{hypotenuse}} = \frac{12}{15}$$

$$\tan(x) = \frac{\text{opposite}}{\text{adjacent}} = \frac{9}{12}$$

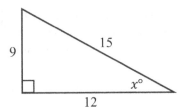

For easy trigonometry questions (usually ones that appear in the first 20 questions), you need to set up the basic trigonometry functions correctly.

Example 1: What is the value of $\cos B$ in the triangle below?

A. $\frac{1}{2}$ B. $\frac{1}{\sqrt{5}}$ C. $\frac{\sqrt{5}}{2}$ D. $\frac{2}{\sqrt{5}}$ E. $\sqrt{5}$

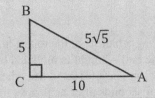

Solution: To find $\cos B$, we need to find the side length adjacent to angle B and the hypotenuse. The side length adjacent to angle B is 5 and the hypotenuse is $5\sqrt{5}$, so we set up the cosine equation and simplify.

$$\cos B = \frac{5}{5\sqrt{5}} = \frac{1}{\sqrt{5}}$$

The answer is B. The ACT sometimes leaves answer choices with the square root in the denominator.

For other similar questions, we may need to use the Pythagorean theorem to find the third side of a triangle and then find the sine, cosine, or tangent.

Example 2: What is the value of $\tan A$ in the triangle below?

A. $\frac{4}{3}$ B. $\frac{4}{\sqrt{33}}$ C. $\frac{\sqrt{33}}{4}$ D. $\frac{3}{4}$ E. $\frac{\sqrt{33}}{7}$

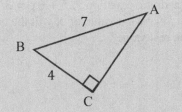

Solution: To find $\tan A$, we need to know the side lengths opposite angle A and adjacent to angle A. The side length opposite angle A is 4. The side length adjacent to angle A, side AC, is currently unknown. To solve for AC, we use the Pythagorean theorem.

$$4^2 + AC^2 = 7^2$$

$$16 + AC^2 = 49$$

$$AC^2 = 33$$

- 146 -

$$AC = \sqrt{33}$$

Now, we can label all sides of triangle ABC and find tan A. The opposite side length is 4, and the adjacent side length is $\sqrt{33}$ so

$$\tan A = \frac{opposite}{adjactent} = \frac{4}{\sqrt{33}}$$

The answer is B.

Both examples we have done so far gave us a triangle. **What if we see a basic trigonometry question and a no triangle given? We can draw our own right triangle!** Remember that SOH-CAH-TOA only applies to right triangles.

> **Example 3:** For an angle with a measure of q in a right triangle, $\sin q = \frac{9}{15}$ and $\tan q = \frac{9}{12}$, what is the value of $\cos q$?
>
> A. $\frac{6}{\sqrt{369}}$ B. $\frac{6}{\sqrt{205}}$ C. $\frac{12}{9}$ D. $\frac{15}{9}$ E. $\frac{12}{15}$

Solution: We can draw a right triangle, label one of the acute angles as q, and then use the trigonometry functions to label the sides.

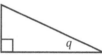

Since $\sin q = \frac{9}{15}$, we can first label the opposite side as 9 and the hypotenuse as 15. Since $\tan q = \frac{9}{12}$ and the opposite side is already labelled as 9, we now also label the adjacent sides as 12. As a result, the triangle now looks like this:

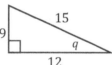

Now, we can see that $\cos q = \frac{12}{15}$. **The answer is E.**

Using Trigonometry to Find Side Lengths in Right Triangles

The second very common type of easy trigonometry question asks us to use trigonometry to solve for an unknown side of a right triangle. To solve these questions correctly, we need to use SOH-CAH-TOA and then solve for the unknown side.

> **Example 4:** In the triangle below, which of the following expressions is equal to x?
>
> A. $9 \sin 67°$
> B. $9 \cos 67°$
> C. $9 \tan 67°$
> D. $\frac{9}{9 \sin 67°}$
> E. $\frac{9}{9 \cos 67°}$
>
>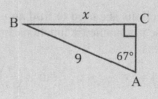

Solution: The first step is to identify which trigonometric function involves the values we are given and x. We know angle A, the hypotenuse, and are solving for the opposite, so we use the sine function. We can set up the sine function and plug in the values we are given.

$$\sin A = \frac{opposite}{hypotenuse} \quad \rightarrow \quad \sin 67° = \frac{x}{9}$$

- 147 -

Next, we solve for x by multiplying both sides by 9 and get

$$x = 9 \sin 67°$$

The answer is A.

If the question asks for the numerical value of x, we can plug $9 \sin 67°$ into the calculator to find the actual length, which here is 8.28.

Another version of a question testing this concept gives us no angle but tells us the value of the sine, cosine, or tangent. With no angle, using trigonometry seems confusing at first, but, if we know how to set up trigonometric functions, we solve with the same SOH-CAH-TOA knowledge we used in Example 4.

Example 5: In triangle ABC shown below, $\cos B = \frac{2}{3}$ and the length of AB is 6. What is the length of AC?

A. 2
B. 4
C. $3\sqrt{5}$
D. 9
E. $3\sqrt{13}$

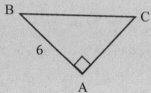

Solution: In this question, we are not given any angles, but we are told what the $\cos B = \frac{2}{3}$. We also know that $\cos B = \frac{6}{BC}$, so we can set these equal and solve for BC:

$$\frac{6}{BC} = \frac{2}{3}$$

$$2BC = 18$$

$$BC = 9$$

Now that we know $BC = 9$, we can use the Pythagorean theorem to solve for AC.

$$AC^2 + 6^2 = 9^2$$

$$AC^2 = 45$$

$$AC = \sqrt{45} = 3\sqrt{5}$$

The answer is C.

Inverse Trigonometric Functions

Inverse trigonometric functions are used to find an unknown angle in a right triangle when the side lengths are known. Inverse trigonometric functions are just like SOH-CAH-TOA except that the angle is switched with the side lengths.

$$\sin^{-1}\left(\frac{\text{opposite}}{\text{hypotenuse}}\right) = x° \quad \rightarrow \quad \sin^{-1}\left(\frac{9}{15}\right) = x°$$

$$\cos^{-1}\left(\frac{\text{adjacent}}{\text{hypotenuse}}\right) = x° \quad \rightarrow \quad \cos^{-1}\left(\frac{12}{15}\right) = x°$$

$$\tan^{-1}\left(\frac{\text{opposite}}{\text{adjacent}}\right) = x° \quad \rightarrow \quad \tan^{-1}\left(\frac{9}{12}\right) = x°$$

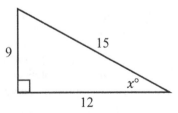

In the example triangle, we can use inverse trigonometry to solve for the unknown angle $x°$. Using a calculator and any of the inverse trigonometric functions, we can find that angle $x = 36.9°$. Most questions on the ACT do not ask you to solve for the actual angle and instead give you answer choices with the inverse trigonometric functions, so these questions are usually easy to spot on test day.

Example 6: Which of the following expressions gives the degree measure of ∠A in the triangle below?

A. $\tan^{-1}\left(\frac{30}{55}\right)$
B. $\tan^{-1}\left(\frac{55}{30}\right)$
C. $\sin^{-1}\left(\frac{55}{30}\right)$
D. $\sin^{-1}\left(\frac{30}{55}\right)$
E. $\cos^{-1}\left(\frac{30}{55}\right)$

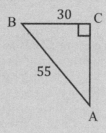

Solution: To start, let's figure out which function (sine, cosine, or tangent) we should use. 30 is the opposite side and 55 is the hypotenuse, so we need to use the inverse sine functions. Sine is opposite over hypotenuse, so the correct expression is $\sin^{-1}\left(\frac{30}{55}\right)$. **The answer is D.**

Trigonometric Identity To Know

You may not so fondly remember trigonometric identities from math class. Or, if you have never heard of that term, you will likely dislike them when you learn them in class. The good news is that for the ACT you only need to know this simple trigonometric identity:

$$\sin^2\theta + \cos^2\theta = 1$$

This identity is a rule for all values of θ, which is a term that just represents an angle. You need to memorize this equation for test day. If you ever see a $\sin^2\theta$ or $\cos^2\theta$ term in a question, you are going to need to use this identity.

Example 7: If $3\sin^2\theta + 3\cos^2\theta = a$, what is the value of a?

A. $\frac{1}{3}$ B. 1   C. 3   D. 6   E. 9

Solution: To solve, we need to use the trigonometric identity $\sin^2\theta + \cos^2\theta = 1$. If we factor 3 out from the left side, we get

$$3(\sin^2\theta + \cos^2\theta) = a$$

Since $\sin^2\theta + \cos^2\theta = 1$, we can plug in 1 for $\sin^2\theta + \cos^2\theta$ and solve for a.

$$3(1) = a$$
$$3 = a$$

The answer is C.

As you can see in this example, we only need to use the identity to solve. When you see a $\sin^2\theta$ or $\cos^2\theta$ term in a question, do not think of SOH-CAH-TOA. Instead, find how you can use the identity to solve as we did in Example 7.

Cheat Method – Substitution: We can also solve this question by picking a value and using a calculator. We can pick any value for θ, plug it into equation $3\sin^2\theta + 3\cos^2\theta$, and see what you get for a. As long as you enter the equation into your calculator correctly, you will always get 3. Go ahead and try it! If you need to review Substitution, go to Chapter 2.

PrepPros

Graphing Cosine and Sine Functions

Cosine and sine are periodic functions, meaning that the functions repeat over and over again. To start, you need to know the basics of what a sine and cosine function look like when graphed. If you have never learned sine and cosine functions, memorize the basics about each function listed below. This will help you solve most questions on this topic on test day.

To start, let's learn what the simplest form of cosine and cosine functions look like and learn some general characteristics.

$$f(x) = \cos x$$

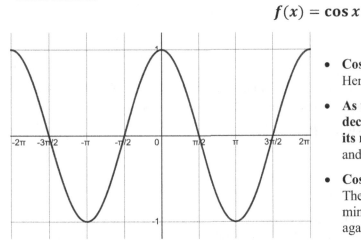

Basics To Know

- **Cosine functions start at its maximum when $x = 0$.** Here, the function starts at the point $(0, 1)$.

- **As the function moves to the right, the function decreases to its minimum value and then returns to its maximum value.** Here, the minimum is at $(\pi, -1)$ and the maximum value is at $(2\pi, 1)$.

- **Cosine functions repeat infinitely in both directions.** The cosine function continues to go between its minimum and maximum in both directions over and over again.

$$f(x) = \sin x$$

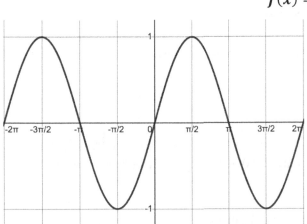

Basics To Know

- **Sine functions start at the midline.** Here, the function starts at the point $(0, 0)$.

- **As the function moves to the right, the function increases to its maximum value, returns to 0, decreases to its minimum value, and then returns to 0.** Here, the maximum is at $(\frac{\pi}{2}, 1)$ and the maximum value is at $(\frac{3\pi}{2}, -1)$.

- **Sine functions repeat infinitely in both directions.**

Notice that the x-axis labels are not numbers – instead, the labels are in radians. If you have never learned radians, do not focus too much on this, as you only need to understand the basics for the ACT. Radians are just another way to measure an angle. The conversion is **π radians = 180 degrees**. Trigonometric functions are most commonly graphed with radians on the x-axis.

*Note that the "basics to know" listed above only apply are for sine and cosine functions where only the amplitude and period (more on those shortly) are changed. Horizontal shifts can change the start and end points of the functions. The good news for anyone just learning how to graph sine and cosine for the first time in this book is that horizonal shifts are not commonly tested on the ACT.

Now that we know the basics, let's learn two more important characteristics of these functions: amplitude and period.

Chapter 17: Trigonometry

Amplitude

The amplitude of function is the amount by which the function travels above or below the midline. You can think of the amplitude as the height of the function.

The amplitude of a function is defined by $|A|$, where A is the leading coefficient in front of the sine or cosine function.

$$f(x) = A\cos x \qquad f(x) = A\sin x$$

To make this clearer, let's look the graphs of 2 cosine and 2 sine functions.

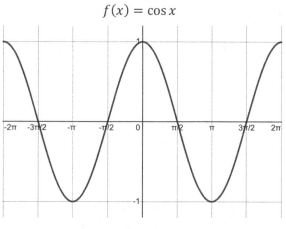

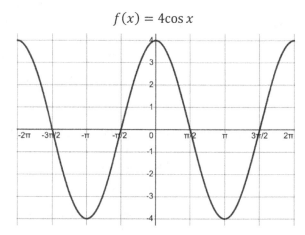

Amplitude = 1   *Amplitude = 4*

$f(x) = \cos x$ is the same as $f(x) = 1\cos x$, so for the graph on the left, $A = 1$. The graph goes up 1 unit from the midpoint to a maximum value of $y = 1$ and down 1 unit to the minimum value of $y = -1$. In the graph on the right, $A = 4$, so the graph goes up 4 units to a maximum value at $y = 4$ and down 4 units to a minimum value of $y = -4$.

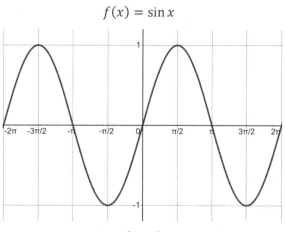

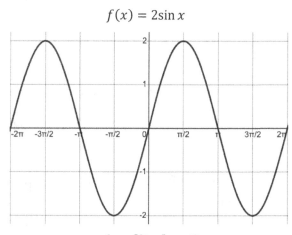

Amplitude = 1   *Amplitude = 2*

$f(x) = \sin x$ is the same as $f(x) = 1\sin x$, so for the graph on the left, $A = 1$. We see the graph going up 1 unit from the midline to a maximum value of $y = 1$ and down 1 unit to a minimum value of $y = -1$. For the graph on the right, $A = 2$, so the graph goes up 2 units to a maximum value at $y = 2$ and down 2 units to a minimum value at $y = -2$.

Now that you know the rules for amplitude and the basic shapes of sine and cosine functions, any amplitude question on the ACT should be easy!

Example 8: For the graph shown below, what is the amplitude of the function?

A. -5
B. -2
C. 1
D. 2
E. 5

Solution: The graph goes up and down 5 units from the midline, so the amplitude is 5. **The answer is E.**

It is also important to note that amplitude can never be a negative number, so we know answer choices A and B are incorrect immediately.

Period

The period of a function is equal to the length of one complete cycle of the function. For the sine and cosine functions, the period is equal to the length of one full wave, which can be found by finding the distance between the peaks of the function.

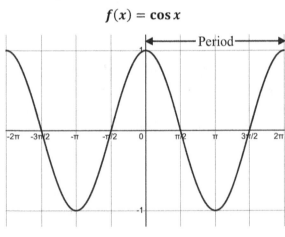

$f(x) = \cos x$

$Period = 2\pi$

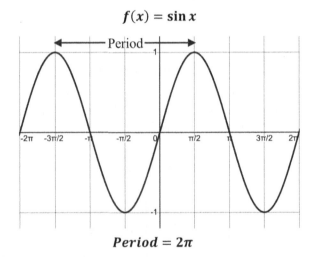

$f(x) = \sin x$

$Period = 2\pi$

As shown above, the period of a basic cosine and sine function is 2π. So, what causes the period of a function to change?

The period of a function is defined by $\left|\frac{2\pi}{B}\right|$, where B is the constant that x is multiplied by in the function.

$$f(x) = A\cos(Bx) \qquad f(x) = A\sin(Bx)$$

Let's see how this works.

For the cosine function $f(x) = \cos x$, $B = 1$, so the period is equal to $\left|\frac{2\pi}{1}\right| = 2\pi$. For the sine function $f(x) = \sin x$, $B = 1$, so the period is equal to $\left|\frac{2\pi}{1}\right| = 2\pi$. These match the periods we see in the graphs above.

Now, what happens if we have $f(x) = \cos 2x$. Well here $B = 2$, so the period is equal to $\left|\frac{2\pi}{2}\right| = \pi$. Let's look at the graph of this function.

$$f(x) = \cos 2x$$

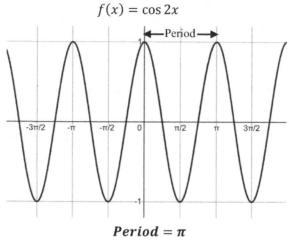

$$Period = \pi$$

Notice how the repeating units of the function now repeat faster. Changing the B-value in cosine and sine functions changes the period, which can either squeeze together the function or stretch it out.

Example 9: Which of the following equations properly describes the function $f(x)$ shown below?

A. $f(x) = 3 \sin\left(\frac{x}{2}\right)$
B. $f(x) = 6 \sin(4x)$
C. $f(x) = 3 \cos\left(\frac{x}{2}\right)$
D. $f(x) = 3 \cos(4x)$
E. $f(x) = 6 \cos(4x)$

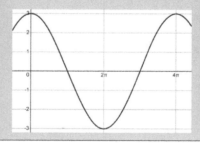

Solution: To start, we can see that this is a cosine function because the function is at a maximum value when $x = 0$ (and there is no horizontal shift...more on this in the next section), so we know that A and B are incorrect. We can also see that the amplitude is 3, so we can eliminate E.

To determine if the correct answer is C or D, we need to find the period. Looking at the graph, we see that the period is 4π. Remember, the easiest way to find the period from a graph is to look for the distance between the peaks of the function. In the graph, we see peaks of the function at $x = 0$ and $x = 4\pi$, so the period is 4π.

To find which answer choice is correct, we can use the B-values from the answer choices to see which one gives us the correct period of 4π:

For $f(x) = 3 \cos\left(\frac{x}{2}\right)$, $B = \frac{1}{2}$, so

$$Period = \left|\frac{2\pi}{(1/2)}\right| = 4\pi$$

For $f(x) = 3 \cos(4x)$, $B = 4$, so

$$Period = \left|\frac{2\pi}{(4)}\right| = \frac{\pi}{2}$$

Answer choice C gives a period of 4π. Answer choice D gives a period of $\frac{\pi}{2}$. **The answer is C.**

Vertical and Horizontal Shifts

Trigonometric functions follow the same vertical and horizontal shifting rules that we use for all other types of functions (you can learn more about these in Chapter 33). We will cover the basics for cosine and sine functions in this chapter. Advanced sine and cosine graphing questions can include vertical or horizonal shifts.

Vertical Shifts

A constant added or subtracted to a sine or cosine function causes a vertical shift. Using the equations below, the D-value shows the vertical shift of a function.

The vertical shift of a function occurs when a constant, D, is added to or subtracted from the function.

$$f(x) = A\cos(Bx) + D \qquad f(x) = A\sin(Bx) + D$$

To see how this works, consider the two functions below.

$f(x) = \cos x \qquad\qquad\qquad\qquad f(x) = \cos x + 3$

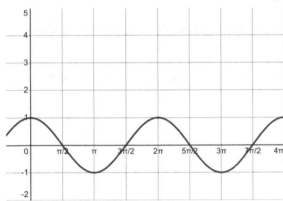
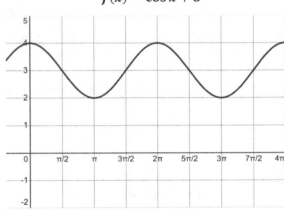

Vertical Shift Up 3 Units

Notice how the cosine function is shifted 3 units up on the graph on the right. **A positive value of D, such as 3 in the example above, shifts the function up. A negative value of D shifts the function down.**

> **Example 10:** When $f(x) = 2\sin(x) + C$ is graphed, the function has no x-intercepts. If C is a positive constant, which of the following statements about C must be true?
>
> A. $C = 2$ B. $C < 2$ C. $C > 2$ D. $C \leq 2$ E. $C \geq 2$

Solution: The best way to solve this question is to draw it out. If you need help drawing it out, you can reference the graph of $f(x) = 2\sin(x)$ on page 151. The amplitude of $f(x)$ is 2, so the minimum value of the function is a $y = -2$.

To have no x-intercepts, we must shift the function up by more than 2 units, so **the answer is C**. If we shift $f(x)$ up exactly 2 units, the minimum points will be on the x-axis, so there will still be x-intercepts. If we shift $f(x)$ up by less than 2 units, there will be even more multiple x-intercepts.

This is a more advanced question that would appear at the end of the ACT, so do not worry too much if this seems challenging…it is supposed to!

Horizontal Shifts

A constant added to or subtracted from the *x*-value inside the parentheses causes a horizonal shift to the sine and cosine functions. Using the equations below, the C-value shows the horizontal shift of a function.

The horizontal shift of a function occurs when a constant, C, is added or subtracted to the function.

$$f(x) = A\cos(Bx + C) \qquad f(x) = A\sin(Bx + C)$$

For horizontal shifting, you need to memorize the following rules:

1. **The horizontal shift is equal to $\frac{C}{B}$.** When $B = 1$ (most common on the ACT), the horizonal shift is equal to C.
2. **A positive value of C shifts the function to the left.**
3. **A negative value of C shifts the function to the right.**

Now, we know that seems confusing, so let's see how this works with the functions below.

Solid Line: $f(x) = \sin x$ 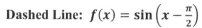 Dashed Line: $f(x) = \sin\left(x - \frac{\pi}{2}\right)$

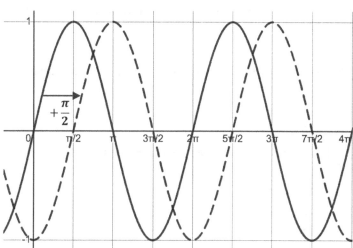

What To Notice

- Horizonal Shift of $\frac{\pi}{2}$ units to the right.

- Negative value of C, so the function shifts to the right.

- Horizontal shifts change the where the function is at $x = 0$. Normally, the sine function passes through the origin. However, if the function shifts horizontally, it may no longer pass through the origin (as seen with the dashed line here)

Horizontal shifts are the least common type of transformation with sine and cosine functions on the ACT.

Summary of Transformation Rules for Sine and Cosine Functions

All the transformation rules we have covered in this chapter are summarized below:

$$y = A\cos(Bx + C) + D \qquad y = A\sin(Bx + C) + D$$

- $|A|$ is the amplitude of the function (half of the total height of the graph).

- The period of the function for sine, cosine, secant, and cosecant is equal to $\left|\frac{2\pi}{B}\right|$. For tangent and cotangent graphs, the period is equal to $\left|\frac{\pi}{B}\right|$.

- **C shifts the graph horizontally.** A positive value of C shifts the graph left, and a negative value of C shifts the graph to the right. The magnitude of the shift is equal to $\frac{C}{B}$.

- **D shifts the graph vertically.** A positive value of D shifts the graph up, and a negative value of D shifts the graph down. The magnitude of the shift is equal to D.

Graphing Tangent Functions

Tangent functions are very rarely tested on the ACT, but they have appeared on the test before and will appear again. **You should only study this if you feel confident on the other trigonometry topics or are aiming for a top ACT Math score.**

Tangent functions look quite different from the sine and cosine functions we just learned, but if you know what a tangent function generally looks like, you should be able to answer any tangent graphing questions correctly on test day.

$$y = \tan x$$

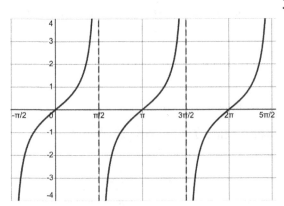

Basics To Know

- Tangent functions cross the origin.
- Tangent functions do not have an amplitude.
- Tangent functions have vertical asymptotes (shown as dotted lines in the graph) that occur regularly π units apart.
- Tangent functions repeat infinitely in both directions.

*Note that the "basics to know" listed above are for $y = \tan x$. Horizontal and vertical shifts can change the characteristics of a tangent function.

Period of Tangent Functions

The period of a tangent function is defined by $\left|\frac{\pi}{B}\right|$, where B is the constant that x is multiplied by in the function.

$$f(x) = \tan(Bx)$$

Using the graph above, notice that the period is equal to π. The easiest way to find the period of a tangent function is to find the distance between the vertical asymptotes.

Transformations of Tangent Functions

Tangent functions follow the same rules as sine and cosine functions for vertical and horizontal shifting that we summarized on the previous page.

That covers pretty much everything you need to know for tangent graphs on the ACT! If you know the basics of what a tangent graph looks like, how to find the period of a tangent function, and the rules for vertical and horizontal shifting, you should be able to solve a tangent graphing question if it appears on your ACT.

Example 11: Which of the following equations properly describes the function shown below?

A. $y = \tan 2x - 1$
B. $y = \tan 4x - 1$
C. $y = \tan x - 2$
D. $y = \tan\frac{x}{2} - 1$
E. $y = \tan\frac{x}{4} - 2$

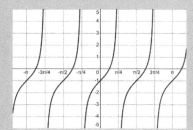

Solution: To solve, we need to find (1) the vertical shift and (2) the period.

The vertical shift is the easier part, so we will start with that. A tangent function normally intersects the origin, but we see the tangent function passing through the point $(0, -1)$. Therefore, we know the function is shifted down 1 unit, so we must see -1 as the D-value. We can eliminate answer choices C and E because the vertical shift is incorrect.

To find the period of a tangent function, we find the distance between two vertical asymptotes. We see two vertical asymptotes at $x = -\frac{\pi}{4}$ and $x = \frac{\pi}{4}$, so we know the period of the function is $\frac{\pi}{2}$.

Now that we know the period, we need to use the B-values in the answer choices to find which one has a period of $\frac{\pi}{2}$. Remember, we use $\left|\frac{\pi}{B}\right|$ to find the period for tangent functions, not $\left|\frac{2\pi}{B}\right|$!

For $y = \tan 2x - 1$, $B = 2$ so

$Period = \left|\frac{\pi}{2}\right| = \frac{\pi}{2}$

For $y = \tan 4x - 1$, $B = 4$ so

$Period = \left|\frac{\pi}{4}\right| = \frac{\pi}{4}$

For $y = \tan\frac{x}{2} - 1$, $B = \frac{1}{2}$ so

$Period = \left|\frac{\pi}{1/2}\right| = = 2\pi$

The answer is A.

Questions like this have only appeared at the end of ACTs as part of the hard questions from 45-60 and are not common. If you are preparing for test day in a more of a rush, graphing tangents is not an important topic to prioritize.

For students who are aiming for top scores, make sure you understand how to solve a question like this, as it is not too technically hard if you understand the basics.

Advanced Trigonometry

The ACT LOVES to test you on two advanced trigonometry rules: Law of Sines and Law of Cosines. Many of you will have never learned these before, so we will teach you everything you need to know in this chapter. **These two topics are very common on the ACT, so you need to memorize both the law of sines and law of cosines equations for test day.**

Law of Sines

The Law of Sines rules written below is true for any type of triangle. **It is important to note that Law of Sines can be used for non-right triangles.**

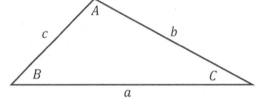

$$\frac{\sin(A)}{a} = \frac{\sin(B)}{b} = \frac{\sin(C)}{c}$$

The Law of Sines is a property for any triangle. For Law of Sines (and Law of Cosines), we no longer use SOH-CAH-TOA. So, for the sines in the equation above, do not think opposite over hypotenuse. Instead, remember that an expression such as $\sin(20°)$ has a numerical value, so we treat it as a number.

Law of Sines can also be written as:

$$\frac{a}{\sin(A)} = \frac{b}{\sin(B)} = \frac{c}{\sin(C)}$$

This equation is the same as the one above – everything is just flipped. **You can memorize and use either equation**. Both are equally effective. You need to memorize the equation because the ACT does not always give it to you on the test.

We use the Law of Sines to solve for an unknown side or angle in a triangle.

Example 12: Which of the following correctly solve for the value of x in the triangle below?

A) $850 \sin(28°)$
B) $\dfrac{\sin(110°)}{850\sin(28°)}$
C) $850 \sin(110°) \sin(28°)$
D) $\dfrac{850}{\tan(110°)}$
E) $\dfrac{850\sin(28°)}{\sin(110°)}$

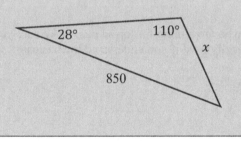

Solution: When solving Law of Sines questions, we want to look for pairs of angles and opposite side lengths. Here, we have two pairs: 110° and 850 and 28° and x. To solve, we set up the Law of Sines equation.

$$\frac{\sin(110°)}{850} = \frac{\sin(28°)}{x}$$

Now, we solve for x. To do so, we first cross-multiply and then divide by $\sin(110°)$.

$$x \sin(110°) = 850 \sin(28°)$$

$$x = \frac{850 \sin(28°)}{\sin(110°)}$$

The answer is E.

Note: For Law of Sines questions on the ACT, the answer choices usually give away that you need to use Law of Sines. If you ever see answer choices like the ones in Example 12, you are looking at a Law of Sines question. Most questions do not ask you to solve for a numerical value. Usually, you are asked to find which expression in the answer choices correctly solves for the unknown as we did in the example above.

That first example was a simpler example, as we were asked to solve for a side length. What if we were asked to solve for an angle instead?

Example 13: In the triangle shown below, which of the following expressions correctly solves for k?

A. $\sin^{-1}\left(\frac{125\sin(86°)}{92}\right)$

B. $\sin^{-1}\left(\frac{92\sin(86°)}{125}\right)$

C. $\sin^{-1}(92\sin(86°) - 125)$

D. $\sin^{-1}\left(\frac{101}{92}\right)$

E. $\sin^{-1}\left(\frac{92}{125}\right)$

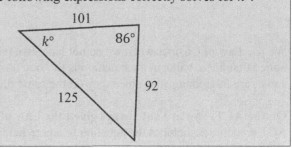

Solution: We have two pairs of sides and angles to use in the Law of Sines equation: $k°$ and 92 and 86° and 125. To solve, we start by setting up the Law of Sines equation.

$$\frac{\sin(k°)}{92} = \frac{\sin(86°)}{125}$$

We want to solve for k, so first we need to multiply both sides by 92.

$$\sin(k°) = \frac{92\sin(86°)}{125}$$

Ok, now for the fun (hard) part! We know what $\sin(k°)$ is equal to, so to solve for k we need to use the inverse sine function. If you need to review inverse functions, we covered them on page 148.

$$k = \sin^{-1}\left(\frac{92\sin(86°)}{125}\right)$$

The answer is B. Now if you are thinking, woah, that was hard! Yes, it absolutely was. Questions like this are often some that students find most difficult on the ACT. A question like Example 13 would be one that is meant to challenge the best math students. If you have never done any of this advanced trigonometry before and find this extremely difficult, you can always skip these questions on test day and save them for last.

Law of Cosines

As with the Law of Sines rules we just learned, the Law of Cosines is a property of any triangle. **Law of Cosines is used to find a missing side or angle in a non-right triangle.** The Law of Cosines equation is show below:

$$a^2 = b^2 + c^2 - 2bc\cos(A)$$

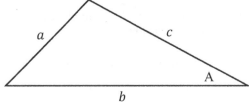

We use Law of Cosines when we do not have two pairs of angles and opposite side lengths. It is important to notice that the a-value in the equation is the side length opposite the angle A. The other two side lengths, b and c, are interchangeable since they do the same thing in the equation.

On the ACT, you are not always given the Law of Cosines, so you need to memorize the equation. The ACT sometimes includes the equation in a note below the question, but it is not always provided.

You need to know how to set up the Law of Cosines correctly. Depending on the difficult of the question, you may need to perform additional algebra to solve for the unknown value, as we did in the Law of Sines examples.

Example 14: Three dancers, Alex, Bialy, and Charlie, are standing on stage at the points shown by the corners of the triangle below. Alex is standing 35 feet from Bialy, 31 feet from Charlie, and the angle formed where Alex is standing has a measure of 28°. Which of the following equations solves for the distance, in feet, between Bialy and Charlie?

A. $35 \sin 28°$

B. $31 \tan 28°$

C. $\frac{31}{\cos 28°} + 35$

D. $\sqrt{35^2 + 31^2 - 2(35)(31)\cos 28°}$

E. $\sqrt{-\frac{35^2 - 31^2}{2(35)(31)\cos(28°)}}$

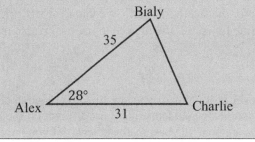

Solution: For this question, we must use Law of Cosines. The triangle is not a right triangle, so we cannot use normal SOH-CAH-TOA. We are not provided two pairs of angles and opposite side lengths, so we cannot use Law of Sines.

The side length we are solving for is opposite the angle that we are given, so the length between Bialy and Charlie is the a-value. 35 and 31 are b and c. Plugging these values into the Law of Cosines equation, we get:

$$a^2 = 35^2 + 31^2 - 2(35)(31)\cos 28°$$

To solve for a, we take the square root of both sides.

$$a = \sqrt{35^2 + 31^2 - 2(35)(31)\cos 28°}$$

The answer is D.

*****Note:** For Law of Cosines questions on the ACT, the answer choices usually give away that you need to use Law of Cosines. If you see any complicated looking answer choices with cosines, like D and E in Example 14, you are looking at a Law of Cosines question.

Unit Circle

Remember the unit circle? The one your math teacher made you memorize all of those points for? Well, it's back. However, **the unit circle is NOT a commonly tested topic on the ACT (and the least commonly tested trigonometry topic). You should only study this if you feel confident on the other trigonometry topics or are aiming for a top ACT Math score.**

You do not need to memorize all the points but should know the basics of the unit circle for the ACT. **For students aiming for top math scores, we recommend memorizing the entire unit circle.**

A complete unit circle is shown below.

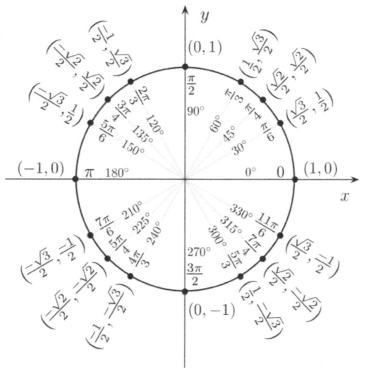

Angles on the unit circle can be expressed in degrees or radians. Just as we can describe the temperature in Fahrenheit or Celsius, we can describe an angle in degree or radians. If you have not worked with radians before, all you need to know is that **π radians = 180 degrees**. It is important to memorize this conversion for test day.

There are a few important principles to know with the unit circle.

1. **The cosine of any angle on the unit circle is equal to the *x*-coordinate of the corresponding point.** For example, $\cos(60°) = \frac{1}{2}$.

2. **The sine of any angle on the unit circle is equal to the *y*-coordinate of the corresponding point.** For example, $\sin(60°) = \frac{\sqrt{3}}{2}$.

3. **The tangent of any angle on the unit circle is equal to $\frac{y-coordinate}{x-coordinate}$.** For example, $\tan(60°) = \frac{\sqrt{3}/2}{1/2}$, which simplifies to $\tan(60°) = \sqrt{3}$.

Understanding these three principles and memorizing the unit circle can make many unit circle questions easy.

Example 15: On the interval $0 \leq \theta < 2\pi$, $\sin \theta = \frac{\sqrt{2}}{2}$ is true for what value(s) of θ?

A. $\frac{\pi}{4}, \frac{5\pi}{4}$ B. $\frac{\pi}{4}, \frac{3\pi}{4}$ C. $\frac{\pi}{4}, \frac{7\pi}{4}$ D. $\frac{\pi}{4}$ E. $\frac{\pi}{2}, \frac{3\pi}{2}$

Solution: For this question, we need to find the values of θ, in radians, on the unit circle for which $\sin \theta = \frac{\sqrt{2}}{2}$. The interval from $0 \leq \theta < 2\pi$ includes the entire unit circle, but sometimes the ACT limits which portion of the unit circle we should look at with a smaller interval.

Remember, the sine of any angle is equal to the y-coordinate of the point. So, we need to look at the unit circle and find the point(s) that have $\frac{\sqrt{2}}{2}$ as the y-coordinate. If we look at the unit circle (or have it memorized), we see that $\frac{\pi}{4}$ and $\frac{3\pi}{4}$ have $\frac{\sqrt{2}}{2}$ as the y-coordinate, so we know

$$\sin \frac{\pi}{4} = \frac{\sqrt{2}}{2} \quad \text{and} \quad \sin \frac{3\pi}{4} = \frac{\sqrt{2}}{2}$$

The answer is B.

The other important thing to know for the unit circle is which quadrants cosine, sine, and tangent are positive or negative. The unit circle below shows the values (positive or negative) for cosine, sine, and tangent.

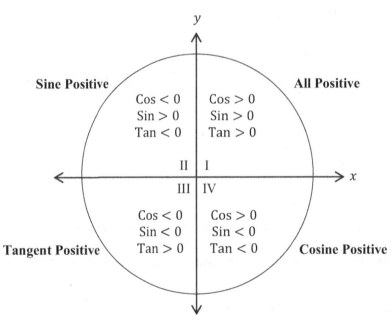

A common moniker to memorize this is "**A**ll **S**tudent **T**ake **C**alculus." "**All**" tells us all 3 values are positive in the 1st quadrant. "**S**tudents" stands for **S**ine and tells us only sine is positive in the 2nd quadrant and the other values are negative. "**T**ake" stands for **T**angent and tells us only tangent is positive in the 3rd quadrant. "**C**alculus" tells us only **C**osine is positive in the 4th quadrant.

The most common way the ACT tests this knowledge is with a more advanced version of Example 3 that we solved earlier in this chapter.

> **Example 16:** For an angle with a measure of q in a right triangle, $\sin q = \frac{9}{15}$ and $\tan q = -\frac{9}{12}$, what is the value of $\cos q$?
>
> A. $-\frac{12}{15}$ B. $-\frac{12}{9}$ C. $\frac{12}{9}$ D. $\frac{15}{9}$ E. $\frac{12}{15}$

Solution: This question is identical to Example 3 except that $\tan q$ is now negative instead of positive? How does that change the question? Well, since $\sin > 0$ and $\tan < 0$, we know that q must be in the 2nd quadrant. In the 2nd quadrant, $\cos < 0$, so we already know that C, D, and E are incorrect.

The rest of the solution is the same as we already did for Example 3, so we will not show it again here. The only difference is that when we solve for $\cos q = \frac{12}{15}$ from the triangle we drew, we make the value negative since we are in the 2nd quadrant, so **the answer is A**.

PrepPros

Trigonometry Practice Problems: Answers on page 329.

1. The side lengths of a triangle are given in the figure below. What is $\sin C$?

   A. $\frac{12}{6}$
   B. $\frac{6}{9}$
   C. $\frac{9}{6}$
   D. $\frac{6}{12}$ ⊙
   E. $\frac{9}{12}$

   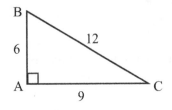

2. Two of the side lengths of a right triangle are given in the figure below. What is $\cos C$?

   A. $\frac{3}{5}$
   B. $\frac{5}{3}$
   C. $\frac{5}{4}$
   D. $\frac{4}{5}$ ⊙
   E. $\frac{4}{3}$

3. For an angle with measure θ, $\sin \theta = \frac{12}{13}$ and $\cos \theta = \frac{5}{13}$. What is the value of $\tan \theta$?

   SOH CAH TOA
   $\frac{12}{5}$

   A. $\frac{5}{12}$
   B. $\frac{13}{12}$
   C. $\frac{12}{5}$ ⊙
   D. $\frac{5}{13}$
   E. $\frac{13}{5}$

4. The side lengths of a triangle are given below. Which of the following expressions gives the measure of the angle θ ?

   A. $\tan^{-1}\left(\frac{5}{12}\right)$
   B. $\tan^{-1}\left(\frac{5}{13}\right)$
   C. $\sin^{-1}\left(\frac{5}{13}\right)$
   D. $\tan^{-1}\left(\frac{12}{5}\right)$ ⊙
   E. $\cos^{-1}\left(\frac{12}{13}\right)$

   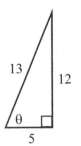

5. If $\sin \theta = 0.8$ then in the triangle below, what is the value of x?

   A. 3.6
   B. 14.4 ⊙
   C. 21.6
   D. 22.5
   E. 24

   $\frac{x}{18} = .8$

   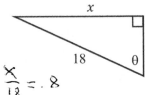

6. The figure below shows a 7-foot ladder leaning against a vertical wall. The ladder makes a 47° angle. Which of the following expressions gives the height where the top of the ladder hits the wall?

   A. $7 \cos 47°$
   B. $7 \tan 47°$
   C. $7 \sin 47°$ ⊙
   D. $\frac{7}{\cos 47°}$
   E. $\frac{7}{\sin 47°}$

   $\sin 47 = \frac{x}{7}$
   $7 \sin 47$

   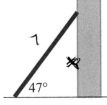

7. The triangle below has side lengths given in meters:

Which of the following expressions is equal to x?

A. $18 \sin 68°$
B. $18 \tan 68°$
C. $\dfrac{18}{\sin 68°}$
D. $\dfrac{18}{\tan 68°}$
E. $\dfrac{18}{\cos 68°}$

8. $5\sin^2\theta + 5\cos^2\theta = x$

For the function above, what is the value of x?

A. -5
B. 1
C. 5
D. 8
E. 10

9. A right triangle is shown in the figure below. What is the value for $\cos C$?

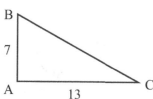

A. $\dfrac{7}{13}$
B. $\dfrac{13}{7}$
C. $\dfrac{13}{\sqrt{218}}$
D. $\dfrac{7}{\sqrt{218}}$
E. $\dfrac{\sqrt{218}}{13}$

10. $y = 0.75 \tan(\pi x) - 3.75$

What is the period for the function above?

A. 0.75
B. 1
C. 1.5
D. 2
E. π

11. Which expression correctly solves for the measure of angle θ in the figure below?

A. $\sin^{-1}\left(\dfrac{17}{15}\right)$
B. $\sin^{-1}\left(\dfrac{15}{17}\right)$
C. $\cos^{-1}\left(\dfrac{17}{8}\right)$
D. $\tan^{-1}\left(\dfrac{8}{15}\right)$
E. $\tan^{-1}\left(\dfrac{15}{17}\right)$

12. For the function $y = -5\sin(2.5x) + 12$, what is the amplitude?

A. -12
B. -5
C. 1
D. 2.5
E. 5

13. If $0° < \theta < 180°$ and $\tan\theta = \dfrac{5}{12}$, then $\sin\theta = ?$

A. $-\dfrac{5}{13}$
B. $-\dfrac{12}{13}$
C. $\dfrac{5}{13}$
D. $\dfrac{5}{12}$
E. $\dfrac{12}{13}$

14. $g(x) = -2\csc(6x) + 7$

What is the period for the function $g(x)$?

A. -2
B. $\frac{\pi}{3}$
C. $\frac{2\pi}{3}$
D. 2
E. 3π

15.

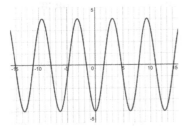

The graph above shows the function $p(x) = q\cos(x)$. What is the amplitude for the $p(x)$?

A. -4
B. -1
C. 1
D. 4
E. 12

16. If $90° < \theta < 180°$ and $\sin\theta = \frac{8}{17}$, then $\cos\theta = ?$

A. $-\frac{17}{15}$
B. $-\frac{15}{17}$
C. $-\frac{8}{17}$
D. $\frac{8}{15}$
E. $\frac{15}{17}$

17. If $\sin^2\theta = \frac{9}{11}$, what does $\cos^2\theta$ equal?

A. $\frac{-9}{11}$
B. $\frac{2}{11}$
C. $\frac{3}{\sqrt{11}}$
D. $\frac{6}{11}$
E. $\frac{11}{9}$

18. What is the sum of the amplitude and period of the function $y = \frac{5}{2}\sin\left(\frac{x}{2} + 10\right) + 1$?

A. $\frac{5}{2} + 4\pi$
B. $\frac{5}{2} + \frac{\pi}{2}$
C. $10 + 4\pi$
D. $10 + \frac{\pi}{2}$
E. $\frac{25}{2}$

19. The function $f(x)$ and three points on the function are shown below.

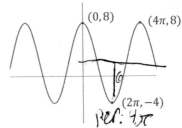

Which of the following equations correctly described the function $f(x)$?

A. $y = 12\sin 2x$
B. $y = 6\sin\frac{x}{2}$
C. $y = 12\cos 2x$
D. $y = 6\cos\frac{x}{2}$
E. $y = 6\cos 2x$

20. If angle A is equal to $520°$, then which of the following expresses $\frac{A}{2}$ in terms of radians?

A. $\frac{26}{9}\pi$
B. $\frac{13}{9}\pi$
C. $\frac{9}{13}\pi$
D. $\frac{9}{4}\pi$
E. $\frac{8}{9}\pi$

Chapter 17: Trigonometry

21. The lengths of the sides of the triangle below are given in feet. Which of the following gives the measure of θ?

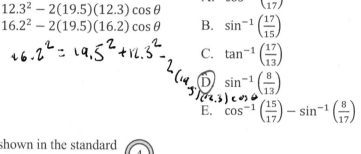

side opposite θ, Not "a"
$a^2 = b^2 + c^2 - 2bc\cos\theta$

A. $19.5^2 = 12.3^2 + 16.2^2 - 2(12.3)(16.2)\cos\theta$
B. $16.2^2 = 19.5^2 + 12.3^2 - 2(19.5)(12.3)\cos\theta$
C. $12.3^2 = 19.5^2 + 16.2^2 - 2(19.5)(16.2)\cos\theta$
D. $\tan\theta = \frac{12.3}{16.2}$
E. $\cos\theta = \frac{12.3}{19.5}$

$16.2^2 = 19.5^2 + 12.3^2 - 2(19.5)(12.3)\cos\theta$

22. A tangent function is shown in the standard (x, y) coordinate plane below.

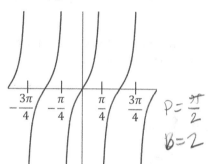

$P = \frac{\pi}{2}$
$b = 2$

Which of the following equations correctly represents this function?

A. $y = \tan 4x$
B. $y = \tan 2x$
C. $y = \tan x$
D. $y = \tan \frac{x}{2}$
E. $y = \tan \frac{x}{4}$

23. In the triangle below, point D is 15 units from point C. Which of the following expressions is equal to the measure of angle B?

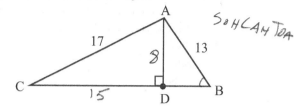

SOHCAHTOA

A. $\cos^{-1}\left(\frac{13}{17}\right)$
B. $\sin^{-1}\left(\frac{17}{15}\right)$
C. $\tan^{-1}\left(\frac{17}{13}\right)$
D. $\sin^{-1}\left(\frac{8}{13}\right)$
E. $\cos^{-1}\left(\frac{15}{17}\right) - \sin^{-1}\left(\frac{8}{17}\right)$

24. Andrew is standing in the front corner of the end zone. His friend Sam is standing on the same sideline at the 45-yard line. Both of them are trying to throw a football into a trashcan placed in the middle of the field as shown below.

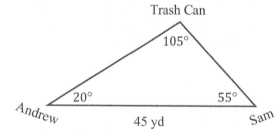

Which of the following solves for how many yards Andrew has to throw the football for it to land in the trash can?

A. $\frac{\sin(105°)}{45}$
B. $45\cos(55°)$
C. $\frac{45\sin(105°)}{\sin(55°)}$
D. $\frac{\sin(55°)}{45\sin(20°)}$
E. $\frac{45\sin(55°)}{\sin(105°)}$

$\frac{\sin 55}{x} = \frac{\sin 105}{45}$

$45 \sin 55 = x \sin 105$

- 167 -

25. Kim is standing 15 feet from a basketball hoop that is 17 feet from Jodie, as shown in the figure below, in which the measure of an angle is given. Which of the following equations, when solved, gives the distance between Kim and Jodie?

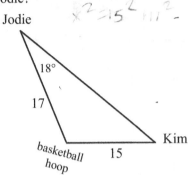

A. $15^2 = x^2 + 17^2 - 2x(17)(\cos 18°)$
B. $15^2 = x^2 + 17^2 - 2(15)(17)(\cos 18°)$
C. $17^2 = x^2 + 15^2 - 2x(17)(\cos 18°)$
D. $x^2 = 15^2 + 17^2 - 2x(17)(\cos 18°)$
E. $x^2 = 15^2 + 17^2 - 2(15)(17)(\cos 18°)$

26. The functions $y = \sin x$ and $y = \sin(x - a) - b$, where a and b are constants, are graphed in the standard (x, y) coordinate plane below. The functions have the same maximum value. Which of the following statements about a and b is true?

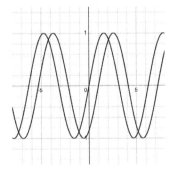

A. $a < 0$ and $b > 0$
B. $a > 0$ and $b < 0$
C. $a = 0$ and $b > 0$
D. $a < 0$ and $b = 0$
E. $a = 0$ and $b = 0$

27. The diagram below shows three friends who are spaced out throwing a frisbee in a field. All distances are displayed in feet. Which of the following expressions is equal to the distance, in feet, between Jamal and Aditya?

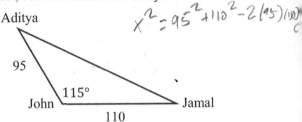

A. $\dfrac{205}{\cos 115°}$
B. $\dfrac{205}{\cos 115°} + 110$
C. $\dfrac{205}{\sin 115°} + 95$
D. $\sqrt{95^2 + 110^2 - 2(95)(110)\cos 115°}$
E. $\sqrt{95^2 + 110^2 - 2(95)(110)\cos 65°}$

28. On the interval $0 < \theta < 2\pi$, for what value(s) of θ does $\tan \theta = -1$?

A. $\dfrac{3\pi}{4}$
B. $\dfrac{3\pi}{4}$ and $\dfrac{7\pi}{4}$
C. $\dfrac{\pi}{2}$ and $\dfrac{3\pi}{2}$
D. $\dfrac{5\pi}{4}$ and $\dfrac{7\pi}{4}$
E. $\dfrac{7\pi}{4}$

29. A triangular field has been set up for grazing cows. All lengths are in meters. What is the area of the field below in square meters?

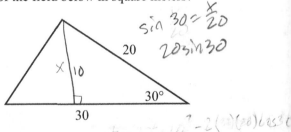

A. 150
B. 180
C. 200
D. 300
E. 600

30. In the figure below, the distances between 2 cabins are shown as well as the angle formed at the campground. Which of the following values is closest to the distance, in feet, from Cabin A to Cabin B?
(Note $\cos 113° \approx -0.39$; $\sin 113° \approx 0.92$)

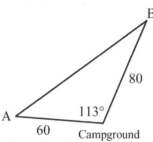

A. 96
B. 100
C. 117
D. 122
E. 140

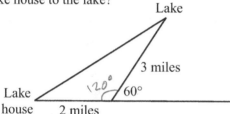

31. The figure below shows a map of Josiah's lake house and pathways to get to the lake. Which of the following expressions represents the straight-line distance, in miles, from Josiah's lake house to the lake?

A. $\dfrac{2\sin(120°)}{3\sin(30°)}$
B. $\dfrac{3\sin(120°)}{2\sin(30°)}$
C. $\sqrt{2^2 + 3^2 - 2(2)(3)\cos(30°)}$
D. $\sqrt{2^2 + 3^2 - 2(2)(3)\cos(60°)}$
E. $\sqrt{2^2 + 3^2 - 2(2)(3)\cos(120°)}$

32. For every angle θ, measured in radians, which of the following is equal to $\cos(2\pi + \theta)$?

A. $\cos(\pi - \theta)$
B. $\cos\theta$
C. $\cos\left(\dfrac{\pi}{2} - \theta\right)$
D. $\cos\left(\dfrac{3\pi}{4} - \theta\right)$
E. $\cos(\pi + \theta)$

33. Which of the following equations when solved would give the value of x, in feet, of the missing side length of the triangle below?

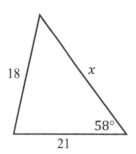

A. $18^2 = x^2 + 21^2 - 2x(18)(\cos 58°)$
B. $18^2 = x^2 + 21^2 - 2x(21)(\cos 58°)$
C. $21^2 = x^2 + 18^2 - 2x(18)(\cos 58°)$
D. $x^2 = 18^2 + 21^2 - 2x(21)(\cos 58°)$
E. $x^2 = 18^2 + 21^2 - 2(18)(21)(\cos 58°)$

34. In the figure below, the given side lengths of △ABC are in inches. Which of the following is the closest to the area, in square inches of △ABC?

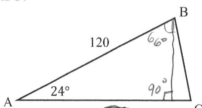

A. 3,295
B. 3,600
C. 6,580
D. 8,100
E. 16,200

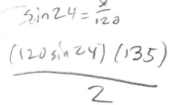

35. In the figure below, BE bisects ∠ACD. What is the length of AB on the figure below?

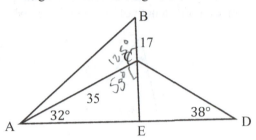

A. $\dfrac{35 \sin 38°}{\sin 32°}$

B. $\dfrac{35 \sin 110°}{\sin 32°}$

C. $\dfrac{35 \sin 55°}{\sin 32°}$

D. $\sqrt{35^2 + 17^2 - 2(35)(17)\cos 110°}$

E. $\sqrt{35^2 + 17^2 - 2(35)(17)\cos 125°}$

36. Given that $3 \sin a = 3$ and $4 \cos(\tfrac{\pi}{4} - b) = 4$. Which of the following could be a value, in radians, of $a + b$?

A. 0
B. $\dfrac{\pi}{4}$
C. $\dfrac{\pi}{2}$
D. $\dfrac{3\pi}{4}$
E. π

37. Consider the family of functions $f(x) = 3 \sin x + c$, where c is a real number. Which of the following inequalities represents the graph of all the possible values of c for which the graph of $f(x)$ has no x-intercepts?

A. $c \geq 3$
B. $c > 3$
C. $-3 < c < 3$
D. $|c| < 3$
E. $|c| > 3$

38. As shown below, James walks 570 feet due east of the entrance to the zoo and stopped at the snack stand and then walks 370 feet in a straight line 55° north of east to the big cat exhibit. Which of the following expressions is equal to the distance, in feet, between the entrance and the big cat exhibit?

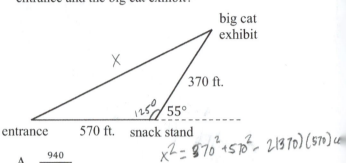

A. $\dfrac{940}{\cos 55°}$

B. $\dfrac{370}{\cos 55°} + 570$

C. $\dfrac{370}{\sin 125°} + 570$

D. $\sqrt{370^2 + 570^2 - 2(370)(570) \cos 55°}$

E. $\sqrt{370^2 + 570^2 - 2(370)(570) \cos 125°}$

39. In triangle ABC shown below, the given side lengths are in feet. Which of the following expressions gives the area, in square feet, of triangle ABC?

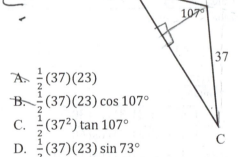

A. $\tfrac{1}{2}(37)(23)$

B. $\tfrac{1}{2}(37)(23) \cos 107°$

C. $\tfrac{1}{2}(37^2) \tan 107°$

D. $\tfrac{1}{2}(37)(23) \sin 73°$

E. $\sqrt{23^2 + 37^2 - 2(23)(37) \cos 107°}$

40. A sine function is shown in the standard (x, y) coordinate plane below.

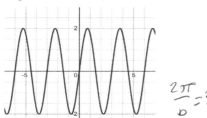

One of the following equations represents this function. Which one?

A. $y = 2\sin\left(\frac{2}{3}\pi x\right)$
B. $y = 2\sin\left(\frac{3}{2}\pi x\right)$
C. $y = 2\sin\left(\frac{2}{3}x\right)$
D. $y = 3\sin\left(\frac{2}{3}\pi x\right)$
E. $y = 3\sin(2x)$

41. Deshaun is backpacking and needs to find the length of $\overline{BC}$. The measurements of which side lengths and angles are sufficient for Deshaun to determine the length of $\overline{BC}$ using law of sines?

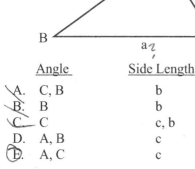

	Angle	Side Length
A.	C, B	b
B.	B	b
C.	C	c, b
D.	A, B	c
E.	A, C	c

42. The sides of an acute triangle measure 9 feet, 10 feet, and 12 feet. Which of the following equations solves for the largest angle in the triangle?

A. $9^2 = 10^2 + 11^2 - 2(10)(11)\sin x$
B. $9^2 = 10^2 + 11^2 - 2(10)(11)\cos x$
C. $12^2 = 9^2 + 10^2 - 2(9)(10)\sin x$
D. $12^2 = 9^2 + 10^2 - 2(9)(10)\cos x$
E. $10^2 = 9^2 + 12^2 - 2(9)(12)\cos x$

43. The figure below shows a drone. At a certain moment, the drone forms an angle of elevation 65° from point A on the ground. At the same moment, the angle of elevation of the drone from point B, 170 feet from A on level ground is 57°. Which of the following is closest to the length, in feet, of the straight-line distance from point B to the drone?

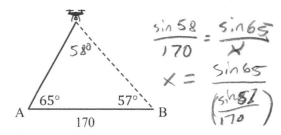

A. 152
B. 160
C. 182
D. 184
E. 205

44. In the figure below, which of the following expressions correctly solves for $\angle ABD$?

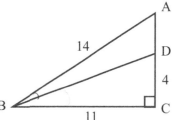

A. $\sin^{-1}\left(\frac{4}{14}\right)$
B. $\cos^{-1}\left(\frac{11}{14}\right)$
C. $\sin^{-1}\left(\frac{4}{14}\right) - \cos^{-1}\left(\frac{11}{14}\right)$
D. $\cos^{-1}\left(\frac{11}{14}\right) - \tan^{-1}\left(\frac{4}{11}\right)$
E. $\cos^{-1}\left(\frac{11}{14}\right) - \sin^{-1}\left(\frac{4}{11}\right)$

45. A team of researchers is installing motion capture cameras on the perimeter of a portion of the Sequoia National Park to study the number of black bears in the area. If motion cameras are installed every 40 feet, which of the following equations solves for the total number of motion cameras that will be installed?

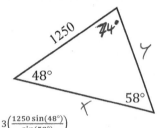

A. $\dfrac{3\left(\dfrac{1250\sin(48°)}{\sin(58°)}\right)}{40}$

B. $\dfrac{1250 + 1250\sin(48°) + 1250\sin(58°)}{40}$

C. $\dfrac{1250 + \left(\dfrac{1250\sin(48°)}{\sin(58°)}\right) + \left(\dfrac{1250(\sin 74°)}{\sin(58°)}\right)}{40}$

D. $\dfrac{1250 + \left(\dfrac{1250\sin(58°)}{\sin(48°)}\right) + \left(\dfrac{1250(\sin 58°)}{\sin(74°)}\right)}{40}$

E. $1250 + \left(\dfrac{1250\sin(48°)}{\sin(58°)}\right) + \left(\dfrac{1250(\sin 74°)}{\sin(58°)}\right)$

46. In an acute triangle with side lengths 19, 17, and 10, the largest angle is 83°. Which of the following expressions correctly solves for the smallest angle?

A. $\sin^{-1}\left(\dfrac{19\sin(83°)}{10}\right)$

B. $\sin^{-1}\left(\dfrac{10\sin(83°)}{19}\right)$

C. $\sin^{-1}\left(\dfrac{17\sin(83°)}{19}\right)$

D. $\sin^{-1}\left(\dfrac{19}{17}\right)$

E. $\sin^{-1}\left(\dfrac{10}{19}\right)$

Chapter 18: Absolute Value

Absolute value is defined as a number's distance from zero. Since a distance can never be negative, **the absolute value is always positive.**

$$|3| = 3 \text{ (3 is three units from zero)}$$

$$|-3| = 3 \text{ (}-3 \text{ is three units from zero)}$$

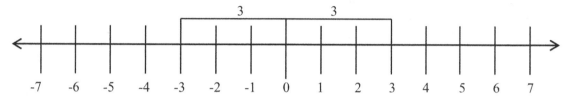

For equations with absolute value bars, complete any math inside the absolute value bars first. Then, solve the rest of the equation. For example, to solve

$$|3 - 7| + 2$$

start by working inside the absolute value bars to get

$$|-4| + 2$$

$|-4| = 4$, so the equation becomes $4 + 2 = 6$.

> **Example 1:** What is the value of $|2 + 11| - 2|3 - 5|$?
>   A. 9   B. 13   C. 17   D. 22   E. 28

Solution: We start by working inside the absolute value bars. The equation becomes

$$a = |13| - 2|-2|$$

$|13| = 13$ and $|-2| = 2$, so we get

$$a = 13 - 2(2)$$
$$a = 9$$

The answer is A.

Absolute Value and Unknown Variables

What if there is a variable inside the absolute value bars? Let's consider the equation below.

$$|x - 3| = 5$$

For any equation like this, **there will be two answers.** Since $|5| = 5$ and $|-5| = 5$, we need to solve for the values of x when $x - 3 = 5$ and $x - 3 = -5$.

$$x - 3 = 5 \qquad\qquad x - 3 = -5$$
$$x = 8 \qquad\qquad x = -2$$

Both $x = -2$ and $x = 8$ are correct answers.

For any question with an unknown variable inside the absolute value bar, there will be multiple solutions. There are three steps to solve these questions.

1. Move all terms outside of the absolute value bars to the right side of the equation.

2. Set the expression inside the absolute value bar equal to the positive value (1st equation) and negative value (2nd equation) of the number on the right side.

3. Solve the equations to get the values of the unknown variable.

Example 2: What is the solution set to the equation $|2x + 1| - 6 = 11$?
   A. $\{-9\}$ B. $\{8\}$ C. $\{2, 8\}$ D. $\{-3, 2\}$ E. $\{-9, 8\}$

Solution: First, we need to move terms outside of the absolute value bars to the right side, so we add 6 to both sides to get
$$|2x + 1| = 17$$
Next, we set the expression inside the absolute value bars equal to 17 and -17 and solve.

$$2x + 1 = 17 \qquad\qquad 2x + 1 = -17$$
$$2x = 16 \qquad\qquad 2x = -18$$
$$x = 8 \qquad\qquad x = -9$$

The answer is E. Notice here that there are two solutions! As we stated earlier, this will always be the case when the unknown variable is inside the absolute value bars.

Absolute Value and Inequalities

Absolute value with inequalities questions are the most difficult type of absolute value question you will face on the ACT. Whenever solving these questions, **the solution is an interval**. To see how this works, let's start with a simple example:
$$|x| < 3$$
We need to find all x-values that are less than 3 units away from zero in either direction. On a number line, this is all points that are less than $+3$ and greater than -3.

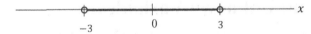

The solution would be the interval $-3 < x < 3$. We do not include $+3$ or -3 because they are exactly 3 units from zero and not less than 3 units from zero.

What if instead we had
$$|x| \geq 3$$
Now, we need to find all x-values that are greater than or equal to 3 units from zero in either direction. On a number line, this is all points that are less than or equal to -3 and greater than or equal to $+3$.

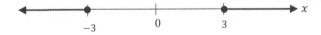

The solution would be the interval $x \leq -3$ and $x \geq 3$. Here, we include the $+3$ and -3 because they are exactly 3 units from zero.

Chapter 18: Absolute Value

For any questions with an unknown in the absolute value bars and an inequality, the solution is an interval. There are 4 steps to solve these questions.

1. **Move all terms outside of the absolute value bars to the right side of the equation.** For example, given $|x + 3| - 2 < 5$, we need to add 2 to both sides to get $|x + 3| < 7$

2. **Determine where on a number line the inequality is true.** For $|x + 3| < 7$, the value in the absolute value bars, $x + 3$, must be greater than -7 and less than $+7$.

3. **Set the expression inside the absolute value bar in an inequality equation(s).** For $|x| < a$ or $|x| \leq a$, set up the equation as $-a < x < a$ or $-a \leq x \leq a$. For $|x| > a$ or $|x| \geq a$, set up the equation as $x < -a$ and $x > a$ or $x \leq -a$ and $x \geq a$. For $|x + 3| < 7$, we set up our inequality equations as $-7 < x + 3 < 7$.

4. **Solve the equations to get the intervals for the unknown variable.** For $-7 < x + 3 < 7$, we solve by subtracting 3 from all terms. The final answer is $-10 < x < 4$.

Example 3: The set of all values of x that satisfies $|x + 3| - 4 < 1$ is the same as the set of all values of x that satisfies:

A. $0 < x < 2$ B. $0 < x < 5$ C. $-2 < x < 2$ D. $-8 < x < 2$ E. $-8 < x < 5$

Solution: First, we need to move all the terms outside of the absolute value bars to the right side. After adding 4 to both sides, we get

$$|x + 3| < 5$$

This tells us that $x + 3$ must be less than 5 units from zero, so on a number line $x + 3$ must be greater than -5 and less than $+5$. We can now set up the inequality and remove the absolute value bars:

$$-5 < x + 3 < 5$$

From here, we just do algebra. To get x by itself, we subtract 3 from all terms and get

$$-8 < x < 2$$

The answer is D.

Example 4: The set of all values of x that satisfies $\left|\frac{1}{2}x + 2\right| > 3$ is the same as the set of all values of x that satisfies:

A. $x < -10$ and $x > 2$ B. $x < -5$ and $x > 5$ C. $x < -10$ and $x > 0$ D. $x > 2$ E. $x < 5$

Solution: All of the numbers outside of the absolute value bars are already on the right side. The equation tells us that $\frac{1}{2}x + 2$ must be greater than 3 units away from zero, so on a number line $\frac{1}{2}x + 2$ must be less than -3 and greater than $+3$. We can now set up the inequalities and remove the absolute value bars:

$$\frac{1}{2}x + 2 < -3 \quad \text{and} \quad \frac{1}{2}x + 2 > 3$$

From here, we just do algebra. First, we need to subtract 2 from both sides to get

$$\frac{1}{2}x < -5 \quad \text{and} \quad \frac{1}{2}x > 1$$

Now, we multiply by 2 and get

$$x < -10 \quad \text{and} \quad x > 2$$

The answer is A.

Absolute Value Practice: Answers on pages 329-330.

1. What is the value of $|8 - 5| - |4 - 8|$?

   A. -9
   B. -1
   C. 0
   D. 3
   E. 7

2. $|5(-3) + 4|$ is equal to:

   A. -11
   B. 4
   C. 11
   D. 17
   E. 19

3. When $x = -7$, $|3x - 4| + 5$ is equal to:

   A. -30
   B. -20
   C. 10
   D. 25
   E. 30

4. What is the solution set to $|x + 4| = 8$?

   A. $x = 4$
   B. $x = -4$
   C. $x = -12$
   D. $x = 4, -12$
   E. $x = 4, -4, -12$

5. The value of one solution to the equation $|9 - x| = 6$ is $x = 3$. What is the value of the other solution?

   A. -6
   B. -3
   C. 6
   D. 12
   E. 15

6. If $x = 4$, $|3x - 6| + |-4x + 8|$ is equal to:

   A. -18
   B. 4
   C. 14
   D. 24
   E. 28

7. What is the solution set to $|3x + 6| > 24$?

   A. $x > 6$
   B. $x < -10$
   C. $x < -10$ and $x > 6$
   D. $x < -6$ and $x > 6$
   E. $x < -6$ and $x > 10$

8. What is the sum of the solutions to the equation $|36 - 3x| = 18$?

   A. -24
   B. -12
   C. 6
   D. 12
   E. 24

9. If x and y are the solutions to the equation $|4a + 4| - 4 = 12$, what is the $|xy|$?

   A. 8
   B. 15
   C. 16
   D. 32
   E. 120

10. If $|a| = -a$, which of the following statements must be true?

    A. $a \leq 0$
    B. $a \geq 0$
    C. $a = 0$
    D. $a \neq 0$
    E. a is not a real number

Chapter 18: Absolute Value

11. For real numbers $a, b,$ and c such that $a > b > c$ where $b < 0$, which of the statements below is(are) always true?

    I. $|a| > |b|$
    II. $|a| > |c|$
    III. $|c| > |b|$

    A. I only
    B. III only
    C. I and II only
    D. I and III only
    E. II and III only

12. If $|4x - 3| + 2 = 15$ and $|5y + 3| = 17$, what is the smallest possible value of xy?

    A. -20
    B. -16
    C. -11
    D. -4
    E. -2.5

13. For some positive integer p, the sum of the absolute values of all integers from $-p$ to p is 30. What is the value of p?

    A. 2
    B. 3
    C. 4
    D. 5
    E. Cannot be determined from the given information

14. For all real numbers $x, y,$ and z, which of the following expressions is equal to $|x - y - z|$?

    A. $|x + y + z|$
    B. $|x + y - z|$
    C. $|x - y + z|$
    D. $|-x + y + z|$
    E. $|-x - y - z|$

15. For real numbers $a, b,$ and c such that $a < b < c$ and $c > 0$, which of the statements below is(are) always true?

    I. $|a| > |b|$
    II. $|c| > |a|$
    III. $\left|\frac{a}{c}\right| > \left|\frac{b}{c}\right|$

    A. I, II, and III
    B. I and III
    C. II and III
    D. I
    E. None of the statements

16. If x and y are real numbers such that $x > 0$ and $y < 0$, which of the following is equivalent to $|x| - |y|$?

    A. $|x - y|$
    B. $|x + y|$
    C. $|x| + |y|$
    D. $x - y$
    E. $x + y$

17. What is the solution set of the equation $\frac{5}{3}|-3x + 1| + 15 < 12$?

    A. $-2 < x < \frac{4}{3}$
    B. $-\frac{4}{3} < x < 2$
    C. $x < \frac{4}{3}$ and $x < -2$
    D. $x > 2$
    E. No solution

18. Which of the following is equivalent to the equation $|2x + 5| + 4 = 7$?

    A. $2x + 5 = 7$
       $2x + 5 = -7$
    B. $2x + 5 = 3$
       $2x + 5 = -11$
    C. $2x + 5 = 3$
       $-(2x + 5) = 3$
    D. $2x + 5 = -3$
       $-2x + 5 = 11$
    E. $2x + 5 = 11$
       $2x + 5 = -11$

- 177 -

PrepPros

19. If a and b are real numbers such that $a < 0$ and $b < 0$ and $b < a$, then which of the following is equivalent to $a - b$?

   A. $|a| - |b|$
   B. $|a| + |b|$
   C. $|b| + |a|$
   D. $b + a$
   E. $|b - a|$

20. The solution set of the equation $|3x - 2| = 3x - 2$ is the set of all values of x such that:

   A. $x \leq \frac{2}{3}$
   B. $x \geq \frac{2}{3}$
   C. $x \leq 0$
   D. $x \geq 0$
   E. x is a rational number

21. Given that a is a positive number, b is a negative number and $|a| < |b|$, which of the following expressions has the greatest value?

   A. $\left|\frac{a-b}{b}\right|$
   B. $\left|\frac{a-b}{a}\right|$
   C. $\left|\frac{a+b}{b-a}\right|$
   D. $\left|\frac{a+b}{b}\right|$
   E. $\left|\frac{a+b}{a}\right|$

22. The solution set of which of the following equations is the set of real numbers that are 8 units from -2 ?

   A. $|x + 8| = -2$
   B. $|x - 8| = 2$
   C. $|x + 8| = 2$
   D. $|x + 2| = 8$
   E. $|x - 2| = 8$

23. Given that a is a negative number with an absolute value greater than 1 and b is a positive number less than one, which of the following expressions has the greatest value?

   A. $|b - a|$
   B. $\left|\frac{a+b}{b}\right|$
   C. ab
   D. $\left|\frac{ab}{a}\right|$
   E. $\left|\frac{a-b}{b}\right|$

24. If $|x| - 1 = |x + 1|$, which of the following must be true?

   A. $x \geq 0$
   B. $x \leq 0$
   C. $x \geq 1$
   D. $x \leq -1$
   E. $x \neq 0$

- 178 -

Chapter 19: Matrices

Matrices are one of the most common advanced topics on the ACT. This is not because matrices are especially difficult; instead, it is because many students have never worked with matrices before! While matrices may seem intimidating at first, they are actually quite simple once you learn the rules for how to add, subtract, and multiply matrices.

What is a Matrix?

A matrix is a rectangular arrangement of numbers into rows and columns. Matrices are useful in math because they allow more complex equations to be reduced into a simpler form with fewer variables. To show you an example of what we mean, let's see how a system of equations below can be represented in a matrix.

$$10x - 3y = 40$$
$$4x + 8y = 18$$

$$\Rightarrow \begin{bmatrix} 10 & -3 & 40 \\ 4 & 8 & 18 \end{bmatrix}$$

$$\uparrow \quad \uparrow \quad \uparrow$$
$$x \quad y \quad \text{constants}$$

As you can see, the system of equations can be represented by numbers in the matrix. The easiest type of matrix question on the ACT could ask you to understand this concept.

Matrix Dimensions

The dimensions of a matrix refer to the number of rows and number of columns in the matrix. Matrix dimensions are written as (rows × columns). You can also think of this as (height × width). The examples below show you some matrices of various dimensions.

$$(\mathbf{2 \times 1}): \begin{bmatrix} 8 \\ 1 \end{bmatrix} \qquad (\mathbf{2 \times 2}): \begin{bmatrix} -5 & 7 \\ -4 & -2 \end{bmatrix} \qquad (\mathbf{1 \times 3}): \begin{bmatrix} 10 & 1 & -9 \end{bmatrix}$$

ACT questions do not ask directly about matrix dimensions, but we need to understand matrix dimensions for the other topics that we will learn in this chapter.

Matrix Addition and Subtraction

Matrix addition and subtraction is just simple arithmetic. Using matrices with the same dimensions, you complete the arithmetic for each position in the matrix. Take a look at the example below to see how it's done!

$$\begin{bmatrix} -5 & 4 \\ -1 & 7 \end{bmatrix} + \begin{bmatrix} 10 & 7 \\ -5 & -2 \end{bmatrix} = \begin{bmatrix} 5 & 11 \\ -6 & 5 \end{bmatrix}$$

Top Left: $-5 + 10 = 5$ Top Right: $4 + 7 = 11$

Bottom Left: $-1 + (-5) = -6$ Bottom Right: $7 + (-2) = 5$

To solve for top left position, use the values in the top left. The top left of the first matrix, -5, plus the top left in the second matrix, 10, gives us the value in the top left of the resulting matrix 5. We repeat this process for all other spots in the matrix to solve for the entire matrix.

> **Example 1:** In the matrices shown below, what is the value of $a + b$?
>
> $$\begin{bmatrix} 11 & 14 \\ -9 & -5 \end{bmatrix} + \begin{bmatrix} 10 & a \\ 6 & 8 \end{bmatrix} = \begin{bmatrix} 21 & 9 \\ b & 3 \end{bmatrix}$$
>
> A. 8   B. 2   C. -2 D. -5 E. -8

Solution: To find $a + b$, we need to find the values of a and b. Let's start with a. To find a, we need to look at the values in the top right position. We can see that

$$14 + a = 9$$

Solving this equation by subtracting 14 from both sides, we find

$$a = -5$$

To find b, we look at values in the bottom left position. We see that

$$-9 + 6 = b$$
$$-3 = b$$

Now that we know the values of a and b, we can solve.

$$a + b = (-5) + (-3)$$
$$a + b = -8$$

The answer is E.

If there are coefficients included in front of a matrix, we distribute the coefficient to the values in the matrix just as we would in normal arithmetic. In the example below, we distribute the 3 into the first matrix and then complete the subtraction for each position in the matrix to solve.

$$3\begin{bmatrix} 4 & 1 \\ -11 & 6 \end{bmatrix} - \begin{bmatrix} 12 & -3 \\ 1 & 8 \end{bmatrix} = \begin{bmatrix} 0 & 6 \\ -34 & 10 \end{bmatrix}$$

Top Left: $3(4) - 12 = 0$ Top Right: $3(1) - (-3) = 6$

Bottom Left: $3(-11) - 1 = -34$ Bottom Right: $3(6) - 8 = 10$

Example 2: $3\begin{bmatrix} 2 & -10 \\ -8 & 4 \end{bmatrix} - 4\begin{bmatrix} -5 & -8 \\ 9 & 3 \end{bmatrix} =$

A. $\begin{bmatrix} 26 & -62 \\ 60 & 24 \end{bmatrix}$ B. $\begin{bmatrix} 26 & 2 \\ -60 & 0 \end{bmatrix}$ C. $\begin{bmatrix} -14 & -62 \\ -12 & 0 \end{bmatrix}$ D. $\begin{bmatrix} -14 & -30 \\ -24 & 12 \end{bmatrix}$ E. $\begin{bmatrix} -3 & -18 \\ -17 & -11 \end{bmatrix}$

Solution: To solve, we distribute the coefficients into each matrix and complete the subtraction.

Top Left: $3(2) - 4(-5) = 26$ Top Right: $3(-10) - 4(-8) = 2$

Bottom Left: $3(-8) - 4(9) = -60$ Bottom Right: $3(4) - 4(3) = 0$

The answer is B.

*****Test-Taking Tip:** When solving any matrix question, check the answer choices once you find the value for any position in the matrix. You can often find the correct answer after solving for only 1 or 2 positions in the matrix.

*One Rule to Know About Matrix Addition and Subtraction

We can only add and subtract matrices of the same dimensions. If you are even asked to add or subtract matrices that have different dimensions, the resulting matrix will be undefined. The correct answer would either say "Undefined" or [ ] (the empty set), which is a fancy math way of saying there is no answer.

"Advanced" Matrices Topics

Matrix addition and subtraction questions are generally pretty easy and will appear in the first 30 question of ACT Math Test. All other topics for matrices are "advanced" and almost always appear somewhere in questions 40-60. While these topics are "advanced," many matrices questions are not too difficult once you know the rules for how to solve them. The rest of this chapter will cover the more "advanced" topics that commonly appear on the ACT and how to solve them.

Finding the Determinant of a (2 × 2) Matrix

On the ACT, you need to know how to find the determinant of a (2 × 2) matrix. The determinant of a matrix is just a property of a matrix. All you need to know about the determinant is how to find it in case the ACT asks you a question about it. Determinant questions are generally not very difficult as long as you memorize the formula below:

For a (2 × 2) matrix $\begin{bmatrix} a & b \\ c & d \end{bmatrix}$, **the determinant** $= ad - bc$

To find the determinant, all you need to do is multiply top left (a) × bottom right (d) and subtract top right (b) × bottom left (c). To show you how this works with numbers, let's use the matrix below.

$$\begin{bmatrix} 2 & -6 \\ 3 & 12 \end{bmatrix}$$

To find the determinant, we plug the values from the matrix into the equation $ad - bc$:

$$\text{Determinant} = (2)(12) - (-6)(3)$$
$$= (24) - (-18)$$
$$= 24 + 18$$
$$\text{Determinant} = 42$$

On the ACT, a determinant question could be that simple! However, the ACT more commonly includes a variable as show in Example 3.

Example 3: The determinant of matrix B is equal to 10. What is the value of x?

$$B = \begin{bmatrix} -4 & 1 \\ 6 & x \end{bmatrix}$$

A. 4   B. 1   C. 0   D. −1   E. −4

Solution: To solve for x, we need to set up the determinant equation and solve for x. We are told that the determinant of matrix B is equal to 10, so the determinant equation is

$$-4(x) - 6(1) = 10$$
$$-4x - 6 = 10$$
$$-4x = 16$$
$$x = -4$$

The answer is E.

Determinant questions appear occasionally on the ACT. However, the far more commonly tested "advanced" matrix questions involve matrix multiplication, which we will learn next.

Matrix Multiplication

The most common type of "advanced" matrix question on the ACT is matrix multiplication. There are two steps in matrix multiplication: (1) determining whether multiplication will be defined or undefined and (2) completing the multiplication.

Defined vs. Undefined Results from Matrix Multiplication

The first step in matrix multiplication is determining if the result of matrix multiplication will be defined or undefined and, if the result is defined, what the resulting matrix's dimensions will be. To do this, we use the dimensions of the matrices and the following steps.

1. **Write down the dimensions of the two matrices that you are multiplying together.** For example, if you are multiplying matrix A, a (1×2) matrix, and matrix B, a (2×3) matrix, we write:

$$AB = (1 \times 2) \times (2 \times 3)$$

2. **Draw a box around the middle 2 numbers and see if those 2 numbers match.** This tells you if the matrix is defined or undefined. For our example, we would put a box like this:

$$AB = (1 \times \boxed{2) \times (2} \times 3)$$

   a. **If the numbers do not match, the matrix is undefined.** You can stop here, as there is no more math that needs to be done.

   b. **If the numbers match, the matrix is defined. For a matrix to be defined, the number of columns in the first matrix must be equal to the number of rows in the second matrix.** Continue to step 3 to find the dimensions of the resulting matrix. Our example above is defined, so we will continue to step 3.

3. **Bring down the first and last numbers (the 2 numbers outside the box) to find the dimensions of the resulting matrix.** With our example, we bring down the 1 and 3 to see the resulting matrix will be a (1×3) matrix, as shown below:

$$(1 \times \boxed{2) \times (2} \times 3)$$
$$\downarrow \qquad \swarrow$$
$$AB = (1 \times 3)$$

4. Now that we know that the matrix AB is a (1×3) matrix. The second step, which we will learn next in this chapter, is to complete the matrix multiplication to find the values that will be in the matrix.

Example 4: Using the matrices shown below, which of the following is a (2×3) matrix?

$$A = \begin{bmatrix} 2 \\ 5 \end{bmatrix} \qquad B = \begin{bmatrix} -2 & 3 \\ 7 & 4 \end{bmatrix} \qquad C = \begin{bmatrix} 1 & -3 & 8 \\ 10 & 5 & -4 \end{bmatrix}$$

A. AB B. CB C. BC D. CA E. BA

Solution: To find which matrix will be a (2×3) matrix, we need to first know the dimensions of the matrices presented in the question. Matrix A is (2×1), matrix B is (2×2), and matrix C is (2×3). Now, we need to set up the matrix multiplication for all the answer choices.

We can start with answer choice A, matrix AB.

$$AB = (2 \times \boxed{1) \times (2} \times 2)$$

The middle numbers in the box do not match, so AB is undefined.

Next, let's try answer choice B, matrix CB.

$$CB = (2 \times \boxed{3)\times (2} \times 2)$$

The middle numbers in the box do not match, so CB is undefined.

Next, let's try answer choice C, matrix BC.

$$BC = (2 \times \boxed{2) \times (2} \times 3)$$
$$BC = (2 \times 3)$$

BC is a (2 × 3) matrix, so C is correct. To finish explaining the answer choices, let's go over answer choices D and E as well.

For answer choice D, we get

$$CA = (2 \times \boxed{3) \times (2} \times 1)$$

The middle numbers in the box do not match, so CA is undefined.

For answer choice E, we get

$$BA = (2 \times \boxed{2) \times (2} \times 1)$$
$$BA = (2 \times 1)$$

BA is defined and is a (2 × 1) matrix. The only answer choice that results in a (2 × 3) matrix is BC, so **the answer is C.**

Questions like Example 4 appear occasionally on the ACT, so make sure you understand this before moving on to the next topic.

You will more commonly use this skill as the first step in matrix multiplication, a topic that the ACT loves to test in the more difficult questions that appear towards the back of the test.

Matrix Multiplication – How To Find The Values In The Matrix

Multiplying matrices is a tricky task that can be broken down into two major steps: (1) finding out if the matrix is defined or undefined (the skill we just learned on the last two pages) and (2) determining the resulting values in the matrix. We have already learned step 1, so now we need to learn step 2.

To learn how this works, let's work through the entire process using the matrices below to find matrix AB.

$$A = \begin{bmatrix} 2 & -4 \\ -6 & 1 \end{bmatrix} \qquad B = \begin{bmatrix} 3 & 1 \\ -2 & 9 \end{bmatrix}$$

1. Determine if AB is defined or undefined.

   $AB = (2 \times \boxed{2}) \times (\boxed{2} \times 2)$ The middle numbers match, so the matrix is defined.

   $AB = (2 \times 2)$ AB is a (2×2) matrix.

2. Multiply AB and find the values in the new matrix.

To find the values in the matrix AB, we work horizontally ACROSS the first matrix, matrix A, and DOWN the second matrix, matrix B. To find the values that go in matrix AB, we do a combination of multiplication and addition.

To start, let's solve for top left spot in matrix AB, which is labeled as w below. To solve for the top left, we use the top row in matrix A and the left column in matrix B, as shown by the gray boxes below. **When multiplying matrices, always start at the left of the row and the top of the column.** We multiply the 1st terms, 2 and 3, together. We then go to the 2nd terms, -4 and -2, and multiply those together. Finally, we sum those two products to get the value for the top left spot in matrix AB, as shown below.

Top Left: $\begin{bmatrix} 2 & -4 \\ -6 & 1 \end{bmatrix} \times \begin{bmatrix} 3 & 1 \\ -2 & 9 \end{bmatrix} = \begin{bmatrix} w & \end{bmatrix}$ $w = (2)(3) + (-4)(-2) = 14$

$\begin{bmatrix} 2 & -4 \\ -6 & 1 \end{bmatrix} \times \begin{bmatrix} 3 & 1 \\ -2 & 9 \end{bmatrix} = \begin{bmatrix} \mathbf{14} & \end{bmatrix}$

To solve for the top right spot in matrix AB, which is labeled as x below, we repeat that process except now we use the top row in matrix A and the right column in matrix B. We multiply the 1st terms, 2 and 1, together. We then go to the 2nd terms, -4 and 9, and multiply those together. Finally, we sum those two products to get the value for the top right spot in matrix AB, as shown below.

Top Right: $\begin{bmatrix} 2 & -4 \\ -6 & 1 \end{bmatrix} \times \begin{bmatrix} 3 & 1 \\ -2 & 9 \end{bmatrix} = \begin{bmatrix} 14 & x \end{bmatrix}$ $x = (2)(1) + (-4)(9) = \mathbf{-34}$

$\begin{bmatrix} 2 & -4 \\ -6 & 1 \end{bmatrix} \times \begin{bmatrix} 3 & 1 \\ -2 & 9 \end{bmatrix} = \begin{bmatrix} 14 & \mathbf{-34} \end{bmatrix}$

To solve for the bottom left spot in matrix AB, which is labeled as y below, we repeat that process except now we use the bottom row in matrix A and the left column in matrix B. We multiply the 1st terms, -6 and 3, together. We then go to the 2nd terms, 1 and -2, and multiply those together. Finally, we sum those two products to get the value for the top right spot in matrix AB, as shown below.

Bottom Left: $\begin{bmatrix} 2 & -4 \\ -6 & 1 \end{bmatrix} \times \begin{bmatrix} 3 & 1 \\ -2 & 9 \end{bmatrix} = \begin{bmatrix} 14 & -34 \\ y & \end{bmatrix}$ $y = (-6)(3) + (1)(-2) = \mathbf{-20}$

$\begin{bmatrix} 2 & -4 \\ -6 & 1 \end{bmatrix} \times \begin{bmatrix} 3 & 1 \\ -2 & 9 \end{bmatrix} = \begin{bmatrix} 14 & -34 \\ \mathbf{-20} & \end{bmatrix}$

Finally, to solve for the bottom right spot in matrix AB, which is labeled as z below, we repeat that process except now we use the bottom row in matrix A and the right column in matrix B.

Bottom Right: $\begin{bmatrix} 2 & -4 \\ \boxed{-6} & \boxed{1} \end{bmatrix} \times \begin{bmatrix} 3 & \boxed{1} \\ -2 & \boxed{9} \end{bmatrix} = \begin{bmatrix} 14 & -34 \\ -20 & z \end{bmatrix}$ $z = (-6)(1) + (1)(9) = 3$

$$\begin{bmatrix} 2 & -4 \\ -6 & 1 \end{bmatrix} \times \begin{bmatrix} 3 & 1 \\ -2 & 9 \end{bmatrix} = \begin{bmatrix} 14 & -34 \\ -20 & \mathbf{3} \end{bmatrix}$$

Now, we are done and have solved for matrix AB.

*Test-Taking Tip: When solving any matrix question, check the answer choices once you find the value for any position in the matrix. You can often find the correct answer after solving for only 1 or 2 positions in the matrix.

Next, let's work through an example where the matrices had different dimensions. Note that the steps for matrix multiplication are always the same no matter what the matrices involved look like, so we will follow the same process we did for the previous example.

Example 5: Using the matrices below, XY is equal to:

$$X = \begin{bmatrix} -5 & 6 \\ 2 & -1 \\ 3 & -2 \end{bmatrix} \qquad Y = \begin{bmatrix} 3 \\ -4 \end{bmatrix}$$

A. $\begin{bmatrix} 39 & 10 & 17 \end{bmatrix}$ B. $\begin{bmatrix} -42 & -14 & 1 \end{bmatrix}$ C. $\begin{bmatrix} -15 & -24 \\ 6 & 4 \\ 9 & 8 \end{bmatrix}$ D. $\begin{bmatrix} -39 \\ 10 \\ 17 \end{bmatrix}$ E. $\begin{bmatrix} -42 \\ -14 \\ 1 \end{bmatrix}$

Solution: To solve, we first need to find the dimensions of matrix XY.

$XY = (3 \times 2) \times (2 \times 1)$ The middle numbers match, so the matrix is defined.

$XY = (3 \times 1)$ XY is a (3×1) matrix.

We know that XY is a (3×1) matrix, so we already know the correct answer is D or E. Even if you find multiplying matrices difficult, if you can master this first step, you will likely be guessing between only 2 or 3 answer choices on test day.

Next, we need to multiply XY to find the values in matrix. Remember, we work across our first matrix, X, and down our second matrix, Y.

Let's start with the top spot in matrix XY, which is labeled as a below. To solve for the top, we use the top row in matrix X and the only column in matrix Y, as shown by the gray boxes below. **When multiplying matrices, we start at the left of the row and the top of the column.** We multiply the 1st terms, -5 and 3, together. We then go to the 2nd terms, 6 and -4, and multiply those together. Finally, we sum those two products to get the value for the top spot in matrix XY, as shown below.

Top: $\begin{bmatrix} \boxed{-5 \quad 6} \\ 2 & -1 \\ 3 & -2 \end{bmatrix} \times \begin{bmatrix} \boxed{3} \\ \boxed{-4} \end{bmatrix} = \begin{bmatrix} a \\ \\ \end{bmatrix}$ $a = (-5)(3) + (6)(-4) = \mathbf{-39}$

$$\begin{bmatrix} -5 & 6 \\ 2 & -1 \\ 3 & -2 \end{bmatrix} \times \begin{bmatrix} 3 \\ -4 \end{bmatrix} = \begin{bmatrix} -39 \\ \\ \end{bmatrix}$$

At this point, we should check the answer choices. We see that only answer choice D has 39 in the top position, so we already know **the correct answer is D**. On the ACT, you almost never actually need to solve the entire matrix, so check the answer choices right away after you find the value for any position in the matrix to save time.

For practice, let's go over how to find the other values in matrix XY.

To solve for the middle spot in matrix XY, which is labeled as b below, we use the middle row in matrix X and the column in matrix Y. We multiply the 1st terms, 2 and 3, together. We then go to the 2nd terms, -1 and -4, and multiply those together. Finally, we sum those two products to get the value for the top spot in matrix XY, as shown below.

Middle: $\begin{bmatrix} -5 & 6 \\ 2 & -1 \\ 3 & -2 \end{bmatrix} \times \begin{bmatrix} 3 \\ -4 \end{bmatrix} = \begin{bmatrix} -39 \\ b \\ \end{bmatrix}$ $\quad b = (2)(3) + (-1)(-4) = \mathbf{10}$

$\begin{bmatrix} -5 & 6 \\ 2 & -1 \\ 3 & -2 \end{bmatrix} \times \begin{bmatrix} 3 \\ -4 \end{bmatrix} = \begin{bmatrix} -39 \\ \mathbf{10} \\ \end{bmatrix}$

To solve for the bottom spot in matrix XY, which is labeled as c below, we use the bottom row in matrix X and the column in matrix Y. We multiply the 1st terms, 3 and 3, together. We then go to the 2nd terms, -2 and -4, and multiply those together. Finally, we sum those two products to get the value for the top spot in matrix XY, as shown below.

Bottom: $\begin{bmatrix} -5 & 6 \\ 2 & -1 \\ 3 & -2 \end{bmatrix} \times \begin{bmatrix} 3 \\ -4 \end{bmatrix} = \begin{bmatrix} -39 \\ 10 \\ c \end{bmatrix}$ $\quad c = (3)(3) + (-2)(-4) = \mathbf{17}$

$\begin{bmatrix} -5 & 6 \\ 2 & -1 \\ 3 & -2 \end{bmatrix} \times \begin{bmatrix} 3 \\ -4 \end{bmatrix} = \begin{bmatrix} -39 \\ 10 \\ \mathbf{17} \end{bmatrix}$

Let Your Calculator Help!

Did you know that some calculators can do matrix multiplication for you? If you own a TI-83, TI-84, TI-Nspire (non-CAS), or most versions of Casio calculators, your calculator can do matrix multiplication! To learn how, go to YouTube and look up a tutorial. It is good to know how your calculator can help in case you get stuck on test day.

We still recommend that you understand how matrix multiplication works and do not rely on your calculator, as it is faster to solve matrices on test day with the methods we just learned. Additionally, some matrix multiplication questions will involve variables that you cannot enter in your calculator.

Chapter 19: Matrices

Matrices Practice: Answers on page 330.

1. What is the value of $x + y$?

   $$\begin{bmatrix} x & 4 \\ 2 & 8 \end{bmatrix} + \begin{bmatrix} 3 & y \\ 3 & 2 \end{bmatrix} = \begin{bmatrix} 6 & 9 \\ 5 & 10 \end{bmatrix}$$

   A. 0
   B. 3
   C. 5
   D. 8 *(circled)*
   E. 9

2. What is the value of $x + y + z$?

   $$3\begin{bmatrix} x \\ 2y \\ 5z \end{bmatrix} = 6\begin{bmatrix} 5 \\ 3 \\ 10 \end{bmatrix}$$

   handwritten: $x=10$, $3x \quad 30$, $y=3$, $6y=18$, $z=4$, $15z \quad 60$

   A. 7
   B. 11
   C. 13
   D. 17 *(circled)*
   E. 18

3. Which of the following matrices properly represents the system of equations below?

   $$3x - 11y = 18$$
   $$12x + 2y = 90$$

   A. $\begin{bmatrix} 3 & -11 & 18 \\ 12 & 2 & 90 \end{bmatrix}$ *(circled)*
   B. $\begin{bmatrix} 3 & 11 & -18 \\ 12 & -2 & 90 \end{bmatrix}$
   C. $\begin{bmatrix} 3 & -11 & -18 \\ 12 & 2 & -90 \end{bmatrix}$
   D. $\begin{bmatrix} -3 & 11 & -18 \\ -12 & -2 & -90 \end{bmatrix}$
   E. $\begin{bmatrix} -3 & -11 & 18 \\ -12 & 2 & 90 \end{bmatrix}$

4. What is $\begin{bmatrix} 1 & 4 \\ 2 & 6 \end{bmatrix} + \begin{bmatrix} 7 & 8 \\ 9 & 10 \end{bmatrix}$ equal to?

   A. $\begin{bmatrix} 11 & 9 \\ 15 & 12 \end{bmatrix}$
   B. $\begin{bmatrix} 7 & 12 \\ 11 & 16 \end{bmatrix}$
   C. $\begin{bmatrix} 8 & 12 \\ 11 & 16 \end{bmatrix}$ *(circled)*
   D. $\begin{bmatrix} 8 & 10 \\ 13 & 16 \end{bmatrix}$
   E. $\begin{bmatrix} 9 & 11 \\ 12 & 15 \end{bmatrix}$

   handwritten: $\begin{bmatrix} 8 & 12 \\ 11 & 16 \end{bmatrix}$

5. What is the determinant of the matrix shown below?

   $$\begin{bmatrix} 9 & 6 \\ 2 & -3 \end{bmatrix}$$ *handwritten: $-27 - 12 = -39$*

   A. -39 *(circled)*
   B. -15
   C. 14
   D. 15
   E. 48

6. What is the value of $a - b$?

   $$3\begin{bmatrix} -4 & 2 \\ 12 & b \end{bmatrix} - \begin{bmatrix} -7 & a \\ 2 & 10 \end{bmatrix} = \begin{bmatrix} -5 & 9 \\ 34 & 8 \end{bmatrix}$$

   A. -25
   B. -9 *(circled)*
   C. -3
   D. 6
   E. 12

   handwritten: $3b - 10 = 8$, $3b = 18$, $b = 6$; $6 - a = 9$, $-a = 3$, $a = -3$; $-3 - 6 = -9$

7. Matrixes A and B are displayed below. If Matrix $C = 2A + 2B$, which of the following gives Matrix C?

   $$A = \begin{bmatrix} 1 & 7 \\ 3 & 4 \end{bmatrix} \quad B = \begin{bmatrix} 4 & 2 \\ 5 & 6 \end{bmatrix}$$

   A. $\begin{bmatrix} 5 & 9 \\ 8 & 10 \end{bmatrix}$
   B. $\begin{bmatrix} 6 & 16 \\ 11 & 14 \end{bmatrix}$
   C. $\begin{bmatrix} 10 & 18 \\ 16 & 20 \end{bmatrix}$ *(circled)*
   D. $\begin{bmatrix} 9 & 11 \\ 13 & 16 \end{bmatrix}$
   E. $\begin{bmatrix} 3 & 11 \\ 9 & 9 \end{bmatrix}$

   handwritten: $\begin{bmatrix} 2 & 14 \\ 6 & 8 \end{bmatrix} + \begin{bmatrix} 8 & 4 \\ 10 & 12 \end{bmatrix} = \begin{bmatrix} 10 & 18 \\ & \end{bmatrix}$

8. What is the value of the determinant of the matrix below?

   $$\begin{bmatrix} 2 & 3 \\ 7 & 8 \end{bmatrix}$$ *handwritten: $16 - 21 = -5$*

   A. -50
   B. -10
   C. -5 *(circled)*
   D. 37
   E. 38

- 187 -

9. Which of the following matrices is equal to the product of the matrices below?

$$\begin{bmatrix} 3 & 4 \\ 7 & 4 \end{bmatrix} \begin{bmatrix} 2 \\ 4 \end{bmatrix} = \begin{bmatrix} 22 \\ \end{bmatrix}$$

(2×2) (2×1) (2×1)

A. $\begin{bmatrix} 22 \\ 30 \end{bmatrix}$

B. $\begin{bmatrix} 13 \\ 19 \end{bmatrix}$

C. $\begin{bmatrix} 6 & 8 \\ 28 & 16 \end{bmatrix}$

D. $\begin{bmatrix} 25 \\ 37 \end{bmatrix}$

E. The product is undefined.

10. The determinant of the matrix below is equal to:

$$\begin{bmatrix} 4 & -3 \\ 6 & 5 \end{bmatrix}$$ 20 − (−18)

A. −32
B. 2
C. 12
D. 38
E. 39

11. For what values of x is the determinant of the matrix below equal to 0?

$$\begin{bmatrix} (x-6) & 8 \\ x & (x+4) \end{bmatrix}$$

A. −2 and 12
B. −6 and −4
C. 6 and 4
D. 2 and −12
E. −8, −4, and 6

12. What are the dimensions of the product of the matrices below?

$$\begin{bmatrix} 5 & 4 & 0 \\ 3 & 6 & 4 \end{bmatrix} \times \begin{bmatrix} 3 & 6 \\ 4 & 3 \\ 2 & 5 \end{bmatrix} =$$

(2×3)   (3×2)

A. (2 × 3)
B. (2 × 2)
C. (3 × 2)
D. (3 × 3)
E. The product is undefined.

13. If the value of the determinant for the matrix below is 54, what is the value of a?

$$\begin{bmatrix} 3 & 9 \\ a & 12 \end{bmatrix}$$

36 − 9a = 54
−9a = 18
a = −2

A. −18
B. −2
C. 6
D. 2
E. 18

14. There are two schools on a field trip at the San Diego Zoo. The first school has 10 adult chaperones and 50 students. The second school has 6 adult chaperones and 35 students. If adult tickets are $50 and student tickets are $25, which of the following matrix products represents the ticket costs, in dollars for each school?

10(50)

A. $[50 \ 25] \begin{bmatrix} 50 & 35 \\ 10 & 6 \end{bmatrix}$

B. $[50 \ 25] \begin{bmatrix} 50 & 10 \\ 35 & 6 \end{bmatrix}$

C. $[50 \ 25] \begin{bmatrix} 10 & 6 \\ 50 & 35 \end{bmatrix}$

D. $\begin{bmatrix} 50 \\ 25 \end{bmatrix} \begin{bmatrix} 50 & 35 \\ 10 & 6 \end{bmatrix}$

E. $\begin{bmatrix} 50 \\ 25 \end{bmatrix} \begin{bmatrix} 10 & 6 \\ 50 & 35 \end{bmatrix}$

15. For what value of x will the determinant of the matrix $\begin{bmatrix} 4+x & -6 \\ x & 3 \end{bmatrix}$ have a value of 39?

A. −18
B. −3
C. 3
D. $\frac{54}{4}$
E. 18

3(4+x) + 6x = 39
12 + 3x + 6x = 39
9x = 27

- 188 -

Chapter 19: Matrices

For questions 16-18, use the four matrices below.

$$A = \begin{bmatrix} 7 \\ 3 \\ 4 \end{bmatrix} \quad B = \begin{bmatrix} 2 & -25 \\ 13 & 7 \end{bmatrix}$$

$$C = \begin{bmatrix} 1 & 0 & 4 \\ 3 & 8 & 5 \end{bmatrix} \quad D = \begin{bmatrix} 1 & 9 \\ 3 & 8 \\ 6 & 4 \end{bmatrix}$$

16. Which of the following matrix products is undefined?

    A. CA
    B. CD
    C. BC
    D. DA
    E. DB

17. Which matrix or matrices can be added to the resulting matrix from the matrix multiplication below?

$$\begin{bmatrix} a & b \\ c & d \\ e & f \end{bmatrix} \times \begin{bmatrix} w & x \\ y & z \end{bmatrix} = \begin{bmatrix} - & - \\ - & - \\ - & - \end{bmatrix}$$

    A. D only
    B. B only
    C. C only
    D. D and B
    E. A and B

18. What is the value of $CD + B$?

    A. $\begin{bmatrix} 25 & 25 \\ 57 & 111 \end{bmatrix}$
    B. $\begin{bmatrix} 27 & 0 \\ 70 & 118 \end{bmatrix}$
    C. $\begin{bmatrix} 52 & 80 \\ 173 & 343 \end{bmatrix}$
    D. $\begin{bmatrix} 3 & 0 & -25 \\ 16 & 46 & 35 \end{bmatrix}$
    E. $\begin{bmatrix} 7 & -16 & -40 \\ 44 & 1 & 9 \end{bmatrix}$

19. Flour costs $30 per bag and sugar costs $18 per bag. If Bakery A orders 10 bags of flour and 7 bags of sugar each week and Bakery B orders 18 bags of flour and 13 bags of sugar each week, which of the following matrix products represents the weekly spend, in dollars, for each bakery?

    A. $[18 \ \ 30] \begin{bmatrix} 7 & 13 \\ 10 & 18 \end{bmatrix}$
    B. $[18 \ \ 30] \begin{bmatrix} 7 & 10 \\ 13 & 18 \end{bmatrix}$
    C. $[18 \ \ 30] \begin{bmatrix} 10 & 18 \\ 7 & 13 \end{bmatrix}$
    D. $\begin{bmatrix} 18 \\ 30 \end{bmatrix} \begin{bmatrix} 7 & 10 \\ 13 & 18 \end{bmatrix}$
    E. $\begin{bmatrix} 18 \\ 30 \end{bmatrix} \begin{bmatrix} 7 & 13 \\ 10 & 18 \end{bmatrix}$

20. An ice cream parlor sells single scoops for $3, double scoops for $5, and sundaes for $7. If the ice cream parlor sold 300 single scoops, 400 double scoops, and 190 sundaes on a Saturday, which of the following matrix products yields their total daily sales for that Saturday?

    A. $[3 \ \ 5 \ \ 7] \begin{bmatrix} 190 \\ 400 \\ 300 \end{bmatrix}$
    B. $[3 \ \ 5 \ \ 7] \begin{bmatrix} 300 \\ 400 \\ 190 \end{bmatrix}$
    C. $[3 \ \ 5 \ \ 7] \begin{bmatrix} 400 \\ 300 \\ 190 \end{bmatrix}$
    D. $\begin{bmatrix} 300 \\ 400 \\ 190 \end{bmatrix} [3 \ \ 5 \ \ 7]$
    E. $\begin{bmatrix} 190 \\ 400 \\ 300 \end{bmatrix} [3 \ \ 5 \ \ 7]$

PrepPros

21. What is the matrix product of
$\begin{bmatrix} a & b \\ c & d \end{bmatrix} \begin{bmatrix} e & f \\ g & h \end{bmatrix}$?

A. $\begin{bmatrix} ae & cf \\ bg & bh \end{bmatrix}$

B. $\begin{bmatrix} ae & bf \\ ag & dh \end{bmatrix}$

C. $\begin{bmatrix} ae+bg & af+bh \\ ce+dg & cf+dh \end{bmatrix}$

D. $\begin{bmatrix} ae+cf & bf+dh \\ ae+cg & cf+dh \end{bmatrix}$

E. Cannot be determined

22. What is the matrix product of
$\begin{bmatrix} 3 & 4 & 5 \\ 0 & 2 & 1 \end{bmatrix} \begin{bmatrix} 2 & 5 \\ 1 & 3 \\ 3 & 4 \end{bmatrix}$?

A. $\begin{bmatrix} 6 & 0 \\ 4 & 6 \\ 15 & 4 \end{bmatrix}$

B. $\begin{bmatrix} 29 & 32 \\ 5 & 10 \end{bmatrix}$

C. $\begin{bmatrix} 37 & 25 \\ 10 & 5 \end{bmatrix}$

D. $\begin{bmatrix} 25 & 47 \\ 5 & 10 \end{bmatrix}$

E. $\begin{bmatrix} 6 & 4 & 15 \\ 0 & 6 & 4 \end{bmatrix}$

23. What is the matrix product of
$\begin{bmatrix} 3a & -2 \end{bmatrix} \begin{bmatrix} 5e & 4 \\ 2g & -6h \end{bmatrix}$?

A. $\begin{bmatrix} 15ae & 12a \\ -4g & 12h \end{bmatrix}$

B. $\begin{bmatrix} 15ae & -8 \\ 6ag & 12h \end{bmatrix}$

C. $\begin{bmatrix} 8ae - 4g & 7a - 4h \end{bmatrix}$

D. $\begin{bmatrix} 15a - 10e & 12a + 8h \end{bmatrix}$

E. $\begin{bmatrix} 15ae - 4g & 12a + 12h \end{bmatrix}$

Chapter 20: Repeating Patterns

Any idea what number is the 307th decimal place after the decimal point of $0.\overline{34562}$ or what the units digit of 7^{103} is? Questions like this appear quite often on the ACT, and they seem almost impossible to solve at first glance. However, once you learn the trick to solving repeating patterns questions, they are actually easy!

Repeating Decimals

The first and easiest type of repeating patterns question is one with a repeating decimal. Remember, a line above a decimal shows the decimal repeats over and over again without ending. For example,

$$0.\overline{1234} = 0.1234123412341234\ldots$$

As you will see in the following example, we can use the repeating pattern to find values that occur way later in the decimal without actually writing it out.

> **Example 1:** What is the 307th place after the decimal point in the repeating decimal $0.\overline{34562}$?
> A. 2   B. 3   C. 4   D. 5   E. 6

Solution: The trick to solving repeating decimals questions is using the repeating pattern to our advantage. To show you how this works, let's write out the decimal in repeating form.

$$0.\overline{34562} = 0.345623456234562\ldots$$

We want to go to the end of the repeating unit, which here is the 2. Since the pattern repeats every 5 places, every 5th place after the decimal point will be a 2.

$$0.\overline{34562} = 0.345623456234562\ldots$$

      ↑   ↑ ↑ ↑

          5th 10th 15th

The 5th place, the 10th place, the 15th place are all 2. As the repeating decimal continues, every digit that is a multiple of 5 will be a 2. 25 places, 50 places, 500 places…all of these will be 2.

We are looking for the 307th place after the decimal point. To find that value, we need to find a multiple of 5 near 307. The closest multiple of 5 is 305, which will be a 2. Once we know that the 305th place is a 2, we can count forward in our sequence.

The 306th digit is a 3, and the 307th digit is a 4. **The answer is C.**

> **Example 2:** What is the 703rd place after the decimal point in the repeating decimal $0.\overline{596127}$?
> A. 1   B. 5   C. 6   D. 7   E. 9

Solution: Let's use the same trick we just learned in Example 1. Here, we have 6 digits repeating. We go to the end of the repeating unit, which here is a 7.

$$0.\overline{596127} = 0.596127596127\ldots$$

      ↑   ↑ ↑

         6th 12th

Every number that is a multiple of 6 after the decimal point will be a 7. We are looking for the 703rd place after the decimal point. To find that value, we need to find a multiple of 6 near 703. The closest multiple is 702, which is a 7. Once we know the 702nd place is a 7, we can count forward in the sequence. The 703rd term is 5. **The answer is B.**

Repeating Patterns with Powers and the Units Digit

What is the units digit of 7^{123}? This is an example of second and more difficult type of repeating patterns question. Before we learn how to solve these questions, let's make sure that you know what the units digit refers to.

The units digit of a number is the digit in the one's place. For example, the units digit in 945 is 5, and the units digit of 10,381 is 1.

Now that we know what the units digit (or one's place) is, let's get back to learning how to solve repeating powers questions that ask about the units digit.

Example 3: What is the units digit of 7^{122} ?
A. 1   B. 2   C. 3   D. 7   E. 9

Solution: If we try to enter this into the calculator, most calculators will either give us an error or will show us a number in scientific notation. Either way, we cannot see the number in the units digit, so we need to take another approach.

To solve, we need to identify the repeating pattern as the exponent increases. Take a look at the powers of 7 written below and see if you can spot the pattern.

$$7^1 = 7 \qquad 7^5 = 16,807$$
$$7^2 = 49 \qquad 7^6 = 117,649$$
$$7^3 = 243 \qquad 7^7 = 823,543$$
$$7^4 = 2,401 \qquad 7^8 = 5,764,801$$

As the powers increase, we see a repeating pattern with the units digit. The units digits above are in the pattern

$$7, 9, 3, 1, 7, 9, 3, 1\ldots$$

The units digits repeat in the pattern of 7, 9, 3, 1 over and over again as the powers increase. Now that we see the pattern, we can use the same technique we did with repeating decimals: go to the end of the repeating unit.

$$7, 9, 3, 1, 7, 9, 3, 1\ldots$$
$$\qquad\uparrow\qquad\quad\uparrow$$
$$\qquad\text{4th}\qquad\text{8th}$$

The 4th power and the 8th power have a units digit of 1. As the repeating pattern continues, all powers that are a multiple of 4 will have a units digit of 1. $7^{12}, 7^{40}, 7^{400}$ will all have a units digit of 1.

We are looking for 7^{122}, so we need to find out what number is the 122nd term in the pattern. To do this, we want to see if 122 is a multiple of 4 and, if it is not, find the closest multiple of 4 near 122. 122 is not a multiple of 4, and the closest multiple of 4 is 120. This tells us that 7^{120} has a 1 in the units digit.

Counting forward in the pattern, 7^{121} has a 7 in the units digit and 7^{122} has a 9 in the units digit. **The answer is E.**

Chapter 20: Repeating Patterns

Example 4: 3^x has a 9 in the ones place. What digit does 3^{x+3} have in the ones place?
A. 1   B. 3   C. 6   D. 7   E. 9

Solution: To solve this question, we need to know the repeating pattern in the units digit for the powers of 3. The pattern with the powers of 3 is shown below:

$$3^1 = 3 \qquad\qquad 3^5 = 243$$
$$3^2 = 9 \qquad\qquad 3^6 = 729$$
$$3^3 = 27 \qquad\qquad 3^7 = 2,187$$
$$3^4 = 81 \qquad\qquad 3^8 = 6,561$$

As the powers increase, we see a repeating pattern in the units digit. The units above follow the pattern

$$3, 9, 7, 1, 3, 9, 7, 1 \ldots$$

The pattern of 3, 9, 7, 1 repeats over and over again as the powers increase.

In this question, 3^x has a 9 in the ones place. The easiest method to find out what digit is in the ones place of 3^{x+3} is to pick a value for x and use the pattern above. Since $3^2 = 9$, we can use $x = 2$. This works because the 9 is in the ones place.

Now, we need to find out what 3^{x+3} has in the ones place. Since we picked $x = 2$, 3^{x+3} becomes 3^5. $3^5 = 243$, so there is a 3 in the ones place. **The answer is B.**

We could have picked any value of x that made 3^x have a 9 in the ones place. Since $3^6 = 729$, we could have used $x = 6$ and solved from there. 3^{x+3} becomes 3^9. $3^9 = 19,683$, which has a 3 in the ones place. The term 3^{x+3} is telling us to go 3 terms forward in the repeating pattern. If we start at any term that has a 9 in the units digit and count 3 terms forward, we will always get to a term with a 3 in the units digit.

Commonly Tested Repeating Patterns with Powers and the Units Digit

There are a variety of numbers that have a repeating pattern in the units digit as the power increases. **The most commonly tested repeating patterns with powers repeat every 4 terms.** You should memorize the patterns for the numbers below.

$$2^1 = 2 \qquad 2^5 = 32 \qquad\qquad 3^1 = 3 \qquad 3^5 = 243$$
$$2^2 = 4 \qquad 2^6 = 64 \qquad\qquad 3^2 = 9 \qquad 3^6 = 729$$
$$2^3 = 8 \qquad 2^7 = 128 \qquad\qquad 3^3 = 27 \qquad 3^7 = 2,187$$
$$2^4 = 16 \qquad 2^8 = 256 \qquad\qquad 3^4 = 81 \qquad 3^8 = 6,561$$

$$7^1 = 7 \qquad 7^5 = 16,807 \qquad\qquad 8^1 = 8 \qquad 8^5 = 32,768$$
$$7^2 = 49 \qquad 7^6 = 117,649 \qquad\qquad 8^2 = 64 \qquad 8^6 = 262,144$$
$$7^3 = 243 \qquad 7^7 = 823,543 \qquad\qquad 8^3 = 512 \qquad 8^7 = 2,097,152$$
$$7^4 = 2,401 \qquad 7^8 = 5,764,801 \qquad\qquad 8^4 = 4,096 \qquad 8^8 = 16,777,216$$

If you ever see other numbers on the ACT in questions like examples 3 and 4, write out the powers until you see a repeating pattern. Once you spot the pattern, you can use the same methods we used in these examples to solve.

Repeating Patterns with Powers of i

The final repeating pattern we need to know is with the powers of i. For those of you who have not learned about complex numbers yet, this will be covered in Chapter 25. All you need to know for now is that $i = \sqrt{-1}$. The pattern for the powers of i is shown below.

$$i^1 = i \qquad\qquad i^5 = i$$
$$i^2 = -1 \qquad\qquad i^6 = -1$$
$$i^3 = -i \qquad\qquad i^7 = -i$$
$$i^4 = 1 \qquad\qquad i^8 = 1$$

As the powers increase, this pattern of $i, -1, -i, 1$ repeats over and over again every 4 terms. You should memorize this pattern. Since the pattern is every 4 terms, we will use the same method we just used with repeating powers.

> **Example 5:** $10i^{47} - 7$ is equal to:
>
> A. $-10i - 7$ B. $10i + 7$ C. $3i$ D. 3 E. 17

Solution: To solve, we need to find out what i^{46} is equal to. From the pattern above, we know power of i follow a repeating pattern. We can go to the end of the repeating unit.

$$i, -1, -i, 1, i, -1, -i, 1 \dots$$
$$\uparrow\uparrow$$
$$\text{4th}\text{8th}$$

i^4 and i^8 are equal to 1. As the repeating pattern continues, all powers that are a multiple of 4 will be equal to 1. i^{12}, i^{20}, i^{40} are all equal to 1.

We are looking for i^{47}, so we need to find out what number is the 47th term in the pattern. To do this, we want to find the closest multiple of 4 near 47. The closest multiples of 4 near 47 are 44 and 48. This tells us that $i^{44} = 1$ and $i^{48} = 1$.

If we use i^{44} and count forward in the pattern, $i^{45} = i$, $i^{46} = -1$, and $i^{47} = -i$. If we use i^{48} and count backwards, we see $i^{47} = -i$. Now that we know $i^{47} = -i$, we can plug in $-i$ for i^{47} and solve.

$$10i^{47} - 7 = 10(-i) - 7 = -10i - 7$$

The answer is A.

> **Example 6:** If k is a multiple of 4, i^{4k+1} equals:
>
> A. 1 B. $i + 1$ C. i D. $-i$ E. -1

Solution: The easiest way to solve this question is to pick a value for k. We can pick any multiple of 4. To make this as simple as possible, let's pick $k = 4$.

Next, plug in $k = 4$ and solve.

$$i^{4k+1} = i^{4(4)+1} = i^{17}$$

Now, we use the repeating pattern that we used in Example 5 to solve for i^{17}. All powers that are multiples of 4 are equal to 1, so we want to find a multiple of 4 close to 17. The closest multiple of 4 is 16, so $i^{16} = 1$. Counting forward in the sequence, we find that $i^{17} = i$. **The answer is C.**

How to Solve Repeating Patterns Questions

For any repeating patterns question, use the following steps:

1. **Identify the repeating unit.** For repeating decimals, this should be easy. For repeating powers, you will need to have the pattern memorized or write out the powers until you see the pattern repeat.

2. **Find the number of items in the repeating unit.** For example, $0.\overline{235638}$ has 6 items. All of the powers and i examples had 4 items.

3. **Go to the end of the repeating unit.** In $0.\overline{235638}$, the end of the repeating unit is the 8. In the powers patterns, the end of the repeating unit is the 4th term. This is the value of the term we will find in step 4.

4. **Find a multiple of the number of items in the repeating unit (step 2) closest to the target number.** For example, if you want to find the 103rd number after the decimal point in $0.\overline{235638}$, find a multiple of 6 near 103. The closest one is 102. The 102nd term is an 8.

5. **Count forwards or backwards in the repeating pattern to find target term.** In $0.\overline{235638}$, the 102nd term is 8 and the 103rd term is 2.

Repeating Patterns Practice: Answers on page 330.

1. What is the 81st digit after the decimal point in $0.\overline{46981}$?

   A. 1
   B. 4
   C. 6
   D. 8
   E. 9

2. What is the 331st digit after the decimal point in the repeating decimal $0.\overline{1679}$?

   A. 0
   B. 1
   C. 3
   D. 7
   E. 8

3. i^{77} is equal to:

   A. -1
   B. $-i$
   C. i
   D. 1
   E. 77

4. Given that today is Sunday, what day of the week will it be 132 days from today?

   A. Monday
   B. Wednesday
   C. Thursday
   D. Friday
   E. Saturday

5. What is the 297th digit after the decimal point in the repeating decimal $0.\overline{39765}$?

   A. 3
   B. 5
   C. 6
   D. 7
   E. 9

6. Given that today is Thursday, what day of the week was 205 days ago?

   A. Friday
   B. Saturday
   C. Sunday
   D. Monday
   E. Tuesday

7. What is the 52nd digit after the decimal point in the repeating decimal $0.\overline{80345}$?

   A. 0
   B. 3
   C. 4
   D. 5
   E. 8

8. What is $10i^{16} - 4i^6$ equal to?

   A. 4
   B. 6
   C. 10
   D. 14
   E. 40

PrepPros

9. What is the 217th digit after the decimal point in the repeating decimal $0.\overline{217657}$?

   A. 1
   B. 2
   C. 5
   D. 6
   E. 7

10. When 7^{217} is multiplied out, what is the digit in the ones place?

    A. 1
    B. 2
    C. 3
    D. 7
    E. 9

11. Given that today is Friday, what day of the week will it be in 157 days?

    A. Sunday
    B. Saturday
    C. Monday
    D. Tuesday
    E. Wednesday

12. What is the value of i^{263}?

    A. i
    B. -1
    C. $-i$
    D. 1
    E. Cannot be determined

13. When 3^{106} is multiplied out, what is the digit in the ones place?

    A. 1
    B. 3
    C. 4
    D. 7
    E. 9

14. When 2^{132} is multiplied out, what is the digit in the ones place?

    A. 0
    B. 2
    C. 4
    D. 6
    E. 8

15. If 8^{90} has a 4 in the units digit, what number does 8^{92} have in the units digit?

    A. 0
    B. 2
    C. 4
    D. 6
    E. 8

16. If m is an integer, what does i^{8m-3} equal?

    A. i
    B. $-i$
    C. -1
    D. 1
    E. Cannot be determined.

17. $\dfrac{i^{102}}{i^{80}} =$

    A. i^{12}
    B. i^{13}
    C. i^{14}
    D. i^{15}
    E. i^{16}

18. Barney purchased a new laptop in June that is estimated to stop working in 90 months. What month is his laptop estimated to stop working?

    A. February
    B. March
    C. July
    D. October
    E. December

19. If 7^{x-2} has a 3 in the ones place, what digit does 7^{x+3} have in the ones place?

    A. 1
    B. 3
    C. 7
    D. 9
    E. Cannot be determined.

20. If $i^{7k-3} = i$, which of the following statements must be true?

A. When $7k - 3$ is divided by 4, the remainder is 0.
B. When $7k - 3$ is divided by 4, the remainder is 1.
C. When $7k - 3$ is divided by 4, the remainder is 2.
D. When $7k - 3$ is divided by 4, the remainder is 3.
E. Cannot be determined from the given information.

Chapter 21: Circles, Ellipses, and Hyperbolas

We can almost guarantee that you will see at least one circle question on the ACT. Ellipses are a commonly tested topic at the end of the test and appear in questions 45-60. Hyperbolas appear rarely on the ACT, but they have appeared more in recent years and will certainly be on the ACT again in the future.

Circles

In order to answer circles questions on the ACT, you need to be familiar with the equation for a circle and how to graph a circle.

Equation for a Circle

The equation for a circle with a center at the origin and a radius r is

$$x^2 + y^2 = r^2$$

Just to make sure you understand this, let's go over this equation with some numbers. Let's start with

$$x^2 + y^2 = 16$$

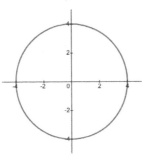

This equation is a circle with its center at the origin and a radius of 4. Make sure that you remember that the number represents r^2. Many students forget this and mistakenly think the radius here is 16.

The equation for a circle with a center at (h, k) and a radius r is

$$(x - h)^2 + (y - k)^2 = r^2$$

We call this the standard form of a circle. This is the equation that you need to memorize for test day, as questions using this form come up far more often. Again, let's put some numbers in to make sure we understand how this works.

$$(x - 3)^2 + (y + 5)^2 = 49$$

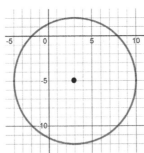

This equation is a circle with a center at $(3, -5)$ and a radius of 7. Make sure that you notice the sign of the h and k values in the equation is the opposite of the actual coordinate of the center (h, k). The expression $(x - 3)^2$ shows the x-coordinate is at $x = 3$, not $x = -3$. The experssion $(y + 5)^2$ shows the y-coordinate is at $y = -5$ not $y = 5$. A common mistake is to think the center of this circle is at $(-3, 5)$.

Chapter 21: Circles, Ellipses, and Hyperbolas

Example 1: A circle in the (x, y) coordinate plane has a center $(-9, 4)$ and a radius of 6. Which of the following is the equation of the circle?

A. $(x - 9)^2 + (y + 4)^2 = 36$
B. $(x + 9)^2 + (y - 4)^2 = 36$
C. $(x + 9)^2 + (y + 4)^2 = 36$
D. $(x - 9)^2 + (y + 4)^2 = 6$
E. $(x + 9)^2 + (y - 4)^2 = 6$

Solution: For this question, we need to properly use the equation of a circle. The radius is 6, so the right side must equal r^2, which here is 36. Since the center is at $(-9, 4)$, we need to see the opposite signs of h and k, which here are $+9$ and -4 respectively, in the circle equation. **The answer is B.**

Example 2: In the (x, y) coordinate plane, which of the following equations is that of a circle that has a center $(3, -5)$ and a radius of $\sqrt{10}$?

A. $(x - 3)^2 + (y - 5)^2 = \sqrt{10}$
B. $(x - 3)^2 + (y + 5)^2 = \sqrt{10}$
C. $(x + 3)^2 + (y - 5)^2 = 10$
D. $(x - 3)^2 + (y + 5)^2 = 10$
E. $(x - 9)^2 + (y + 5)^2 = 100$

Solution: As in the last example, we need to properly use the equation of a circle. The radius is $\sqrt{10}$, so the right side must equal r^2, which here is 10. Since the center is at $(3, -5)$, we need to see the opposite signs of h and k, which here are -3 and $+5$ respectively, in the circle equation. **The answer is D.**

Advanced Circle Questions

For more difficult circle questions, the ACT requires a deeper understanding of some basic principles of how circles work. While these principles may at times seem simple, recognizing these principles will be critical to solving more advanced circle questions.

Principle #1: The two endpoints of any diameter on a circle have their midpoint at the center of the circle.

Try this on your own. Grab a piece of paper and draw a circle. No matter how you draw the diameter, the center of the circle will be the midpoint of the diameter.

Example 3: Circle P has its center at $(2, 7)$. If AB is a diameter of circle P and point A is at $(-3, 4)$, which of the following is point B?

A. $(7, 10)$ B. $(-8, 1)$ C. $(-\frac{1}{2}, \frac{11}{2})$ D. $(6, 8)$ E. $(8, 11)$

Solution: Using principle #1, we know that the center of the circle must be the midpoint of AB. Since we are given point A, we can use the midpoint formula to solve for point B. To solve for the x-coordinate, we set up

$$\frac{x+(-3)}{2} = 2$$
$$x - 3 = 4$$
$$x = 7$$

At this point if we check the answer choices, we already know that **the answer is A**. Be sure to always check the answer choices once you find either the x-coordinate or y-coordinate of a point.

To finish solving this question algebraically, we solve for the y-coordinate.
$$\frac{y+(4)}{2} = 7$$
$$y + 4 = 14$$
$$y = 10$$

Point B is at (7,10), so **the answer is A.** If you need to review how to use the midpoint formula, go back to Chapter 5.

Principle #2: The distance between the center and any endpoint of a diameter of a circle is equal to the radius of the circle.

If this principle seems obvious, it is because it is. It is just the definition of a radius! However, it is helpful to recognize if you are only given two endpoints of a diameter and are asked to find the equation of the circle.

Example 4: In the xy-plane, points $(4, 2)$ and $(6, 10)$ are the endpoints of a diameter on circle. Which of the following is the equation of the circle?

A. $(x-1)^2 + (y-4)^2 = 68$
B. $(x-4)^2 + (y-2)^2 = 68$
C. $(x-1)^2 + (y-4)^2 = 17$
D. $(x-5)^2 + (y-6)^2 = 68$
E. $(x-5)^2 + (y-6)^2 = 17$

Solution: To find the equation of the circle, we need to find the center and the radius. To find the center, we need to find the midpoint of the two endpoints of the diameter. The x-coordinate of the center is at
$$\frac{4+6}{2} = x$$
$$x = 5$$

The y-coordinate of the center is at
$$\frac{2+10}{2} = y$$
$$y = 6$$

The center of the circle is at $(5, 6)$. From this, we know that answer choices A, B, and C are incorrect. Now that we know the center, we can find the radius using principle #2. The distance from the center to either of the endpoints is equal to the radius. Here, we will use point $(4, 2)$ to find the radius using the distance formula.
$$r = \sqrt{(5-4)^2 + (6-2)^2}$$
$$r = \sqrt{(1)^2 + (4)^2}$$
$$r = \sqrt{17}$$

If you need to review the distance formula, go back to Chapter 5.

Now that we know the radius, we can finish this question. The right side of a circle equation is equal to r^2. Since $(\sqrt{17})^2 = 17$, **the answer is E.**

TIP – Draw It Out: For any questions like this, we recommend making a drawing. Sketching a coordinate plane, labeling the endpoints of the diameter, and drawing the circle can help you identify what steps you need to take to solve the question. Even if you still cannot find the exact answer, you can often at least eliminate some incorrect answer choices and make a more educated guess after drawing it out.

Ellipses

For ellipses questions on the ACT, you need to be familiar with the equation for an ellipse and know how draw the graph of an ellipse.

Standard Equation of an Ellipse

The equation of an ellipse with a center at the origin is

$$\frac{x^2}{a^2} + \frac{y^2}{b^2} = 1$$

Here, we can think of **a as the x-radius**, which shows us how far left and right the ellipse goes from the center, and **b as the y-radius**, which tells you how far up and down the ellipse goes from the center. Many textbooks switch a and b depending on the shape of the ellipse, but we will just think of a as the x-radius and b as the y-radius in this book to make this topic simpler to teach.

When written in standard form, **ellipses always have a + sign in the middle and are always equal to 1.** Instead of having a diameter, ellipses have a major and minor axis. The major axis is the longer diameter of the ellipse, and the minor axis is the shorter diameter of the ellipse. It is important to remember that the lengths of the axes are equal to 2a and 2b.

All of that probably seems very confusing to any of you who have not done ellipses before, so let's go over this equation with some numbers.

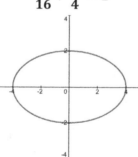

$$\frac{x^2}{16} + \frac{y^2}{4} = 1$$

The center of this ellipse is at the origin. For this ellipse $a = 4$ and $b = 2$. a is the x-radius, so the ellipse goes 4 units to the left from the center to the point $(-4, 0)$ and 4 units to the right of the center to the point $(4,0)$. b is the y-radius, so the ellipse goes 2 units up from the center to the point $(0,2)$ and 2 units down from the center to the point $(0, -2)$. These four points are called the **vertices**.

The length of the major axis is 8 and the length of the minor axis is 4.

Example 5: Which of the following equations describes the ellipse shown in the standard (x, y) coordinate plane below?

A. $\frac{x^2}{4} + \frac{y^2}{6} = 1$

B. $\frac{x^2}{16} + \frac{y^2}{36} = 1$

C. $\frac{x^2}{4} + \frac{y^2}{-6} = 1$

D. $x^2 + y^2 = 36$

E. $\frac{x^2}{16} + \frac{y^2}{36} = 52$

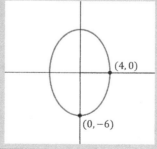

Solution: The ellipse has its center at the origin. The ellipse goes 4 units right of the center and 6 units down from the center, so $a = 4$ and $b = 6$. The values in the denominator should be a^2, which here is 16, and b^2, which here is 36, so the answer is B.

Answer choice D is a circle. Answer choice E is incorrect since it is equal to 52, and ellipses must always be equal to 1.

The equation for an ellipse with the center at (h, k) is

$$\frac{(x-h)^2}{a^2} + \frac{(y-k)^2}{b^2} = 1$$

This is the equation that you need to memorize for test day, as questions using this form come up more often on test day. Again, let's put some numbers in to make sure we understand how this works.

$$\frac{(x-2)^2}{4} + \frac{(y+3)^2}{25} = 1$$

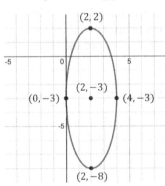

The center of the ellipse is at $(2, -3)$. Just like in circles, the sign of the h and k values in the equation is the opposite of the actual coordinate of the center (h, k). $a = 2$, so two of the vertices are 2 units left and right of the center at points $(0, -3)$ and $(4, -3)$. $b = 5$, so the other two vertices are 5 units up and down from the center at points $(2, 2)$ and $(2, -8)$.

Example 6: Shown below is an ellipse in the standard (x, y) coordinate plane. If the ellipse is described by the equation $\frac{(x+4)^2}{4} + \frac{(y+3)^2}{16} = 1$, what are the coordinates of points A and B?

	Point A	Point B
A.	$(-6, -3)$	$(-4, -7)$
B.	$(-6, -3)$	$(-4, -19)$
C.	$(-6, -7)$	$(-4, -7)$
D.	$(-8, -7)$	$(-4, -20)$
E.	$(-8, -3)$	$(-4, -7)$

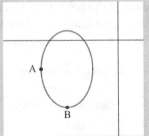

Solution: From the equation, we can see the center of the ellipse is at $(-4, -3)$. Since $a^2 = 4$, $a = 2$, which means point A will be 2 units left of the center at $(-6, -3)$. Since $b^2 = 16$, $b = 4$, which means point B will be 4 units down from the center at $(-4, -7)$. **The answer is A.**

As you see with this example, if you know the general equation of an ellipse and how to graph an ellipse on the coordinate plane, you should be able to solve ellipse questions pretty quickly and easily!

Chapter 21: Circles, Ellipses, and Hyperbolas

Foci on an Ellipse

Each ellipse has two foci (plural of focus) on its major axis. The major axis is the longest diameter of the ellipse. The two focus points are equal distances from the center. On the ACT, you do not need to know how to find the foci, but you do need to know what they are and where they generally appear on an ellipse. If you understand the diagrams below, you will be able to answer any foci questions on test day.

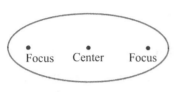
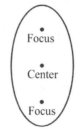

As long as you know where foci are generally located on an ellipse, you can solve any foci questions on test day.

Example 7: For an ellipse with the equation $\frac{(x+2)^2}{25} + \frac{(y-8)^2}{9} = 1$, which of the following ordered pairs are the foci of the ellipse?

- A. $(-2, 8)$ and $(-7, 8)$
- B. $(-7, 8)$ and $(3, 8)$
- C. $(-6, 8)$ and $(2, 8)$
- D. $(-2, 13)$ and $(3, 8)$
- E. $(-7, 8)$ and $(-2, 3)$

Solution: First, we need to draw the ellipse on the coordinate plane. The ellipse has a center at $(-2, 8)$. Since $a^2 = 25$, $a = 5$, which means two of the vertices are 5 units left and right of the center at points $(-7, 8)$ and $(3, 8)$. Since $b^2 = 9$, $b = 3$, which means two of the vertices are 3 units up and down from the center at points $(-2, 11)$ and $(-2, 5)$.

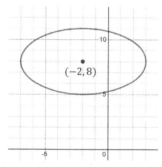

Once we have drawn the ellipse, we can use the answer choices to see which points will match with where the foci should be. We know the foci are on the major axis, so the y-value of both points should be at $y = 8$. Therefore, we know answer choices D and E are incorrect. Point $(-2, 8)$ is the center, so A is incorrect. Points $(-7, 8)$ and $(3, 8)$ are vertices, so B is incorrect. The foci should be a bit inside the ellipse, so **the answer is C.**

Example 7 is more difficult than any foci question that has ever been on the ACT as of the writing of this book. The ACT usually includes a picture of the ellipse for foci questions. Therefore, it is much easier for us to see where the foci are located and use the answer choices to find the correct coordinates of the foci.

Hyperbolas

Hyperbolas rarely appear on the ACT. In recent years, the ACT has been adding more questions with advanced topics, so we certainly expect hyperbolas to appear more frequently on future ACTs. If you see any hyperbolas questions on the ACT, you need to be familiar with the equations for vertical and horizontal hyperbolas and how to graph a hyperbola on the coordinate plane.

Standard Equation of a Hyperbola

The standard equation for a vertical hyperbola and horizontal hyperbola with center $(0, 0)$ are shown below.

Horizontal Hyperbola
$$\frac{x^2}{a^2} - \frac{y^2}{b^2} = 1$$

Vertical Hyperbola
$$\frac{y^2}{a^2} - \frac{x^2}{b^2} = 1$$

When written in standard form, **hyperbolas always have a negative sign in the middle and are always equal to 1. The a-value shows how many units from the center the two vertices will be.** We will see how this appears on graphs in the examples below. For the ACT, you do not need to know what b represents or how to find the foci.

Let's plug in some number and see how hyperbolas appear on a graph.

Horizontal Hyperbola
$$\frac{x^2}{4} - \frac{y^2}{9} = 1$$

Vertical Hyperbola
$$\frac{y^2}{4} - \frac{x^2}{9} = 1$$

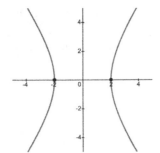
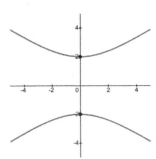

Notice how the sign of the x^2 and y^2 terms determine the direction of the hyperbolas. When the x^2 term is positive and the y^2 term is negative, the hyperbola is horizontal. When the y^2 term is positive and the x^2 term is negative, the hyperbola is vertical.

For both hyperbolas above, $a = 2$, so the vertices are 2 units from the center. The center is at the origin for both hyperbolas. For the horizontal hyperbola, the vertices are at $(-2, 0)$ and $(2, 0)$. For the vertical hyperbola, the vertices are at $(0, -2)$ and $(0, 2)$.

For any hyperbola with center (h, k), the equation is

Horizontal Hyperbola
$$\frac{(x-h)^2}{a^2} - \frac{(y-k)^2}{b^2} = 1$$

Vertical Hyperbola
$$\frac{(y-k)^2}{a^2} - \frac{(x-h)^2}{b^2} = 1$$

For a horizontal hyperbola, the vertices are located at $(h \pm a, k)$. For a vertical hyperbola, the vertices are located at $(h, k \pm a)$.

Let's plug in some numbers and see how these appear in the coordinate plane.

$$\frac{(x-3)^2}{16} - \frac{(y-1)^2}{4} = 1$$

$$\frac{(y+4)^2}{9} - \frac{(x-2)^2}{25} = 1$$

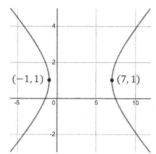
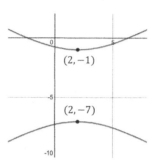

For the horizontal hyperbola, the center (not shown) is at $(3, 1)$. $a = 4$, so the vertices are 4 units left and right of the center (not shown) at points $(-1, 1)$ and $(7, 1)$. For the vertical parabolas, the center (not shown) is at $(2, -4)$. $a = 3$, so the vertices are 3 units up and down from the center at points $(2, -1)$ and $(2, -7)$. Make sure that you do not mistakenly think the center is at $(-4, 2)$. Remember, in the equation for vertical parabolas, the order of the h and k values for the center are switched.

Example 8: A hyperbola that has vertices $(2, 4)$ and $(2, 10)$ is shown below in the standard (x, y) coordinate plane. The hyperbola has which of the following equations?

A. $\frac{(y-4)^2}{9} - \frac{(x-2)^2}{16} = 1$

B. $\frac{(y-7)^2}{9} - \frac{(x-2)^2}{16} = 1$

C. $\frac{(y-7)^2}{16} - \frac{(x-2)^2}{16} = 1$

D. $\frac{(x-2)^2}{9} - \frac{(y-7)^2}{16} = 1$

E. $\frac{(x-2)^2}{9} + \frac{(y-7)^2}{16} = 1$

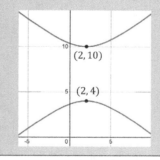

Solution: We need a vertical hyperbola, so D, which is a horizontal parabola, and E, which is an ellipse, are incorrect. The center must be the midpoint between the two vertices. To solve for the center, use the midpoint formula.

$$\text{Center} = \left(\frac{2+2}{2}, \frac{10+4}{2}\right) = (2, 7)$$

Answer choice A incorrectly has the center at $(2, 4)$. The vertices are 3 units up and down from the center, so $a = 3$ and therefore $a^2 = 9$. **The answer is B.**

PrepPros

Circles, Ellipses, and Hyperbolas Practice: Answers on page 330.

 1. In the standard (x, y) plane, what is the center of the circle $(x - 3)^2 + (y + 4)^2 = 16$?

A. $(-3, 4)$
B. $(3, 4)$
C. $(3, -4)$
D. $(4, 4)$
E. $(-4, 4)$

 2. In the standard (x, y) plane, what is diameter of the circle $(x + 5)^2 + (y - 3)^2 = 36$?

A. 6
B. 6π
C. 12
D. 12π
E. 36π

 3. Which of the following equations is that of a circle that is in the standard (x, y) coordinate plane, has a center at $(4, -7)$, and has a radius of 8?

A. $(x + 4)^2 + (y - 7)^2 = 8$
B. $(x - 4)^2 + (y + 7)^2 = 8$
C. $(x - 4)^2 + (y + 7)^2 = 2\sqrt{2}$
D. $(x + 4)^2 + (y - 7)^2 = 64$
E. $(x - 4)^2 + (y + 7)^2 = 64$

 4. In the standard (x, y) coordinate plane, what is the area of the following circle?

$$(x + 2)^2 + (y - 3)^2 = 144$$

A. 12
B. 12π
C. 64π
D. 144
E. 144π

 5. In the (x, y) coordinate plane, what is the radius of a circle having points $(-2, 1)$ and $(4, 9)$ as endpoints of a diameter?

A. 5
B. 6
C. 8
D. 10
E. 25

 6. Which of the following equations is that of a circle that is in the standard (x, y) coordinate plane, has a center at $(-11, 5)$, and has a radius of 4?

A. $(x + 11)^2 + (y - 5)^2 = 4$
B. $(x - 11)^2 + (y + 5)^2 = 4$
C. $(x - 11)^2 + (y + 5)^2 = 2$
D. $(x + 11)^2 + (y - 5)^2 = 16$
E. $(x - 11)^2 + (y + 5)^2 = 16$

 7. Michelle is standing at the center of a field swinging a ball attached to a 12-foot string. To graph the path of the ball on the (x, y) coordinate plane, Michelle decides the point where she is standing is the origin and each coordinate unit represents 1 foot. Which of the following equations best models the path of the ball during 1 full swing?

A. $x^2 + y^2 = 144$
B. $x^2 + y^2 = 12$
C. $x^2 + y^2 = \sqrt{12}$
D. $\frac{x^2}{12} + \frac{y^2}{8} = 1$
E. $\frac{x^2}{12} + \frac{y^2}{8} = 144$

 8. A circle in the standard (x, y) coordinate plane has a radius of $2\sqrt{3}$ and a center at $(0, 5)$. Which of the following is the equation of the circle?

A. $x^2 + (y + 5)^2 = 2\sqrt{3}$
B. $x^2 + (y - 5)^2 = 2\sqrt{3}$
C. $x^2 + (y + 5)^2 = 12$
D. $x^2 + (y - 5)^2 = 12$
E. $x^2 + (y - 5)^2 = 36$

9. Which of the following gives the equation of a circle tangent to $y = 6$ with a center of $(6, 3)$?

A. $(x - 3)^2 + (y + 6)^2 = 3$
B. $(x - 6)^2 + (y - 3)^2 = 3$
C. $(x - 6)^2 + (y - 3)^2 = 9$
D. $(x + 6)^2 + (y + 3)^2 = 9$
E. $(x - 6)^2 + (y - 3)^2 = 36$

10. In the standard (x, y) coordinate plane, the circle centered at the origin that passes through $(8, 6)$ is the set of all points that are:

   A. 10 coordinate units from the origin
   B. 10 coordinate units from the origin and $(8,6)$
   C. Equidistant from the origin and $(8,6)$
   D. Equidistant from the line segment with endpoints at the origin and $(8,6)$
   E. Cannot be determined

11. One of the following equations determines the graph below. Which one?

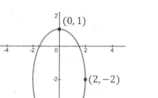

   A. $\frac{x^2}{2} + \frac{(y-2)^2}{3} = 1$
   B. $\frac{x^2}{4} + \frac{(y-2)^2}{9} = 1$
   C. $\frac{x^2}{4} + \frac{(y+2)^2}{9} = 1$
   D. $\frac{x^2}{9} + \frac{(y-2)^2}{4} = 1$
   E. $\frac{x^2}{9} + \frac{(y+2)^2}{4} = 1$

12. Which of the following equations determines the ellipse shown in the standard (x, y) coordinate plane below?

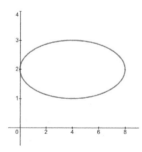

   A. $\frac{(x-4)^2}{16} + \frac{(y-2)^2}{4} = 1$
   B. $\frac{(x-4)^2}{16} + \frac{(y-2)^2}{1} = 1$
   C. $\frac{(x-4)^2}{4} + \frac{(y-2)^2}{2} = 1$
   D. $\frac{(x-4)^2}{1} + \frac{(y-2)^2}{16} = 1$
   E. $\frac{(x-4)^2}{16} - \frac{(y-2)^2}{2} = 1$

13. Shown below is an ellipse in the standard (x, y) coordinate plane. If the ellipse is described by the equation $\frac{(x-1)^2}{49} + \frac{(y-6)^2}{16} = 1$, what are the coordinates of vertices A and B?

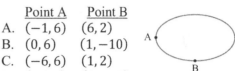

	Point A	Point B
A.	$(-1, 6)$	$(6, 2)$
B.	$(0, 6)$	$(1, -10)$
C.	$(-6, 6)$	$(1, 2)$
D.	$(-6, 2)$	$(1, -10)$
E.	$(8, 6)$	$(-1, 6)$

14. For an ellipse with the equation $\frac{(x-5)^2}{16} + \frac{(y-5)^2}{25} = 1$, which of the following ordered pairs are the foci of the ellipse?

   A. $(2, 5)$ and $(8, 5)$
   B. $(5, 2)$ and $(5, 8)$
   C. $(-2, 8)$ and $(5, 5)$
   D. $(5, 0)$ and $(5, 10)$
   E. $(5, 0)$ and $(1, 5)$

15. Suppose the equations $(x - 10)^2 + y^2 = 16$ and $(x - 5)^2 + y^2 = 100$ are graphed in the same standard (x, y) coordine plane. How many points of intersection do these graphs share?

   A. 0
   B. 1
   C. 2
   D. 3
   E. 4

16. A circle in the standard (x, y) coordinate plane has a center $(3, 6)$. One endpoint of a diameter of the circle has y-coordinate 10. What is the y-coordinate of the other endpoint of the diameter?

   A. 0
   B. 1
   C. 2
   D. 3
   E. 6

17. A hyperbola is shown below in the standard (x, y) coordinate plane. The hyperbola has which of the following equations?

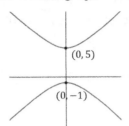

A. $\frac{(y-2)^2}{9} - \frac{x^2}{16} = 1$
B. $\frac{(y-2)^2}{36} - \frac{x^2}{16} = 1$
C. $\frac{y^2}{9} - \frac{(x-2)^2}{16} = 1$
D. $\frac{y^2}{36} - \frac{(x-2)^2}{16} = 1$
E. $\frac{x^2}{9} - \frac{(y-2)^2}{16} = 1$

18. Suppose the equations $(x+1)^2 + (y-3)^2 = 9$ and $\frac{(x-2)^2}{25} + \frac{(y-3)^2}{4} = 1$ are graphed in the same standard (x, y) coordinate plane. How many points of intersection do these graphs share?

A. 0
B. 1
C. 2
D. 3
E. 4

19. A circle in the standard (x, y) coordinate plane contains two points that are 10 coordinate units apart and make a diameter. Which of the following could be the equation of the circle?

A. $(x-10)^2 + (y-10)^2 = 100$
B. $(x+100)^2 + (y-30)^2 = 10$
C. $\left(x+\sqrt{10}\right)^2 + \left(y-\sqrt{10}\right)^2 = 10$
D. $(x+225)^2 + (y-100)^2 = 500$
E. $(x-95)^2 + (y-107)^2 = 25$

20. In the (x, y) coordinate plane, the points $(-4, 3)$ and $(4, -3)$ are the endpoints of the diameter of a circle. Which of the following is the equation of the circle?

A. $x^2 + y^2 = 25$
B. $x + y^2 = 100$
C. $(x-4)^2 + (y+3)^2 = 25$
D. $(x-4)^2 + (y+3)^2 = 100$
E. $(x+4)^2 + (y-3)^2 = 25$

21. A circle in the standard (x, y) coordinate plane intersects the y-axis at $(0, 5)$ and $(0, 11)$. The radius of the circle is 5 coordinate units. Which of the following could be the center of the circle?

I. $(-4, 8)$
II. $(0, 8)$
III. $(4, 8)$

A. I only
B. II only
C. III only
D. I and III only
E. I, II, and III

22. The point $(3, b)$ lies on the ellipse with the given equation of $\frac{(x+3)^2}{36} + \frac{(y+4)^2}{25} = 1$. What is the value of b?

A. -4
B. -3
C. 1
D. 4
E. 5

23. Which of the following points represents an endpoint of the major axis of the ellipse with the equation $\frac{(x-3)^2}{9} + \frac{(y+4)^2}{25} = 1$?

A. $(3, -4)$
B. $(3, -29)$
C. $(3, 1)$
D. $(0, 4)$
E. $(0, 1)$

- 208 -

24. Graphed in the standard (x, y) coordinate plane is an ellipse. The center of the ellipse is $(0, 0)$. What is the value of a?

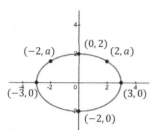

A. $\frac{4}{3}$
B. $\frac{2\sqrt{5}}{3}$
C. $\frac{4\sqrt{3}}{2}$
D. 4
E. $2\sqrt{5}$

25. Which of the following equations determines the ellipse shown in the standard (x, y) coordinate plane below?

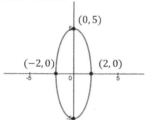

A. $2x^2 + 5y^2 = 10$
B. $5x^2 + 2y^2 = 10$
C. $10x^2 + 4y^2 = 40$
D. $25x^2 + 4y^2 = 100$
E. $75x^2 + 40y^2 = 3{,}000$

26. Points A and B represent the foci of the ellipse. Which of the following points represent A and B of the ellipse with the equation $\frac{x^2}{25} + \frac{y^2}{16} = 1$?

	Point A	Point B
A.	$(0, 0)$	$(0, 4)$
B.	$(0, -3)$	$(0, 3)$
C.	$(5, 0)$	$(-5, 0)$
D.	$(-3, 0)$	$(3, 0)$
E.	$(-3, 0)$	$(0, 4)$

27. A hyperbola that has vertices $(-1, -2)$ and $(3, -2)$ and that passes through the point $(-3, 0)$ is shown below in the standard (x, y) coordinate plane. The hyperbola has which of the following equations?

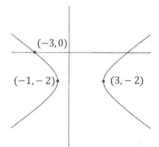

A. $\frac{(x-1)^2}{4} + \frac{3(y+2)^2}{4} = 1$
B. $\frac{(x-1)^2}{4} + \frac{4(y+2)^2}{3} = 1$
C. $\frac{(x+1)^2}{4} - \frac{3(y+2)^2}{4} = 1$
D. $\frac{(x-1)^2}{4} - \frac{3(y+2)^2}{4} = 1$
E. $\frac{(x-1)^2}{4} - \frac{4(y+2)^2}{3} = 1$

28. A hyperbola passes through the points $(0, -1)$, $(0, 1)$, and $(4, 5)$ on the standard (x, y) coordinate plane. The hyperbola has which of the following equations?

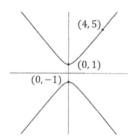

A. $4y^2 - 6x^2 = 4$
B. $4y^2 - 6x^2 = 6$
C. $5y^2 - 4x^2 = 4$
D. $4x^2 - 6y^2 = 6$
E. $4x^2 - 6y^2 = 4$

29. Points $(4, a)$ and $(b, 3)$ lie on the ellipse with the equation $\frac{x^2}{16} + \frac{y^2}{36} = 1$. Which of the following gives the value of $a + b$?

A. 2
B. $\sqrt{7}$
C. 3
D. $\sqrt{12}$
E. $2\sqrt{21}$

Chapter 22: Probability

The Basics of Probability

Probability is the likelihood of a desired outcome occurring compared to the total number of possible outcomes. On the ACT, probability is usually listed as a fraction or, less commonly, a decimal or a percentage.

$$\text{Probability} = \frac{\text{Desired Outcome}}{\text{All Possible Outcomes}}$$

The ACT often will phrase probability questions by asking you the probability of an event occurring. To answer these questions, consider the event that you are counting and compare it to the total number of possible outcomes.

To learn how probability works, let's work through a few questions with the following example:

Example 1: A bag has a total of 38 chocolate candies. 18 of the candies are blue, 10 are red, 5 are yellow, 3 are green, and 2 are pink.

Question 1: Andy will reach into the bag and pick one candy. What is the probability that he will grab a yellow candy?

A. $\frac{5}{33}$ B. $\frac{5}{18}$ C. $\frac{5}{38}$ D. $\frac{10}{38}$ E. $\frac{5}{19}$

Solution: There is a total of 38 candies in the bag, and there are 5 yellow candies. Therefore, the probability of selecting a yellow candy is $\frac{5}{38}$. **The answer is C.**

Question 2: Evelyn is going to pick one piece of chocolate candy from the bag. What is the probability that she will NOT pick a blue candy?

A. $\frac{9}{19}$ B. $\frac{10}{19}$ C. $\frac{9}{38}$ D. $\frac{10}{38}$ E. $\frac{19}{38}$

Solution: There is a total of 18 blue candies in the bag, which means there are 20 candies that are not blue. The probability of selecting a chocolate candy that is not blue is $\frac{20}{38}$, which simplifies to $\frac{10}{19}$. **The answer is B.**

Pretty easy, right? Now, these questions get a bit more difficult when you have probabilities that involve multiple events. **It is important to remember that with multiple events, we multiply the probabilities of each individual event together.** Make sure that you remember to multiply fractions and not add them, as the most common mistake students make is incorrectly adding the fractions when you are supposed to multiply.

Question 3: Min will select 2 chocolate candies from the bag without replacement. What is the probability that Min will select a red candy and then a green candy?

A. $\frac{13}{75}$ B. $\frac{15}{722}$ C. $\frac{15}{703}$ D. $\frac{13}{76}$ E. $\frac{105}{1444}$

Solution: We have two probabilities. For the first probability, there are a total of 38 candies in the bag and 10 red candies, so the probability of selecting a red candy is $\frac{10}{38}$. For the second probability, there are only 37 candies left in the bag since Min does not replace the first candy. There are still 3 green candies in the bag, so the probability of the second candy being green is $\frac{3}{37}$. Since we have multiple events occurring in a row, we multiply the probabilities together.

$$\frac{10}{38} \times \frac{3}{37} = \frac{30}{1,406}$$

Simplifying the fraction, we get an answer of $\frac{15}{703}$. **The answer is C.**

For questions like #3, **make sure to read carefully to see if the selection is with replacement or without replacement, as it changes the answer.** If Min instead replaced the chocolate candy he selected the first time, there would still be a total of 38 candies in the bag for the 2nd piece of candy he draws from the bag, so the total probability instead would be

$$\frac{10}{38} \times \frac{3}{38} = \frac{30}{1,444}$$

Questions like this are one of the most common types of probability questions, so make sure you understand the difference between replacement and no replacement and how it affects the probability!

Example 2: Two fair six-sided dice are repeatedly rolled simultaneously. What is the probability that two 6's are rolled on the 15th roll?

  A. $\frac{1}{3}$ B. $\frac{1}{6}$ C. $\frac{1}{12}$ D. $\frac{1}{36}$ E. $\frac{1}{60}$

Solution: The probabilities of rolling a 6 on each die is $\frac{1}{6}$. Since we have multiple events occurring, we must multiply the probabilities together to solve.

$$\frac{1}{6} \times \frac{1}{6} = \frac{1}{36}$$

The answer is D. The fact that the question says this is the 15th roll has no effect on the probability. It is just there to confuse you!

3 Probability Rules to Know

There are three probability rules that you need to know for test day.

Rule #1 – The sum of the probabilities of all possible outcomes is equal to 1.

For example, let's think of a flipping a coin. The probability of flipping a head is $\frac{1}{2}$, and the probability of flipping a tail is $\frac{1}{2}$. Of course, $\frac{1}{2} + \frac{1}{2} = 1$. All coin flips must end in a head or a tail, so the sum of the probabilities of those events must equal 1.

Example 3: In a class of fifth graders, students were asked to pick their favorite lunch, and no student was allowed to select more than one lunch as their favorite: $\frac{1}{2}$ picked pizza, $\frac{1}{5}$ picked chicken nuggets, $\frac{1}{10}$ picked pasta, and $\frac{3}{20}$ picked tacos. What is the probability that a randomly selected student did not select any of these lunches?

  A. 0   B. $\frac{3}{1600}$ C. $\frac{1}{20}$ D. $\frac{5}{60}$ E. $\frac{1}{60}$

Solution: All fifth graders selected a favorite lunch, so the sum of the fractions must add up to 1. We can use the given fractions to find the fraction of students, x, who did not select any of the lunches.

$$\frac{1}{2} + \frac{1}{5} + \frac{1}{10} + \frac{3}{20} + x = 1$$

To solve, we need to make the fractions all have a common denominator. Here, the least common denominator is 20. If you need to review adding fractions, go back to Chapter 6.

$$\frac{10}{20} + \frac{4}{20} + \frac{2}{20} + \frac{3}{20} + x = 1 \rightarrow \frac{19}{20} + x = 1$$

$$x = \frac{1}{20}$$

The fraction of students who selected none of the lunches is $\frac{1}{20}$, so the probability that a randomly selected student picked none of the lunches is also $\frac{1}{20}$. **The answer is C.**

Rule #2 – The probability of Event A OR Event B occurring is the sum of the probabilities of the individual events.

$$P(A \text{ or } B) = P(A) + P(B)$$

Example 4: Kristina is on a game show where she plays three games for three different prizes. The first game is for a toaster, the second game is for a couch, and the third game is for a new car. The probability that she wins a toaster is 0.5, the probability that she wins a couch is 0.2, and the probability that she wins a new car is 0.05. What is the probability that she wins a new car or a toaster?

A. 0.025   B. 0.1   C. 0.25   D. 0.5   E. 0.55

Solution: Since we are finding the probability of winning a new car OR a toaster, we add the probabilities of both events. The probability of winning a car or a toaster is the sum of the probability of winning a car, 0.05, and the probability of winning a toaster, 0.5.

$$P(\text{car or toaster}) = P(\text{car}) + P(\text{toaster}) = 0.05 + 0.5 = 0.55$$

The answer is E.

Rule #3 – The probability of Event A AND Event B occurring is the product of the probabilities of the individual events.

$$P(A \text{ and } B) = P(A) \times P(B)$$

Example 5: The probability that Event A will occur is 0.3. The probability that Event B will occur is 0.7. Given that Events A and B are mutually exclusive, what is the probability that Event A *and* Event B will occur?

A. 0.21   B. 0.3   C. 0.5   D. 0.7   E. 1.0

Solution: We are finding the probability that Events A AND B occur, so we multiply the probabilities of the individual events.

$$P(A \text{ and } B) = P(A) \times P(B) = 0.3 \times 0.7 = 0.21$$

The answer is A.

Make sure that you memorize all 3 of these rules, especially rules #2 and #3, as those have appeared very often on recent ACTs. As long as you know the rules, any probability questions with these rules should be easy!

Chapter 22: Probability

Probability and Data Tables

The ACT can also give you a data table and ask you to identify the probability of a certain event occurring. It is critical to read the question carefully and consider (1) what are the events that you are being asked to identify (the numerator) and (2) what are the total events you are choosing from (the denominator). For these questions, probability can be defined as

$$\text{Probability} = \frac{\text{Number In Target Group}}{\text{Total Number To Select From}}$$

Let's see how to handle this with the example below:

The table below shows the results of a survey asking high school students in two different classrooms about their preferred lunch.

	Tacos	Chicken Tenders	Vegetable Pasta	Total
Period 1	24	3	6	33
Period 2	9	5	15	29
Total	33	8	21	62

Example 6: Given that a student is in period 2, what is the probability that he or she picked chicken tenders on the survey?

A. $\frac{5}{62}$ B. $\frac{5}{29}$ C. $\frac{8}{29}$ D. $\frac{29}{62}$ E. $\frac{33}{62}$

Solution: We are asked to consider students from period 2, so we only look at the 29 students in period 2 not at all students at the school. Of the students in period 2, 5 selected chicken tenders.

$$\frac{\text{Selected Chicken Tenders in Period 2}}{\text{Total Students in Period 2}} = \frac{5}{29}$$

The answer is B.

Example 7: If a student's favorite school lunch is vegetable pasta, what is the probability that student is in period 2?

A. $\frac{15}{62}$ B. $\frac{21}{62}$ C. $\frac{15}{29}$ D. $\frac{21}{29}$ E. $\frac{15}{21}$

Solution: For this question, we only look at the 21 students who selected vegetable pasta as their favorite. Of those 21 students, 15 are in period 2.

$$\frac{\text{In Period 2 and Selected Vegeable Pasta}}{\text{Total Students who Selected Vegetable Pasta}} = \frac{15}{21}$$

The answer is E.

Questions like these are the least common type of probability question on the ACT. That being said, they have been on the test before and are 100% fair game to be on the test again. Whenever they do pop up, they are usually easy to answer as long as you know how to read the table correctly.

PrepPros

Advanced Probability Questions

Advanced probability questions require you to find the probability for more complex events. These very commonly appear at the end of the math test in questions 45-60. There is a high likelihood you will see one of these questions on test day!

We will cover how to solve the most common types in the following examples.

Example 8: A fair spinner with 5 equally sized regions and an arrow has regions numbered 1, 2, 3, 4, and 5 respectively. A second fair spinner with 3 equally sized regions and an arrow has regions numbered 1, 2, and 3 respectively. The arrows are both spun at the same time and the numbers the two arrows land on are added together. What is the probability that the sum is odd?

A. $\frac{1}{5}$ B. $\frac{1}{3}$ C. $\frac{5}{8}$ D. $\frac{7}{15}$ E. $\frac{8}{15}$

Solution: To find the probability that the sum is odd, we need to find two things: (1) the number of outcomes that add to an odd number and (2) the total number of possible outcomes. Let's start by finding the total number of possible outcomes.

The first spinner has 5 possible outcomes while the second spinner has 3 possible outcomes. To find the total number of possible outcomes, we multiply

$$\underset{\text{1st spinner Outcomes}}{5} \times \underset{\text{2nd spinner Outcomes}}{3} = \underset{\text{Total Outcomes}}{15}$$

That's the easy part. Now for the hard part. We need to find the total number of outcomes that add to an odd number. The most reliable way to do this is to find an organized way to count the outcomes and keep a tally of the odd numbers. To make our tally, we will use the following rule:

Odd + Odd = Even
Even + Even = Even
Odd + Even = Odd

To start, let's say the first spinner lands on a 1. The second spinner could land on a 1, 2, or 3. Of these three possible outcomes, only 1 + 2 sums up to an odd number, so we have 1 outcome in the tally.

Next, let's say the first spinner lands on a 2. The second spinner could land on a 1, 2, or 3. Of these possible outcomes, 2 + 1 and 2 + 3 add to an odd number, so we have 2 more outcomes to add to our tally (so 3 total).

Now, let's say the first spinner lands on a 3. There is going to be 1 outcome that sums to an odd number. How do we know this so quickly? Well, 1 and 3 are both odd, so we know that 3 will follow the same pattern that 1 did and will only have 1 outcome that sums to an odd number (3 + 2) We add 1 more to our tally (so 4 total).

What if the first spinner lands on a 4? Since 4 is even, we can use the pattern we found for 2. There are going to be 2 outcomes (4 + 1 and 4 + 3) that sum to an odd number. We add 2 more to our tally (so 6 total).

Finally, if the first spinner lands on a 5, there is going to be 1 outcome (5 + 2) that sums to an odd number. We add 1 more to our tally and find that there are 7 total outcomes that sum to an odd number.

So to find the probability, we do

$$\text{Probability of Odd Sum} = \frac{\text{Outcomes with Odd Sum}}{\text{Total Outcomes}} = \frac{7}{15}$$

The answer is D.

For any question like this, it is critical to have an organized way of going through the possible outcomes and tallying the ones we want to count. Example 8 just shows one type of question and one approach to solve, but different questions will require different approaches. A good first step is to always draw a diagram and start listing outcomes. If there is a pattern, as there was in Example 8, you will be able to spot it. If not, you can just brute force your way to the answer by listing all possible outcomes and finding the probability from there.

Example 9: Kenji and David are members of a dinner club that will be meeting tonight. The 8 members of the dinner club will be seated randomly around a table. What is the probability that Kenji and David will be sitting next to each other at dinner?

A. $\frac{1}{15}$ B. $\frac{1}{7}$ C. $\frac{1}{5}$ D. $\frac{2}{7}$ E. $\frac{3}{7}$

Solution: At first, this question seems extremely difficult to solve. There are so many places that Kenji and David can sit and so many possible outcomes to deal with! You may be thinking about permutations and combinations. No need for any of that complicated math. **There is a quick and easy way to solve this question: draw a diagram and assign one person a seat.**

In the diagram below, each dash represents a chair. Let's put Kenji in a chair.

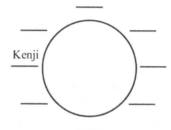

Now that Kenji is in a chair, what is the probability that David is randomly seated next to Kenji? Well, there are 2 seats next to Kenji and a total of 7 seats left, so the probability that David is sitting next to Kenji is $\frac{2}{7}$. **The answer is D.**

Notice that the chair we put Kenji in does not matter. No matter what chair Kenji is randomly assigned to, there are 2 seats next to him and 7 total seats left. We could have also assigned David to a seat and then done the same thing with where Kenji can sit: there would be 2 seats next to David and 7 seats total. No matter how we set this up, the probability that Kenji and David are sitting next to each other is always $\frac{2}{7}$!

Example 10: Six volleyball players are going to be randomly split into two teams of 3. If Kim and Mary are among the 6 players, what is the probability that they will be on the same team?

A. $\frac{1}{30}$ B. $\frac{1}{10}$ C. $\frac{1}{5}$ D. $\frac{1}{3}$ E. $\frac{2}{5}$

Solution: Draw a diagram of the situation and place one of the players on a team. Here, we will place Kim on the 1st team.

Kim ___ ___   ___ ___ ___

What is the probability that Mary will be on the same team as Kim? There are 2 spots left on Kim's team and 5 spots left overall, so the probability they will be on the same team is $\frac{2}{5}$. **The answer is E.**

Just like in our last example, no matter where we put Kim, there will be 2 spots left on that team and 5 spots overall, so the probability will always be $\frac{2}{5}$.

- 215 -

PrepPros

Advanced probability questions like examples 8-10 commonly appear at the end of the ACT, usually in questions 45-60, and most students find them very difficult. However, using this simple diagram trick makes questions like this quick and easy to solve!

Expected Value

The expected value is the outcome you expect for a probability based event, like how many questions you might answer correctly if you guess on a multiply choice test. For example, if you guess randomly on a 60-question multiple-choice math test which choices A, B, C, D, and E (sounds familiar right?!), you can expect to get 20% correct (12 out of 60).

The calculation behind this is simple: take the probability of an event occurring and multiply by the number of events.

$$\text{Expected Value} = P(A) \times A$$

Where $P(A)$ is the probability that event A occurs and A is the number of times event A occurs. For our multiple-choice test example, the probability of guessing an answer correctly is $\frac{1}{5}$ and the number of questions is 60, so

$$\text{Expected Value} = P(\text{guess correctly}) \times \text{number of questions} = \frac{1}{5} \times 60 = 12$$

If you guess randomly on the ACT math test, the expected number of correct answers is 12.

Example 11: A bag contains 12 identically sized, solid-colored balls. 3 balls are black, 5 are green, 2 are blue, and 2 are yellow. A ball is drawn at random and returned to the bag, and the results are recorded. If this experiment is conducted 600 times, how many times would a green ball be expected to be selected?

A. 100 B. 150 C. 250 D. 300 E. 500

Solution: The probability of drawing a green ball is $\frac{5}{12}$, and the experiment will be conducted 600 times, so

$$\text{Expected Value} = \frac{5}{12} \times 600 = 250$$

The answer is C.

This is the easy type of expected value question that would appear somewhere in the first 30 questions. More advanced expected value questions will include <u>multiple possible outcomes from the same event</u>.

For example, let's say that there are three cards on the table facedown. Each card has a number written on it, which represents the amount of money the winner gets. If one card has a 1, one card has a 3, and one card has a 11, what is the expected value of playing the game?

The approach is the same as before, except that now we need to add the sum of all the expected values using the equation

$$\text{Expected Value} = P(A) \times A + P(B) \times B + P(C) \times C \ldots$$

$P(A)$ is probability that events A occurs, and A is the payout for event A. $P(B)$ is probability that events B occurs, and B is the payout for event B, and so on for however many events there are. For our example, the probability of selecting each card is $\frac{1}{3}$. The payout for each event is the number on the card.

$$\text{Expected Value} = \frac{1}{3} \times 1 + \frac{1}{3} \times 3 + \frac{1}{3} \times 11 = \frac{15}{3}$$

The expected value of drawing a card is $\frac{15}{3}$, or $5.00. Since the card numbers are only 1, 3, and 11, the winner will never get exactly $5.00, but that is the average payout expected based on the probability and payouts.

Chapter 22: Probability

> **Example 12:** Terry is playing a game involving ten identical cards in a deck. Each card has a single number written on it: 4 cards have a 2, 3 cards have a 5, 2 cards have a 10, and 1 card has a 25. Terry will choose a card at random, and he will be awarded the number of points equal to the number written on the card. What is the expected value for the number of points that Terry will be awarded if he draws 1 card?
>
> A. 2   B. 4.4   C. 5   D. 6.8   E. 7.5

Solution: To find the expected value, we need to multiply the probability of each event occurring by the points awarded from each event, which is just the number on the card. The probability of drawing a 2 is $\frac{4}{10}$, the probability of drawing a 5 is $\frac{3}{10}$, probability of drawing a 10 is $\frac{2}{10}$, and probability of drawing a 25 is $\frac{1}{10}$.

$$\text{Expected Value} = \frac{4}{10} \times 2 + \frac{3}{10} \times 5 + \frac{2}{10} \times 10 + \frac{1}{10} \times 25 = 6.8$$

The answer is D.

Advanced expected value questions like Example 12 will most likely appear at the end of the test in questions 45-60. This is not very commonly tested but expected value questions have appeared on a few recent tests. Students aiming for top math scores should memorize how to set this up.

Probability Practice: Answers on page 331.

1. Andy has a big bag of marbles. If the bag has 30 blue marbles, 25 red marbles, and 15 green marbles, what is the probability that he will randomly select a red marble?

   A. $\frac{5}{14}$
   B. $\frac{6}{15}$
   C. $\frac{3}{7}$
   D. $\frac{5}{7}$
   E. $\frac{5}{6}$

2. Jerry is in a rush and needs to grab one of the premade sandwiches at the market. Jerry's favorite is the Italian sub, but the sandwiches have no labels on them. If there are 15 turkey sandwiches, 12 veggie subs, and 10 Italian subs, what is the probability that he does NOT get an Italian sub?

   A. $\frac{1}{10}$
   B. $\frac{10}{27}$
   C. $\frac{15}{27}$
   D. $\frac{10}{37}$
   E. $\frac{27}{37}$

3. A bag contains 13 flavored pieces of candy: 5 lemon, 2 strawberry, 3 orange and 3 grape. What is the probability that one piece of randomly selected candy is flavored strawberry or grape?

   A. $\frac{3}{13}$
   B. $\frac{5}{13}$
   C. $\frac{8}{13}$
   D. $\frac{5}{8}$
   E. $\frac{10}{13}$

4. The table below shows the grades that 50 students received on the Chemistry exam.

Exam Grade	Number of Students
A	11
B	23
C	12
D	3
F	1

   What is the probability that a randomly selected student's exam score is less than a B?

   A. 0.24
   B. 0.32
   C. 0.46
   D. 0.52
   E. 0.68

5. A box contains 1 red bead, 6 white beads, and 3 blue beads. Jorge will randomly remove one bead from the box, record its color, and place it back in the box. If Jorge repeats this experiment 150 times, what is the expected number of times Jorge will record a bead that is blue?

   A. 30
   B. 45
   C. 75
   D. 105
   E. 120

6. A group of backpackers were asked to pick their favorite country in Europe. No backpacker was allowed to pick more than one country. $\frac{1}{4}$ picked Italy, $\frac{1}{5}$ picked Spain, $\frac{1}{6}$ picked France, and $\frac{1}{20}$ pick Portugal. If a random backpacker from the group is selected, what is the probability that he or she did not pick any of these 4 countries?

   A. $\frac{3}{20}$
   B. $\frac{1}{3}$
   C. $\frac{4}{10}$
   D. $\frac{1}{2}$
   E. $\frac{2}{3}$

Chapter 22: Probability

7. A box contains 12 solid-colored marbles: 5 blue, 4 red, 1 yellow, and 2 pink. Which of the following expressions gives the probability of drawing, at random and without replacement, a pink marble on the 1st draw and a red marble on the 2nd draw, and a pink marble on the 3rd draw?

   A. $\left(\frac{2}{12}\right)\left(\frac{4}{11}\right)\left(\frac{2}{10}\right)$
   B. $\left(\frac{2}{12}\right)\left(\frac{4}{11}\right)\left(\frac{1}{10}\right)$
   C. $\left(\frac{2}{12}\right)\left(\frac{1}{11}\right)\left(\frac{4}{11}\right)$
   D. $\left(\frac{2}{12}\right)\left(\frac{4}{12}\right)\left(\frac{2}{12}\right)$
   E. $\left(\frac{2}{12}\right)\left(\frac{4}{12}\right)\left(\frac{1}{12}\right)$

8. A pencil will be randomly selected from a bag. The probability of selecting a white pencil is $\frac{3}{13}$. The probability of selecting a blue pencil is $\frac{2}{13}$. What is the probability of selecting a white *or* blue pencil?

   A. $\frac{1}{13}$
   B. $\frac{5}{13}$
   C. $\frac{5}{26}$
   D. $\frac{6}{26}$
   E. $\frac{6}{169}$

9. A bowl contains 12 red marbles, 6 blue marbles and an unknown number of black marbles. The probability of choosing a blue marble out of the bowl is $\frac{1}{7}$. How many black marbles are in the bowl?

   A. 6
   B. 8
   C. 12
   D. 18
   E. 24

Use the information below for questions 10 and 11.

The table below shows the results of two diets on the weight of dogs.

Diet	Weight of Dogs		Total
	Gained	Lost	
A	50	100	150
B	75	75	150

10. Based on the results in the table, what fraction of the dogs who lost weight received diet B?

    A. $\frac{75}{175}$
    B. $\frac{75}{150}$
    C. $\frac{100}{175}$
    D. $\frac{175}{300}$
    E. $\frac{100}{300}$

11. Based on the results in the table, what fraction of the dogs received diet A and gained weight?

    A. $\frac{1}{2}$
    B. $\frac{1}{3}$
    C. $\frac{1}{6}$
    D. $\frac{5}{12}$
    E. $\frac{5}{6}$

12. Three squares with the same center have side lengths of 1, 2, and 3 respectively. What is the probability that a point randomly chosen in the interior of the largest square is also in the interior of the smallest square?

    A. $\frac{1}{9}$
    B. $\frac{2}{9}$
    C. $\frac{1}{3}$
    D. $\frac{4}{9}$
    E. $\frac{6}{9}$

13. Julia runs out of time on her test and needs to guess on the last 4 questions. Each question has 5 answers. If Julia answers each one randomly, what is the probability she answers all 4 questions correctly?

    A. $\frac{1}{625}$
    B. $\frac{4}{625}$
    C. $\frac{1}{125}$
    D. $\frac{1}{25}$
    E. $\frac{25}{125}$

14. The probability that each of two independent events will occur is given in the table below.

Event	Probability
X	0.3
Y	0.5

    What is the probability that Event X or Event Y occur?

    A. 0.15
    B. 0.3
    C. 0.4
    D. 0.7
    E. 0.8

15. At the regional baseball tournament, two games are played simultaneously. In the first game, team A has a 35% chance of winning. In the second game, team C has a 60% chance of winning. What is the probability that both team A and C win?
    (Note: Neither game can result in a tie.)

    A. 14%
    B. 21%
    C. 26%
    D. 47.5%
    E. 95%

Use the information below for questions 16-18.

	Crust Style		
	Thin	Deep Dish	Gluten Free
Topping — Cheese	12	19	7
Topping — Pepperoni	8	25	9

The table above shows the pizza orders at Pete's Pizzeria from 1-2pm on a Saturday afternoon.

16. What is the probability that a pizza ordered was a thin crust pizza?

    A. $\frac{1}{5}$
    B. $\frac{1}{4}$
    C. $\frac{2}{5}$
    D. $\frac{19}{40}$
    E. $\frac{3}{5}$

17. What is the probability that a pizza ordered was thin crust or gluten free?

    A. $\frac{19}{28}$
    B. $\frac{21}{40}$
    C. $\frac{1}{2}$
    D. $\frac{19}{40}$
    E. $\frac{9}{20}$

18. Max and Amelia are picking up 2 pizzas from Pete's Pizzeria for lunch. If 2 pizzas are randomly selected from the pizzas ordered from 1-2pm at Pete's Pizzeria, what is the probability that Max and Amelia get 2 deep dish pepperoni pizzas or 2 thin crust cheese pizzas?

    A. $\left(\frac{25}{80}\right)\left(\frac{25}{80}\right) + \left(\frac{12}{80}\right)\left(\frac{12}{80}\right)$
    B. $\left(\frac{25}{80}\right)\left(\frac{12}{79}\right) + \left(\frac{24}{80}\right)\left(\frac{11}{80}\right)$
    C. $\left(\frac{25}{80}\right)\left(\frac{24}{79}\right) + \left(\frac{12}{80}\right)\left(\frac{11}{79}\right)$
    D. $\left(\frac{25}{44}\right)\left(\frac{12}{20}\right)$
    E. $\left(\frac{25}{80}\right) + \left(\frac{7}{80}\right)$

19. A box of donated toys has ten toys left. 3 are blue stuffed animals, 3 are colored balls, of which 2 are red and 1 is blue, and 4 are frisbees, of which 3 are blue and 1 is red. If the probability of drawing each object is the same, what is the probability that the next toy drawn from the box is red or a ball?

   A. $\frac{1}{5}$
   B. $\frac{3}{10}$
   C. $\frac{2}{5}$
   D. $\frac{1}{2}$
   E. $\frac{3}{5}$

20. A San Diego high school football team will play three games in a tournament to get to the final. The local newspaper gives them an 80% chance of winning the first game, a 60% chance of winning the second game, and a 20% chance of winning the third game. What is the probability that the team will win the first two games and lose the third game?

   A. 6.4%
   B. 9.6%
   C. 25.6%
   D. 38.4%
   E. 80%

21. There are 52 cards in a deck of cards. There are 4 suits, spades, hearts, diamonds, and clubs, and each suit has 13 cards numbered 1 through 13. What is the probability that a randomly selected card is numbered 7 or a heart?

   A. $\frac{4}{52}$
   B. $\frac{10}{52}$
   C. $\frac{13}{52}$
   D. $\frac{16}{52}$
   E. $\frac{17}{52}$

22. Billy, Randal, Mike, and Shaun are at the waterpark. They are randomly assigned into pairs at the top of a two-person waterslide. What is the probability that Billy and Shaun will be paired together?

   A. $\frac{1}{12}$
   B. $\frac{1}{8}$
   C. $\frac{1}{6}$
   D. $\frac{1}{4}$
   E. $\frac{1}{3}$

23. A slot machine has two buttons you press. The first button will randomly give you a number from 1 to 5. The second button will randomly give you a number from 1 to 3. What is the probability that the product of the two buttons is even?

   A. $\frac{2}{3}$
   B. $\frac{3}{5}$
   C. $\frac{8}{15}$
   D. $\frac{7}{15}$
   E. $\frac{2}{5}$

24. At casino night, James will play a game in which he rolls three six-sided dice numbered 1 through 6. He will be awarded 4 points for each die that lands on an odd number. Let the random variable x represent the total number of points awarded on any roll of the dice. What is the expected value of x?

   A. 1
   B. 2
   C. 4
   D. 6
   E. 12

- 221 -

PrepPros

25. There are 12 seats at a large conference table, all of which will be filled. Adam and Jane will both attend the conference and do not like each other. If all members are randomly seated, what is the probability that Adam and Jane will not be sitting next to each other?

   A. $\frac{1}{12} \cdot \frac{1}{11}$
   B. $\frac{2}{12} \cdot \frac{2}{11}$
   C. $\frac{10}{12} \cdot \frac{9}{11}$
   D. $\frac{1}{12} \cdot \frac{9}{11}$
   E. $\frac{9}{11}$

26. Two six-sided dice numbered 1 through 6 are rolled simultaneously. What is the probability that the sum of the faces that land up will be between greater than 4 and less than and 8?

   A. $\frac{7}{36}$
   B. $\frac{9}{36}$
   C. $\frac{15}{36}$
   D. $\frac{16}{36}$
   E. $\frac{18}{36}$

27. There are six students in a class. The six students will be randomly be split into two groups of 3. If Shoba and Shanice are two students in the class, what is the probability that they will end up in the same group?

   A. $\frac{1}{9}$
   B. $\frac{2}{9}$
   C. $\frac{1}{5}$
   D. $\frac{1}{3}$
   E. $\frac{2}{5}$

28. Given that x will be chosen randomly from $\{3, 4, 6, 7, 9\}$ and y will be chosen randomly from $\{5, 6, 7, 8, 9, 10\}$, what is the probability that xy is odd?

   A. $\frac{1}{5}$
   B. $\frac{3}{10}$
   C. $\frac{11}{30}$
   D. $\frac{1}{2}$
   E. $\frac{13}{30}$

29. Wanda is on a game show. There are 8 identical envelopes on the table with different amounts of money inside: 3 have $6, 4 have $15, and 1 has $50. Wanda gets to keep the money in the envelope she selects. What is the expected value for the amount of money, in dollars, Wanda will get from selecting one envelope?

   A. 12
   B. 13.5
   C. 14.45
   D. 16
   E. 18.7

30. A box contains 12 bagels of 3 types. There are 6 sesame bagels, 4 blueberry bagels, and 2 everything bagels. You reach into the box and grab a bagel at random and then, without replacing the first bagel, reach into the box and choose another bagel at random. What is the probability that both of the bagels you choose are the same type?

   A. $\frac{2}{12}$
   B. $\frac{12}{19}$
   C. $\frac{44}{132}$
   D. $\frac{44}{144}$
   E. $\frac{36}{1320}$

Use the following information to answer questions 31-33.

Data from a random sample of 245 customers of a certain clothing company are listed below. The table indicates the number of customers in 3 age brackets (16-25, 26-35, 36-45) and the number of items of clothing from the company each customer owns.

Age (in years)	Items of Clothing			
	1–3	4–6	7+	Total
16-25	71	17	2	90
26-35	43	32	60	135
36-45	11	6	3	20
Total	125	55	65	245

31. If two customers are chosen at random, what is the probability that they are both above the age of 25 and own less than 4 items of clothing?

   A. $\frac{155}{245}$
   B. $\frac{54(53)}{245(244)}$
   C. $\frac{43(42)}{245(244)}$
   D. $\frac{54(53)}{125(124)}$
   E. $\frac{43}{135} + \frac{11}{20}$

32. Three customers that are below the age of 36 are chosen at random. Given that the first customer is 17 years old and owns 6 items of clothing, what is the probability that the next 2 customers are in the 16-25 age bracket and own 4-6 items of clothing?

   A. $\frac{17(16)}{245(244)}$
   B. $\frac{16(15)}{245(244)}$
   C. $\frac{17(16)}{90(89)}$
   D. $\frac{16(15)}{224(223)}$
   E. $\frac{49(48)}{225(224)}$

33. Two customers from this sample will be chosen at random. Given that no customer is chosen twice, what is the probability that both customers chosen will be from the same age bracket?

   A. $\left(\frac{90}{245}\right)\left(\frac{135}{245}\right)\left(\frac{20}{245}\right)$
   B. $\left(\frac{90}{245}\right)\left(\frac{135}{244}\right)\left(\frac{20}{243}\right)$
   C. $\frac{90}{245} + \frac{135}{245} + \frac{20}{245}$
   D. $\frac{90(89)}{245(244)} + \frac{135(134)}{245(244)} + \frac{20(19)}{245(244)}$
   E. $\frac{125(124)}{245(244)} + \frac{55(54)}{245(244)} + \frac{65(54)}{245(244)}$

34. To win a carnival game, a contestant must remember which of the five differently colored balls are hidden under five separate boxes. John can remember where one of the colored balls is but cannot remember where the other four are and will need to randomly guess. What is the probability that John will win the game?

   A. $\frac{1}{120}$
   B. $\frac{1}{60}$
   C. $\frac{1}{24}$
   D. $\frac{1}{5}$
   E. $\frac{1}{4}$

35. There are two twins in a family. At a family reunion, Zach is sitting at the head of the table with 7 seats. The twins are not allowed to sit next to Zach, but the seating has already been randomly assigned. What is the probability the twins are not sitting next to Zach?

   A. $\frac{1}{6} \cdot \frac{1}{5}$
   B. $\frac{4}{6} \cdot \frac{3}{5}$
   C. $\frac{4}{6} \cdot \frac{4}{5}$
   D. $\frac{5}{6} \cdot \frac{4}{5}$
   E. $\frac{4}{6}$

Chapter 23: Factorial, Permutations, Combinations, and Organized Counting

On the ACT, you will have to answer a variety of "how many" questions, such as "how many outfits can a person create with 3 shirts, 4 shoes, and 5 pairs of pants?" or "if a lock code consists of 3 numbers and 2 letters, how many different lock codes are possible?" To successfully answer these questions, you must understand the differences in how to setup and solve using permutations, combinations, and organized counting and know how factorials work.

Factorial

The factorial, symbolized by the "!", is a function that multiplies an integer by every integer below it. For example,

$$5! = 5 \times 4 \times 3 \times 2 \times 1$$
$$3! = 3 \times 2 \times 1$$

For easy factorial questions on the ACT, that is all you need to know!

Example 1: The expression $2! + 4!$ is equal to:

A. 6   B. 24   C. 26   D. 720   E. 40,320

Solution: Rewriting the factorial expression in terms of multiplication, we get

$$2! + 4! = (2 \times 1) + (4 \times 3 \times 2 \times 1)$$
$$2! + 4! = 2 + 24$$
$$2! + 4! = 26$$

The answer is C. Many calculators also have a "!" button and can solve factorial questions for you. If you are unsure if your calculator has a "!" button, go look it up online.

Questions like Example 1 are the most common way factorials are tested on the ACT. However, more advanced questions do appear at the end of the ACT, so if you are a stronger math student, make sure you understand the equation below.

The factorial $n!$ for a positive integer n is defined as $n! = n(n-1)(n-2)\ldots(2)(1)$

This equation is the exact same rule that we learned above, but now it is written in fancy math terms. For any integer n, you multiply n by every integer below it until you get to 1. Understanding this equation is important for solving advanced factorial questions.

Example 2: $\dfrac{3!n!}{(n+1)!} = ?$

A. $\dfrac{1}{n+1}$ B. $\dfrac{6}{n+1}$ C. $3n$ D. $\dfrac{6n}{n+1}$ E. $3n^2 + 3n$

Solution: We can solve this question algebraically or can substitute in number.

Method #1 – Math Teacher Way: We can use the definition of factorial to write out the equation.

$$\frac{(3!)(n)(n-1)(n-2)\ldots(2)(1)}{(n+1)(n)(n-1)(n-2)\ldots(2)(1)}$$

- 224 -

Do you notice what cancels out once we have written it out in this form? The entire $n!$ in the numerator cancels out because we have an (n) on top and bottom, $(n-1)$ on top and bottom, and so on. The only terms that do not cancel out are 3! and $(n+1)$.

$$\frac{(3!)\cancel{(n)(n-1)(n-2)\dots(2)(1)}}{(n+1)\cancel{(n)(n-1)(n-2)\dots(2)(1)}} = \frac{3 \times 2 \times 1}{n+1} = \frac{6}{n+1}$$

The answer is B. Okay, so that was confusing. What is an easier way to solve this question?

Method #2 – Substitution (Cheat Method): We can pick a value to plug in for n and solve. To make the numbers easy, let's pick $n = 2$. Plugging in 2 for n we get:

$$\frac{3!\,2!}{3!} = \frac{(3 \times 2 \times 1)(2 \times 1)}{3 \times 2 \times 1} = \frac{12}{6} = 2$$

Our answer is 2. To tell which answer choice is correct, we plug in $n = 2$ to the answer choices and see which one is equal to 2. The only one that give us 2 is B, so we can tell that **the answer is B.** Much easier, right? Always look to use substitution when you see variables in the answer choices.

That is a difficult question that would appear late on the ACT Math Test, so if you find that confusing and are not a strong math student, do not worry too much. You are not likely going to see a question like this on test day.

Permutations

In permutations, the order matters. If the order in which the objects are selected makes the outcome different, we use a permutation to solve.

> **Example 3:** A class with 15 students is selecting 3 different students for the positions of president, vice president, and party planner. How many possible different selections can be made?
>   A. 45   B. 135   C. 225   D. 455   E. 2,730

Solution: The order matters here because a different order of students being selected first, second, and third leads to a different outcome of who is president, vice president, and party planner. We need to count every possible selection, so we must use a permutation.

To solve a permutation, we use:

$$_nP_r = \frac{n!}{(n-r)!}$$

where n is the number of items we are choosing from and r is number of items we actually choose. Most calculators have nPr programmed into them, so you likely do not need to memorize the equation. If your calculator does not have it, you will need to memorize the equation.

For Example 3, $n = 15$ since we are selecting from 15 students, and $r = 3$ since we are choosing 3 students for the positions.

$$_{15}P_3 = \frac{15!}{(15-3)!} = 2{,}730$$

The answer is E.

Combinations

In combinations, the order does not matter. In other words, if the order that you select the objects does not affect the final outcome, we use a combination to solve.

> **Example 4:** Andrew has 5 tickets to a baseball game and is going to invite 4 of his friends to go with him. If Andrew has 12 friends, how many different combinations of 4 people can he invite?
>
> A. 495   B. 792   C. 1,320   D. 11,880   E. 20,736

Solution: The order does not matter here. Let's say Andrew texts 4 friends to invite them to the game. As long as Andrew asks the same 4 friends to go to the game with him, it does not matter who he texts first, second, third, or fourth. The outcome (who attends the baseball game) is the same, so we use a combination.

To solve a combination, we use:

$$_nC_r = \frac{n!}{r!\,(n-r)!}$$

where n is the number of items we are choosing from and r is number of items we actually choose. As with permutations, most calculators have nCr programmed into them, so you do not need to memorize the equation.

For example 4, $n = 12$ since we are selecting from 12 friends, and $r = 4$ since we are choosing 4 students to give tickets to.

$$_{12}C_4 = \frac{12!}{4!\,(12-4)!} = 495$$

The answer is A.

Permutations and combinations do appear on the ACT, but these are not as commonly tested as the organized counting questions we are about to cover.

Organized Counting

Most "how many" questions on the ACT are not permutations or combinations, so we need to use a different method to solve. **For these questions, we can answer the question "how many choices do I have" for each position where we need to select an item.** To see how this works, let's work through the examples below:

> **Example 5:** For his graduation dinner, Eric needs to select his outfit. If Eric has 6 dress shirts, 5 pairs of dress pants, 7 ties, and 3 pairs of shoes, how many different outfits could Eric put on?
>
> A. 19   B. 30   C. 210   D. 630   E. 1,260

Solution: This example is the simplest type of organized counting question. We recommend drawing out a sketch with positions for each item as shown below:

$$\underset{\text{Shirts}}{\underline{}} \times \underset{\text{Pants}}{\underline{}} \times \underset{\text{Ties}}{\underline{}} \times \underset{\text{Shoes}}{\underline{}} = \text{Total Outfits}$$

All we need to do now is put the number of choices in each position. Since Eric has 6 shirts, we put a 6 in the position for shirts. Since Eric has 5 pairs of pants, we put a 5 in the position from pants, and so on.

$$\underset{\text{Shirts}}{\underline{6}} \times \underset{\text{Pants}}{\underline{5}} \times \underset{\text{Ties}}{\underline{7}} \times \underset{\text{Shoes}}{\underline{3}} = \underset{\text{Total Outfits}}{630}$$

To solve, multiply all the numbers together to find the total number of possibilities.

Eric has 630 possible outfits. **The answer is D.**

More advanced organized counting questions may at first seem far more difficult, but we can solve them in the exact same way as example 5.

> **Example 6:** Bertha's Beans labels a 7-character code on each can of beans it produces? Each code contains 2 letters followed by 5 numbers. The letters and numbers may repeat. How many 7-character codes are possible?
>
> A. 26(25)(10)(9)(8)(7)(6) B. $26^2(10^5)$ C. $26^5(10^2)$ D. 2(26)(10) E. (7)(6)(5)(4)(3)

Solution: To start, sketch a diagram of the 7-character code.

$$\underset{\text{letter}}{\_\_\_\_} \times \underset{\text{letter}}{\_\_\_\_} \times \underset{\text{number}}{\_\_\_\_} \times \underset{\text{number}}{\_\_\_\_} \times \underset{\text{number}}{\_\_\_\_} \times \underset{\text{number}}{\_\_\_\_} \times \underset{\text{number}}{\_\_\_\_} =$$

Now, label how many choices we have at each spot. For the first spot in the code, we have 26 letters in the alphabet, so there are 26 possible letters for that position. Since the letters can repeat, we can also have 26 possible letters for the second spot in the code. For the numbers, we have 10 numbers to pick from (0 through 9). Since the numbers can repeat, there are 10 possible options for all 5 number spots in the code.

Filling in the number of choices for each position, we get:

$$\underset{\text{letter}}{26} \times \underset{\text{letter}}{26} \times \underset{\text{number}}{10} \times \underset{\text{number}}{10} \times \underset{\text{number}}{10} \times \underset{\text{number}}{10} \times \underset{\text{number}}{10} =$$

To solve, multiply all the numbers together. There are $26^2(10^5)$ or 67,600,000 possible 7-character codes. **The answer is B**.

> **Example 7:** The LockTight Safe Company just released its brand new safe. To access the safe, the correct 6-character code must be entered. The first and last characters must be different letters. The middle characters are all numbers, the numbers can be repeated, and the second character must be either a 0 or a 1. How many combinations are possible for the safe?
>
> A. 655,200 B. 936,000 C. 1,300,000 D. 1,352,000 E. 6,500,000

Solution: To start, sketch a diagram of the 6-character code:

$$\underset{\text{letter}}{\_\_\_\_} \times \underset{\text{0 or 1}}{\_\_\_\_} \times \underset{\text{number}}{\_\_\_\_} \times \underset{\text{number}}{\_\_\_\_} \times \underset{\text{number}}{\_\_\_\_} \times \underset{\text{letter}}{\_\_\_\_} =$$

Let's start with the letters. For the first character in the code, there are 26 possible options. The first and last characters must be different letters. Once a letter is selected for the first character, there are only 25 other letters left to choose from, so there are 25 possible options for the last character in the code.

$$\underset{\text{letter}}{26} \times \underset{\text{0 or 1}}{\_\_\_\_} \times \underset{\text{number}}{\_\_\_\_} \times \underset{\text{number}}{\_\_\_\_} \times \underset{\text{number}}{\_\_\_\_} \times \underset{\text{letter}}{25} =$$

Next, let's deal with the numbers. The second character in the code must be a 0 or a 1, so there are only 2 possible options for this spot. The numbers can be repeated, so the other characters have 10 possible options. Filling in the numbers, we get

$$\underset{\text{letter}}{26} \times \underset{\text{0 or 1}}{2} \times \underset{\text{number}}{10} \times \underset{\text{number}}{10} \times \underset{\text{number}}{10} \times \underset{\text{letter}}{25} =$$

Multiply the numbers together to solve. There are 1,300,000 possible combinations for the safe. **The answer is C**.

Questions like examples 6 and 7 are very common on the ACT. Easier versions of these questions appear in the middle of the test anywhere from questions 20-40 while more advanced ones appear in the last 20 questions. Use the "draw a diagram and label the spots" method that we used for these examples and solving these questions should be quick and easy!

④ Advanced Combinations, Permutations, and Organized Counting

Advanced combinations, permutations, and organized counting questions are some of the most difficult on the ACT Math Test, so this section is only for strong math students aiming for top ACT Math Scores. If you are not a strong math student, do not worry about mastering this section.

There are a variety of ways the ACT can test you on these topics, so in the rest of this chapter we will cover the most common ways the ACT has tested these in the past. Understanding the following examples will give you the skills you need to handle these challenging questions in case you see them on test day.

④ Question Type #1 – Advanced Organized Counting

Example 8: At the end of a men's basketball game, all 5 players on the court high five each other player and the coach. What was the total number of high fives given?
  A. 36   B. 25   C. 21   D. 15   E. 11

Solution: We can solve this questions using combinations or organized counting. Both methods are shown, so you can find out which seems easier to you.

Method #1 – Combinations: A high five takes a pair of people, so this question is actually just asking us to find out how many pairs of 2 people can be selected from the 5 players and the coach. The order does not matter, so we use a combination. We have 6 total people, so $n = 6$, and need to select 2, so $r = 2$.

$$_6C_2 = \frac{6!}{2!\,(6-2)!} = 15$$

The answer is D. If that seems confusing or you do not feel confident with combinations, you may prefer using method #2.

Method #2 – Organized Counting: The key to solving this question is to have an organized approach and to recognize the pattern to save time. To make this simpler, let's call the players A, B, C, D, E. Now, let's consider the first player A.

To high five the 4 other players and the coach, player A must make 5 high fives. We can show the high fives as $\leftrightarrow$ to give a visual as well.

$A \leftrightarrow B$ $A \leftrightarrow C$ $A \leftrightarrow D$ $A \leftrightarrow E$ $A \leftrightarrow$ Coach   Total High Fives $= 5$

Now, let's consider player B. Player B has already high fived player A, so he only needs to high five players C, D, and E and the coach.

$B \leftrightarrow C$ $B \leftrightarrow D$ $B \leftrightarrow E$ $B \leftrightarrow$ Coach   Total High Fives $= 5 + 4$

What about player C? Well, player C has already high fived players A and B, so he only needs to high five placed D and E and the coach.

$C \leftrightarrow D$ $C \leftrightarrow E$ $C \leftrightarrow$ Coach   Total High Fives $= 5 + 4 + 3$

Player D has already high fived players A, B, and C, so he only needs to high five player E and the coach.

$D \leftrightarrow E$ $C \leftrightarrow$ Coach   Total High Fives $= 5 + 4 + 3 + 2$

Player E has already high fived players A, B, C, and D, so he only needs to high five the coach.

$E \leftrightarrow$ Coach   Total High Fives $= 5 + 4 + 3 + 2 + 1$

Everyone has already high fived the coach, so we are done.

$$\text{Total High Fives} = 5 + 4 + 3 + 2 + 1 = 15$$

The answer is D. You likely recognized the pattern pretty quickly, so these questions can be solved pretty quickly with this method. The organized counting method and pattern can appear in any similar questions where we are being asked about the various ways to count events that involve making pairs.

Question Type #2 – Advanced Combinations and Counting Multiple Outcomes

Example 9: There are 12 donuts in a box in the break room. 7 of the donuts are glazed, 3 are chocolate, and 2 are cinnamon sugar. If Trace randomly selects two donuts, what is the probability that he gets 1 chocolate donut and 1 cinnamon sugar donut?

A. $\frac{5}{12}$ B. $\frac{1}{24}$ C. $\frac{1}{22}$ D. $\frac{1}{12}$ E. $\frac{1}{11}$

Solution: The key to solving this question is understanding that we need to count two separate outcomes that both end up with Trace getting 1 chocolate donut and 1 cinnamon sugar donut:

	1st Donut Selected	**2nd Donut Selected**
Outcome #1	Chocolate	Cinnamon Sugar
Outcome #2	Cinnamon Sugar	Chocolate

We now need to find the probabilities for outcome #1 and outcome #2. The big mistake most students make is only counting one of these outcomes. For the outcome #1, we need to find the probability of first getting a chocolate donut and then getting a cinnamon sugar donut:

$$\text{Probability (Outcome \#1)} = \text{P(Chocolate)} \times \text{P(Cinnamon Sugar)} = \frac{3}{12} \times \frac{2}{11} = \frac{6}{132}$$

For outcome #2, we need to find the probability of first getting a cinnamon sugar donut and then getting a chocolate donut:

$$\text{Probability (Outcome \#2)} = \text{P(Cinnamon Sugar)} \times \text{P(Chocolate)} = \frac{2}{12} \times \frac{3}{11} = \frac{6}{132}$$

To get our final answer, we add the probabilities of both outcomes and simplify:

$$\frac{6}{132} + \frac{6}{132} = \frac{12}{132} = \frac{1}{11}$$

The correct answer is E. Anytime you see a question like this asking you to find the probability of a specific event, make sure that you remember that various orders can lead to the desired outcome and, to solve correctly, you may need to solve for the probabilities of multiple outcomes.

PrepPros

Factorial, Permutations, Combinations, and Organized Counting Practice: Answers on page 331.

 1. To decorate his room, Eric has decided to buy one lamp, one landscape photograph, and one sports poster. At the bookstore, there are ten types of lamps, four landscape photographs, and six sports posters. How many different ways can Eric decorate his room?

A. 20
B. 40
C. 200
D. 240
E. 460

 2. Veronica is setting the table for dinner and needs to choose a tablecloth, a placemat, and a type of plate. She has 5 tablecloths, 4 types of placemats, and 2 sets of plates. How many possible ways can Veronica set the table?

A. 9
B. 10
C. 11
D. 20
E. 40

3. What is the value of $\frac{7!(10)}{5!}$?

A. 5
B. 2!(10)
C. 42
D. 420
E. 14!

 4. Tessa has five tickets to the Padres game. She is going to invite four of her ten friends to go to the game with her. Which of the following describes how many different groups of five people can go to the game?

A. 10^5
B. $_{10}P_5$
C. $_{10}P_4$
D. $_{10}C_5$
E. $_{10}C_4$

 5. Andrea is planting some new types of flowers in her new flowerbed. In her flowerbed, she has room for only four new plants. The plants must be planted side-by-side in one row. Her husband Mark accidentally purchased eight different types of flowers. How many different ways can Andrea plant her new flowerbed?

A. 32
B. 70
C. 256
D. 1,680
E. 4,096

 6. Trey is selecting a 6-digit passcode for his new phone. The first number will be 8 but all of the other numbers can be any digit. How many passcodes could he select?

A. 10^6
B. 10^5
C. $10(9)(8)(7)(6)$
D. 9^6
E. 9^5

 7. There are 9 candidates in the running for the town hall elections. The candidate with the most votes will become President; the candidate with the second-most votes will be Vice President, and the candidate with the third most votes will be the Chairman. Assuming there are no ties, how many outcomes are possible from the election?

A. $_9P_3$
B. $_9C_3$
C. $_9P_8\ _9P_7\ _9P_6$
D. $9(8)(7)(6)$
E. 9^3

 8. $\frac{7!}{4!} = ?$

A. $\frac{7}{4}$
B. 24
C. 168
D. 210
E. 1,260

- 230 -

9. There are thirty-five members who signed up for the Carlsbad Bowling League. 20 of the members are men and the remaining 15 are women. The members will be split into 16 teams and each team will have a team captain. 9 of the team captains will be men and 7 of the team captains will be women. Which of the following describes how many different sets of team captains could be selected?

   A. $_{35}C_{16}$
   B. $_{35}C_{16}\ _{20}C_9$
   C. $_{20}C_9\ _{15}C_7$
   D. $_{35}P_{16}$
   E. $_{20}P_9\ _{15}P_7$

10. Tamika lives in Carlsbad. The area code for her phone will start with (858). For the remaining seven digits, she will randomly be assigned numbers from 0 – 9. Which of the following expressions gives the number of different possible combinations for the last seven digits of her phone number?

    A. 10(7)
    B. 10(9)(8)(7)(6)(5)(4)
    C. 7^{10}
    D. 10^7
    E. 10^{10}

11. The code for each item in Warsham's Grocery store is 4 characters long. Each code has two letters followed by two numbers. No codes contain the letters O, W, or Z or the numbers 0 or 2. Any of the other letters and digits may be used up to 2 times. Which of the following expressions represents how many different item codes are possible?

    A. 23(23)(10)(10)
    B. 23(22)(10)(9)
    C. 23(23)(8)(8)
    D. 23(22)(8)(7)
    E. 26(26)(10)(10)

12. If you place the letters in NUMBER into a machine that organizes them into a random order, what is the probability that it will spell the word "number" correctly?

    A. $\dfrac{1}{6(5)(4)(3)(2)(1)}$
    B. $\dfrac{1}{6^6}$
    C. $\dfrac{6}{6(5)(4)(3)(2)}$
    D. $\dfrac{6^6}{6(5)(4)(3)}$
    E. $\dfrac{1}{6^5}$

13. A group of 11 teams are being divided into two divisions: one division with 5 teams and one division with 6 teams. Which of the following expressions gives the number of different divisions that could be selected with these 11 teams?

    A. $_{11}P_5$
    B. $_{11}P_6\ _{11}P_5$
    C. $_{11}C_6$
    D. $_{11}C_6\ _{11}C_5$
    E. 11(10)

14. The ID code at Cyrus Technologies must be seven characters long and consist of the following sequence: 1 letter, 4 digits, 2 letters. For any 1 code, the letters may be the repeated but the digits (0 – 9) must be different. Which of the following expressions give the number of passwords possible?

    A. $10^4(26^3)$
    B. 26(10)(9)(8)(7)
    C. $26^3(10)(9)(8)(7)$
    D. $10^4(26)(25)(24)$
    E. $10^4(26^3)(4)(3)(2)(1)$

15. Pinewood camp prints ID cards for its campers. Each 7-character code consists of the letters OAC followed by 4 digits from 0 to 9. The digits may not repeat. Which of the following expressions gives the total number of different 7-character codes?

   A. 1(1)(1)(10)(9)(8)(7)
   B. 1(1)(1)(10)(10)(10)(10)
   C. 3(1)(10)(9)(8)(7)
   D. 3(1)(10)(10)(10)(10)
   E. 3(2)(1)(10)(9)(8)(7)

16. 150 students are up for election for their class president, vice president, and chairman. If the same student cannot hold two positions, which of the following expressions gives the maximum number of distinct election outcomes that can occur?

   A. 3(150)
   B. 150^3
   C. 150(149)(148)(3)(2)(1)
   D. 150(149)(148)
   E. $\frac{150(149)(148)}{3(2)(1)}$

17. At Tom's Sub Shop, each sandwich comes with one types of meat, one type of spread, one type of cheese, and one type of bread. Tom is very particular about his sandwiches, so you cannot pick specific vegetables. Customers can get a sandwich Tom's way, which has lettuce, tomato, onions, and pickles, or with no vegetables. If Tom's Sub Shop has 4 types of meat, 7 spreads, 5 types of cheese, and 3 types of bread, how many different sandwiches can a customer order at Tom's Sub Shop?

   A. 19
   B. 38
   C. 140
   D. 420
   E. 840

18. How many seating arrangements are possible for 5 people to sit at a rectangular table with 2 people on each side and one person at the head of the table if one person sits in each seat and only 2 people are allowed to sit at the head of the table?

   A. 12
   B. 24
   C. 48
   D. 120
   E. 240

19. At a certain business, employee identification badges are made up of the first letter of their first, middle, and last names followed by 7 digits from 0 to 9. For example, a badge could be MDS1496853. If the letter and numbers can repeat, how many possible combinations are there for the company's identification badges?

   A. $26^3(9^7)$
   B. $26^3(10^7)$
   C. 26(25)(24)(9^7)
   D. 26(25)(24)(10^7)
   E. $26^3(8)(7)(6)(5)(4)(3)(2)$

20. Six boys are randomly assigned into two groups of 3 for a group project. One group will present on Monday and the other will present on Tuesday. If Marcus, Jay, and Allen are part of the group of boys, what is the probability that Marcus, Jay, and Allen will be paired together and will present on Tuesday?

   A. $\frac{1}{20}$
   B. $\frac{1}{30}$
   C. $\frac{1}{40}$
   D. $\frac{1}{60}$
   E. $\frac{1}{120}$

21. There are 7 points in a plane, and no 3 of the points are collinear. These 7 points, taken 2 points at a time, determine how many distinct lines?

   A. 7
   B. 14
   C. 21
   D. 28
   E. 42

22. Which of the following is equivalent to $\frac{5!(x-1)!}{3!x!}$?

   A. $\frac{20}{x}$
   B. $\frac{5}{3x}$
   C. $\frac{(5x-5)!}{(3x)!}$
   D. 20
   E. $20(x-1)$

23. Three sisters are going shopping with their mom, and they walk into a dessert shop. There are 6 kinds of cookies, 5 kinds of croissants, and 5 kinds of brownies. Their mom will choose three different desserts at random for her daughters. What is the probability that the mom will choose 1 of each of the 3 kinds of desserts?

   (Note: The same dessert cannot be selected multiple times.)

   A. $\frac{1}{3}$
   B. $\frac{1}{16}$
   C. $\frac{3}{16}$
   D. $\frac{15}{56}$
   E. $\frac{15}{112}$

24. 22 students are playing doubles beach volleyball. What is the maximum number of different 2-player teams possible?

   A. 11
   B. 44
   C. 231
   D. 462
   E. 924

25. At a coworking space, the entrance code consists of the following sequence: 1 digit, 5 letters, 2 digits. For any 1 code, the digits (0-9) may be the same, but the letters, each from the English alphabet must all be different. Which of the following expressions correctly gives the probability that a randomly generated entrance code contains the word GRAIN?

   A. $\frac{5!(10^3)}{10^3(26)(25)(24)(23)(22)}$
   B. $\frac{10^3}{10^3(26)(25)(24)(23)(22)}$
   C. $\frac{(4)(3)(2)(1)10^3}{10^3(26)(25)(24)(23)(22)}$
   D. $\frac{10^3}{10(9)(8)(26^4)}$
   E. $\frac{5^5(10^3)}{10(26)(25)(24)(23)(22)}$

26. Samantha is creating a series of pictures with increasing numbers of colored circles and pieces of string. Her design has a piece of string connecting each circle to every other circle in the picture with a colored piece of string. Her design for the picture with 4 circles is shown below.

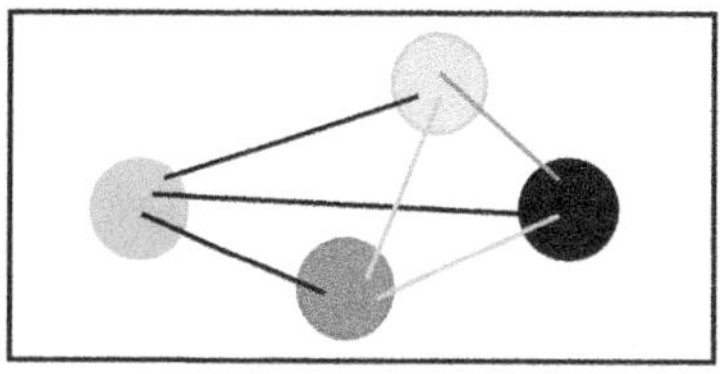

   How many pieces of string will Samantha need to use for the picture with 9 circles?

   A. 18
   B. 36
   C. 45
   D. 64
   E. 72

27. How many seating arrangements are possible for 8 people to sit in the 8 seats of a SUV if 1 person sits in each seat and only 3 of the 8 people can sit in the driver's seat?

   A. 16
   B. 7!
   C. 8!
   D. 3(7!)
   E. 3(8!)

28. A new housing complex will have 10 condos. The condos will all be connected by a path so guests can walk directly from one condo to any of the other condos. If each of the paths connecting two condos are separate from any other path, how many total paths will there be in the housing complex?

   A. 10
   B. 20
   C. 45
   D. 55
   E. 90

29. If $\frac{(n+2)!}{n!} = 42$, then $(n+1)! = ?$

   A. 21
   B. 24
   C. 120
   D. 720
   E. 5,040

30. Of the 18 kayaks to rent in La Jolla, 4 are 1 person kayaks, 6 are 2 person kayaks, 2 are 3 person kayaks, and 6 are 4 person kayaks. A travel agent randomly chooses 4 kayaks for a business trip without realizing there are different types of kayaks. What is the probability the travel agent will randomly pick 1 of each of the 4 types of kayaks?

   A. $\frac{1}{3}$
   B. $\frac{1}{4}$
   C. $\frac{1}{12}$
   D. $\frac{8}{85}$
   E. $\frac{16}{85}$

31. After a business meeting, all attendees shook hands with every other person at the meeting. If there were a total of 66 handshakes, how many people were at the meeting?

   A. 11
   B. 12
   C. 22
   D. 33
   E. 132

Chapter 24: Sequences

For test day, you need to know how to handle arithmetic, geometric, and recursive sequences. In this chapter, we will review the basics of these three types of sequences, the equations that you need to memorize, and how to solve any sequence questions.

Arithmetic Sequences

Arithmetic sequences are sequences using addition and subtraction between terms. The common difference, which is the number that is added or subtracted between consecutive terms, is constant. For example, let's consider the arithmetic sequence below:

$$4, 8, 12, 16, 20, 24 \ldots$$

For this sequence, the **common difference** is $+4$ because we see 4 is the difference between consecutive terms. For easier arithmetic sequence questions, which commonly appear in the first 30 questions of the ACT, you need to be able to find the common difference in a sequence and use that to find a later term in the sequence.

> **Example 1:** In a certain arithmetic sequence, the 1st and 4th terms are 3 and 24 respectively. What is the 5th term of the arithmetic sequence?
>
> A. 27   B. 30   C. 31   D. 37   E. 45

Solution: For any arithmetic sequence questions, we recommend drawing out the sequence and filling in any numbers in the sequence you are given. A simple visual can make it much easier to solve these questions correctly.

$$\underset{\text{1st term}}{\underline{3}} \quad \underset{\text{2nd term}}{\underline{}} \quad \underset{\text{3rd term}}{\underline{}} \quad \underset{\text{4th term}}{\underline{24}} \quad \underset{\text{5th term}}{\underline{}}$$

Now that we have a diagram, we can more easily see how to solve for the common difference. To go from the 1st to 4th term, we must add the common difference 3 times. The total difference between the 1st and 4th terms is 21, so the common difference is 7.

The find the 5th term, we add 7 to the 24 to get 31. **The answer is C.**

More difficult arithmetic sequence questions will ask you to solve for a term much later in the sequence. What if you were asked to find the 88th term in the sequence above? You do not want to add the common difference over and over and over again…we need a faster way! To solve this quickly, we use the equation

$$t_n = t_1 + d(n-1)$$

where t_1 is the first term in the sequence, d is the common difference, t_n is the nth term, and n is the term number. You need to memorize this equation for test day.

Let's use the equation to find the 88th term in the sequence for example 1. The first term is 3, the common difference is 7, and we are looking for the 88th term, so we get

$$t_{88} = 3 + 7(88-1) = 612$$

The 88th term in the sequence is 612.

> **Example 2:** The 3rd and 5th terms in an arithmetic sequence are -4 and 11 respectively. What is the 45th term of this sequence?
>
> A. 311   B. 318.5   C. 326   D. 329   E. 333.5

Solution: First, we need to find the common difference. It is always best to draw out a diagram to help visualize the sequence.

$$\underline{}\quad \underline{}\quad \underline{-4}\quad \underline{}\quad \underline{11}$$
$$\text{1st term}\quad \text{2nd term}\quad \text{3rd term}\quad \text{4th term}\quad \text{5th term}$$

To go from the 3rd to 5th term, we must add the common difference 2 times. The difference between the 3rd and 5th terms is 15, so the common difference is $\frac{15}{2}$ or 7.5. Now that we know the common difference, we can fill in the rest of the terms in our diagram.

$$\underline{-19}\quad \underline{-11.5}\quad \underline{-4}\quad \underline{3.5}\quad \underline{11}$$
$$\text{1st term}\quad \text{2nd term}\quad \text{3rd term}\quad \text{4th term}\quad \text{5th term}$$

Now that we know the 1st term, we can use our equation to solve for the 45th term.

$$t_{45} = -19 + 7.5(45 - 1) = 311$$

The answer is A.

1-4 Geometric Sequences

Geometric sequences are sequences using multiplication and division between terms. The common ratio, which is the number that each consecutive term is multiplied or divided by, is constant. For example, let's consider the geometric sequence below:

$$3, 6, 12, 24, 48, 96 \ldots$$

For this sequence, the **common ratio** is × 2 because we multiply by 2 between consecutive terms. For geometric sequence questions on the ACT, you need to find the common ratio and use that to find other terms in the sequence.

Example 3: The 1st term in a geometric sequence is 560 and the second term is −280. What is the 5th term of the geometric sequence?

A. 70   B. 35   C. 17.5   D. −35   E. −70

Solution: To start, let's make a diagram of the sequence.

$$\underline{560}\quad \underline{-280}\quad \underline{}\quad \underline{}\quad \underline{}$$
$$\text{1st term}\quad \text{2nd term}\quad \text{3rd term}\quad \text{4th term}\quad \text{5th term}$$

Now, we need to find the common ratio. To find a common ratio, you can take any term in a geometric sequence, here we will use −280, and divide it by the previous term, which here is 560. So, the common ratio is $\frac{-280}{560} = -\frac{1}{2}$.

Once we know the common ratio, we can use it to find the other terms in the sequence. To find the 3rd term, we multiply the second term by $-\frac{1}{2}$. The 3rd term is $-\frac{1}{2}(-280) = 140$. We then repeat this process to find the 4th and the 5th terms.

$$\underline{560}\quad \underline{-280}\quad \underline{140}\quad \underline{-70}\quad \underline{35}$$
$$\text{1st term}\quad \text{2nd term}\quad \text{3rd term}\quad \text{4th term}\quad \text{5th term}$$

The 5th term is 35. **The answer is B.**

Geometric sequences questions are generally not too difficult. For geometric sequences, the ACT has never asked you to find a term way later in a sequence. Just in case they do, you can memorize the formula below.

$$t_n = t_1 \times r^{n-1}$$

where t_1 is the first term in the sequence, r is the common ratio, t_n is the nth term, and n is the term number.

Chapter 24: Sequences

Recursive Sequences

A recursive sequence is a sequence in which terms are defined using previous terms and a given formula. In recursive sequences, we cannot find the current term until we know the previous term. We cannot find the 3rd term until we know the 2nd term, we cannot find the 4th term until we know the 3rd term, and so on. That means that we need to solve for the terms in a recursive sequence one term at a time.

If you have never done recursive sequences before, that may all seem very confusing, so let's use the example formula below to make it clearer.

$$a_n = 2a_{n-1} + 2 \quad \text{and} \quad a_1 = 3$$

nth term $\quad (n-1)$th term $\quad$ 1st term

a_n is the nth term in the sequence, and a_{n-1} is the previous term right before a_n. In a recursive sequence, you are always given the 1st term, which in this example is $a_1 = 3$. To solve for the 2nd term, we use the formula and plug in $n = 2$ and get

$$a_2 = 2a_1 + 2$$

In words, the formula says the 2nd term, a_2, is equal to 2 times the 1st term, a_1, plus 2. Since we know that $a_1 = 3$, we can solve a_2.

$$a_2 = 2(3) + 2 = 8$$

Now that we know the 2nd term, we can solve for the 3rd term, a_3. Since we are solving for the 3rd term, we use the formula and $n = 3$ and get

$$a_3 = 2a_2 + 2 \rightarrow a_3 = 2(8) + 2 = 18$$

Below, we use the same steps to solve for the 4th term, a_4, the 5th term, a_5, and the 6th term, a_6.

$$a_4 = 2a_3 + 2 \rightarrow a_4 = 2(18) + 2 = 38$$

$$a_5 = 2a_4 + 2 \rightarrow a_5 = 2(38) + 2 = 78$$

$$a_6 = 2a_5 + 2 \rightarrow a_6 = 2(78) + 2 = 158$$

We can continue this pattern as long as necessary to find the answer. Most recursive sequence questions on the ACT will ask you to solve for the 4th, 5th, or 6th term.

Example 4: A sequence is defined for all integers by $s_n = 3s_{n-1} + n + 5$ and $s_1 = 1$. What is s_4?

A. 10   B. 38   C. 114   D. 123   E. 379

Solution: In order to find the 4th term, s_4, we need to start by finding the 2nd term, then the 3rd, and then finally the 4th term. To solve for the 2nd term, we set $n = 2$ and use the formula and the 1st term, which the question tells us is equal to 1.

$$s_2 = 3s_1 + 2 + 5 \rightarrow s_2 = 3(1) + 2 + 5$$

$$s_2 = 10$$

Now that we know the 2nd term, we can find the 3rd term.

$$s_3 = 3s_2 + 3 + 5 \rightarrow s_3 = 3(10) + 3 + 5$$

$$s_3 = 38$$

Once we know the 3rd term, we can find the 4th term.

$$s_4 = 3s_3 + 4 + 5 \rightarrow s_4 = 3(38) + 4 + 5$$

$$s_4 = 123$$

The 4th term is 123. **The answer is D.**

PrepPros

Explicit Formula for Recursive Sequences

An explicit formula is an equation that gives the value of a term based on the position in the sequence. With the explicit formula, you do not need to know the previous terms and can just input the value in the equation to find the value. For example, if we had the explicit formula:

$$a_n = 2n + 5$$

We can find any nth term using the equation. To find the 4th term, a_4, we plug in $n = 4$ and solve.

$$a_4 = 2(4) + 5 = 13$$

Some recursive sequences follow a distinct pattern can be expressed as an explicit formula. The most common way the ACT tests explicit formulas for sequences is to provide a recursive sequence and ask you to find the explicit formula.

> **Example 5:** Given the recursive formula below, which of the following equations is a correct explicit formula for the sequence?
>
> A. $a_n = 10 + 4n$
> B. $a_n = 6 + 4n$
> C. $a_n = -4 + 14n$ $a_1 = 10$
> D. $a_n = 6 + 8n$ $a_n = a_{n-1} + 4$
> E. $a_n = 14 + 4n$

Solution: To solve, let's start finding the values in the recursive formula. We already know the first term is 10, so when $n = 1$, $a_1 = 10$. We can find the following terms in the sequence.

$$a_2 = a_1 + 4 \rightarrow a_2 = 10 + 4 = 14$$
$$a_3 = a_2 + 4 \rightarrow a_3 = 14 + 4 = 18$$
$$a_4 = a_3 + 4 \rightarrow a_3 = 18 + 4 = 22$$

At this point, we can notice the pattern: the value increases by 4 as you go from one term to the next. This means that the slope of the equation must be 4, so we must see $4n$ in the explicit formula. We can eliminate answer choices C and D.

To find the constant (the number) in the explicit formula, we can test using the point(s) that we found. An easy value to start with is $a_1 = 10$. If we plug in $n = 1$, the correct explicit formula must give $a_1 = 10$.

$$\text{For A: } a_1 = 10 + 4(1) = 14$$
$$\text{For B: } a_1 = 6 + 4(1) = 10$$
$$\text{For E: } a_1 = 14 + 4(1) = 18$$

Only B gives us the correct value of 10, so we can tell that **the answer is B**. Notice that if we plug other values of n directly into the explicit equation, we get the values of a_2, a_3, and a_4 that we solved for above.

Shortcut Method: If you ever see a question like this on the ACT, start by using the 1st term in the sequence as a test point. In Example 5, we are given $a_1 = 10$, so immediate plug in $n = 1$ to the explicit answer choices and eliminate any that do not give you 10. Often on the ACT, only 1 answer works with this shortcut method, and you can tell the correct answer without finding any other terms in the sequence.

For the example above, we could eliminate A, D and E immediately. To then tell which answer choice is correct, find 2nd term and use that as a test point. Once we find $a_2 = 14$, only B works, so we can tell that **the correct answer is B**.

Chapter 24: Sequences

Sequences Practice: Answers on page 331.

1. The 1st term is 5 in the arithmetic sequence 5, 12, 19, 26, ···. What is the eighth term of the arithmetic sequence?

    A. 33
    B. 40
    C. 47
    D. 54
    E. 61

2. The 3rd and 5th terms in an arithmetic sequence are 21 and 15 respectively. What is the 1st term of the sequence?

    A. 30
    B. 28
    C. 27
    D. 12
    E. 9

3. What is the missing term in the geometric sequence below?

    $$1, 3, \_\_, 27, 81$$

    A. 6
    B. 9
    C. 12
    D. 15
    E. 18

4. The first four terms in an arithmetic sequence are 7, 10, 13, and 16. What is the general expression for the nth term?

    A. $2n + 5$
    B. $3n + 4$
    C. $3n + 7$
    D. $4n + 3$
    E. $5n + 1$

5. For a geometric sequence, the 1st and 4th terms are 2 and 16 respectively. What is the 6th term of the geometric sequence?

    A. 2
    B. 18
    C. 24
    D. 36
    E. 64

6. The 1st and 2nd terms of a geometric sequence are 20 and -10 respectively. What is the 5th term in the geometric sequence?

    A. $\frac{5}{2}$
    B. $\frac{5}{4}$
    C. $\frac{5}{8}$
    D. $-\frac{5}{4}$
    E. $-\frac{5}{2}$

7. For an arithmetic sequence the 10th term is 5 and the 15th term is 8.75. What is the first term of the sequence?

    A. -3.25
    B. -1.75
    C. 0
    D. 0.75
    E. 1.25

8. The first term in an arithmetic sequence is 12 and the sequence has 5 terms. What is the difference between the mean and median values for the terms in this sequence?

    A. 0
    B. 1
    C. 4
    D. 5
    E. 12

9. A sequence is defined for all positive integers by $a_n = -2a_{n-1} + 3$ and $a_1 = 3$. What is a_5?

    A. -27
    B. -15
    C. -3
    D. 9
    E. 33

10. The money in Anish's account increases in a geometric sequence each year. If Anish's account started with $240 and he had $300 after one year, approximately how much money, in dollars, is in Anish's account after 5 years?

   A. 450
   B. 480
   C. 540
   D. 585
   E. 730

11. In an arithmetic sequence, the first term is $\frac{5}{4}$ and the third term is $\frac{1}{2}$. What is the sixth term?

   A. $\frac{19}{8}$
   B. $\frac{9}{4}$
   C. $-\frac{1}{2}$
   D. $-\frac{5}{8}$
   E. -1

12. A recursive sequence is defined as $s_n = 3s_{n-1} - 2n + 1$ and $s_1 = 2$. What is s_4?

   A. 4
   B. 5
   C. 6
   D. 8
   E. 11

13. The recursive formula for a sequence is given below.
$$a_1 = 8$$
$$a_n = a_{n-1} + 10$$
Which of the following equations is an explicit formula for this sequence that gives the nth term?

   A. $a_n = -10n + 10$
   B. $a_n = -8n + 10$
   C. $a_n = 8n + 10$
   D. $a_n = 10n - 2$
   E. $a_n = 10n + 8$

14. The second term in an arithmetic sequence is -42. If the fifth term is 6, what is the value of the 60th term?

   A. 870
   B. 886
   C. 902
   D. 918
   E. 934

15. Given the recursive formula below, which of the following is a correct explicit formula for the sequence?
$$a_1 = 8$$
$$a_{n+1} = 3a_n$$

   A. $a_n = 5 + 3n$
   B. $a_n = 7 + n$
   C. $a_n = 5 + 3^n$
   D. $a_n = 8(3^n)$
   E. $a_n = 8(3^{n-1})$

16. What is the sum of the first 3 terms of the arithmetic sequence in which the 5th term is 15 and the 8th term is 19?

   A. 29
   B. 31
   C. 33
   D. 35
   E. 37

17. Consecutive terms in an arithmetic sequence have a negative common difference. The sum of the first four terms in the sequence is 60. Which of the following values could be the first term of the sequence?

   A. -3
   B. 6.5
   C. 13.25
   D. 15
   E. 18

Chapter 25: Complex Numbers

Complex numbers are a combination of real and imaginary components expressed in the form $a + bi$, where a and b are real numbers and i is the imaginary unit. The imaginary unit is defined as

$$i = \sqrt{-1}$$

Since part of complex numbers are "imaginary," it is difficult to grasp how they work. But do not worry, you only need to learn a few methods for how to handle complex numbers when they appear on the ACT.

Adding and Subtracting Complex Numbers

For addition and subtraction with complex numbers, we combine like terms. For example,

$$(8 + 5i) + (5 - 2i) = 13 + 3i$$

Simple right? For subtraction questions, always make sure that you distribute the negative sign to both terms.

$$(2 - 3i) - (5 - 7i) = 2 - 3i - 5 + 7i = -3 + 4i$$

Many students make the mistake of forgetting to distribute the negative sign and get an answer of $-3 - 10i$. Be careful because the ACT will have this common mistake as an incorrect answer choice.

> **Example 1:** What is the difference of complex numbers $22 - 14i$ and $7 - 3i$?
>
> A. $15 - 17i$ B. $15 - 11i$ C. $-15 + 11i$ D. $29 - 17i$ E. $-15 + 17i$

Solution: Set up the equation and combine like terms.

$$a - b = (22 - 14i) - (7 - 3i) = 22 - 14i - 7 + 3i$$

$$a - b = 15 - 11i$$

The answer is B.

Multiplying Complex Numbers

Before we go into the details of how to multiply complex numbers, you need to know that

$$i^2 = -1$$

Multiplying complex numbers is just like multiplying binomials: use FOIL, which stands for First, Outer, Inner, Last. For example,

$$(3 - 5i)(2 - 2i) = 6 - 6i - 10i + 10i^2 = 6 - 16i + 10i^2$$

We are not done yet. Since there is an i^2 term when we multiply complex numbers and $i^2 = -1$, we must plug in -1 for i^2.

$$6 - 16i + 10(-1)$$

Combining the numbers, we get the answer of

$$-4 - 16i$$

> **Example 2:** What is the product of complex numbers $1 - 3i$ and $11 + 2i$?
>
> A. $11 - 6i$ B. $12 - i$ C. $11 - 38i$ D. $17 - 31i$ E. $5 - 33i$

Solution: Multiply the two imaginary numbers together and combine like terms.

$$(1 - 3i)(11 + 2i) = 11 + 2i - 33i - 6i^2 = 11 - 31i - 6i^2$$

Now, plug in -1 for i^2 and combine the numbers.
$$11 - 31i - 6(-1) = 17 - 31i$$

The answer is D.

2-4 The Complex Conjugate

All complex numbers have a complex conjugate. The complex conjugate is a complex number with an identical real part and an imaginary part with the opposite sign. In algebra terms,

$$a + bi \text{ and } a - bi \text{ are complex conjugates.}$$

If you prefer numbers,

$$2 + 3i \text{ and } 2 - 3i \text{ are complex conjugates.}$$

To find the complex conjugate of any complex number, switch the sign of the imaginary part.

So why does this matter? The complex conjugate is important because **the product of any complex number and its complex conjugate is a real number**.

$$(a + bi)(a - bi) = a^2 + b^2$$

With numbers, we can see how the imaginary terms cancel out and we just get numbers.

$$(2 + 3i)(2 - 3i) = 4 - 6i + 6i - 9i^2 = 4 - 9i^2 = 4 - 9(-1) = 13$$

Notice that $2^2 + 3^2 = 13$, so we can skip all that math if we memorize the shortcut for the product of complex conjugates.

Complex conjugates are most often used when complex numbers are fractions with the imaginary part in the denominator. Fractions are not allowed to have the i in the denominator. To fix this problem, we can multiply the top and bottom of the fraction by the complex conjugate. For example, if we are given

$$\frac{10}{1 - 2i}$$

we need to multiply the top and bottom of the fraction by the complex conjugate, which here is $1 + 2i$.

$$\frac{10}{1 - 2i} \times \frac{1 + 2i}{1 + 2i}$$

We get
$$\frac{10 + 20i}{5}$$

We can now simplify and get
$$2 + 4i$$

Example 3: Which of the following is equivalent to the equation below?

$$\frac{5}{3 - 4i}$$

A. $\frac{3}{5} + \frac{4}{5}i$ B. $\frac{5}{3} - \frac{5}{4}i$ C. $\frac{15}{7} - \frac{20}{7}i$ D. $\frac{4}{5} - \frac{4}{25}i$ E. $\frac{5}{3} + \frac{4}{7}i$

Solution: To simplify, multiply the top and bottom of the fraction by the complex conjugate of $3 + 4i$.

$$\frac{5}{3 - 4i} \times \frac{3 + 4i}{3 + 4i}$$

We get
$$\frac{15 + 20i}{25}$$
We can now split the fraction and simplify to get
$$\frac{3}{5} + \frac{4}{5}i$$

The answer is A.

> **TIP – Use Your Calculator**
>
> If you calculator has an *i* button, **you can type most complex numbers questions into your calculator, and it will tell you the answer**. You do not need to do any math! For those of you with a TI-83, TI-84 TI-Nspire (non CAS), and many Casio calculators, you can enter complex numbers in your calculator! If you have a different type of calculator, it is worth looking up if you have an *i* button.
>
> To see how this trick works, go back to Examples 1–3 that we just solved and plug them into your calculator. When you press ENTER, the calculator will show you the correct answer!

The Powers of *i*

You should memorize the following pattern of *i* powers.

$$i^1 = i$$
$$i^2 = -1$$
$$i^3 = -i$$
$$i^4 = 1$$

Knowing this pattern will be essential to solving certain imaginary numbers questions that ask you to solve for a higher power of *i*, such as i^{102}. The method for solving these questions is covered in Chapter 20 on p. 194, so you can go to that chapter to learn how to solve questions with higher powers of *i*.

For most students, that is all that you need to know about complex numbers!

The ACT will also rarely include questions that involve the complex plane, which we will discuss next. Since it is very rarely tested, the complex plane can be skipped for students on a time crunch to get ready for the ACT. In general, it is only important for students aiming for top math scores who want to know everything that can be on the ACT.

Advanced Complex Number Topics

The following advanced complex number topics are rarely tested on the ACT. If these topics do appear on the test, they are usually later in questions 40-60. The good news is these questions are usually pretty easy to solve as long as you know the rules that you will learn in the rest of this chapter.

 ## The Complex Plane

The complex plane is a way to represent complex numbers on a coordinate plane. The complex plane works just like the standard (x, y) coordinate plane, except that now the x-axis is "real" and the y-axis is "imaginary." For graphing complex numbers, you need to know the following rule:

Any complex number $a + bi$ is graphed on the complex plane at point (a, b).

Let's graph $3 + 4i$, $1 - 3i$, and $-1 + 2i$ in the complex plane.

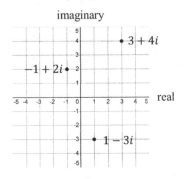

For $3 + 4i$, the point is at $(3, 4)$. This makes sense because the complex number has a value of 3 for the real number, which is on the x-axis, and a value of 4 for the imaginary number, which is on the y-axis. For the same reasoning, $1 - 3i$ is at $(1, -3)$ and $-1 + 2i$ is at $(-1, 2)$.

> **Example 4:** When graphed in the complex plane, the sum of complex numbers $-2 + 4i$ and $-3 - 2i$ appears in which quadrant?
>
> A. I   B. II   C. III   D. IV   E. Cannot be determined

Solution: First, we need to add the complex numbers together.

$$(-2 + 4i) + (-3 - 2i) = -5 + 2i$$

The complex number $-5 + 2i$ will be at point $(-5, 2)$ in the complex plane, which is in quadrant II. **The answer is B.**

 ## Absolute Value of a Complex Number

The absolute value of a complex number is equal to its distance from the origin in the complex plane.

$$|a + bi| = \sqrt{a^2 + b^2}$$

As an example, for the complex number $3 + 4i$, we get

$$|3 + 4i| = \sqrt{3^2 + 4^2} = \sqrt{9 + 16} = \sqrt{25} = 5$$

This equation is just the Pythagorean theorem in disguise. $3 + 4i$ is at $(3, 4)$ in the complex plane. To find the distance from the origin to the point $(3, 4)$, we can draw a triangle. The triangle will have a base of 3 and a height of 4 and $3^2 + 4^2 = 5^2$, which tells the distance from the origin is 5.

> **Example 5:** $|7 - 4i| = ?$
>
> A. 3   B. $\sqrt{33}$ C. $3\sqrt{5}$ D. $\sqrt{65}$ E. 28

Solution:
$$|7 - 4i| = \sqrt{7^2 + 4^2} = \sqrt{65}$$

The answer is D.

Distance Between Complex Numbers

To solve for the distance between two complex numbers, we find the distance between the numbers on the complex plane. In other words, we just use the distance formula!

For any two complex number $a + bi$ and $c + di$, distance $= \sqrt{(a - c)^2 + (b - d)^2}$

Let's try this with complex numbers $2 + 4i$ and $-3 + i$.

$$\text{Distance} = \sqrt{(2 - (-3))^2 + (4 - 1)^2} = \sqrt{5^2 + 3^2} = \sqrt{25 + 9} = \sqrt{34}$$

We can also solve for the distance between complex number by graphing them in the complex plane. Once we have the points graphed, we can draw a triangle and solve for the distance.

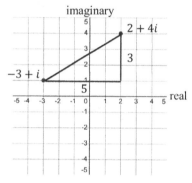

From the diagram above, we know the base of the triangle is 5 and the height is 3, so we can use the Pythagorean theorem to find the hypotenuse, which is the distance between the two complex numbers.

$$\text{Distance} = \sqrt{5^2 + 3^2} = \sqrt{25 + 9} = \sqrt{34}$$

> **Example 6:** What is the distance, in coordinate units, between $6 - 3i$ and $2 + 7i$ on the complex plane?
>
> A. 4   B. $4\sqrt{5}$ C. $2\sqrt{29}$ D. $2\sqrt{41}$ E. $\sqrt{186}$

Solution: Distance $= \sqrt{(6 - 2)^2 + ((-3) - 7)^2} = \sqrt{4^2 + (-10)^2} = \sqrt{16 + 100} = \sqrt{116} = 2\sqrt{29}$

The answer is C.

Complex Numbers Practice: Answers on pages 331-332.

1. Which of the following gives the correct answer when you subtract x from z?

   $$x = -3 + 2i$$
   $$z = 5 + 4i$$

   A. $-2 + 6i$
   B. $2 + 6i$
   C. $8 + 2i$
   D. $8 + 6i$
   E. $2 - 6i$

2. What is the sum of the complex numbers $8 + 2i$ and $3 + 3i$?

   A. 16
   B. $16i$
   C. $11 + 5i$
   D. $13 + 3i$
   E. $24 + 6i$

3. What is the sum of the complex numbers $2 + 7i$ and $6 + 5i$?

   A. $8 + 12i$
   B. $20i$
   C. $9 + 11i$
   D. $12 + 35i$
   E. $8 + 35i$

4. Which of the following complex numbers is equal to $(3 + 6i) - (-5 + 3i)$?

   A. $-8 + 3i$
   B. $-2 + 3i$
   C. $-2 + 9i$
   D. $8 + 3i$
   E. $8 + 9i$

5. $(-4 + 6i) - (1 + 3i) = ?$

   A. $-5 + 9i$
   B. $5 + 3i$
   C. $-5 + 3i$
   D. $-3 + 9i$
   E. $3 + 3i$

6. What is the difference between complex numbers $(6 + 5i)$ and $(2i + 3)$?

   A. $8 + 2i$
   B. $3 + 3i$
   C. $3 + 7i$
   D. $9 + 3i$
   E. $8 + 8i$

7. $4(3 + 2i) - 0.5(-8 + 6i) = ?$

   A. $8 + 8i$
   B. $8 + 5i$
   C. $16 + 5i$
   D. $12 + 8i$
   E. $16 + 8i$

8. Which of the following complex numbers is equal to $(5 + 4i) - (8i^2 - 8i)$?

   A. $-13 - 4i$
   B. $-3 - 4i$
   C. $13 - 4i$
   D. $13 + 12i$
   E. $-3 + 12i$

9. What is the product of the complex numbers $(3 + 4i)$ and $(3 - 4i)$?

   A. 25
   B. 7
   C. 1
   D. $9 - 16i$
   E. $9 + 16i$

10. What is the product of the complex numbers $(4 + 5i)$ and $(-3 + 3i)$?

    A. $27 + 3i$
    B. $-27 - 3i$
    C. $2 + 11i$
    D. $-27 + 11i$
    E. $-12 + 15i$

11. In the complex numbers, where $i^2 = -1$, $\frac{4}{1-3i} = ?$

    A. $-\frac{1}{2} - \frac{3}{2}i$
    B. $\frac{2}{5} + \frac{6}{5}i$
    C. $\frac{2}{5} - \frac{6}{5}i$
    D. $\frac{4}{5} - \frac{12}{5}i$
    E. $\frac{4}{5} + \frac{3}{2}i$

12. $|-6i + 2| = ?$

    A. -4
    B. 4
    C. $4\sqrt{2}$
    D. $2\sqrt{10}$
    E. 8

13. What is the product of the complex numbers $(6 + 3i)$ and $(2 + i)$?

    A. $8 + 4i$
    B. $15 + 12i$
    C. $9 + 12i$
    D. $12 + 9i$
    E. $9 + 6i$

14. For $i = \sqrt{-1}$, $(5 - 5i)(-5 + 5i) = ?$

    A. $-25 - 25i$
    B. $-25 - 50i$
    C. 0
    D. $25i$
    E. $50i$

15. The product of 2 complex numbers is 53. If one of the complex numbers is $7 + 2i$, what is the other number?

    A. $46 - 2i$
    B. $371 + 106i$
    C. $\frac{371}{9} - \frac{106}{9}i$
    D. $\frac{7}{53} + \frac{2}{53}i$
    E. $7 - 2i$

16. What is the distance, in coordinate units, between $-4 + i$ and $1 + 2i$ in the complex plane?

    A. $\sqrt{34}$
    B. $\sqrt{26}$
    C. $\sqrt{17}$
    D. 4
    E. 6

17. If $i = \sqrt{-1}$, what is the value of the expression $12i^4 + 8i^2 + 12$?

    A. 32
    B. 24
    C. 16
    D. 8
    E. 0

18. For all real numbers x and imaginary number i, which of the following expressions is equivalent to $(x + 4i)(2x - 5i)$?

    A. $2x^2 - 3xi + 20$
    B. $2x^2 - 13xi + 20$
    C. $2x^2 + 3xi - 20$
    D. $2x^2 + 13xi - 20$
    E. $2x^2 + 3xi + 20$

For the questions 19-21, use the complex plane below.

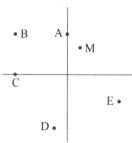

19. In the complex plane above, points A and C represent two complex numbers. Which point represents the sum of A and C?

    A. A
    B. B
    C. M
    D. D
    E. E

20. In the complex plane above, point M is at the point $p + qi$. If $-2(p + qi)$ was graphed on the complex plane, it would be at which of the following points?

    A. A
    B. B
    C. C
    D. D
    E. E

21. The product of two complex numbers is represented by point E in the complex plane above. If one complex number is $-3 + 6i$, which of the following could be the other complex number?

    A. $-3 - 6i$
    B. $6 + 2i$
    C. $3 + 4i$
    D. $2i$
    E. $-4 - 4i$

22. The product of $a + bi$ and which of the following complex numbers results in a real number?

    A. $b + ai$
    B. abi
    C. $a - bi$
    D. $b - ai$
    E. $(a + b)i$

23. Given that a is a positive integer and that $i^a = -i$, which of the following must be true about a? (Note: $i^2 = -1$)

    A. When a is divided by four the remainder is 0
    B. When a is divided by four the remainder is 1
    C. When a is divided by four the remainder is 2
    D. When a is divided by four the remainder is 3
    E. Cannot be determined

24. In the complex numbers, where $i^2 = -1$, $(-2 + 4i)^3 - 5i + 2 = ?$

    A. $88 - 16i$
    B. $90 - 21i$
    C. $-8 + 64i$
    D. $-6 + 59i$
    E. $-10 - 21i$

25. Given that $i = \sqrt{-1}$, which of the following complex numbers is equal to $\frac{4+5i}{5-4i}$?

    A. $\frac{4}{5} - \frac{5}{4}i$
    B. i
    C. 1
    D. $\frac{40+41i}{41}$
    E. $\frac{41}{9}$

26. Which of the following complex numbers equals $(4 + 3i)(\pi - 2i)$?

    A. $4\pi + 6$
    B. $4\pi - 6i$
    C. $(4 + \pi) - 5i$
    D. $(4\pi + 6) + (-8 + 3\pi)i$
    E. $(4\pi - 6) + (-8 + 3\pi)i$

27. In the complex numbers, where $i^2 = -1$, $\frac{5}{2-4i} = ?$

    A. $\frac{1}{2} + i$
    B. $-\frac{5}{6} - \frac{10}{6}i$
    C. $\frac{5}{2} - \frac{5}{4}i$
    D. $\frac{5}{9} + \frac{10}{9}i$
    E. $\frac{7}{9} + \frac{5}{9}i$

28. In the complex numbers, where $i^2 = -1$, what complex number x is the solution to the equation $x(3 - 3i) + 5 = 8$?

    A. $\frac{1}{6} + \frac{1}{2}i$

    B. $\frac{1}{4} + \frac{3}{4}i$

    C. $\frac{1}{2} + \frac{1}{2}i$

    D. $1 + i$

    E. 1

Chapter 26: Word Problems

One of the challenges of the ACT Math Test is dealing with everyone's least favorite questions: word problems. Word problems are often written in a way that makes it confusing to figure out exactly what is happening in the question. Word problems include a wide variety of math topics that we have already learned in this book, so we will not cover any specific type of word problem in this chapter. Instead, we will focus on the tips that can help you solve all types of word problems more effectively and efficiently.

Tip #1 – Do Not Be Intimidated

Word problems look scary. Many students see a big paragraph and say, "no way, I can't solve that." They feel intimidated before even trying to solve the question. Do not let this be you! Word problems at their core are no more difficult than any other ACT Math questions. When you see a big paragraph on test day, take a deep breath and solve it one step at a time.

Tip #2 – Turn Words into Equations

When approaching a word problem, take it one sentence at a time. As you read through the question, identify each piece of key information and write it down in an equation. If you can convert the question from a word problem into an equation or equation(s), the question will be much easier to solve.

One of the most common types of word problems is a system of equations question, which we covered in Chapter 15 on page 130. For these questions, you will need to turn the word problem into two equations. Once you have converted the word problem into two equations, you will be able to solve the question with the methods we learned in Chapter 15.

Tip #3 – Backsolve with the Answer Choices

For some word problems, writing your own equation(s) is very difficult and may not be the fastest or easiest way to solve. If you cannot write out the equation(s) or are not sure if the equation(s) that you wrote are correct, try backsolving. Sometimes it is faster and easier to take the answer choices, go through the steps of the word problem, and see if you have the correct answer. Even if you cannot tell which answer is correct, backsolving can often help you eliminate some answer choices and make a better guess. If you need to review how to backsolve, go back to Chapter 1.

Tip #4 – Guess and Move on (If You Have To)

If you get to a word problem, try using the tips above, and still have no idea how to solve it, circle the question, bubble in your best guess, and move on! It is easy to waste a lot of time reading and rereading long, confusing word problems. Students who do this often end up running out of time. Save those precious minutes to answer more questions that you know how to solve. We know it sounds backwards but giving up quickly on a word problem that you have no idea how to solve may help you actually get a better score.

If you complete the rest of the questions in the section and have time remaining, you can always come back to any questions that you guessed on. Sometimes, when re-reading the question, you will realize how to solve it. It is easier to think more clearly when you are no longer worried about finishing the rest of the questions on the test.

Chapter 26: Word Problems

Word Problems Practice: Answers on page 332.

1. The total price of a pie bought by Alex and her friends was $23.80. The pie was cut into 7 equal slices, and Alex ate 2 slices. Alex paid the portion of the price that was equal to the portion of the pie she ate. What portion of the total price did Alex pay?

   A. $2.64
   B. $3.40
   C. $5.95
   D. $6.80
   E. $9.00

2. Amin bought a new motorcycle. He made an initial payment of $500 and then made 48 equal monthly payments. The total that Amin paid for the motorcycle was $7,700. What was the amount of each of his monthly payments?

   A. $10.42
   B. $150.00
   C. $160.42
   D. $172.92
   E. $240.00

3. A fish tank has dimensions, in inches, of 50 by 21 by 33. A hose is filling the tank at a rate of 200 cubic inches per minute. Which of the following is closest to the numbers of minutes it will take the fill the tank?

   A. 6
   B. 56
   C. 173
   D. 347
   E. 544

4. On the first day of school, Mrs. Rusher gave her fourth-grade students 9 new Spanish words to learn. On each day of school after that, she gave the students 6 new Spanish words to learn. How many new Spanish words has she given the students to learn by the 17th day of school?

   A. 117
   B. 111
   C. 105
   D. 99
   E. 93

5. To build a model rocket, Sebastian spent 3 hours on each of 6 workdays. On the 7th day, he spent $\frac{3}{4}$ of the time he had worked each of the previous workdays to complete the project. How many total hours did it take Sebastian to complete the model rocket?

   A. $20\frac{1}{4}$
   B. $20\frac{3}{4}$
   C. 21
   D. $23\frac{1}{4}$
   E. $23\frac{3}{4}$

6. Silvia received $100 as a present on her 15th birthday and decided to deposit the money in a savings account. To continue to increase her savings, Silvia decides on a savings plan: for each successive birthday, she will deposit $100 more than the amount deposited for the previous birthday. This is the only money deposited into the account. What is the total amount of money that Silvia has in the account on the day after her 19th birthday?

   A. $600
   B. $800
   C. $1,000
   D. $1,100
   E. $1,500

7. John and Matt each ordered food at their favorite restaurant in Italy. The price of John's meal was y dollars and the price of Matt's meal was $6 more than John's meal. Since John is nice, they split the cost of the meal evenly. There was no tip or sales tax. Which of the following expressions represents the amount, in dollars, each of them paid?

   A. y
   B. $y + 6$
   C. $y + 3$
   D. $2y$
   E. $2y + 6$

8. On a canvas, Malik painted a triangle whose width is half the width of the canvas and whose height is the same as the height of the canvas. What is the ratio of the area of the triangle to the area of the entire canvas?

A. $\frac{1}{4}$
B. $\frac{1}{3}$
C. $\frac{1}{2}$
D. $\frac{3}{4}$
E. 1

9. Rectangle X has a length of 48 inches and a width of 30 inches. Rectangle Y has a length and width that are both $\frac{2}{3}$ the length and width of Rectangle X. Rectangle Z has a length and width that are both $\frac{1}{2}$ the length and width of Rectangle Y. What is the perimeter, in inches, of Rectangle Z?

A. 156
B. 78
C. 52
D. 40
E. 26

10. The number of a certain type of bacteria increases exponentially, tripling every 40 minutes. What is the mass, in grams, of the bacterial exactly 2 hours after the mass first reaches 5 grams?

A. 50
B. 135
C. 200
D. 405
E. 8,000

11. Of 30 students selected, 14 students play soccer, 10 play baseball, and 4 play both soccer and baseball. How many students play neither soccer nor baseball?

A. 26
B. 20
C. 18
D. 10
E. 2

12. A cup of hot coffee that is 84 °C is placed into a freezer at the same time as can of soda at −3 °C is taken out of a cooler. If the coffee temperature drops by 41 °C and the soda temperature increases by 41 °C, how do the temperatures compare?

A. The coffee is 10 °C cooler than the soda.
B. The coffee is 1 °C cooler than the soda.
C. The temperatures are the same.
D. The coffee is 5 °C warmer than the soda.
E. The coffee is 87 °C warmer than the soda.

13. This week Dan's Donuts sold 6 times as many cinnamon crumb donuts as maple glazed donuts. If this week 168 maple glazed and cinnamon crumb donuts were sold, how many cinnamon crumb donuts were sold?

A. 24
B. 28
C. 42
D. 120
E. 144

14. On Monday, the temperature at 7:00 am was 52 °F and rose at a constant rate of $\frac{3}{2}$ °F per hour until 11:00 am. Then the temperature rose at a rate of 2 °F per hour. The temperature first passed above 65 °F between:

A. 12:00pm and 1:00pm
B. 1:00pm and 2:00pm
C. 2:00pm and 3:00pm
D. 4:00pm and 5:00pm
E. 5:00pm and 6:00pm

15. Two Sundays ago, Daniel purchased 10 bagels and three tubs of cream cheese for $24.40. Last Sunday, Daniel purchased 16 bagels for $22.72. Today, he only has a $20 bill. What is the maximum number of tubs of cream cheese that he can purchase?

(Note: No sales tax is charged.)

A. 3
B. 4
C. 5
D. 6
E. 7

16. Jasmine and Shandra start running laps from the same starting line at the same time and in the same direction on an outdoor track. Jasmine completes a lap in 60 seconds and Shandra completes a lap in 45 seconds. Both continue running at their same respective rates and in the same direction for 8 minutes. What is the fewest number of seconds after starting that they will both be back at the starting line at the same time?

    A. 135
    B. 180
    C. 225
    D. 240
    E. 360

17. Jamie makes pies and cookies. It takes her 20 minutes to make a pie and 30 minutes to make a tray of cookies. This weekend Jamie is going to spend 8 hours making pies and cookies. She will make twice as many trays of cookies as pies. How many trays of cookies will she make?

    A. 6
    B. 8
    C. 10
    D. 12
    E. 14

18. After the majority of students struggled on the midterm, a U.S history teacher decided to give a second test for students to be able to improve. However, the final score would not be the better of the two tests; instead, the final score would be based upon how much the student improved. The new midterm score would be calculated as $\frac{4}{5}$ times the difference of the two tests added on to the first test score. If Matthew originally scored 63 points on his first test and 83 points on his second test, what would his new midterm score be rounded to the nearest whole number?

    A. 66
    B. 73
    C. 79
    D. 87
    E. 99

19. Alice's construction company is building a new modern house with a fence on the north side of the property with a length of 780 feet. If Alice wants to place a total of 13 cameras that are evenly spaced out with two on the ends of the fence, how many feet apart should each camera be?

    A. 55
    B. 60
    C. 65
    D. 70
    E. 75

20. To accommodate the guests at a concert, the stage manager, Frank, tried 3 different seating configurations. One configuration was to have only rows of 9, one was to have only rows of 15, and one was to have only rows of 20. None of these configurations work because for each, the last row had 2 fewer people than the other rows. What is the lowest possible numbers of guests at the concert?

    A. 58
    B. 88
    C. 133
    D. 178
    E. 358

21. Bubba's Ice cream shop sells only chocolate, vanilla, and strawberry ice cream bars. On Saturday, they sold a total of 85 ice cream bars. They sold 13 more strawberry bars than chocolate bars and 11 fewer strawberry bars than vanilla. How many strawberry bars did they sell?

    A. 16
    B. 18
    C. 29
    D. 40
    E. 51

22. Jake and Chandler are both standing at the starting line on a 400-meter track when they begin to run at the same time in the same direction around the track. Jake runs at a constant rate of 40 seconds per lap while Chandler runs at a constant rate of 70 seconds per lap. How many seconds after beginning to run will Jake have run exactly 1.5 more laps than Chandler?

A. 30
B. 55
C. 105
D. 140
E. 210

23. Jonathan is working as a delivery driver for a trucking company. He starts and ends all of his trips at the same loading dock. Jonathan began his last trip on Friday at 5:00 am when he left the loading dock. During his driving time, he drove 840 miles at an average speed of 40 miles per hour. His driving time was 3 times as long as his unloading time, and his resting time was 16 hours. When did Jonathan end his last trip?

A. Saturday at 1:00 am
B. Sunday at 1:00 am
C. Sunday at 9:00 am
D. Monday at 1:00 am
E. Tuesday at 9:00 am

24. There are a total of 1,920 calories in a batch of cookies made by John and 230 of those calories are from fat. When making a batch of cookies, John includes 2 sticks of butter. If each stick is equal to 8 tablespoons of butter and if 80% of the calories from fat in the batch of cookies are from the 2 sticks of butter, which of the following is closest to the number of calories from fat per tablespoon of butter?

A. 12
B. 23
C. 46
D. 96
E. 170

25. Julia and Caroline plan to attend a concert in Indio. Julia will drive 225 miles at a constant speed of 45 miles per hour, stopping one time for a 15-minute break. Caroline will drive 360 miles and for the first 4 hours at 65 miles per hour and then take a 30-minute break before driving at a constant speed of 50 miles per hour for the rest of her trip. How much earlier, in minutes, must Caroline leave before Julia so they arrive at the same time?

A. 60
B. 60.25
C. 75
D. 125
E. 135

26. A t-shirt company sells their signature t-shirt for $18. At this price, 24 t-shirts are sold each day. For every $1 decrease in price, the company will sell 2 extra t-shirts per day. The company will adjust the price to maximize revenue. What is the maximum possible revenue for 1 day?

A. $432.00
B. $440.00
C. $450.00
D. $880.00
E. $900.00

27. Jasmine and Demarcus are going to going to start a cupcake stand at a local farmers market. They estimate it will cost $5 per batch of cupcakes, $80 for the mixer, and $25 for the farmers market stand. If they sell each batch of cupcakes for $12, which of the following equations represents the profit, y dollars, they will make on selling x batches of cupcakes?

A. $y = 5x - 105$
B. $y = 7x - 105$
C. $y = 12x - 105$
D. $y = 7x + 105$
E. $y = 12x + 105$

28. Gary's watersport shop rents out 1-person, 2-person, and 4-person kayaks for a day. 1-person kayaks cost $75 per day, 2-person kayaks cost $125 per day, and 4-person kayaks cost $175 per day. Yesterday, Gary made $12,250 by renting 120 kayaks. He rented out twice as many 1-person kayaks as 2-person kayaks. How many 4-person kayaks were rented out?

   A. 15
   B. 30
   C. 35
   D. 55
   E. 70

Chapter 27: Inequalities

In math, two values are not always equal. Sometimes, we just know that one value is bigger or smaller when compared to another value. In these situations, we use inequalities.

Algebra with Inequalities

To solve inequalities on the ACT, treat the inequality signs ($<, >, \leq, \geq$) like an $=$ sign and solve using algebra. Inequalities can be solved as normal algebraic expressions with the exception of one very important rule:

When multiplying or dividing by a negative number, switch the direction of the inequality sign.

This rule is the most important thing to remember from this section and where students most commonly make mistakes on inequalities questions. As a quick example, let's see how to solve the equation below.

$$-2x + 5 \leq 11$$
$$-2x \leq 6$$

When dividing by -2, we switch the direction inequality sign, so

$$x \geq -3$$

Let's see a second example:

$$3x + 6 > x - 4$$

The first step is combining like terms. We subtract x from both sides to get the x-terms on the left side. We then subtract 6 from both sides to get the numbers on the right side.

$$3x - x > -4 - 6$$
$$2x > -10$$
$$x > -5$$

In this example, we never multiply or divide by a negative number, so the inequality sign stays the same. Just because we are working with a negative number does not mean we need to flip the inequality sign. Some students flip the sign whenever they divide and see a negative sign. Don't make that mistake! Only flip the inequality when you multiply or divide both sides by a negative number.

> **Example 1:** Which of the following inequalities describes the solution set for $6x + 12 \leq 9x + 17$?
>
> A. $x \geq \frac{29}{3}$ B. $x \leq \frac{29}{3}$ C. $x \leq -\frac{5}{3}$ D. $x \geq -\frac{5}{3}$ E. $x \geq -\frac{3}{5}$

Solution: To solve, we need to isolate x. Here, let's move all the x-terms to the left side and all the numbers to the right side. To do this, we subtract $9x$ from both sides and 12 from both sides to get

$$6x - 9x \leq 17 - 12$$
$$-3x \leq 5$$

Now we divide both sides by -3. Since we are dividing by a negative number, we switch the direction of the inequality sign.

$$x \geq -\frac{5}{3}$$

The answer is D.

Example 2: Which of the following graphs shows the solution set for the inequality $2x - 4 \geq -x + 6$?

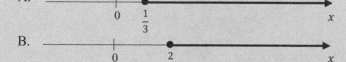

Solution: Now is a good time to review how to draw inequalities on a number line.

1. **For greater than and less than (> and <), use an open circle.**
2. **For greater than or equal to and less than or equal to ($\geq$ and $\leq$), use solid circles.**

For this question, we need to solve the inequality. Let's move all the x-terms to the left side and all the numbers to the right side. To do this, we add x to both sides and add 4 to both sides to get

$$2x + x \geq 6 + 4$$
$$3x \geq 10$$

Now, we divide both sides by 3. Since we are dividing by a positive number, the inequality sign does not change. We get

$$x \geq \frac{10}{3}$$

Since the inequality sign is greater than or equal to, we put a solid dot a $\frac{10}{3}$ and shade to the right of $\frac{10}{3}$. **The answer is C.**

Graphing Linear Inequalities

When graphing linear inequalities in the coordinate plane, you need to remember three simple steps:

1. **Rearrange the equation into $y = mx + b$ form.**
2. **Plot the line. For greater than and less than (> and <), draw a dashed line. For greater than or equal to and less than or equal to ($\geq$ and $\leq$), draw a solid line.**
3. **Shade to show the solution. For greater than and greater than or equal to (> and $\geq$), shade above the line. For less than and less than or equal to (< and $\leq$), shade below the line.**

Let's start by graphing the inequality $2x + 3y \geq 6$.

First, we need to rearrange this into slope-intercept form to isolate y. If we do this correctly, we will get

$$y \geq -\frac{2}{3}x + 2$$

Since this is greater than or equal to, we draw a solid line and shade above the line, so the graph looks like

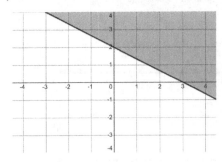

The solution set is the shaded area of the graph.

For a system of inequalities in the coordinate plane, the solution is where the shaded regions overlap. For example, let's consider the system of inequalities $4x - 2y > 8$ and $x + 3y > -2$.

To graph these inequalities, we need to rearrange them into slope-intercept form to isolate y. If we do this correctly, we get

$$y < 2x - 4 \quad \text{and} \quad y > -\frac{1}{3}x - \frac{2}{3}$$

For the $y < 2x - 4$ line, we draw a dashed line and shade below the line. For the $y > -\frac{1}{3}x - \frac{2}{3}$ line, we draw a dashed line and shade above the line.

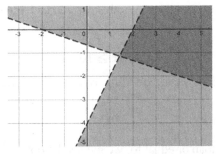

The solution set to this system of equations is the dark area in the top right where the shaded regions overlap.

Example 3: The dark shaded region in the graph below represents the solution set to which of the following systems of inequalities?

A. $y > 2x - 1$
$y > \frac{1}{2}x + 2$

B. $y < 2x - 1$
$y > \frac{1}{2}x + 2$

C. $y > 2x - 1$
$y < \frac{1}{2}x + 2$

D. $y < 2x + 2$
$y > \frac{1}{2}x - 1$

E. $y > 2x + 2$
$y < x - 1$

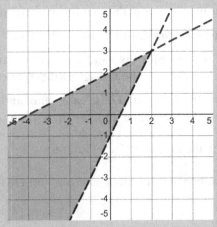

Solution: First, we need to find the equations of the lines. The steeper line has a slope of 2 and a y-intercept at -1. The shaded region is above the line and the line is dashed, so the first equation is $y > 2x - 1$. The flatter line has a slope of $\frac{1}{2}$ and a y-intercept at 2. The shaded region is below the line and the line is dashed, so the second equation is $y < \frac{1}{2}x + 2$. **The answer is C.**

Advanced Graphing Inequalities

On more difficult questions, the ACT will ask you how to graph inequalities with parabolas, circles, and even ellipses. All these graphs still follow the same rules we just discussed for the solid lines vs. dashed lines. Students most commonly get confused about where to shade for these inequalities.

Parabolas

Parabolas shade just like lines do. **For greater than and greater than or equal to (> and ≥), shade above the line. For less than and less than or equal to (< and ≤), shade below the line.** To see how this works, take a look at the examples below.

$y \geq \frac{1}{2}x^2 - 2$

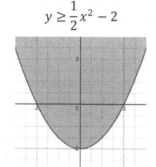

$y < \frac{1}{2}x^2 - 2$

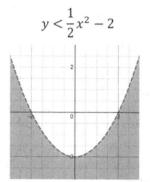

Circles and Ellipses

For inequalities with circles and ellipses, remember the following rule: **for greater than and greater than or equal to (> and ≥), shade outside of the circle or ellipse. For less than and less than or equal to (< and ≤), shade inside the circle or ellipse.**

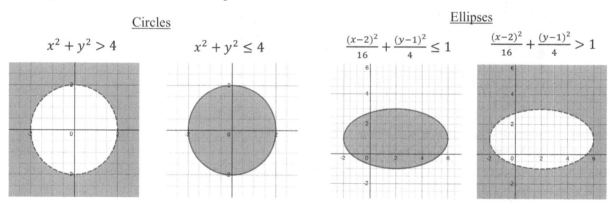

As long as you know how to shade all of these various lines and shapes, you will be ready for the most difficult inequalities questions that appear towards the end of the ACT math section. In addition to shading, you also need to know how to properly draw circles, and ellipses to answer these questions correctly. If you need to learn or review how to graph circles and ellipses, go to chapter 21.

Example 4: The shaded region in the standard (x, y) coordinate plane below is bounded by a parabola and a line. The shaded region and its boundary is the solution set to which of the following systems of inequalities?

A. $y \leq -2x + 2$
   $y \geq x^2 - 2x - 1$
B. $y \geq -2x + 2$
   $y \geq x^2 - 2x - 1$
C. $y \leq -2x + 2$
   $y \leq x^2 - 2x - 1$
D. $y \leq -2x - 2$
   $y \geq x^2 - 2x - 1$
E. $y \leq -2x - 2$
   $y \leq x^2 - 2x - 1$

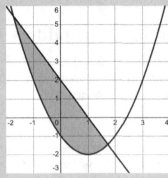

Solution: For any questions like these, look at the answer choices right away. In this question, the equation of the line must be $y = -2x + 2$ or $y = -2x - 2$. The y-intercept is at 2, so we know D and E are incorrect. We need to shade below the line, so the equation for the line must be $y \leq -2x + 2$. C is also incorrect.

Notice that the equation of the parabola is the same in all of the answer choices. On questions like this, you do not need to be able to write the equation of the parabola yourself. You just need to know which inequality sign to use based on where the solution set is. Here, the solution set is above the parabola, so the inequality sign must be $\geq$. The parabola equation is $y \geq x^2 - 2x - 1$. **The answer is A.**

Example 5: The shaded region in the graph below represents the solution set to which of the following systems of inequalities?

A. $y \leq 3x - 4$
   $x^2 + y^2 > 9$
B. $y \geq 3x - 4$
   $x^2 + y^2 < 9$
C. $y \leq -\frac{1}{2}x - 1$
   $x^2 + y^2 > 9$
D. $y \leq 3x - 4$
   $x^2 + y^2 < 9$
E. $y \leq -\frac{1}{2}x - 1$
   $x^2 + y^2 < 9$

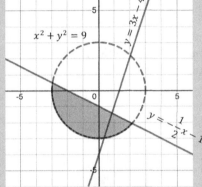

Solution: As with the last example, we want to look at the answer choices right away. The solution set is inside of the circle and the circle is drawn with a dotted line, so the circle equation must be $x^2 + y^2 < 9$. The shaded region is directly below the line $y = -\frac{1}{2}x - 1$, which is a solid line, so the second inequality must be $y \leq -\frac{1}{2}x - 1$. **The answer is E.**

The other line $y = 3x - 4$ does not affect the solution set, so it should not be part of our system of inequalities. If you ever see a line that is not directly bordered by the shaded region, ignore it! The ACT just puts it there to confuse you.

Chapter 27: Inequalities

Inequalities Practice: Answers on page 332.

1. Which of the following inequalities describes the solution set for $4x - 2 \geq 10x - 14$?

   A. $x \leq 2$
   B. $x \geq 2$
   C. $x \geq \frac{8}{3}$
   D. $x \leq -1$
   E. $x \geq -2$

2. The solution set to $3x + 4 > -11$ is all real values of x such that:

   A. $x > -15$
   B. $x < -15$
   C. $x > -11$
   D. $x > -5$
   E. $x < -5$

3. Which of the following graphs shows the solution set for $5 - 3x \geq -2x + 11$?

   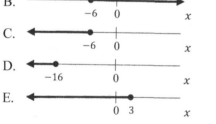

4. What is the greatest integer solution to $-3x + 4 > 19.4$?

   A. -3
   B. -4
   C. -5
   D. -6
   E. -7

5. Which of the following is the solution set for $\frac{2}{5}x + 6 \leq x + 10$?

   A. $x \leq -\frac{20}{3}$
   B. $x \geq -\frac{20}{3}$
   C. $x \geq \frac{4}{7}$
   D. $x \leq \frac{20}{3}$
   E. $x \leq 10$

6. The solution set to $\frac{1}{3}x < \frac{3}{2}x + \frac{11}{6}$ is all real values of x such that:

   A. $x > -\frac{11}{7}$
   B. $x < -\frac{11}{7}$
   C. $x > \frac{11}{7}$
   D. $x > 2$
   E. $x < 2$

7. Which of the following inequalities is equivalent to $5x + 9y \leq 2x - 6$?

   A. $x \geq -3y - 2$
   B. $x \leq -3y - 2$
   C. $x \geq 3y - 2$
   D. $x \leq 3y - 2$
   E. $x \geq 3y + 2$

8. Which of the following number line graphs shows the solution set to the inequality $4 < 3x - 5 < 13$?

   A. [number line with open circles at 3 and 6, ray right from 6]
   B. [number line with open circles at 3 and 6, segment between]
   C. [number line with open circles at 3 and 6, ray left from 3]
   D. [number line with open circles at 3 and 6, rays outward]
   E. [number line at 3 and 6] (empty set)

9. If $x \geq -14$ and $y \leq 19$, what is the greatest possible value of $2y - x$?

   A. 5
   B. 24
   C. 33
   D. 38
   E. 52

PrepPros

10. Which of the following is the solution statement for the inequality shown below?

$$-3 < -2x + 1 < 11$$

A. $-5 < x < 2$
B. $-3 < x < 11$
C. $-2 < x < 5$
D. $-2 < x$
E. $x < -5$ or $x > 2$

11. One of the following inequalities is graphed below in the standard (x, y) coordinate plane. Which one?

A. $y > x - 4$
B. $y < x - 4$
C. $y > -2x - 4$
D. $y < -2x - 4$
E. $y > 2x - 4$

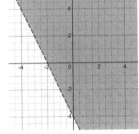

12. Which of the following inequalities is true for all positive integers q?

A. $q \leq q - 1$
B. $q \leq -q^2$
C. $q \leq \frac{1}{q}$
D. $q \leq \sqrt{q^2 + 2}$
E. $q^2 \leq (q-1)^2$

13. The shaded region in the standard (x, y) coordinate plane is the solution set to which of the following systems of inequalities?

A. $\begin{cases} y \geq x + 3 \\ y \geq -\frac{2}{3}x + 1 \end{cases}$
B. $\begin{cases} y \geq x + 3 \\ y \leq -\frac{2}{3}x + 1 \end{cases}$
C. $\begin{cases} y \leq x + 3 \\ y \geq -\frac{2}{3}x + 1 \end{cases}$
D. $\begin{cases} y \geq x + 3 \\ y \leq -\frac{3}{2}x + 1 \end{cases}$
E. $\begin{cases} y \leq x + 3 \\ y \geq -\frac{3}{2}x + 1 \end{cases}$

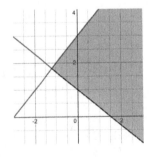

14. The shaded region in the graph below represents the solution set to which of the following systems of inequalities?

A. $\begin{cases} y \geq \frac{1}{2}x - 1 \\ y \geq (x+2)^2 - 1 \end{cases}$
B. $\begin{cases} y \leq \frac{1}{2}x - 1 \\ y \geq (x+2)^2 - 1 \end{cases}$
C. $\begin{cases} y \geq \frac{1}{2}x + 1 \\ y \leq (x+2)^2 - 1 \end{cases}$
D. $\begin{cases} y \leq \frac{1}{2}x + 1 \\ y \geq (x+2)^2 - 1 \end{cases}$
E. $\begin{cases} y \geq \frac{1}{2}x + 1 \\ y \geq (x+2)^2 - 1 \end{cases}$

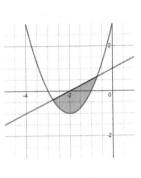

15. If $0 > y > -1 > x$, then which of the following inequalities CANNOT be true?

A. $x^2 > y^2$
B. $x^3 > y^3$
C. $-\frac{1}{y} > -\frac{1}{x}$
D. $\frac{x}{y} > 3$
E. $0 < xy < 1$

16. The shaded region is the solution set to one of the following systems of inequalities. Which system is it?

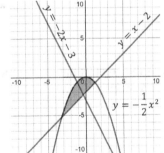

A. $y \geq x - 2$
$y \geq -\frac{1}{2}x^2$

B. $y \leq -2x - 3$
$y \geq -\frac{1}{2}x^2$

C. $y \geq x - 2$
$y \leq -\frac{1}{2}x^2$

D. $y \leq x - 2$
$y \geq -\frac{1}{2}x^2$

E. $y \leq -2x - 3$
$y \leq -\frac{1}{2}x^2$

- 262 -

17. The shaded region is the solution set to one of the following systems of inequalities. Which system is it?

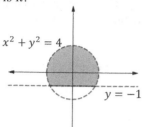

A. $y < -1$
   $4 < x^2 + y^2$
B. $y < -1$
   $4 > x^2 + y^2$
C. $y > -1$
   $4 > x^2 + y^2$
D. $y > -1$
   $4 < x^2 + y^2$
E. $y < 2$
   $x < 2$

18. Which of the following inequalities is equivalent to $(x + 2)^2 \le 9$?

A. $-5 \le x \le 1$
B. $-3 \le x \le 3$
C. $-1 \le x \le 3$
D. $-1 \le x \le 1$
E. $0 \le x \le 3$

19. The shaded region in the graph below represents the solution set to which of the following systems of inequalities?

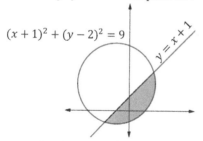

A. $\begin{cases} y \ge x + 1 \\ (x+1)^2 + (y-2)^2 \le 9 \end{cases}$
B. $\begin{cases} y \le x + 1 \\ (x+1)^2 + (y-2)^2 \le 9 \end{cases}$
C. $\begin{cases} y \ge x + 1 \\ (x+1)^2 + (y-2)^2 \ge 9 \end{cases}$
D. $\begin{cases} y \le x + 1 \\ (x+1)^2 + (y-2)^2 \ge 9 \end{cases}$
E. $\begin{cases} x + 1 \le 3 \\ y - 2 \le 3 \end{cases}$

20. If x and y are real numbers such that $x > 1$ and $y < -1$, then which of the following inequalities *must* be true?

A. $\frac{x}{y} < -1$
B. $x^2 - 3 > y^2 - 3$
C. $x + y > 0$
D. $\frac{1}{5}x + 1 > \frac{1}{5}y + 1$
E. $3x^{-2} > 3y^{-2}$

21. The inequality $x^2 - 2 < -3$ is true for the values of x in which of the following sets?

A. $\{-1, 1\}$
B. $\{1\}$
C. $\{x \mid -1 < x < 1\}$
D. $\{x \mid 0 < x < 1\}$
E. The empty set

22. The shaded region in the standard (x, y) coordinate plane is the solution set to which of the following systems of inequalities?

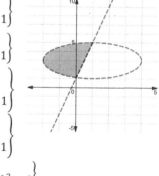

A. $\begin{cases} y > 4x + 1 \\ \frac{(x-1)^2}{9} + \frac{(y-3)^2}{4} < 1 \end{cases}$
B. $\begin{cases} y < 4x + 1 \\ \frac{(x-1)^2}{9} + \frac{(y-3)^2}{4} < 1 \end{cases}$
C. $\begin{cases} y > \frac{1}{4}x + 1 \\ \frac{(x-1)^2}{9} + \frac{(y-3)^2}{4} < 1 \end{cases}$
D. $\begin{cases} y < \frac{1}{4}x + 1 \\ \frac{(x-1)^2}{9} + \frac{(y-3)^2}{4} > 1 \end{cases}$
E. $\begin{cases} y > 4x + 1 \\ (x-1)^2 + (y-3)^2 < 1 \end{cases}$

23. Which of the following inequalities is the solution set for $10 - 3x^2 > -8$?

A. $x < \sqrt{6}$
B. $x > \sqrt{6}$
C. $x > -\sqrt{6}$
D. $-\sqrt{6} < x < \sqrt{6}$
E. $x < -\sqrt{6}$ and $x > \sqrt{6}$

Chapter 28: Exponential Growth and Decay

Any quantity that grows or decays at a fixed rate over time is said to experience exponential growth or decay. Some examples that you may be familiar with include money in a bank account earning 8% interest each year or the number of bacteria on a plate doubling every week.

For most questions on the ACT, we use the simpler form of the exponential growth and decay equations shown below:

Growth: $A = P(1 + r)^t$

Decay: $A = P(1 - r)^t$

P = initial value
A = current value
r = rate of the growth or decay
t = time interval

We use the simple form of the equation above when the time interval is in years, which is most common on the ACT. At the end of this chapter, we will introduce you to the more complex form just in case it appears on your ACT.

Exponential Growth

To see how these equations work and appear on a graph, let's examine the equation for a bank account that has an initial balance of $100 and an 8% annual interest rate.

$$A = 100(1 + 0.08)^t$$

$$A = 100(1.08)^t$$

The $100 is the initial value, and the 8% is the growth rate. 8% is expressed as 0.08 in decimal form, so we get a value of 1.08 inside the parentheses. A represents the current value after t time intervals. Since the amount of money in the bank account is increasing at a non-linear rate over time, we have **exponential growth**.

Now, let's see how this exponential growth equation appears on a graph.

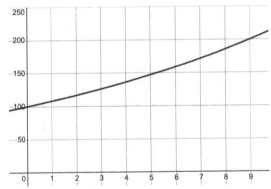

For any exponential growth equation, the graph will have an upward curve like this one. **The y-intercept of the graph shows the initial value**, which in this example is $100.

Note that **the graph is NOT linear.** Even though the growth rate remains constant at 8%, the annual increase in the amount of money in the account will not be the same. In the first year, the $100 grows by 8%, which is $8, so the final amount in the account at the end of year 1 is $108. For the second year, the money is growing at 8% but the starting value is now $108, so the amount of money will increase by 8% of $108, which is $8.64. This explains why a constant rate of change does NOT lead to a constant amount of change and why exponential graphs are not linear.

> **Example 1:** Julia estimates that the numbers of bees in a hive increases by 30% every month. If Julia buys a hive with 50 bees, which of the following properly models Julia's estimate for how many bees, B, will live in the hive in m months?
>
> A. $B = 50 + 30m$ B. $B = 50(0.3)^m$ C. $B = 50m^2 + 30$ D. $B = 50(1.3)^m$ E. $B = 50 + 130m$

Solution: The initial number of bees in the colony is 50, and the growth rate is 30%. Since the growth is 30% each month and not a fixed numerical value, we have exponential growth and not linear growth. A, which is linear, and C, which is quadratic, are incorrect. The value in the parentheses must be 1.3 and not 0.3 since the growth rate is 30%. The 1.3 comes from the $(1 + 0.3)$ in the growth equation. **The answer is D.**

Exponential Decay

Now let's consider an example of **exponential decay**. A new car purchased for $20,000 loses 10% of its value each year after the purchase date.

$$A = 20{,}000(1 - 0.1)^t$$
$$A = 20{,}000(0.9)^t$$

The $20,000 is the initial value, and the 10% is the rate of decay. 10% can be expressed as 0.1 in decimal form, so we get a value of 0.9 inside the parentheses. A represents the current value after t time intervals.

Now, let's see how this exponential decay equation appears on a graph.

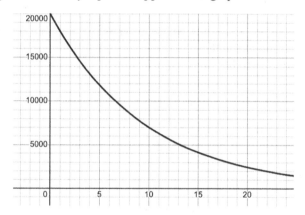

Again, note that the graph is NOT linear. The car continues to lose 10% of its value each year, but the numerical decrease in the car's value is not the same every year. Anytime we have an exponential decay equation, the graph will have a downward curve like this one. **The y-intercept of the graph shows the initial value**, which in this example is the purchase price of $20,000.

> **Example 2:** The Santa Barbara Newspaper is losing subscribers at a rate of 12% per year. If the newspaper currently has 24,000 subscribers, which of the following is closest to the number of subscribers the newspaper will have in 2 years?
>
> A. 5,760 B. 15,360 C. 18,240 D. 18,590 E. 21,120

Solution: The newspaper is losing subscribers at a constant percentage rate, so we can use the exponential decay equation. The 12% decrease can be expressed as 0.12 and, since we asked to find the number of subscribers in 2 years, $t = 2$.

$$\text{Subscribers} = 24{,}000(1 - 0.12)^2 = 24{,}000(0.88)^2 = 18{,}585.6$$

The question says, "closest to," so we are not going to see the exact value in the answer choices. We need to pick the answer closest to the value of 18,585.6. **The answer is D.**

General Exponential Form

Exponential equations can also appear in the general form show below.

$$y = ab^x$$

where $a \neq 0$ and b is a positive number and $b \neq 1$. The a and b values are constants. The main points we need to understand about this general exponential form as listed below:

- a is the y-intercept and shows the initial value of graph when $x = 0$.
- b is the rate of change and shows how much the initial value changes per time interval.
- x is the time interval.
- If $b > 1$, the equation shows exponential growth.
- If $0 < b < 1$, the equation shows exponential decay.

To better understand general form, let's consider two examples with some numbers:

Example 1: A population of 150 endangered Rhinos is doubling every year. Write an equation that models the size of the population, $P(x)$, in x years.

$$P(x) = 150(2)^x$$

The initial Rhino population is 150, so $a = 150$. The population is doubling every year, so the rate of change, b, is 2. x represents the number of years.

Example 2: After a lake is polluted, the population of fish in the lake follow exponential decay. A survey finds that one third of the fish in the lake survived after 1 month. If the estimated initial population of fish in the lake was 12,000, write an equation that models the number of fish, $F(x)$, in m months.

$$F(x) = 12{,}000 \left(\frac{1}{3}\right)^m$$

The initial population of fish in the lake is 12,000, so $a = 12{,}000$. The population is one third of its starting value after 1 month so $b = \frac{1}{3}$. m represents the number of months.

Graphing General Exponential Form (Bonus Topic)

The ACT can include questions where you need to know how to graph exponential equations, but these are very rare and you are extremely unlikely to see it on test day. If you understand the 2 examples below, you should be able to solve any exponential graphing questions that appear on the ACT.

Exponential Growth ($b > 1$)

$$y = 2^x$$

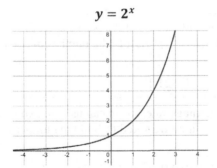

- y-interecept at $(0, a)$
- Graph increasing from left to right when $b > 1$.
- Horizontal asymptote at $y = 0$.

Exponential Decay ($0 < b < 1$)

$$y = 2\left(\frac{1}{2}\right)^x$$

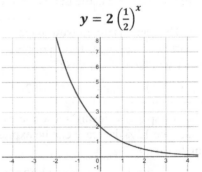

- y-interecept at $(0, a)$
- Graph decreasing from left to right when $0 < b < 1$.
- Horizontal asymptote at $y = 0$.

The most important difference to understand is how the general shape of the graph changes when $b > 1$, where we see exponential growth, compared to when $0 < b < 1$, where we see exponential decay.

Also, note that the y-intercept always appears at the point $(0, a)$. For the graph on the left, $a = 1$, so the y-intercept is at $(0, 1)$. The equation $y = 2^x$ is the same as $y = (1)2^x$, so we do not see the 1 in the equation. For the graph on the right, $a = 2$, so the y-intercept is at $(0, 2)$.

Advanced Exponential Growth and Decay Equations (Bonus Topic)

The exponential growth and decay equations that we learned at the beginning of this chapter are the simplified versions. The ACT very rarely includes questions for which you need to know the compound exponential growth and decay equations listed below. **This topic is rarely tested and advanced, so you should only worry about this if you are aiming for top ACT Math scores.**

Compound Growth: $\quad A = P\left(1 + \frac{r}{n}\right)^{nt}$

Compound Decay: $\quad A = P\left(1 - \frac{r}{n}\right)^{nt}$

P = initial value
A = current value
r = rate of the growth or decay
t = time interval
n = number of times compounded per time interval

Compounding growth or decay equations are most commonly used for calculations involving money. We only need to use these more advanced forms of the equations when the compounding occurs multiple times within each time interval. I know that seems a bit confusing, so let's take a look at an example to make it clearer.

> **Example 3:** Rachel puts $2,000 in a savings account that has an annual interest rate of 4% and compounds every 6 months. Which of the following equations correctly calculates the value of her investment in 3 years?
>
> A. $2,000(1.04)^3$ B. $2,000(1.4)^3$ C. $2,000(1.04)^6$ D. $2,000\left(1 + \frac{0.04}{2}\right)^3$ E. $2,000\left(1 + \frac{0.04}{2}\right)^6$

Solution: Anytime an annual growth or decay rate is provided and the compounding occurs at a rate that is less than a year, we use the compound growth or decay equations. For Example 3, the compounding occurs every 6 months and the interest rate is annual, so we must use the compound growth equation shown above.

Since the compounding occurs 2 times per year (there are 2 6-month periods each year), $n = 2$. The initial value is $2,000, so $P = 2,000$. The rate of growth is 4%, so $r = 0.04$. We are finding the investment value in 3 years, so $t = 3$. Plugging all of these values into the compound growth equation, we get:

$$\text{Value in 3 Years} = 2,000\left(1 + \frac{0.04}{2}\right)^{(2)(3)} = 2,000\left(1 + \frac{0.04}{2}\right)^6$$

The answer is E.

If the question had no compounding and the investment just had an annual interest rate of 4%, we would use the simpler equations we learned at the start of this chapters and the correct answer would be A.

Again, this topic is very rarely tested on the ACT, but it has been on the test before and is fair game. You should memorize both forms of the exponential growth and decay equations we learned in this chapter if you are aiming for top math scores.

Exponential Growth and Decay Practice: Answers on page 332.

1. Trayvon is buying 5,436 fish to start his fish farm. The number of fish in his pond are estimated to increase at a rate of 3% per year. Which equation models the total number of fish, P, in the pond t years from now?

   A. $P(t) = 5,436(1.03)^t$
   B. $P(t) = 5,436(0.03)^t$
   C. $P(t) = 0.03(5,436)^t$
   D. $P(t) = 1.03(5,436)^t$
   E. $P(t) = 1.03t + 5,436$

2. The number of ants in a colony grows exponentially, doubling every 5 days. What is the population of the colony, in thousands, exactly 30 days after the population first reaches a population of 3,000 ants?

   A. 24
   B. 48
   C. 75
   D. 96
   E. 192

3. A surfboard depreciates at an annual rate of 15%. If the initial value of the surfboard is $995, which of the following functions P correctly models the price of the surfboard t years from purchase?

   A. $P(t) = 0.15(995)^t$
   B. $P(t) = 0.85(995)^t$
   C. $P(t) = 995(1.15)^t$
   D. $P(t) = 995(0.85)^t$
   E. $P(t) = 995(0.15)^t$

4. Priscilla selects a random number on Monday. Every day, the number decreases by 40%. If Priscilla selects 340 on Monday, which of the following expressions is equal to the number the following Monday?

   A. $340(0.6)^7$
   B. $340(0.4)^7$
   C. $340(1.4)^7$
   D. $340 - 7(0.4)$
   E. $340 - 7(0.6)$

5. The population of otters in a lake, l, at the beginning of each year can be modeled by the equation $l(x) = 5(2^x)$, where x represents the number of years after the beginning of the year 2010. For example, $x = 0$ represents the beginning of the year 2010, $x = 1$ represents the beginning of the year in 2011, and so on. According to the model, how many otters were in the lake at the beginning of the year 2015?

   A. 160
   B. 320
   C. 640
   D. 1,280
   E. 31,250

6. An invasive species of fish that preys on snails was introduced to Lake Michigan in 2008. Since the introduction of the invasive species, the population of snails has decreased by one third each year. If the population of snails was estimated to be 81,000 in January 2018, what was the population estimated to be in January 2022?

   A. 36,000
   B. 27,000
   C. 24,000
   D. 16,000
   E. 9,000

7. Cocoa Daily sells dark chocolate almonds in bulk online. The price per *pound*, $P(x)$, for a store to purchase x pounds of dark chocolate almonds is given by the function below.

   $$P(x) = 6.5 + 0.95^x$$

   Which of the following dollar values is closest to the total price to purchase 90 pounds of dark chocolate almonds from Cocoa Daily?

   A. $499.50
   B. $586.00
   C. $594.50
   D. $670.50
   E. $720.00

8. The function $f(x) = 75{,}000b^x$ models the annual value for a stock, in dollars, x years after being placed on the stock market, where b is a constant. If the stock's value increases 6% per year, what is the value of b?

   A. 0.06
   B. 0.6
   C. 1.06
   D. 1.6
   E. 6

9. Starting in 1950, the number of people living in Alaska doubled every 20 years. The population of Alaska was 150,000 in 1950. Which of the following expressions gives the population of Alaska in 2010?

   A. $150{,}000(2)^3$
   B. $150{,}000(2)^{20}$
   C. $150{,}000(2)^{60}$
   D. $150{,}000(2)(60)$
   E. $150{,}000 + (60)(2)$

10. Each year after a car is purchased, the price is estimated to be 15% less than the value the previous year. If the initial purchase price of a car was $29,500, which of the following is closest to the price of the car 3 years after it was purchased?

    A. $13,000
    B. $16,000
    C. $16,225
    D. $18,100
    E. $20,650

11. From the 2nd month to the 6th month of its life, a golden retriever experiences exponential growth. The table below shows the weight of a golden retriever every 2 months.

Age (months)	Weight (pounds)
2	8
4	18
6	40.5

    Which of the following equations most closely models the weight of the golden retriever, $W(m)$, m months after 2 months from the ages of 2 months to 6 months?

    A. $W(m) = 8(2.25)^{\frac{m}{2}}$
    B. $W(m) = 8(2.25)^{2m}$
    C. $W(m) = 8(1.25)^{\frac{m}{2}}$
    D. $W(m) = 8(1.25)^{2m}$
    E. $W(m) = 2(8)^m$

12. The amount of nitrogen, in milligrams per kilogram of soil, in a soil sample is given by the formula $N = N_0(3^{2m})$, where N is the total nitrogen in a sample m miles from a site where a water treatment plant just opened and N_0 is the initial amount of nitrogen in the soil before the treatment plant opened. Which of the following expressions gives the number of miles where an initial nitrogen concentration of 4 milligram per kilogram is now measured to be 108 milligrams per kilogram?

    A. 0.5
    B. 1.5
    C. 2
    D. 3
    E. 5

13. The equation below models the number of bacteria, in thousands, on a petri dish h hours after the dish has been inoculated. According to the model, the number of bacteria is predicted to increase by 2% every n minutes. What is the value of n?

$$F(h) = 62(1.02)^{\frac{h}{5}}$$

A. 5
B. 12
C. 60
D. 120
E. 300

14. Mac invests D dollars at the start of 2020 that grows exponentially at a constant interest rate. In 2020, Mac earned $190 in interest. If the interest rate had been 2% higher for this investment, the simple interest would have been $342. What will be the approximate value, to the nearest whole dollar, of Mac's investment on the first day of 2022?

A. $6,992
B. $7,600
C. $7,685
D. $7,980
E. $7,984

Chapter 29: Unit Conversion

You need to know how to properly convert units on the ACT. A few common conversion factors you should know are listed below.

$$1 \text{ foot} = 12 \text{ inches} \qquad 1 \text{ yard} = 3 \text{ feet}$$

$$1 \text{ hour} = 60 \text{ minutes} \qquad 1 \text{ minute} = 60 \text{ seconds}$$

For other conversions, such as pounds to kilograms, the ACT provides the conversion factor as part of the question.

> **Example 1:** A string that is 10 feet and 3 inches long is cut into three pieces of equal length. What is the length of each piece of string?
>
> A. 3 feet 1 inch   B. 3 feet 3 inches   C. 3 feet 5 inches   D. 3 feet 8 inches.   E. 4 feet 1 inch

Solution: First, we need to convert the original length of the string to inches. For a question like this, **you need to convert the length to one unit before dividing.** To convert 10 feet to inches, we multiply by 12:

$$10 \text{ feet} \times \frac{12 \text{ inches}}{1 \text{ foot}} = 120 \text{ inches}$$

So, 10 feet and 3 inches has a total length of 123 inches. To find the length of each piece, we divide by 3:

$$\frac{123 \text{ inches}}{3} = 41 \text{ inches per piece}$$

Now, we need to convert 41 inches to feet. 36 inches = 3 feet, which leaves 5 inches leftover to get to 41 inches. The length of each piece of sting is 3 feet 5 inches. **The answer is C.**

> **Example 2:** A tennis court is 78 feet long and 36 feet wide. What is the area, in *square yards*, of a tennis court?
>
> A. 312   B. 936   C. 2,808   D. 8,424   E. 25,272

Solution: We covered questions like this in Chapter 4 (pg. 15-16), but let's revisit them again since they are a classic unit conversion question that appears commonly on the ACT. **To solve questions involving unit conversion and areas or volumes correctly, convert the units BEFORE solving for any area or volume.**

For this example, we are asked to solve for square yards, so we need to first convert feet to yards:

$$\text{Length} = 78 \text{ feet} \times \frac{1 \text{ yard}}{3 \text{ feet}} = 26 \text{ yards}$$

$$\text{Width} = 36 \text{ feet} \times \frac{1 \text{ yard}}{3 \text{ feet}} = 12 \text{ yards}$$

Now that the units are converted to yards, we can find the area of the tennis court in square yards.

$$A = lw = (36 \text{ yards})(12 \text{ yards}) = 312 \text{ square yards}$$

The answer is A.

*Test-Day Tip: Anytime you see units written in italics, pay close attention and make sure you are solving for the correct units. By putting the units in italics, the ACT is telling you to pay close attention to the units to help make sure you do not accidentally solve for the incorrect units.

Dimensional Analysis

For more advanced unit conversion questions, you need to know dimensional analysis, which uses conversion factors to convert from one unit to another. In the previous examples, we did some dimensions analysis to convert feet to inches and feet to yards.

To set dimensional analysis, complete the following steps:

1. Start with the value given in the question.
2. Use the conversion factor(s) to switch the units.
3. Multiply and divide the numbers to find the answer.

If the conversion factor(s) are setup correctly, the answer will have the correct unit and all other units will cancel! An example of how to do this is shown below:

Example 3: The top speed of Andrew's toy car is 30 meters per second. What is the speed of the toy car in kilometers per hour? (1 kilometer = 1,000 meters)

    A. 1,800   B. 500   C. 108   D. 90   E. 33

Solution: To solve this question, we need to convert meters to kilometers and seconds to hours.

Whenever we are given a rate that includes two units, we can set it up as a fraction. In this question, we are given the speed in meters per second, so we can set up 30 meters per second as:

$$\frac{30 \text{ meters}}{1 \text{ second}}$$

From here, we need to convert the units. Notice how that in each step below, we set up the conversion factor so the units cancel.

$$\frac{30 \text{ m}}{1 \text{ s}} \times \frac{1 \text{ km}}{1,000 \text{ m}} = \frac{30 \text{ km}}{1,000 \text{ s}}$$ 1. Convert meters to kilometers.

$$\frac{30 \text{ km}}{1,000 \text{ s}} \times \frac{60 \text{ s}}{1 \text{ min}} = \frac{1,800 \text{ km}}{1,000 \text{ min}}$$ 2. Convert seconds to minutes.

$$\frac{1800 \text{ km}}{1,000 \text{ min}} \times \frac{60 \text{ min}}{1 \text{ hr}} = \frac{108,000 \text{ km}}{1000 \text{ hr}}$$ 3. Convert minutes to hours.

$$\frac{108,000 \text{ km}}{1,000 \text{ hr}} = \frac{108 \text{ km}}{1 \text{ hr}} = 108 \text{ km/hr}$$ 4. Simplify the answer.

You can also solve this question in one big step as shown below.

$$\frac{30 \text{ m}}{1 \text{ s}} \times \frac{1 \text{ km}}{1,000 \text{ m}} \times \frac{60 \text{ s}}{1 \text{ min}} \times \frac{60 \text{ min}}{1 \text{ hr}} = \frac{108,000 \text{ km}}{1,000 \text{ hr}} = 108 \text{ km/hr}$$

The answer is 108.

The most difficult part of unit conversion questions is setting up the conversion factors correctly, so pay close attention to the units. If the units cancel and you finish with the units the question is asking for, the equation is up properly, and you will have the correct answer.

Example 4: Erica bikes at an average speed of 24 miles per hour for 40 minutes. If Rosie bikes at an average speed of 18 miles per hour, approximately many minutes does it take Rosie to bike the same distance that Erica biked in 40 minutes?

    A. 53   B. 56   C. 60   D. 67   E. 89

Solution: We first need to find out how far Erica bikes in 40 minutes. To solve this, it is important to remember that **distance = speed × time**. We need to multiply the time Erica bikes by her speed to find the distance. But first, we need to convert her speed from miles per hour to miles per minute:

$$\frac{24 \text{ miles}}{1 \text{ hour}} \times \frac{1 \text{ hour}}{60 \text{ minutes}} = 0.4 \text{ miles/minute}$$

Now, we can find the distance using the speed and the time.

$$\text{distance} = \frac{0.4 \text{ miles}}{1 \text{ minute}} \times 40 \text{ minutes} = 16 \text{ miles}$$

To find out how long it takes Rosie to bike 16 miles, we need to convert Rosie's speed from miles per hour to miles per minute:

$$\frac{18 \text{ miles}}{1 \text{ hour}} \times \frac{1 \text{ hour}}{60 \text{ minutes}} = 0.3 \text{ miles/minute}$$

To solve for time, we divide the distance by the speed:

$$\text{Time} = \frac{\text{Distance}}{\text{Speed}} = \frac{16 \text{ miles}}{0.3 \text{ miles/minute}} = 53.3 \text{ minutes}$$

The answer is A. The question says "approximately," so we just round our answer to 53.

Example 5: A metal pipe that is p feet long will be cut into n pieces that are each x inches long. Which of the following expressions correctly describes length, in inches, of each of the n pieces of pipe?

  A. $x = \frac{12p}{n}$ B. $x = \frac{p}{nx}$ C. $x = \frac{px}{12n}$ D. $x = \frac{12n}{px}$ E. $x = \frac{12px}{x}$

Solution #1 - "Math Teacher Way": We first need to convert the length of the metal pipe from feet to inches:

$$p \text{ feet} \times \frac{12 \text{ inches}}{1 \text{ foot}} = 12p \text{ inches}$$

Then, we need to cut it into n pieces, so we will divide the metal pipe by n:

$$\frac{12p \text{ inches}}{n \text{ pieces of pipe}} = x \text{ inches per piece of pipe}$$

The answer is A.

Method #2 – Substitution: If solving algebraically seems tricky, we use substitution and pick numbers to make this question easier. Let's say that the metal pipe is 2 feet long ($p = 2$) and that we will cut it into 3 pieces ($n = 3$). From here, we can easily solve for x, the length of each piece in inches:

$$2 \text{ feet} \times \frac{12 \text{ inches}}{1 \text{ foot}} = 24 \text{ inches}$$

$$\frac{24 \text{ inches}}{3} = 8 \text{ inches per piece}$$

With the numbers we picked, we found that $x = 8$. From here, we plug our values of $p = 2$, $= n = 3$, and $x = 8$ into the answer choices to find out which equation is correct. Let's confirm this works by plugging in our values to answer choice A.

$$8 = \frac{12(2)}{3} \rightarrow 8 = 8$$

The equation works with our numbers, so we know that **the answer is A.**

Unit Conversion Practice: Answers on page 333.

1. If a 6-foot giant sub is cut in half and each half is cut into quarters, how many *inches* long are the resulting pieces of the sub?

   A. 6
   B. 9
   C. 18
   D. 36
   E. 72

2. How many *minutes* would it take a car to travel 140 miles at a constant speed of 50 miles per hour?

   A. 168
   B. 117
   C. 90
   D. 64
   E. 30

3. A piece of string that is 9 feet and 4 inches is cut into 4 equal parts. What is the length, to the nearest inch, of each part?

   A. 2 feet 1 inches
   B. 2 feet 3 inches
   C. 2 feet 4 inches
   D. 2 feet 7 inches
   E. 3 feet 2 inches

4. Julia is wrapping packages for Christmas. If each package requires 20 centimeters of wrapping paper, what is the maximum number of packages that can be wrapped with 4 meters of wrapping paper?

   (Note: 1 meter = 100 centimeters)
   A. 15
   B. 20
   C. 25
   D. 30
   E. 40

5. A log that is 11 feet 6 inches long is cut into two equal segments. What is the length, to the nearest inch, of each part?

   A. 5 feet 6 inches
   B. 5 feet 8 inches
   C. 5 feet 9 inches
   D. 6 feet 9 inches
   E. 6 feet 10 inches

6. A 25-foot plank of wood and a 12-foot plank of wood will be cut into 10-inch pieces. How many 10-inch pieces can be cut from the two planks?

   (1 foot = 12 inches)
   A. 10
   B. 30
   C. 37
   D. 40
   E. 44

7. A category 3 hurricane rains 3 inches per hour for 36 hours. Which of the following is closest to the total *feet* of rain over the 36 hours?

   (1 foot = 12 inches)
   A. 6
   B. 9
   C. 12
   D. 36
   E. 96

8. A bakery purchases flour in 50-gallon bags. The flour is mixed with water to make loaves of bread. Each loaf of bread is made by mixing 3 quarts of flour with 2 quarts of water. What is the maximum number of loaves of bread that can be made from two 50-gallon bags of flour?

   (1 gallon = 4 quarts)
   A. 66
   B. 100
   C. 133
   D. 150
   E. 200

9. James is walking at a speed of 5 miles per hour through downtown Manhattan. If James walks for two hours, how many city blocks does he walked?

   (1 city block = $\frac{1}{20}$ of a mile)

   A. 10
   B. 50
   C. 100
   D. 150
   E. 200

Chapter 29: Unit Conversion

10. Annabel runs 9 miles in $1\frac{1}{2}$ hours. What is the average number of *minutes* it takes her to run 1 mile?

    A. 6
    B. 10
    C. $10\frac{1}{2}$
    D. $13\frac{1}{2}$
    E. 15

11. The yarn store sells blue yard and red yarn. Julie wants to buy 90 feet of red yarn and 45 feet of blue yarn. If red yarn sells for $2 per yard and blue yarn sells for $3 per yard, which of the following is how much Julie will pay for 90 feet of red yarn and 45 feet of blue yarn?

    A. 45
    B. 60
    C. 105
    D. 315
    E. 360

12. Prashant drove from Portland to Sacramento. At 11:00am, he was 340 miles from Sacramento. At 3:00pm, he was 95 miles from Sacramento. Which of the following values is closest to Prashant's average speed, in *miles* per hour, from 11:00am to 3:00pm?

    A. 61
    B. 82
    C. 85
    D. 97
    E. 123

13. The diameter of Pluto is 1,477 miles. Which of the following best approximates the circumference of Pluto in kilometers?

    (1 kilometer = 0.6214 miles)
    A. 2,880
    B. 5,770
    C. 7,470
    D. 10,830
    E. 14,935

14. Ming's flight was originally scheduled to depart at 6:40pm. If his flight was delayed by 436 minutes, what time did Ming's flight eventually depart?

    A. 1:24 a.m.
    B. 1:56 a.m.
    C. 2:12 a.m.
    D. 11:01 p.m.
    E. 11:16 p.m.

15. A cattle farm has a field that has a length of 600 feet and a width of 1,090 feet. Which of the following values is closest to the area, in *acres*, of the field?

    (1 acre = 43,560 square feet)

    A. 15
    B. 210
    C. 330
    D. 218,000
    E. 654,000

16. A car traveling at 40 mph has a leaking oil tank that is losing oil at a rate of 2 ounces per minute. How many *miles* will the car travel before the oil tank, which held 360 fluid ounces when it began to leak, is empty?

    A. 9.4
    B. 20.0
    C. 72.8
    D. 80.0
    E. 120.0

17. A kitchen floor that is $13\frac{1}{3}$ feet wide by 16 feet long is going to be covered with square tiles. If each tile is 16 inches wide by 16 inches long, how many tiles will be needed to cover the entire kitchen floor?

    A. 10
    B. 12
    C. 22
    D. 88
    E. 120

18. Ally has a smartwatch that tracks the number of steps she takes each day. If on Saturday her smartwatch records 8,421 steps and Ally's average step covers a distance of 2.25 feet, how far, to the nearest 0.1 *mile*, did Ally walk on Saturday?

(Note: 1 mile = 5,280 feet)
A. 0.8
B. 1.6
C. 3.6
D. 3.9
E. 7.0

19. A rectangle and a square have the same area. The length of the rectangle is 144 centimeters, and the width of the rectangle is 96 centimeters. What is the approximate length, in *inches*, of a side of the square?

(Note: 1 inch = 2.54 centimeters)
A. 37.8
B. 46.3
C. 47.2
D. 56.7
E. 73.8

20. An Olympic bicyclist broke a record during a race in the French hills. He biked 13 miles in 17 minutes. What was his average speed, to the nearest integer, in *miles* per hour?

A. 4
B. 33
C. 46
D. 52
E. 78

21. One day on the foreign exchange market, 1 U.S. dollar could be exchanged for 20.3 Mexican pesos, and 1 Japanese yen could be exchanged for 0.77 U.S. dollars. On that day, which of the following is closest to how many Japanese yen could be exchanged for 50 pesos?

A. 0.77
B. 2.46
C. 1.90
D. 3.20
E. 64.94

22. Melissa drives 11 miles in 15 minutes at a constant speed and did NOT drive above the speed limit. Which of the following speed limits, in *miles* per hour, is the *lowest* the speed limit could have been?

A. 40
B. 45
C. 50
D. 55
E. 60

23. If it takes an object 1.5 seconds to travel 101.6 feet, to the nearest 0.01 *mile* per hour, what is the speed of the object?

(Note: 1 mile = 5,280 feet)
A. 15.45
B. 46.18
C. 67.73
D. 69.27
E. 152.40

24. A racecar has tires with a radius of 1 foot. The racecar completes one lap of a race in 53 seconds, and the tires rotate at an average rate of 2,876 times per minute. To the closest hundredth of a *mile*, what is the length of the racetrack?

(1 mile = 5,280 feet)
A. 0.48
B. 0.96
C. 1.51
D. 3.02
E. 3.42

Chapter 30: Scientific Notation

Scientific notation is used to express numbers that are too big or too small to be easily written in decimal form. For example, instead of writing 15,000,000, we can write 1.5×10^7. You have likely learned scientific notation before, so in this chapter we will review how to write numbers in scientific notation.

How To Write Numbers in Scientific Notation

Scientific notation is always written as a product of two numbers: the digit term and the exponential term. The base of the exponential term is always 10. Using our example from above, we can identify these different numbers.

$$15{,}000{,}000 = 1.5 \times 10^7$$

The 1.5 is the digit term and the 10^7 is the exponential term. **The digit term must always be greater than or equal to 1 and less than 10.**

So how did we turn 15,000,000 into 1.5×10^7? It's all about counting how many places we move the decimal point, as the number of places we move the decimal point tells us the power in the exponential term. In the original number 15,000,000, the decimal is located at the end of the number. To turn this into scientific notation, we need to move the decimal between the 1 and the 5.

$$15{,}000{,}000. = 1.5 \times 10^7$$

The decimal point moves 7 spots to the left, so the power in the exponential term is 7. **When moving the decimal to the left, the power in the exponential term is positive.** Here are two more examples:

$$201{,}000. = 2.01 \times 10^5 \qquad 8{,}320. = 8.32 \times 10^3$$

> **Example 1:** The MLB estimates that 250,000 baseballs are used during an entire season. Which of the following expressions, when written in scientific notation, correctly represents the number of baseballs used during a season?
>
> A. 2.5×10^4 B. 2.5×10^5 C. 2.5×10^6 D. 25×10^4 E. 25×10^5

Solution: To solve, we need to turn 250,000 into scientific notation. To do so, the decimal point moves 5 spots to the left.

$$250{,}000. = 2.5 \times 10^5$$

The answer is B. Answer choices D and E are incorrect because the digit term, the 25 in these answer choices, is too large. In scientific notation, the digit term must be greater than or equal to 1 and less than 10.

Ok, so we know how to write large numbers in scientific notation. What about small numbers less than 1? We use the same approach, except now we must move the decimal point to the right.

$$0.000916 = 9.16 \times 10^{-4}$$

The decimal point moves 4 spots to the right, so the power in the exponential term is -4. **When moving the decimal to the right, the power in the exponential term is negative.** Here are two more examples:

$$0.0000005 = 5 \times 10^{-7} \qquad 0.000036 = 3.6 \times 10^{-5}$$

Notice how we move the decimal point to the right until we get a number for the digit term that is greater than or equal to 1 and less than 10. Depending on the exact number, you may have to move the decimal all the way to the end, as with 0.0000005 or not, as with 0.000036 and 0.000916.

Example 2: During an experiment, Ronald found that the average weight of an ant is 0.0000029 kg. The average weight of an ant in kilograms is equal to 2.9×10^k. What is the value of k?

A. 7   B. 6   C. 2   D. −6   E. −7

Solution: To solve for k, we need to write the average weight of an ant in scientific notation.

$$0.0000029 = 2.9 \times 10^{-6}$$

We need to move the decimal 6 spots to the right, so the power in the exponential term is −6. **The answer is D.**

Scientific Notation Practice: Answers on page 333.

1. A portion of the Great Wall of China has approximately 1.7 million stone blocks. Which of the following expressions, when written in scientific notation, is equivalent to the number of blocks used to construct the portion of the Great Wall of China?

   A. 1.7×10^4
   B. 1.7×10^5
   C. 1.7×10^6
   D. 17×10^5
   E. 170×10^4

2. A beachfront condo was purchased in 1995 for $210,000. If the condo was sold in 2022 for $1,450,000, which of the following expressions represents the increase in the value of the condo from 1995 to 2022?

   A. 1.24×10^5
   B. 1.24×10^6
   C. 1.66×10^6
   D. 12.4×10^6
   E. 16.6×10^5

3. Which of the following expressions represents the sum of 2.6×10^6 and 7.8×10^5 in scientific notation?

   A. 2.03×10^{11}
   B. 3.38×10^6
   C. 8.06×10^5
   D. 8.06×10^6
   E. 20.28×10^5

4. Which of the following expressions represents the difference of 9.7×10^7 and 4.3×10^6 in scientific notation?

   A. 2.26×10^1
   B. 5.4×10^6
   C. 5.4×10^7
   D. 9.27×10^6
   E. 9.27×10^7

5. $\dfrac{7.5 \times 10^{-3}}{1.5 \times 10^{-5}} = ?$

   A. 5×10^2
   B. 5×10^{-2}
   C. 5×10^{-8}
   D. 6×10^2
   E. 6×10^{-8}

6. $(21.4 \times 10^4)(4 \times 10^6) = ?$

   A. 2.54×10^{10}
   B. 8.56×10^{10}
   C. 2.54×10^{11}
   D. 8.56×10^{11}
   E. 85.6×10^{24}

7. Jordan's average heart rate is 65 beats per minute. In scientific notation, how many times would Jordan's heart beat in 24 hours?

   A. 1.56×10^3
   B. 3.90×10^3
   C. 9.36×10^3
   D. 9.36×10^4
   E. 2.34×10^5

8. What is 8% of 9.02×10^4 ?

   A. 7,216
   B. 11,275
   C. 72,160
   D. 112,750
   E. 721,600

9. The area of Connecticut is 1.44×10^4 square kilometers. The area of Canada is 9.89×10^6 square kilometers. Using these measurements, which of the following is closest to the ratio of the area of Canada to Connecticut?

   A. 48:5
   B. 68:1
   C. 98:14
   D. 144:989
   E. 687:1

10. The value of $x^6(0.2x^2 + 2.2x + 7)$ is between which of the following numbers when $x = 10$?

    A. 4×10^6 and 5×10^6
    B. 4×10^7 and 5×10^7
    C. 4×10^8 and 5×10^8
    D. 1×10^8 and 1×10^9
    E. 1×10^9 and 1×10^{10}

11. A truck can carry 12,480 oranges. If the number of oranges carried by 2,500 trucks can be expressed as 3.12×10^n, what is the value of n?

    A. 5
    B. 6
    C. 7
    D. 8
    E. 9

12. About 9.5×10^4 square miles of Alaska is water. The rest of Alaska, about 5.7×10^5 square miles, is land. If a point in Alaska is randomly selected, what is the probability the selected point is in water?

    A. 14.3%
    B. 16.7%
    C. 27.5%
    D. 60.0%
    E. 62.5%

13. The circumference of the Earth is approximately 131.4 million feet. Which of the following expressions is closest to the radius of the Earth, in feet, when expressed in scientific notation?

    A. 6.47×10^3
    B. 2.09×10^7
    C. 4.18×10^7
    D. 2.09×10^8
    E. 4.18×10^8

14. In a certain state, last year's population was estimated to be 5.6×10^7 and the public debt was estimated to be 7.8×10^{10}. Based on these estimates, what was last year's public debt per person in this state?

    A. $0.72
    B. $43.68
    C. $139.29
    D. $1,392.86
    E. $13,928.57

15. What value of a makes the equation below true?

    $$(3.75 \times 10^{3a+6})(7 \times 10^{12}) = 26{,}250$$

    A. -6
    B. -5
    C. -4
    D. -3
    E. -2

16. A 0.005g sample of an unknown metal is analyzed and is found to be 0.03% silver. Which of the following expressions correctly expresses the mass of silver, in grams, in scientific notation?

    A. 1.5×10^{-2}
    B. 1.5×10^{-3}
    C. 1.5×10^{-4}
    D. 1.5×10^{-5}
    E. 1.5×10^{-6}

Chapter 31: Arcs and Sectors

Arcs and sectors questions occasionally appear on the ACT. This topic is not as commonly tested as the rest of the geometry concepts we covered in Chapters 3-4, but it is one that you should still be familiar with for test day.

Arcs

The arc of a circle is a portion of the circumference. Arcs can be measured in two ways: the degree measure of the arc or the length of the arc itself.

Degree Measure of Arc AB

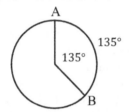

Length of Arc AB

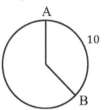

The degree measure of an arc is equal to the measure of the central angle intersecting the arc. The arc length is the actual distance covered moving from point A to point B along the circle.

To solve arc questions, you need to memorize the two equations below. These are different versions of the same equation. Being familiar with both the conceptual idea and the actual equation well help you solve different types of arc questions on the ACT.

$$\frac{\text{Arc Length}}{\text{Circumference}} = \frac{\text{Angle Measure}}{360°} \qquad \frac{L}{2\pi r} = \frac{\theta}{360} \qquad \begin{array}{l} L = \text{arc length} \\ \theta = \text{central angle} \\ r = \text{radius} \end{array}$$

Example 1: In the circle to the right, the length of minor arc BC is 6π and the radius is 8. What is the measure of $\angle A$ in degrees?

A. 270   B. 180   C. 135   D. 100   E. 95

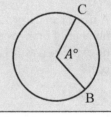

Solution: Using the arc equation, we can setup and solve for the measure of the central angle.

$$\frac{6\pi}{2\pi(8)} = \frac{\theta}{360}$$

$$\frac{6\pi}{16\pi} = \frac{\theta}{360}$$

Next, it is easiest to simplify the fraction on the left-hand side and cancel out the π.

$$\frac{3}{8} = \frac{\theta}{360}$$

$$1080 = 8\theta$$

$$135 = \theta$$

The answer is C.

Chapter 31: Arcs and Sectors

Example 2: Sherry is making a pie chart to represent the favorite ice cream flavor of her classmates. If 5 out of the 25 students in Sherry's class selected strawberry as their favorite flavor, what should the measure of the central angle, in degrees, be for the strawberry sector?

A. 108 B. 95 C. 80 D. 72 E. 60

Solution: The proportion of the students who selected strawberry, 5, to the total students in class, 25, is equal to the proportion of the measure of the central angle to 360°.

$$\frac{5}{25} = \frac{\theta}{360} \rightarrow \frac{1}{5} = \frac{\theta}{360} \rightarrow 360 = 5\theta$$
$$\theta = 72$$

The answer is .

> **TIP – Inscribed Angle Theorem**
>
> An inscribed angle is an angle that has its vertex on a circle and whose sides are chords. While that fancy definition may seem confusing, all you need to know for the ACT is the following rule:
>
> **For an inscribed angle and central angle that intersect the same portion of the arc, the inscribed angle is half the measure of the central angle.**
>
>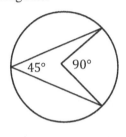
>
> As you can see in the figure, the inscribed angle of 45° is half of the measure of the central angle of 90°. This rule does not come up often on the ACT, but you should still memorize it just in case.

Sectors

The sector is the measure of the area of a portion of a circle. To solve sector questions, you need to memorize the equations below.

$$\frac{\text{Sector Area}}{\text{Area of Circle}} = \frac{\text{Angle Measure}}{360°} \qquad \frac{S}{\pi r^2} = \frac{\theta}{360} \qquad \begin{array}{l} S = \text{sector area} \\ \theta = \text{central angle} \\ r = \text{radius} \end{array}$$

Example 3: For the circle to the right, the radius is 6. If $\angle C = 150°$, what is the area of sector BCD?

A. 8π B. 10π C. 12π D. 15π E. 17π

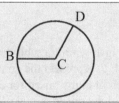

Solution: Using the sector equation above, we can plug in the values from the question and solve to find the area of the sector.

$$\frac{S}{\pi(6)^2} = \frac{150}{360} \rightarrow \frac{S}{36\pi} = \frac{150}{360}$$

Simplify the fraction on the right side we get

$$\frac{S}{36\pi} = \frac{15}{36}$$

- 281 -

Since both sides have 36 in the denominator, we can multiply both sides by 36 and cancel out the 36s to get

$$\frac{S}{\pi} = 15$$

$$S = 15\pi$$

The answer is D.

Example 4: Andrew bought a 12-inch diameter pumpkin pie and cut it into 12 equal slices. After eating 2 slices, he calculates that he consumed 480 calories. How many total calories are in the entire pie?

    A. 960   B. 1,440   C. 1,920   D. 2,400   E. 2,880

Solution: The proportion of calories in two slices to calories in the entire pie is equal to the proportion of the area of the 2 slices of pie to area of the entire pie.

$$\frac{\text{calories in 2 slices}}{\text{calories in whole pie}} = \frac{2 \text{ slices}}{12 \text{ slices}}$$

$$\frac{480}{x} = \frac{2}{12}$$

$$480(12) = 2x$$

$$x = \frac{480(12)}{2} = 2{,}880$$

The answer is E.

Arcs and Sectors Practice: Answers on page 333.

1. The circle below has a circumference of 30π. What is the length of minor arc AB?

   A. 5π
   B. 6π
   C. 8π
   D. 10π
   E. 15π

   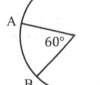

2. Youngstown high school is creating a circle graph to represent the amount of money different clubs raised for a school fundraiser. The clubs raised a total of $15,000. The speech club raised $1,500. What will be the central angle of the sector that displays the money the speech club raised?

   A. 25°
   B. 36°
   C. 45°
   D. 60°
   E. 90

3. The length of AB is 10. What is the perimeter of the semicircle below?

   A. 5π
   B. $5\pi + 10$
   C. $10\pi + 10$
   D. 25
   E. 25π

4. Christine's famous chocolate cake contains 2,700 calories. If the cake is sliced evenly into 9 slices, what is the central angle of each of the slices?

   A. 40°
   B. 45°
   C. 50°
   D. 55°
   E. 60°

5. Dave is making a pie chart to represent the different fruits he currently has in the house. If he has 8 bananas, 6 apples, 4 oranges, and 6 plums, what is the central angle of the portion of the pie chart that represents the apples?

   A. 45°
   B. 60°
   C. 90°
   D. 100°
   E. 120°

6. Adriana's bakery is using a pie chart to display their monthly expenses. Rent is 30% of the monthly expenses. One sector of the chart will be used to display rent. What will be the central angle for that sector?

   A. 30°
   B. 60°
   C. 90°
   D. 108°
   E. 130°

7. Trey's construction company is cutting a circle of concrete into 7 slices. If the original circle of concrete has a diameter of 24 meters, what is the approximate area, in square meters, of one slice of concrete?

   A. 20
   B. 51
   C. 65
   D. 82
   E. 259

8. Jin asked 80 of his classmates to pick their favorite ice cream flavor from 5 options. Jin will represent the results in a circle graph. 20 students picked rocky road, and 24 selected chocolate chip cookie dough. Strawberry, mint chip, and chocolate were chosen as favorites by an equal number of the remaining students. What is the measure of the central angle for mint chip in the circle graph?

   A. 42°
   B. 47.5°
   C. 54°
   D. 58.5°
   E. 60°

9. In the figure below, AC is a diameter of the circle and has a length of 12. What is the length of minor arc AB?

   A. 3π
   B. 4π
   C. 5π
   D. 6π
   E. 8π

   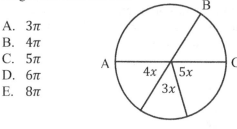

10. Last month, Larissa had total expenditures of $1,200. She spent $750 on a new phone, $275 on her car, $125 on groceries, and $50 on clothing. She will create a circle graph to represent her expenditures from last month. Each sector of the circle graph will represent the percent of her income spent on that category. What will be the measure of the central angle for the car sector?

    A. 76°
    B. 82.5°
    C. 90°
    D. 99.25°
    E. 112°

11. Kristine is building a concrete patio in the shape shown below. The patio has a depth of 8 inches and a radius of 8 feet. If each bag of concrete mix makes 5 cubic feet of concrete, how many bags does Kristine need for the patio?

    A. 12
    B. 15
    C. 18
    D. 21
    E. 23

    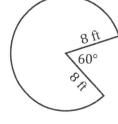

12. Morgan is sharing a pizza with a diameter of 18 inches with 5 of her classmates. Eric eats one quarter of the pizza, and the remaining 5 people share the rest of the pizza evenly. To the nearest integer, how many square inches of pizza did Morgan eat?

    A. 2
    B. 19
    C. 32
    D. 38
    E. 42

13. In the circle shown below, chords LO and MN intersect at point P, which is the center of the circle. The circle has a radius of 6, what is the length of arc NO?

    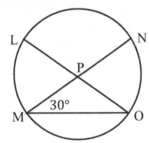

    A. 2π
    B. 3π
    C. 4π
    D. 5π
    E. 6π

14. A circular piece of iron is cut into 12 identical slices. To transport the iron, the slices are loaded onto a truck that can carry a maximum of 3,000 pounds at once. If each truck can carry 2 but not 3 slices of iron, which of the following could have been the weight of the original circular piece of iron in pounds?

    A. 1,500
    B. 4,500
    C. 7,200
    D. 10,600
    E. 14,200

15. Tommy is painting a mural. The shape of the mural is shown below. $\angle BAD = 150°$. For each jar of paint, Tommy can cover 90 square feet. How many jars of paint will Tommy need to paint the entire mural?

    A. 8
    B. 9
    C. 10
    D. 11
    E. 12

    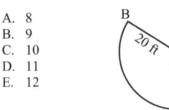

16. The circle below shows the path for a cross country race. In the race, runners start at point C, run to point A, and then run to the finish line at point B. Which of the following is closest to the total distance, in kilometers, of the race?

    A. 7.3
    B. 7.7
    C. 8.5
    D. 8.9
    E. 10.2

    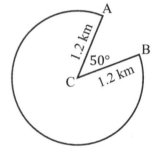

Chapter 32: Vectors

A vector is a quantity that has both a magnitude (length) and direction. Vectors commonly are used to show motion, such as velocity and acceleration. Since vectors are not commonly taught in math class, many students are stumped when vectors appear on the ACT. In this chapter, we will teach you everything you need to know for vectors on the ACT!

What is a Vector?

A vector shows the magnitude and direction of a motion. Vectors are drawn as arrows on the coordinate plane. For example, if a car is driving at 30° east of north at 10 miles per hour, the vector would be:

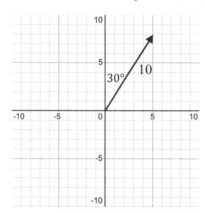

The magnitude (length) of the vector is 10, which shows the speed that the car is traveling. If the car was driving at 20mph, the magnitude (length) of the vector would be 20. The direction is shown by the direction of the vector, which is pointing 30° east of north.

Vectors on the ACT are most commonly written in the following forms:

Standard form: $v = Ai + Bj$

Component Form: $v = \langle A, B \rangle$

In standard form, Ai shows the x-component of the vector and Bj shows the y-component of the vector. In simpler terms, the A shows how far the vector goes left or right and the B shows how far the vector goes up or down. In component form, the A shows the x-component and the B shows the y-component.

The easiest way to teach this is with some examples. Let's consider vectors X and Y below:

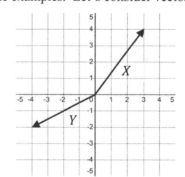

Standard Form

$Vector\ X = 3i + 4j$

$Vector\ Y = -4i - 2j$

Component Form

$Vector\ X = \langle 3, 4 \rangle$

$Vector\ Y = \langle -4, -2 \rangle$

When starting at the origin, a vector written in $Ai + Bj$ or $\langle A, B \rangle$ notation ends at point (A, B). For vector X, we see the vector goes 3 units to the right and 4 units up and ends at the point $(4, 3)$. For vector Y, we see the vector goes 4 units to the left and 2 units down and ends at the point $(-4, -2)$.

Vector Addition and Subtraction

The most common vectors question on the ACT is vector addition and subtraction. The good news is that vector addition and subtraction is simple! When given multiple vectors, all we do is combine like terms.

Example 1: What is the sum of vectors $\langle 2, 5 \rangle$ and $\langle -6, 8 \rangle$?

  A. $\langle 8, 13 \rangle$ B. $\langle -4, 13 \rangle$ C. $\langle -8, -3 \rangle$ D. $\langle -4, 3 \rangle$ E. $\langle -12, 40 \rangle$

Solution: To add vectors in component form, we combine like terms, so we add the A values, the x-components, and B values, the y-components, together.

$$\text{For the } A \text{ values, we get: } 2 + (-6) = -4$$
$$\text{For the } B \text{ values, we get: } 5 + 8 = 13$$

Combining our answers, we get $\langle -4, 13 \rangle$. **The answer is B.**

It's simple arithmetic! The only way the ACT can make these questions slightly more difficult is by adding a coefficient, as shown in Example 2.

Example 2: The vectors A and B can be written as $5i - j$ and $12i - 4j$ respectively. If vector C is equal to $2A - B$, which of the following represents vector C ?

  A. $22i - 6j$ B. $10i - 2j$ C. $-2i + 2j$ D. $2i - 6j$ E. $19i - 9j$

Solution: When there is a coefficient in front of a vector, such as the 2 in $2A$, we distribute the coefficient into in the vector.

$$2A = 2(5i - j) = 10i - 2j$$

Now that we know $2A$, we can subtract B from $2A$ to find vector C:

$$C = 2A - B = (10i - 2j) - (12i - 4j)$$

To solve, we distribute the negative sign and combine like terms.

$$C = 10i - 2j - 12i + 4j = -2i + 2j$$

The answer is C.

Vector Addition and Subtraction On A Graph

For more advanced vectors questions, you need to know how to draw vector addition and subtraction on a graph using the tip-to-tail method. When adding or subtracting vectors, we will use the following steps:

1. **Start at the origin and draw the 1st vector.** For example, if we have 3 vectors A, B, and C and are solving for $A + B + C$, we first draw vector A. The point where the first vector ends, where the top of the arrow is located, is called the tip. This will be our new starting point for drawing the next vector in the equation.

2. **For the 2nd vector, start at the tip of the 1st vector and draw the 2nd vector.** The tail of the second vector (the straight part of the arrow) starts at the tip of the first arrow, hence the name tip-to-tail. For our example, we draw vector B and start from the tip of vector A.

3. **Repeat this process for any additional vectors.** For our example, we have so far done $A + B$. We still need to add vector C, so we start at the tail of vector B and draw vector C.

4. **Draw a vector from the origin to the tip of the final vector in the equation. This vector represents the final vector that you solved for.** For our example, we draw a vector from the origin to the tip of vector C. The vector that we draw is the vector for $A + B + C$.

Let's go through an example to see how this works.

Example 3: For the vectors shown in the graph below, which of the following represents $A + B - C$?

A. D
B. $2E$
C. $A + F$
D. $-3B$
E. $F - C$

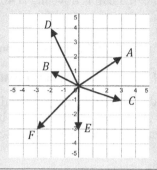

Solution: To find $A + B - C$, we will use the tip-to-tail method. The steps are outlined below.

Step 1: Draw vector A

Start at the origin and draw vector A.

Step 2: Add vector B

Start at the tip of vector A and draw vector B. So far, we have $A + B$.

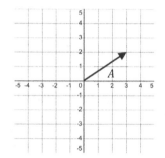

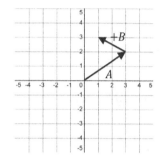

Step 3: Subtract vector C

Start at the tip of vector B and draw $-C$. When subtracting, a vector goes in the opposite direction. $+C$ goes 3 units to the right and down 1 unit, so $-C$ goes 3 units to the left and up 1 unit. We now have $A + B - C$.

Step 4: Draw Vector $A + B - C$

Draw a vector from the origin to the tip of the final vector. Here, we draw a vector from the origin to the end of vector $-C$. This vector, shown as a dashed line below, is equal to vector $A + B - C$.

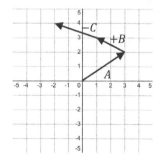

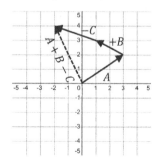

We can see that vector $A + B - C$ goes 2 unit left and 4 units up, which is the same as vector D in the original figure. **The correct answer is A.** This tip-to-tail method takes some practice, so be sure to work through the practice questions to increase your confidence if you have never used this method before.

Magnitude of a Vector

The magnitude of a vector is the length of the vector. Magnitude most commonly comes up on the ACT with questions involving velocity. For example, if a ball is traveling at 40 feet per second, the vector showing this motion would have a magnitude of 40.

The magnitude of a vector can be found using the following equation:

$$\text{For vector } Ai + Bj \text{ or } \langle A, B \rangle, \text{ magnitude} = \sqrt{A^2 + B^2}$$

The magnitude of a vector is rarely tested on the ACT, but you should memorize the equation above just in case. The equation above is the same as the Pythagorean theorem. If you forget the equation on test day, you can draw the vector on the coordinate plane, make a triangle, and use the Pythagorean theorem to solve.

Vectors Practice: Answers on page 333.

1. Given that u and v are vectors such that $u = \langle 5, -3 \rangle$ and $v = \langle 2, 4 \rangle$, what is the component form of the vector $u - v$?

   A. $\langle 7, -7 \rangle$
   B. $\langle 3, 1 \rangle$
   C. $\langle 3, -7 \rangle$
   D. $\langle -3, -7 \rangle$
   E. $\langle 10, 12 \rangle$

2. The vector $4i + 5j$ is added to the vector $-2i + 6j$. What is the sum of the two vectors?

   A. $2i - 1j$
   B. $2i + 11j$
   C. $4i + 11j$
   D. $6i + 11j$
   E. $10i + 3j$

3. Given that u and v are vectors such that $u = \langle 7, 1 \rangle$ and $v = \langle 2, 8 \rangle$, what is the component form of the vector $2u + 3v$?

   A. $\langle 9, 9 \rangle$
   B. $\langle 14, 8 \rangle$
   C. $\langle 16, 10 \rangle$
   D. $\langle 18, 18 \rangle$
   E. $\langle 20, 26 \rangle$

4. When the vector $ai + 4j$ is subtracted from the vector $3i + bj$, the difference is $7i - 3j$. What are the values of a and b?

   A. $a = 0$ and $b = 7$
   B. $a = -10$ and $b = 3$
   C. $a = 4$ and $b = -1$
   D. $a = 10$ and $b = 8$
   E. $a = -4$ and $b = 1$

5. Vector z can be expressed as $ai + bj$, vector w can be expressed as $6i + 2j$, and vector x can be expressed as $14i - j$. If $z + 2w = x$, $a + b$ is equal to:

   A. 8
   B. 5
   C. 2
   D. -3
   E. -7

6. Vince is drawing a vector on the standard (x, y) coordinate plane to show a bus driving 45° north of east at 36 miles per hour. If each coordinate unit represents 1 mile per hour, what is the magnitude of the vector?

   A. 18
   B. $18\sqrt{2}$
   C. 36
   D. $36\sqrt{2}$
   E. 45

Chapter 32: Vectors

7. The vector **i** represents 1 mile per hour east, and the vector **j** represents 1 mile per hour north. Sarah is jogging west at 9 miles per hour. Which of the following vectors represents Sarah's velocity, in miles per hour?

   A. $-9i$
   B. $-9j$
   C. $9i$
   D. $9i$
   E. $9i + 9j$

8. Two vectors are shown in the standard (x, y) coordinate plane below.

   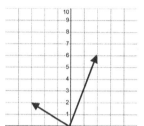

   Which of the following vectors is the sum of these two vectors?

   A. $-i + 8j$
   B. $-i + 4j$
   C. $8j$
   D. $5i + 8j$
   E. $5i + 4j$

9. In the coordinate plane, **i** represents 1 mile east and the vector **j** represents 1 mile north. Tia drives 5 miles south and $5\sqrt{3}$ miles west. Which of the following vectors represents Tia's final location relative to where she began driving?

   A. $-5i + 5\sqrt{3}j$
   B. $-5\sqrt{3}i - 5j$
   C. $-10i$
   D. $5\sqrt{3}i + 5j$
   E. $10j$

For questions 10-13, use the diagram below.

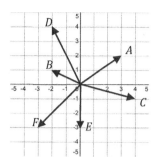

10. Which is the component form of vector $A + F$?

    A. $\langle -1, 0 \rangle$
    B. $\langle 0, -1 \rangle$
    C. $\langle 0, 0 \rangle$
    D. $\langle 6, 5 \rangle$
    E. $\langle 6, -1 \rangle$

11. The vector $F - E + A$ is equal to:

    A. $-4j$
    B. $2j$
    C. $-6i - 5j$
    D. $6i + 2j$
    E. $3i + 5j$

12. Vector $D + E$ is equal to which of the following vectors?

    A. A
    B. B
    C. C
    D. D
    E. None of the above.

13. Which of the following vectors when written in the form $ai + bj$ has $a = 0$ and $b > 0$?

    A. $2B + C$
    B. $A + C$
    C. $2E - B$
    D. $D + A$
    E. $2F$

14. The vectors a, b, and c are represented in the standard (x, y) coordinate plane below. In what general direction will the vector $b - a + c$ point?

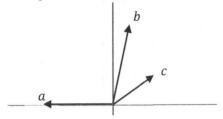

A. Up and to the right.
B. Up and to the left.
C. Down and to the right.
D. Down and to the left.
E. To the left but neither up nor down.

15. The vector i represents 1 mile per hour east, and the vector j represents 1 mile per hour north. According to his car's GPS, at a particular instant, James is driving 30° north of east at 50 miles per hour. Which one of the following vectors represents James' velocity, in miles per hour, at that instant?

A. $-25i - 25\sqrt{3}j$
B. $-25i + 25\sqrt{3}j$
C. $25i - 25\sqrt{3}j$
D. $25i + 25\sqrt{3}j$
E. $25\sqrt{3}i + 25j$

Chapter 33: Shifting and Transforming Functions

On the ACT, you need to know how lines, parabolas, cubics, and other functions shift and transform in the (x, y) coordinate plane.

Rules for Shifting and Transforming Functions

1. **Numbers inside the parentheses shift a function horizontally.** Adding a number shifts a function that many units to the left and subtracting a number shifts a function that many units to the right.

2. **Numbers outside the parentheses shift a function vertically.** Adding a number shifts a function that many units up and subtracting a number shifts a function that many units down.

3. **A negative sign in front of a function flips the function vertically over the x-axis.**

4. **A coefficient in front of the function causes a vertical transformation.** If the coefficient is greater than 1, it causes a vertical stretch. If the coefficient is less than 1, it causes a vertical compression.

All functions follow these same rules. As long as you memorize the rules above, you will be able to solve questions with shifts and transformations of lines, parabolas, cubics, or any other type of function.

Parabolas

We will start by reviewing the shifts and transformations using the parabola function $f(x) = x^2$.

	Horizontal Shift	**Vertical Shift**
$f(x) = x^2$	$f(x) = (x-2)^2$	$f(x) = x^2 - 3$
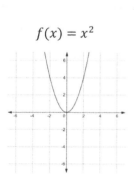	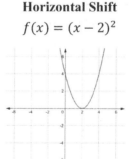	
	Numbers in the parentheses cause a shift right with subtraction (as shown above) and a shift left with addition.	Numbers outside the parentheses cause a shift down with subtraction (as shown above) and a shift up with addition.
Vertical Stretch	**Vertical Compression**	**Vertical Flip**
$f(x) = 4x^2$	$f(x) = \frac{1}{2}x^2$	$f(x) = -x^2$
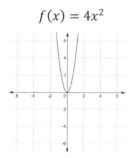	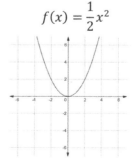	
A coefficient that is greater than 1 causes a vertical stretch.	A coefficient that is less than 1 causes a vertical compression.	A negative sign in the front causes the function to reflect over the x-axis.

Notice how the graph of the original $f(x) = x^2$ function follows the shifting rules we just learned. For the horizontal shift with the -2 in parentheses, we see the graph shift 2 units right. The vertical shift of -3 outside the parentheses shifts the graph 3 units down. The vertical stretch makes the graph steeper while the vertical compression flattens the graph. And finally, the negative sign in from flips the graph over the x-axis.

 ## Cubics

Below, we can see how the cubic function $f(x) = x^3$ follows the same rules for shifts and transformations.

	Horizontal Shift	**Vertical Shift**
$f(x) = x^3$ 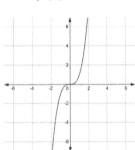	$f(x) = (x+2)^3$ 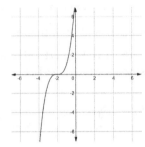	$f(x) = x^3 + 1$ 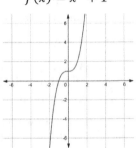
	Numbers in the parentheses cause a shift left with addition (as shown above) and a shift right with subtraction.	Numbers outside the parentheses cause a shift down with subtraction and a shift up with addition (as shown above).
Vertical Stretch	**Vertical Compression**	**Vertical Flip**
$f(x) = 4x^3$ 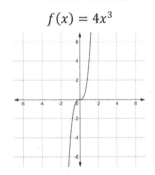	$f(x) = \dfrac{1}{2}x^3$	$f(x) = -x^3$ 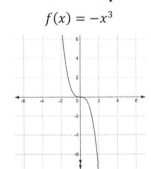
A coefficient that is greater than 1 causes a vertical stretch.	A coefficient that is less than 1 causes a vertical compression.	A negative sign in the front causes the function to reflect over the x-axis.

Let's review the shifts we see in the graphs above. The horizontal shift, the $+2$ in the parentheses, shifts the graph 2 units to the left. The $+1$ outside the parentheses shifts the graph vertically up 1 unit. The vertical stretch makes the graph steeper while the vertical compression flattens the graph. And finally, the negative sign in front flips the graph over the x-axis.

All Other Functions

All functions follow the same basic rules for shifting. The ACT can ask you questions about very weird looking functions. Remember that these functions still follow the same rules for shifts and transformations as the parabolas and cubics that we just reviewed.

$y = f(x)$	**Horizontal Shift** $y = f(x+2)$	**Vertical Shift** $y = f(x) - 3$
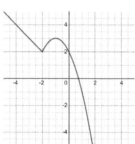	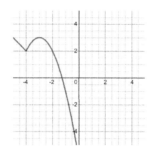	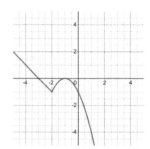
	Numbers in the parentheses cause a shift left with addition (as shown above) and a shift right with subtraction.	Numbers outside the parentheses cause a shift down with subtraction (as shown above) and a shift up with addition.
Vertical Stretch $y = 3f(x)$	**Vertical Compression** $y = \frac{1}{3}f(x)$	**Vertical Flip** $y = -f(x)$
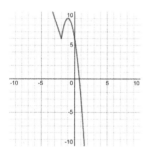	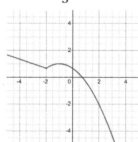	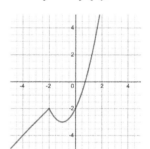
A coefficient that is greater than 1 causes a vertical stretch.	A coefficient that is less than 1 causes a vertical compression.	A negative sign in the front causes the function to reflect over the x-axis.

In function notation, the shifts still follow the same rules. In this example, it is easiest to see the shifts by picking a starting point on the original function $f(x)$. Let's look at the point the corner located at $(-2, 2)$ and see how the function shifts from there.

For the horizontal shift, the $+2$ in the parentheses shifts the function left 2 units, so the corner is now at $(-4, 2)$. The vertical shift, the -3 outside the parentheses, shifts the function down 3 units, so the corner moves to $(-2, -1)$. The vertical stretch makes the function steeper, and the vertical compression makes the function flatter. The negative sign in front causes a vertical flip over the x-axis, so the entire function is flipped upside down and the corner point is now located at $(-2, -2)$.

Shifting and Transforming Functions Practice: Answers on page 334.

1. In the standard (x, y) coordinate plane, point A has coordinates $(5, -9)$. Point A is translated 4 units to the right and 5 units up to Point B. What are the coordinates of Point B?

   A. $(9, -14)$
   B. $(9, -4)$
   C. $(5, -4)$
   D. $(0, -5)$
   E. $(10, -13)$

2. In the standard (x, y) coordinate plane, the graph of the function $y = (x + 11)^2 - 20$ is shifted such that its image is at $y = (x + 11)^2 - 9$. Which of the following describes this shift?

   A. Down 9 units.
   B. Right 11 units.
   C. Left 11 units.
   D. Up 11 units.
   E. Down 11 units.

3. In the standard (x, y) coordinate plane, the graph of the function $y = 2\cos(x) + 3$ undergoes a single translation such that the equation of its image is $y = 2\cos(x) - 7$. Which of the following describes this translation?

   A. Left 10 coordinate units
   B. Right 4 coordinate units
   C. Down 4 coordinate units
   D. Up 10 coordinate units
   E. Down 10 coordinate units

4. $$h(x) = x^2 - 5$$
   $$g(x) = (x - 2)^2 - 1$$

   Which of the following correctly describes the shift required to transform $h(x)$ into $g(x)$?

   A. Shift $h(x)$ right 4 units and down 2 units.
   B. Shift $h(x)$ right 2 units and down 4 units.
   C. Shift $h(x)$ right 2 units and up 4 units.
   D. Shift $h(x)$ left 2 units and down 4 units.
   E. Shift $h(x)$ left 2 units and up 4 units.

5. In the standard (x, y) coordinate plane, the graph of the function $y = |x + 2| + 6$ undergoes two translations such that the equation of its image is $y = |x + 4| + 9$. Which of the following describes these translations?

   A. Left 2 units and down 3 units
   B. Right 2 units and down 3 units
   C. Left 2 units and up 3 units
   D. Right 2 units and up 3 units
   E. Right 2 units and up 6 units

6. $$f(x) = (x + 1)^3 + 2$$

   Which of the following functions $g(x)$ shifts $f(x)$ up by 4 units and left by 1 unit?

   A. $g(x) = x^3 + 6$
   B. $g(x) = (x + 5)^3 + 3$
   C. $g(x) = (x + 2)^3 - 2$
   D. $g(x) = (x + 2)^3 + 6$
   E. $g(x) = (x + 5)^3 + 6$

7.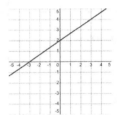

   The graph of $f(x)$ is displayed above. Which of the following is the graph of $y = f(x) - 3$?

   A. 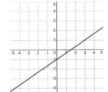   B.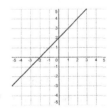

   C. 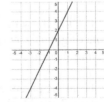   D.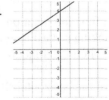

   E.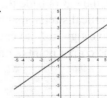

- 294 -

8.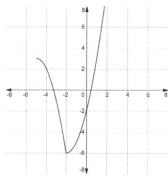

The function $y = f(x+2) + 1$ is show above. What is the y-intercept of $f(x)$?

A. -2
B. -4
C. -5
D. -6
E. -7

9. $g(x) = -(x-2)^2 + 9$
$h(x) = -(x+2)^2 + 11$

Which of the following transformation are required to turn $h(x)$ into $g(x)$?

A. Shift 2 units up.
B. Shift 2 units left and reflect over the x-axis.
C. Shift 4 units left and 2 units up.
D. Shift 4 units right and reflect over the x-axis.
E. Shift 4 units right and 2 units down.

10. In the standard (x, y) coordinate plane, given Parabola P with equation $y = -2x^2$, Parabola Q is the image of Parabola P after a shift of 5 coordinate units up and 8 coordinate units left. Parabola Q has which of the following equations?

A. $y = -2(x+5)^2 - 8$
B. $y = -2(x+8)^2 + 5$
C. $y = -2(x-5)^2 - 8$
D. $y = -2(x+8)^2 - 5$
E. $y = -2(x-8)^2 + 5$

11.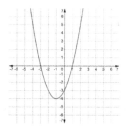

The graph above displays the function $f(x+2) - 3$. Which of the following correctly displays $f(x)$?

A.   B.

C.   D.

E.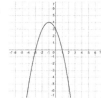

12. The function $f(x)$, when graphed in the standard (x, y) coordinate plane, includes point Z at $(0, 5)$. When function is $-f(x-3) + 4$ is drawn, point Z is located at:

A. $(-3, 9)$
B. $(0, -9)$
C. $(3, -1)$
D. $(-1, 4)$
E. $(3, 9)$

Chapter 34: Statistics

Statistics is not commonly tested on the ACT, but it does appear occasionally. There is a wide range of statistics topics that are included on the ACT, all of which we will cover in this chapter. Most students have learned minimal or no statistics in math class, so these topics usually challenge students simply because they do not know the rules or definitions. If you memorize all the rules and definitions in this chapter, you will be prepared for any statistics questions on the ACT.

Description of A Survey

Imagine we want to find how many pairs of shoes students the average student at a high school owns. To find out, we would conduct a survey where we ask a population of students at the school how many pairs of shoes they own. For this example, let's say there are 500 students at a high school. In statistics, there are a variety of methods of surveying that you need to be familiar with. The common definitions, along with an example for how we would apply it to our pair shoes survey, are listed below.

- **Census: A survey that includes every member of the population.** If we conduct a census for our example, we survey all 500 students at the high school. This method would find the true value for the average number of pairs of shoes students at the high school own.

- **Sample Survey: A survey that includes a selected subset (smaller group) of the population.** If we conduct a sample survey for our example, we survey a small group of students, say 50 students, and would use their answers to make an estimate about the average number of pairs of shoes each student at the high school owns. We would not be able to find the true value – only an estimate.

- **Randomized: Participants are randomly selected from the group. A randomized study/survey produces reliable results.** An example of a randomized survey would be if we randomly selected 50 students at the high school and asked them how many pairs of shoes they own. This would give us an estimate for the average number of pairs of shoes each student at the high school owns.

- **Non-randomized: Participants are not randomly selected from the group. A nonrandomized study/survey can lead to biased results.** An example of a nonrandomized survey would be if we ask the first 50 students who arrive at school how many pairs of shoes they own. This may produce a biased (inaccurate) result because we do not get a random sample of the entire population (all 500 students). For example, if the football team has practice before school, the first 50 students to show up might all be boys who are football players. The average number of pairs of shoes the 50 football players own is not likely representative of how many shoes on average the rest of the students at the high school own.

If you understand these descriptions of a survey, you should be prepared for any questions related to this on test day.

Example 1: Sarah wants to get an estimate of how many seniors plan on attending a 4-year college on the East Coast after graduation. To do so, Sarah plans to ask all the seniors who have lunch during fifth period and record their responses. Seniors who have lunch during other periods were NOT included in the study. Which of the following phrases describes Sarah's method?

  A. Nonrandomized census
  B. Randomized census
  C. Nonrandomized sample survey
  D. Randomized sample survey
  E. Nonrandomized experiment

Solution: Sarah is only surveying students who have lunch in fifth period, so she is not conducting a census. A census would be surveying all seniors at the school. The seniors included in her survey are only the ones who have lunch in fifth period, so she is getting a nonrandomized selection. A randomized selection would use a method, such as picking names from a hat, to randomly select a group of seniors from all seniors at her school. Sarah is asking a subset (small group) of seniors from the entire population, so she is conducting a survey. In an experiment, the person conducting the experiment is manipulating a variable to find out how it influences the results. Sarah is not conducting an experiment. **The answer is C.**

Shapes of Distributions

After collecting data in a survey or census, data points are commonly presented in a graph to show how the points are distributed in the set. When the data points are graphed, we can see the shape of the distribution.

There are 5 common distribution patterns you need to know for the ACT. The shape of the distribution is described by its number of peaks, the possession of symmetry, its tendency to skew, or its uniformity. Each distribution is show below.

Normal Distribution

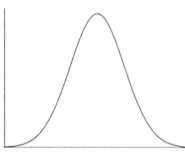

- Symmetric bell shape with one peak
- Mean and median are equal; both are located at the center of the distribution.
- Example: Ask the heights of 1,000 randomly selected men. Most men are near the average height while fewer are shorter or taller than the average.

Uniform Distribution

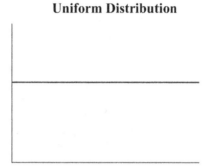

- Equal probability for all outcomes
- Example: Roll a fair dice 200 times and record the results. All number on the dice have an equal probability.

Bimodal Distribution

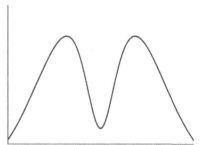

- Two modes (peaks) in the data set
- Example: Number of people at a restaurant at different hours. The two peaks would be during lunch and dinner.

Skewed Left Distribution

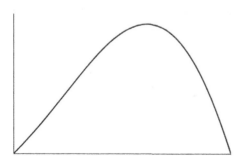

- A graph is skewed left if most of the data is on the right and the tail is skewed left.
- Example: The scores of 80 students on an English test. Most students receive higher scores while fewer have lower scores.

Skewed Right Distribution

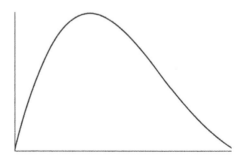

- A graph is skewed right if most of the data is on the left and the tail is skewed right.
- Example: Ask the salary of 500 randomly selected adults. More people have lower and medium salaries while fewer have high salaries.

Example 2: A computer program that randomly selects an integer between 1 and 20 will be run 8,000 times. Each time a number is selected, the number will be recorded. Which of the following will most likely characterize the distribution of the 8,000 recorded numbers?

A. Normal   B. Bimodal   C. Skewed left   D. Skewed right   E. Uniform

Solution: Since the computer program is randomly selecting integers, the probability for each integer being selected is the equal. If we plot the results, we expect to see a uniform distribution. **The answer is E.**

Standard Deviation

Standard deviation is a measure of the spread of values in a data set. A low standard deviation indicates the numbers tend to be closer to the average of a data set while a high standard deviation indicates that numbers tend to be farther from the average of a data set. You do not need to know how to compute standard deviation on the ACT, but you do need to understand the concept. All that you need to know is:

A set of numbers that is closer together has a lower standard deviation, and a set of numbers that is farther apart has a higher standard deviation.

All you need to do to correctly answer standard deviation questions correct is memorize this rule. Let's take a look at two examples to see how this might come up on test day.

Example 3:   Company A: 18, 25, 26, 26, 27, 35, 36, 38
Company B: 64, 66, 66, 66, 68, 68, 68, 70
Company C: 22, 40, 78, 78, 88, 90, 90, 96

Three water filtration companies (A, B, and C) each provided 8 samples of water to be tested for purity. The purity scores are listed above. Which of the following statements about the standard deviation of the purity scores is correct?

A. Company A has the lowest standard deviation.
B. Company B has the lowest standard deviation.
C. Company C has the lowest standard deviation.
D. It cannot be determined which company has the lowest standard deviation.

Solution: To find out which company has the lowest standard deviation, we look for which set of numbers is the closest together. The purity scores for Company B are the closest together, so company B has the lowest standard deviation. **The answer is B.**

Notice that the actual values of the numbers do not affect standard deviation. It does not matter how big or small the numbers are; all that matters is how close the numbers are to each other.

Standard deviation questions can also include a table or graph. If we are given a table or graph, we are still looking for how spread apart the data points are. Data points that are more closely clustered have a lower standard deviation while data points that are more spread apart have a higher standard deviation.

Example 4: The table below give the distribution of weekly rainfall for City A and City B over 17 weeks during the summer of 2021.

Weekly Rainfall	City A	City B
0.00-0.99 inches	6	3
1.00-1.99 inches	2	11
2.00-2.99 inches	3	2
3.00-3.99 inches	1	1
>4 inches	5	0

Which of the following is true about the data shown for these 17 weeks?

A. The standard deviation of weekly rainfall in city A is greater.
B. The standard deviation of weekly rainfall in city B is greater.
C. The standard deviation of weekly rainfall in city A is the same as in city B.
D. The standard deviation of weekly rainfall cannot be calculated with the data provided.

Solution: To determine standard deviation, we need to see how spread out the data points are. The values for the weekly rainfall for city A are very spread out, with 6 weeks having less than 1 inch of rainfall and 5 weeks having greater than 4 inches of rainfall. City B has very consistent rainfall, with 11 of the 17 weeks falling between 1 and 1.99 inches, so the weekly rainfall is not very spread out. City A is much more spread out than city B, so the standard deviation of weekly rainfall in city A is greater. **The answer is A.**

Stem and Leaf Plot

A stem and leaf plot is a method for presenting data in a simple visual form. Data points are split into a "stem," the first digit(s), and a "leaf," the last digit. Stem and leaf plots provide a visual way to represent large data sets and make it easier to observe the frequencies of different events.

To show you how this works, let's consider a family reunion with 14 people in attendance. The ages of everyone at the family reunion are listed below:

17, 21, 24, 25, 30, 41, 45, 45, 48, 49, 54, 61, 77, 79

A stem and leaf plot for the data is shown below.

Stem	Leaf
1	7
2	1, 4, 5
3	0
4	1, 5, 5, 8, 9
5	4
6	1
7	7, 9

The stem and leaf plot shows all the ages. Remember, the "stem" is the first digit, and the leaf is the last digit. Starting at the top of plot, the stem of 1 and leaf of 7 represents the 17 in the data set. Moving down, the stem of 2 has leaf values of 1, 4, and 5, which represents the 21, 24, and 25 in the data set respectively. The 3 and 0 represents the 30, and so on.

As we can see, the stem and leaf plot provides a visual representation of the data and makes it easier to observe the frequencies of the different ages. From the plot, we can clearly see that the highest concentration of people at the family reunion are in their 40s.

There is one more important thing to know for stem and leaf plots: **the number of leaves is equal to the total number of data points.** In our example above, there are a total of 14 leaves to represent the ages of the 14 people in attendance at the family reunion.

Example 5: The stem and leaf plot below shows the heights of 26 lemon trees at Greener Pastures Nursery. If a lemon tree is randomly selected, what is the probability that its height is less than 50 inches?

A. $\frac{5}{13}$
B. $\frac{11}{26}$
C. $\frac{6}{13}$
D. $\frac{1}{2}$
E. $\frac{15}{26}$

Stem	Leaf
3	3, 3, 5, 9
4	0, 1, 3, 6, 6, 8, 9
5	1, 1, 1, 4, 5, 7, 7, 8
6	3, 6, 7, 7, 8
7	0, 2

Solution: To find the probability of selecting a lemon tree with a height less than 50 inches, we need to identify all the lemon trees in the stem and leaf plot that are less than 50 inches tall and divide by the total number of lemon trees. The question tells us there are 26 lemon trees, so we know the total number of lemon trees. If the question did not tell us the total number of lemon trees, we would count the total number of leaves in the stem and leaf plot to find the total.

The lemon trees that have a height less than 50 inches are all ones with a stem of 3 and 4. For the stem of 3, the 4 leaves show the heights of 4 lemons trees to be 33, 33, 35, and 39 inches. For the stem of 4, the 7 leaves show the heights of 7 lemon trees to be 40, 41, 43, 46, 46, 48, and 49 inches. Therefore, there are a total of 11 trees with a height less than 50 inches.

Now, we can find the probability.

$$\frac{\text{Lemon Trees With Height Less Than 50 Inches}}{\text{Total Lemon Trees}} = \frac{11}{26}$$

The answer is B.

Sample Proportion

The sample proportion ($\hat{p}$) describes the proportion of individuals in a sample with a certain characteristic or trait. **To find the sample proportion, we divide the number of individuals who have a certain characteristic or trait by the total number of individuals in the sample.** You can think of the sample proportion as the probability of a certain trait appearing in a randomly selected individual in the sample. Just like probability, sample proportion can be expressed as a fraction or a decimal.

To see how this works, let's look at an example of how this can appear on the ACT.

Example 6: DKMC Fine Woodworking is doing a quality control test on its popular new coffee tables. To conduct the test, the workers selected a random sample of 120 coffee tables out of the 1,000 tables they built in 2022 to inspect and identified 9 of the tables had a poor stability. Let p be the proportion of coffee tables with a poor stability. What is $\hat{p}$, the sample proportion, for this sample?

A. 0.0075   B. 0.009   C. 0.075   D. 0.09   E. 0.12

Solution: The sample proportion is the number of tables with poor stability, 9, out of the entire sample, 120. You can see how this is set up below:

$$\hat{p} = \frac{\text{Tables with poor stability}}{\text{Total tables in the sample}} = \frac{9}{120} = 0.075$$

The total number of tables built in 2022 is irrelevant to finding the sample proportion. **The answer is C.**

Normal Distribution and The Empirical Rule

For a data set that is normally distributed, we need to know something called the empirical rule. This rule is very rarely tested, but, if it does appear on the ACT, questions are pretty easy to solve.

The Empirical Rule

- **68% of the data is within one standard deviation of the mean.**
- **95% of the data is within two standard deviations of the mean.**
- **99.7% of the data is within three standard deviations of the mean.**

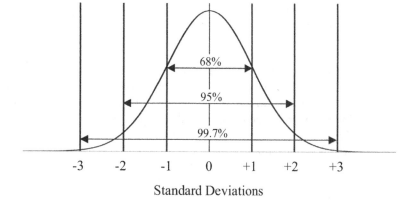

Looking at the normal distribution shown above, the mean is the very middle line. The empirical rule tells us that 68% of the data points lie within 1 standard deviation of the mean. In other words, 68% of the data points are between the -1 and +1 on the graph above. 95% of the data points lie within 2 standard deviations of the mean, which tells us that 95% of the data points are between the -2 and +2 on the graph above. Finally, 99.7% of the data points lie within 3 standard deviations of the mean, so 99.7% of the data points are between the -3 and +3 on the graph above.

As we already said, this is very rarely tested. When this has appeared on the ACT, you have just needed to have the empirical rule memorized. The example below shows how this has been tested in the past. There are a few more advanced examples in the problem set for you to complete in case the ACT presents this is a more difficult way.

Example 7: The scores on a fitness test are normally distributed. The mean score was 110 and the standard deviation was 10. What percentage of the scores on the fitness test are between 90 and 130?

    A. 50%
    B. 68%
    C. 74%
    D. 95%
    E. 99%

Solution: We are told the mean is 110, and the standard deviation is 10. This means that the score of 90, which is 20 points below 110, is exactly 2 standard deviations below the mean, and the score of 130, which is 20 points above 110, is exactly 2 standard deviations above the mean.

The empirical rule tells us that 95% of the data points lie within 2 standard deviations of the mean. Therefore, 95% of the scores are between 90 and 130. **The answer is D.**

PrepPros

Basic Statistics Practice: Answers on page 334.

1. A school librarian wants to predict how often the 500 students at Walker High School will use a new 3D printer. To find out, she randomly selects students 60 students to complete an online survey. Which of the following best describes the method the librarian used?

    A. Randomized study
    B. Nonrandomized study
    C. Randomized survey
    D. Nonrandomized survey
    E. Census

2. A research team in Botswana tagged 50 elephants in a preserve. One month later, the research team returned to the same preserve and observed a random sample of 80 elephants, 15 of which were tagged. Let p be the proportion of elephants in the preserve that are tagged. What is $\hat{p}$, the sample proportion, for this sample?

    A. $\frac{3}{16}$
    B. $\frac{3}{10}$
    C. $\frac{7}{20}$
    D. $\frac{5}{8}$
    E. $\frac{13}{20}$

3. In her science fair experiment, Larissa measures the heights of 8 basil plants, 8 tomato plants, and 8 pepper plants. The heights of all plants, in inches, are listed below.

    Basil: 23, 23, 24, 24, 25, 25, 26, 27, 27
    Tomato: 18, 24, 31, 34, 44, 45, 63, 68
    Pepper: 19, 22, 23, 25, 27, 30, 31, 39

    Larissa calculates the standard deviations for each plant. If b, t, and p represent the standard deviation of the basil, tomato, and pepper plants respectively, which of the following correctly orders the standard deviations from smallest to largest?

    A. $b < t < p$
    B. $p < t < b$
    C. $p < b < t$
    D. $b < p < t$
    E. $t < b < p$

4. Monica is assigned to find out how far seniors at her school drive each day as part of a statistics project. She decides to stand out front of the school and ask every senior how far he or she drives each day. The method that Monica is using can be best described as a:

    A. Census
    B. Nonrandomized study
    C. Randomized study
    D. Nonrandomized survey
    E. Randomized survey

5. 18 balls are placed into a box. Each ball is numbered, and the numbers are shown in stem and leaf plot shown below, what is the probability that a randomly selected ball has a number less than 30?

Stem	Leaf
1	5, 8
2	3, 5, 9
3	0, 0, 1, 3, 4, 7, 7, 9
4	3, 6, 7, 9
5	6

    A. $\frac{5}{18}$
    B. $\frac{8}{18}$
    C. $\frac{13}{18}$
    D. $\frac{5}{23}$
    E. $\frac{7}{23}$

6. For a given set of data, the z-score is given by $z = \frac{x-\mu}{\sigma}$, where μ is the mean of the set and σ is the standard deviation. If, for a set of scores, $\mu = 92$ and $\sigma = 3$, which of the following is the raw score, x, corresponding to $z = 3$?

    A. 85
    B. 89
    C. 95
    D. 98
    E. 101

Use the following information to answer questions 7-9.

In 2015, a poll asked 1,800 households, "On average, how much does your family spent on groceries each week?" The households were split into 2 group, each including 900 households. Group 1 households have children, and group 2 households have no children. The table below lists the percent of each sample that gave each response.

Average amount spent	Group 1	Group 2
Less than $100	3%	3%
$101 to $150	15%	39%
$151 to $200	32%	9%
$201 to $250	33%	11%
$251 to $300	13%	37%
$301 or more	4%	1%

7. Which of the following best characterizes the distribution of the group 1 responses?

    A. Uniform
    B. Normal
    C. Bimodal
    D. Skewed left
    E. Skewed right

8. Which of the following best characterizes the distribution of the group 2 responses?

    A. Uniform
    B. Normal
    C. Bimodal
    D. Skewed left
    E. Skewed right

9. Which of the following statements about standard deviation is correct?

    A. The standard deviation for group 1 is less than the standard deviation for group 2.
    B. The standard deviation for group 2 is less than the standard deviation for group 1.
    C. The standard deviations for groups 1 and 2 are equal.
    D. The standard deviation cannot be determined for either group.
    E. The standard deviation can be determined for group 1 but not for group 2.

10. The scores of 25 students on a fitness test are shown in the stem and leaf plot below.

Stem	Leaf
2	1, 1, 2, 6, 8
3	0, 1, 3, 3, 6, 8, 9
4	1, 2, 2, 4, 4, 5, 8, 9
5	3, 6
6	1, 3, 3

    What percentage of students scored above a 45 on the fitness test?

    A. 52%
    B. 32%
    C. 28%
    D. 20%
    E. 9%

11. Mike has a theory that when asked to pick a random number from 1 to 100, people are more likely to pick values with a single digit than any other number. If Mike's theory is correct, which of the following descriptors will most likely characterize the distribution of the numbers that 10,000 randomly selected people pick if they are asked to pick a number from 1 to 100?

    A. Uniform
    B. Normal
    C. Skewed left
    D. Skewed right
    E. Bimodal

12. Mrs. Pickard is reviewing the test scores of 33 students from last week's test and notices that she accidentally entered the highest score as 92 instead of 95. When she correctly enters the higher score as 95, which of the following value(s) for the test scores must increase?

    I. Mean
    II. Median
    III. Mode
    IV. Range
    V. Standard Deviation

    A. I and III only
    B. I and II only
    C. I, II, and IV only
    D. I, IV, and V only
    E. I, II, IV, and V only

13. The standard normal probability distribution function ($\mu = 0$ and $\sigma = 1$) is shown below in the (x, y) coordinate plane. Which of the following percentages is closest to the percentage of data points that are within 1 standard deviation of the mean in any normal distribution?

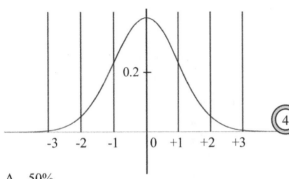

A. 50%
B. 68%
C. 75%
D. 95%
E. 99%

14. Let m, r, and s be the mean, range, and standard deviation of the ages of players on a professional soccer team. Which of the following gives the mean, range, and standard deviation of the ages of the players in 8 years?

	Mean	Range	Standard Deviation
A.	m	r	s
B.	m	r	$s + 8$
C.	$m + 8$	r	s
D.	$m + 8$	r	$s + 8$
E.	$m + 8$	$r + 8$	s

15. The lengths of 10,000 sockeye salmon migrating up the river during the annual salmon run are normally distributed. If the mean length of a sockeye salmon is 25 inches and the standard deviation is 1.75 inches, how many of the 10,000 sockeye salmon migrating up the river are expected to have lengths ranging from 21.5 inches to 28.5 inches?

A. 680
B. 3,400
C. 5,000
D. 6,800
E. 9,500

16. A pair of 6-sided dice are rolled 4,000 times in an experiment. The sum of the numbers rolled is collect after each roll. Which of the following will most likely characterize the distribution of the 4,000 numbers?

A. Uniform
B. Normal
C. Bimodal
D. Skewed left
E. Skewed right

17. A scale created to automatically record the masses of 200 glass jars has a programming error that incorrectly adds 2 ounces to each recorded mass. Using the data from the scale, Arthur computes the mean mass of each glass jar, m, and the standard deviation for the measurements for all glasses, s. After discovering and fixing the programming error, Arthur weighs all 200 glass jars again and recalculates the mean and standard deviation. In terms of m and s, which of the following gives values for the mean and standard deviation that Arthur found after correcting the programming error?

	Mean	Standard Deviation
A.	m	s
B.	$m - 2$	$s - 2$
C.	$m - 2$	s
D.	$m + 2$	$s - 2$
E.	$m + 2$	s

18. The heights of 18,000 students are normally distributed. If the mean height is 66 inches and the standard deviation is 3 inches, what percentage of students are at least 63 inches tall?

A. 50%
B. 68%
C. 84%
D. 95%
E. 97.5%

Chapter 35: Miscellaneous Topics

As we said at the very start of this book, the ACT tests a TON of math topics from algebra, geometry, precalculus, and more. **In this chapter, we will cover all the miscellaneous topics that we have not covered yet in this book. All topics in this chapter have appeared on the ACT before and will appear on the ACT again in the future.** However, none of these miscellaneous topics are commonly tested, so you should only focus on this chapter after you have mastered the other much more commonly tested chapters in the rest of the book. The topics in this chapter progress from the easier and more commonly tested topics to the more difficult and less commonly tested topics.

Venn Diagrams

A Venn diagram is a diagram of overlapping circles that helps visualize the logical relationship between sets and their elements. You have likely seen a Venn diagram before, but if this concept is new to you, let's use the example below to see how it works.

> **Example 1:** Among a group of 23 students, 14 play tennis, 10 play soccer, and 4 play both. Of the 23 students, how many play neither tennis nor soccer?
>
> A. 3   B. 4   C. 5   D. 7   E. 8

Solution: To start, we can draw a Venn diagram and start labeling some numbers.

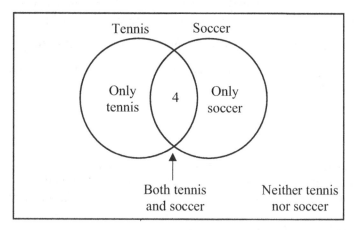

The left circle represents students who play tennis, so we need a total of 14 students inside that circle. The right circle represents students who play soccer, so we need a total of 10 students inside that circle. The overlapping region in the middle represents the students who play both soccer and tennis. We are told that total is 4, so we can label the overlapping region with a 4. The area inside the rectangle and outside of the circles represents the students who play neither tennis nor soccer.

We can fill in the other spots in the Venn diagram with the information from the question.

We are told that there are 14 students total who play tennis and 4 students play both tennis and soccer, so we can subtract to find the number of students who play only tennis.

$$\text{Students who play only tennis} = 14 - 4 = 10$$

We can put a 10 in the left circle, which shows that 10 students play only tennis.

- 305 -

We can repeat this process with the 10 total soccer players, again subtracting the 4 students who play both tennis and soccer to find the students who play only soccer.

$$\text{Students who play only soccer} = 10 - 4 = 6$$

We can put a 6 in the right circle, which shows that 6 students play only soccer.

We can see the updated Venn diagram below.

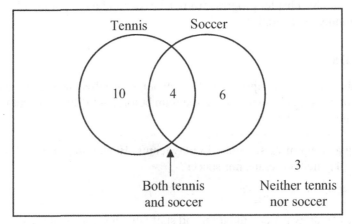

So far, we have a total of 20 students (10 play only tennis, 4 play both, and 6 play only soccer). The question tells that there are 23 students, so we can find the number of students who neither tennis nor soccer.

$$\text{Students who play neither tennis nor soccer} = 23 - 20 = 3$$

The answer is A. Anytime you see a Venn diagram question on the ACT, you should always draw the diagram as we did in this question.

 ## Made-Up Math

The ACT sometimes includes terms or equation that are entirely made-up. While these questions often confuse students on test day because the question includes a term or equation they have never used before, they are most commonly no different than normal functions questions. Let's take a look at an example.

> **Example 2:** If $a \otimes b = 3a^2 - 4b$, what is the value of $5 \otimes 9$?
> A. 39   B. 48   C. 66   D. 189   E. 261

The $\otimes$ is not an actual math term. However, in the question, the $a \otimes b = 3a^2 - 4b$ is defined as a function. To solve, $5 \otimes 9$ we plug in 5 for a, 9 for b, and solve.

$$5 \otimes 9 = 3(5)^2 - 4(9)$$
$$5 \otimes 9 = 75 - 36$$
$$5 \otimes 9 = 39$$

The answer is A. If you ever see a math term on the ACT that you have never seen before, do not freak out! It is probably just made-up math. Stay calm, read the question carefully, and solve.

Logic

Logic questions ask you to think about a given statement and determine which answer choice must also be true.

Example 3: Given the true statement, "if it is Monday, there is bad traffic," which of the following statements *must* be true?

    A. If it is not Monday, there is bad traffic.
    B. If it is not Monday, there is not bad traffic.
    C. If there is bad traffic, it is Monday.
    D. If there is not bad traffic, it is not Monday.
    E. If there is bad traffic, it is not Monday.

These questions often seem confusing until you learn one quick tip: **always look for the contrapositive statement. The contrapositive of a statement must always be true.**

    Original Statement: If A, then B

    Contrapositive Statement: If not B, then not A.

The contrapositive is created by switching the order of the original statement and negating both. Let's apply this to Example 3:

    Original Statement: If it is Monday, there is bad traffic.

    Contrapositive Statement: If there is not be bad traffic, it is not Monday.

The answer is D. This trick always works for any logic question where the original statement is presented in the "if A, then B" pattern and asks which statement must be true.

There can be other logic questions as well on the ACT where this trick does not work. If you see a logic question that is presented in another way, do your best to think through the question carefully. If you are unsure of what the answer is, bubble in your best guess and move on. Do not waste too much time on these types of questions.

Pattern Spotting

Pattern spotting questions present students with a question that seems very overwhelming to solve until you spot the pattern. Once you spot the pattern, solving is easy. The challenge is spotting the pattern. Let's take a look at the example below to see how this works.

Example 4: The first three elements of a pattern are shown below. Each element is composed of small squares with side lengths of 14 inches. Each element is a square with both dimensions 14 inches less than the dimensions of the next element. What is the perimeter, in inches, of the 5th element?

    A. 56
    B. 70
    C. 126
    D. 224
    E. 280

Solution: Following the pattern, the 4th element has a length and width of 4 squares, and the 5th element has a length and width of 5 squares. The length of each side of the squares is 14 inches, so the side total side length for each side of the 5th element is $14 \times 5 = 70$ inches.

The perimeter of the 5th element is all 4 sides added up. Since the shape here is a square, we can use the equation perimeter = $4s$, where s is the length of one side of the square.

$$\text{Perimeter} = 4(70) = 280$$

The answer is E.

Mapping

Mapping questions ask students to map movements and make a conclusion about the final position of an object. For these questions, we always recommend that you draw your own map of the movements.

Example 5: Jimmy normally drives 15 miles on the highway due east to get home from the gym, but the highway is closed due to construction. To take a detour around the construction, Jimmy now needs to leave the gym and drive 2 miles north, turn right and drive 8 miles east, turn right and drive 5 miles south, turn right and drive 2 miles west, turn right and drive 3 miles north, and finally turn right and drive the rest of the way home on the highway. Compared to when there is no construction, how many additional miles does Jimmy now have to drive to get home?

    A. 12   B. 14   C. 16   D. 18   E. 20

To solve, we need to sketch out Jimmy's route home. Normally, Jimmy's normal route on the highway is shown by the thicker line in the middle. The thinner lines show the route Jimmy needs to take to get around the construction and back on the highway.

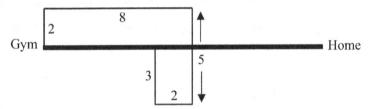

Once we draw our own version of the map, solving this question is much easier. We need to find total number of miles that Jimmy drives when there is construction. To do this, we need to find out where Jimmy gets back on the highway.

We know the entire highway has a length of 15 miles. During his detour, Jimmy travels 8 miles east and then 2 miles west, so when he gets back on the highway, he has moved a total of 6 miles east. When he is getting on the highway at the end of the detour, he is 6 miles away from the gym. Therefore, he still has 9 miles left to drive on the highway to get home. Adding up all of the driving during the detour and the 9 miles on the highway, we can find the total distance Jimmy drives to get home.

$$\text{Jimmy's Drive Home} = 2 + 8 + 5 + 3 + 2 + 9 = 29$$

Jimmy drives a total of 29 miles to get home.

Normally, Jimmy drive 15 miles on the highway to get home. To find how many additional miles he drives, we subtract. $29 - 15 = 14$. **The answer is B.**

Puzzles

The ACT also includes a variety of puzzle questions. Puzzle questions require more problem-solving skills and less traditional math skills. These questions are often some of the most difficult to prepare for on test day and most commonly appear in the last 15 questions of the test. **Puzzle questions can often be very time-consuming to solve, so we advise that you skip any puzzle questions you do not know how to solve immediately and save them for last.**

Example 6: Office Supply Depot sells binders in two ways: a set of 10 binders in a large box and 1 binder in a small box. The large box and small box have the same width and length but different heights. The large box has a height of 12 inches, and the small box has a height of 2.5 inches. Matt has a spot in the corner of his office to store binders. He is going to stack the boxes of binders to a height of 5.5 feet. What is the maximum number binders that he can store?

  A. 66   B. 62   C. 60   D. 52   E. 26

Solution: First, we need to convert the height of 5.5 feet to inches.

$$5.5 \text{ feet} \times \frac{12 \text{ inches}}{1 \text{ foot}} = 66 \text{ inches}$$

Now, we need to figure out the best way to maximize the binders that Matt can store. The large boxes are the more efficient way to store the binders, so we first want to stack as many large boxes as possible. Each large box has a height of 12 inches, so we can stack 5 large boxes. The 5 large boxes have a total height of

$$5 \text{ large boxes} \times 12 \text{ inches per box} = 60 \text{ inches}$$

The 5 large boxes are 60 inches tall, so now we only have 6 inches left. We cannot add any more large boxes because another large box would make the total height over 66 inches.

Next, we have to find out how many small boxes we can add. We have 6 inches of space left and each small box is 2.5 inches, so we can add 2 small boxes.

$$2 \text{ small boxes} \times 2.5 \text{ inches per box} = 5 \text{ inches}$$

We cannot add a third small box because adding another small box would make the total height be over 66 inches.

With 5 large boxes and 2 small boxes, the total height is

$$5 \text{ large boxes}(12 \text{ inches per box}) + 2 \text{ small boxes } (2.5 \text{ inches per box}) = 65 \text{ inches}$$

So, how many binders do we have? Each large box holds 10 binders, and each small box holds 1 binder, so

$$\text{Total binders} = 5(10) + 2(1) = 52$$

The answer is D. As you can see with this example, puzzle questions do not rely on traditional math skills and can be time-consuming. You will have more practice with puzzle questions in the practice questions.

Binomial Theorem and Pascal's Triangle

To expand binomials with powers higher than 2, such as $(2x + 3)^4$, we need to know how to use the binomial theorem and Pascal's triangle. If you have never done this before, this will be a bit tricky at first. However, you do need to know how to do this for some advanced questions that appear in the middle and end of the ACT.

Pascal's triangle (shown below) gives us the coefficients for an expanded binomial in the form of $(a + b)^n$, where n is the row of the triangle. To draw Pascal's triangle, we start with a 1 at the top. The outsides of the triangle are always 1, but the inside numbers are the sum of the two numbers above it. Each row is built from the row above it. The first 5 rows of Pascal's triangle are shown below.

Row	Exponent	Pascal's Triangle
0	$(a+b)^0$	1
1	$(a+b)^1$	1 1
2	$(a+b)^2$	1 2 1
3	$(a+b)^3$	1 3 3 1
4	$(a+b)^4$	1 4 6 4 1
5	$(a+b)^5$	1 5 10 10 5 1

The Binomial Theorem tells us how to use these coefficients to find the entire expanded binomial. To expand a polynomial in the form of $(a + b)^n$, use the following steps.

1. **Find the row of Pascal's triangle to use based on the n-value (the power the binomial is raised to).** For example, for $(2x + 3)^4$, $n = 4$, so we use 4th row of Pascal's Triangle with 1, 4, 6, 4, and 1.

2. **The numbers in Pascal's triangle are the coefficients for each term.** For $(2x + 3)^4$, the first term's coefficient of 1, the second term's coefficient of 4, third term's coefficient is 6, and so on.

3. **The first term is written as $a^n b^0$, which simplifies to a^n.** For $(2x + 3)^4$, the first term is $(2x)^4$, which simplifies to $16x^4$.

4. **As we move right, we subtract one from a's exponent and add 1 to b's exponent. So, the second term is $C \times a^{n-1} b^1$, where C is the coefficient from Pascal's triangle.** For $(2x + 3)^4$, the second term is $4(2x)^3(3)^1$, which simplifies to $96x^3$. Notice how the coefficient of 4 comes from the second spot in the row in Pascal's triangle.

5. **Repeat the process for all middle terms.** For $(2x + 3)^4$, the third term is $6(2x)^2(3)^2$, which simplifies to $216x^2$. The fourth term is $4(2x)^1(3)^3$, which simplifies to $216x$.

6. **The last term is written as $a^0 b^n$, which simplifies to b^n.** For $(2x + 3)^4$, the final term is $(3)^4$, which simplifies to 81.

The fully expanded version of $(2x + 3)^4$ is written below.

$$(2x + 3)^4 = (2x)^4 + 4(2x)^3(3)^1 + 6(2x)^2(3)^2 + 4(2x)^1(3)^3 + (3)^4$$

Notice how the powers of the first term, $2x$, count down and the powers of the second term, 3, count up and how the coefficients come from the 4th row of Pascal's triangle.

With all terms simplified, we get

$$(2x + 3)^4 = 16x^4 + 96x^3 + 216x^2 + 216x + 81$$

Example 7: When $(4x - 3)^3$ is expanded and all like terms are combined, what is the coefficient of the x^3 term?

A. 12   B. 16   C. 36   D. 48   E. 64

Solution: The x^3 term is the first term in the expanded binomial. The first term for a binomial to the third power is always a^3. In this question, the a-value is $4x$, so the first term is equal to

$$(4x)^3 = 64x^3$$

The answer is E. This is the easy version of these types of questions on the ACT, so a question like this can appear in the first 20-30 questions. Make sure you memorize the shortcut rules (steps 3 and 6 on the previous page) for how to find the first and last terms when expanding binomials to solve any question like this quickly and easily!

Example 8: What is the coefficient for the x^2 term in $(5x - 2)^5$ when the term is expanded and all like terms are combined?

A. $-2{,}000$ B. -800 C. -200 D. 400   E. 5,000

Solution: To find the coefficient of the x^2 term, we first need to find which row we are using from Pascal's triangle. Since the binomial is to the 5th power, we use the 5th row. Now, we need to expand the binomial.

$$(5x - 2)^5 = (5x)^5 + 5(5x)^4(-2)^1 + 10(5x)^3(-2)^2 + \mathbf{10(5x)^2(-2)^3} + 5(5x)^1(-2)^4 + (-2)^5$$

Notice how the powers for the first term in the binomial, the $5x$, decrease as we move to the right and the powers for the second term in the binomial, the -2, increase. The coefficients come from the 5th row of Pascal's triangle.

Here, we are looking for the x^2 term, so we only need to simplify the $10(5x)^2(-2)^3$. Recognizing which term to simplify can save you a bunch of time on test day! If you get very skilled at the Binomial Theorem, you can shortcut straight to solving for the x^2 term, which would mean here you would only have to write down and solve $10(5x)^2(-2)^3$ and none of the other terms we set up above.

We have simplified the entire expression below. You should not take the time to do this on the ACT.

$$(5x - 2)^5 = 3{,}125x^5 - 6{,}250x^4 + 5{,}000x^3 - 2{,}000x^2 + 400x - 32$$

The coefficient of the x^2 term is $-2{,}000$. **The answer is A.**

PrepPros

Visual Spatial

Visual spatial questions ask students to manipulate shapes in two-dimensional and three-dimensional space. These questions test non-traditional math skills and often challenge students' problem-solving abilities. We will go through two examples to show you how the ACT may present these types of questions on test day.

Example 9: What is the total number of edges on the 6-sided dice shown below?

A. 9
B. 10
C. 12
D. 16
E. 24

Solution: We can first count the edges that we see. For the front side of the dice, we have 4 edges. **To keep track, we would recommend marking the edges as you go.** Here, we will mark the edges we have counted so far with a black line.

Edges so far = 4

Next, we can mark the edges on the top of the dice. We have already marked one edge, so we can mark the 3 others. Be sure not to double count edges on a question like this!

Edges so far = 7

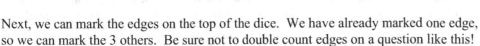

Next, we mark the edges on the right side of the dice. We have already marked two edges, so we mark the 2 others left.

Edges so far = 9

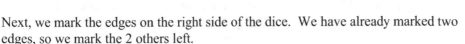

Now for the hard part. We need to visualize the edges that we cannot see. There are 2 more edges that make up the bottom of the dice and 1 more vertical edge on the back left. These edges are shown with the dotted lines.

Total Edges = 12

The answer is C.

Visual spatial questions require you to use your visual spatial skills to manipulate shapes as we did in Example 9. This is only one example of many ways that the ACT can test this skill, but this example is a good introduction to some of the skills you can use that can help you solve these questions correctly. You will see a variety of other common ways the ACT tests your visual spatial skills in the practice questions.

Asymptotes

An asymptote is a line that a function constantly approaches but never touches. You need to know how to find vertical and horizontal asymptotes for a function.

Vertical Asymptotes

Vertical asymptotes occur when the denominator of a rational function is equal to zero. To find where the vertical asymptotes of a function are, we set the denominator equal to zero and solve. For example, let's consider the function $f(x)$ below.

$$f(x) = \frac{x-3}{x^2 - 6x - 7}$$

To find the vertical asymptotes, set the denominator equal to 0 and solve for the value(s) of x.

$$x^2 - 6x - 7 = 0$$

Here, we have a quadratic, so we can factor.

$$(x+1)(x-7) = 0$$

To find the values of x, set each factor equal and solve.

$$x + 1 = 0 \quad x - 7 = 0$$
$$x = -1 \quad x = 7$$

The vertical asymptotes are at $x = -1$ and $x = 7$. Looking at the graph of this function, we can see the vertical asymptotes (shown as dotted lines). Notice how the graph approaches but never crosses the vertical asymptotes.

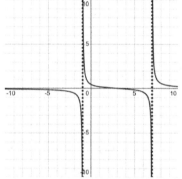

Example 10: On the graph of $y = \frac{5x-7}{3x-9}$ in the standard (x, y) coordinate plane, where is the vertical asymptote?

   A. $x = -9$ B. $y = -3$ C. $x = \frac{5}{3}$ D. $y = \frac{7}{9}$ E. $x = 3$

Solution: To find the vertical asymptote, set the denominator of the function equal to zero and solve.

$$3x - 9 = 0$$
$$3x = 9$$
$$x = 3$$

There is a vertical asymptote at $x = 3$. **The answer is E.**

Horizontal Asymptotes

4

Horizontal asymptotes define the right-end and left-end behaviors on a graph of a function. To find horizontal asymptotes, we look for the degree (the highest power) in the numerator and in the denominator and remember three simple rules:

Rule #1: If the degree of the denominator is larger than the degree of the numerator, the horizontal asymptote is always at $y = 0$.

Consider $f(x)$ shown below.

$$f(x) = \frac{3x^2 + x + 10}{7x^3}$$

The degree of the numerator is 2 since the highest power is the $3x^2$ term. The degree of the denominator, is 3 since the highest power is the $7x^3$ term. The degree of the numerator is greater than the degree of denominator. So, $f(x)$ has a horizontal asymptote is at $y = 0$.

Take a look at the graph of $f(x)$ to see what a horizonal asymptote at $y = 0$ looks like. Notice how the function never crosses the $y = 0$ line, which is the same as the x-axis.

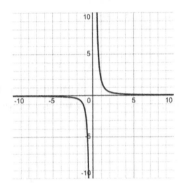

Rule #2: If the degree of the denominator is smaller than the degree of the numerator, there is NO horizontal asymptote.

Consider $g(x)$ shown below.

$$g(x) = \frac{x^3 + 10}{11x^2 - x + 2}$$

The degree of the numerator is 3 since the highest power is the x^3 term. The degree of the denominator is 2 since the highest power is the $11x^2$ term. The degree of the numerator is less than the degree of denominator. So, $g(x)$ has no horizonal asymptote.

Take a look at the graph of $g(x)$. Notice how there is no horizonal asymptote. Functions with a lower degree in the numerator than the denominator have a slant asymptote. You do not need to know how to calculate slant asymptotes for the ACT.

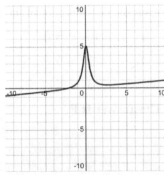

Rule #3: If the degree of the numerator and denominator are equal, the horizontal asymptote is found by dividing the leading coefficients of the polynomials.

Consider $h(x)$ shown below.

$$h(x) = \frac{6x^3 - 2x^2 - 3}{2x^3}$$

The degree of the numerator is 3 since the highest power is the $6x^3$ term. The degree of the denominator is 3 since the highest power is in the $2x^3$ term. Since the degrees of the numerator and denominator are equal, we use the ratio of the leading coefficients to find what the horizontal asymptote will be.

The leading coefficients are the numbers in front of the highest power. In the numerator, the leading coefficient is 6 from the $6x^3$ term. In the denominator, the leading coefficient is 2 from the $2x^3$ term. We divide the coefficients to find the horizontal asymptote.

$$y = \frac{6}{2} = 3$$

So, $h(x)$ has a horizontal asymptote is at $y = 3$.

Take a look at the graph of $h(x)$ to see what a horizonal asymptote at $y = 3$ looks like. Notice how the function never crosses the $y = 3$ line, which is shown as a dotted line below.

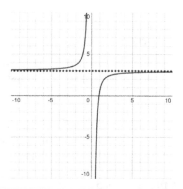

Example 11: The graph of the $f(x) = \frac{-3x^3 + 8x^4 - 7x}{2x^4 + 10x^2 - 9}$ in the standard (x, y) coordinate plane has a horizontal asymptote at what value?

   A. $y = 0$ B. $y = 4$ C. $x = 4$ D. $y = 8$ E. There is no horizontal asymptote.

Solution: To find the horizontal asymptote, we need to find the degree of the numerator and denominator. The degree of the numerator is 4 because we have a $8x^4$ term. The highest power is not always listed first on the ACT, so be sure to look at all terms to find the highest power to find the degree. Make sure you don't fall for the trick that we pulled in this question!

The degree of the denominator is 4 because we have a $2x^4$ term. The degrees of the numerator and denominator are equal, so we follow rule #3 to find the horizontal asymptote: divide by the leading coefficients of the terms with the highest power.

In the numerator, the leading coefficient is 8 from the $8x^4$ term. In the denominator, the leading coefficient is 2 from the $2x^4$ term. We divide the coefficients to find the horizontal asymptote.

$$y = \frac{8}{2} = 4$$

So, $f(x)$ has a horizontal asymptote is at $y = 4$. **The answer is B.**

Miscellaneous Topics Practice: Answers on page 334.

1. 40 residents at an apartment complex in New York City were asked if they owned at least 1 car or at least 1 bike. Data from their answers are recorded below.

Ownership	Number of residents
Bike(s) only	23
Car(s) only	11
Both bike(s) and car(s)	4

   How many of these residents said that they owned NEITHER a bike NOR a car?

   A. 0
   B. 2
   C. 5
   D. 14
   E. 36

2. Given the true statement, "If it is raining, then it is cloudy," which of the following statements *must* be true?

   A. If it is not raining, then it is not cloudy.
   B. If it is not cloudy, then it is not raining.
   C. If it is not raining, it is cloudy.
   D. If it is cloudy, it is raining.
   E. None of the above.

3. For today's workout, Mackenna's first set has 5 squats. For the next set, Mackenna's coach tells her to double the number of squats from the previous set and subtract 4. How many squats will Mackenna do for her fifth set?

   A. 8
   B. 12
   C. 20
   D. 28
   E. 36

4. At a local bakery, there are only 33 sandwiches left with turkey and only 19 sandwiches left with tomato. The number of sandwiches with both turkey and a tomato *must* be:

   A. exactly 52.
   B. exactly 14.
   C. at least 14.
   D. no more than 14.
   E. no more than 19.

5. Mike keeps track of money for the rocketry club. At the end of each day, Mike writes down the total amount of money that the club has. This morning, Mike used $50 to buy some new wiring, but he made a mistake and put the $50 in his notebook as a donation instead of an expense. When Mike calculates the total amount of money that the club has at the end of today, the total will be:

   A. $100 more than it should be.
   B. $75 more than it should be.
   C. $50 more than it should be.
   D. $50 less than it should be.
   E. $100 less than it should be.

6. The course for a race is described in the following sentence. From the starting line, the participants run west for 5 miles, then run north for 2 miles, then run west for 4 miles, then run north for 3 miles to the finish line. Which of the following is closest to the straight-line distance, in miles, from the starting line to the finish line of the race?

   A. 9.9
   B. 10.0
   C. 10.3
   D. 12.8
   E. 13.0

7. Which of the following statements is true for all parallelograms?

   A. The diagonals are perpendicular to one another.
   B. All 4 angles are identical.
   C. The diagonals bisect one other.
   D. There is at least one vertical line of symmetry.
   E. There is at least one horizontal line of symmetry.

8. When $(2x - 1)^5$ is expanded and the like terms are combined, what is the coefficient of the x^5 term?

   A. 8
   B. 10
   C. 32
   D. 50
   E. 64

Chapter 35: Miscellaneous Topics

9. Every graph in one of the following categories has a horizontal line of symmetry regardless of how it is oriented in the standard (x, y) coordinate plane. Which one?

   A. Rectangle
   B. Circle
   C. Isosceles Triangle
   D. Parallelogram
   E. Square

10. The first three elements of a pattern are shown below. Each element is composed of small squares with side lengths of 2 inches. Each element is a square with both dimensions 2 inches less than the dimensions of the next element. What is the area, in square inches, of the 6th element?

   A. 24
   B. 36
   C. 96
   D. 144
   E. 216

11. The graph of $y = \frac{4x^2 - 6}{8x^4 + 6}$ in the standard (x, y) coordinate plane has a horizontal asymptote at $y = ?$

   A. 0
   B. $\frac{1}{2}$
   C. 2
   D. 4
   E. 8

12. Which of the statements is a logical conclusion from the 3 true statements below?

   All zaps are slinks.
   All cricks are snaps.
   All slinks are snaps.

   A. All zaps are cricks
   B. All snaps are zaps.
   C. All zaps are snaps.
   D. No slinks are cricks.
   E. No cricks are zaps.

13. In an AP Biology class with 31 students, 14 students play an instrument, 8 play tennis, and 4 play both. How many students play neither an instrument nor tennis?

   A. 22
   B. 19
   C. 17
   D. 13
   E. 5

14. When graphed in the standard (x, y) coordinate plane, the function $f(x) = \frac{2x^2 + 10}{x^2 - 16x + 60}$ has vertical asymptote(s) at:

   A. $x = 6$ only.
   B. $x = -6$ only.
   C. $x = 10$ only.
   D. $x = 2$ only.
   E. $x = 6$ and $x = 10$.

15. To deliver lunch to my office, the delivery man from Roberto's Burrito Shop must walk a 4-block route to my office. If each different sequence of 4-block-long routes consists of a unique sequence of streets, how many unique routes can the delivery man take to get to my office?

   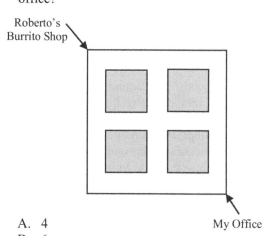

   A. 4
   B. 6
   C. 8
   D. 10
   E. 12

16. Let $a ∴ b = 3ab + b^2$. The value of $3 ∴ (-2 ∴ 5)$ is equal to:

    A. -20
    B. -13
    C. -5
    D. 10
    E. 30

17. Among a group of 25 seniors, 15 are in chemistry, 12 are in computer science, and 10 are in both. How many of the 25 seniors are NOT in either chemistry or computer science?

    A. 15
    B. 11
    C. 8
    D. 7
    E. 6

18. Each of the following shapes has a vertical line of symmetry in at least one orientation except:

    A. Rectangle
    B. Scalene Triangle
    C. Equilateral Triangle
    D. Circle
    E. Ellipse

19. A series of 9 buttons at the Science Museum each play a different sound for a different length of time. The first button plays the sound for 1 second, the second button plays the sound for 2 seconds, the third button plays the sound for three seconds, and so on. Only one sound can play at one. Once a button is pressed, the sound will play and cannot be stopped until the entire sound has played. What is the shortest amount of time, in seconds, that it can take to play 7 different sounds in a row?

    A. 7
    B. 21
    C. 28
    D. 39
    E. 49

20. In certain years, January, a month with 31 days, has exactly 4 Tuesdays and 4 Fridays. The first day of January in those years will be on:

    A. Wednesday.
    B. Thursday.
    C. Friday.
    D. Saturday.
    E. Sunday.

21. There are 50 fractions in the following set.

    $$\left\{\frac{1}{5}, \frac{5}{9}, \frac{9}{13}, \frac{13}{17}, \ldots, \frac{193}{197}, \frac{197}{201}\right\}$$

    Each fraction after the first is found by adding 4 to the preceding fraction's numerator and denominator. What is the product of these 50 fractions?

    A. $\frac{1}{4}$
    B. $\frac{1}{10}$
    C. $\frac{1}{50}$
    D. $\frac{1}{201}$
    E. $\frac{1}{500}$

22. The picture below shows an 8-sided dice. How many total edges are there on the dice?

    A. 9
    B. 11
    C. 12
    D. 14
    E. 16

23. A plane contains 13 horizontal lines and 11 vertical lines. These lines divide the plane into separate regions. How many separate regions have a finite, nonzero area?

    A. 99
    B. 120
    C. 130
    D. 143
    E. 195

Chapter 35: Miscellaneous Topics

24. Let X, Y, and Z represent the hundreds, tens, and ones place, respectively, of a certain 3-digit whole number. Let A, B, and C represent the digits in the hundreds, tens, and ones place of a different 3-digit whole number. The positive difference between the two numbers is greater than 100. Which of the following inequalities *must* be true?

    A. $X - A \geq 1$
    B. $Y - B \geq 1$
    C. $|(A + B) - (X + Y)| = 2$
    D. $|Z - C| \geq 1$
    E. $|A - X| \geq 1$

25. All integers from 1 to 24 are paired with another integer so that the sum of the pair of integers is equal to a perfect square. If all integers can only be used once, what number must 3 be paired with?

    A. 1
    B. 6
    C. 9
    D. 13
    E. 22

26. On his way home, Mark finds out that a street is closed due to a marathon. From his current location, Mark would normally walk 12 blocks south to get home. Now, he must follow a detour to get home. The detour lists the following directions: walk 3 blocks east, 6 blocks south, 1 block west, 1 block north, and 2 blocks west. From the start of the detour, how many blocks does Mark walk to get home?

    A. 20
    B. 19
    C. 18
    D. 17
    E. 16

27. 4 points A, B, C, and D are collinear, and D is between B and C. For A to be between B and C such that $BD + DA + AC = BC$, which of the statements below *must* be true?

    I. A is between B and D
    II. A is between D and C
    III. $BD = DC$
    IV. $DA = AC$

    A. IV only
    B. II only
    C. I and IV only
    D. II and III only.
    E. None of the statements must be true.

28. When $(-4x + 1)^3$ is expanded and the like terms are combined, what is the coefficient of the x term?

    A. -12
    B. -4
    C. -3
    D. 3
    E. 12

29. Shown below are the top, front, and left side views of a stack of 1-inch cubes. The labels T, F, and L specify where the top, front, and left sides are located with respect to the view. What is the volume, in cubic inches, of the stack of cubes?

    top

    front

    left side

    A. 9
    B. 12
    C. 14
    D. 15
    E. 16

30. There are 30 fractions in the following set.
$$\left\{\frac{2}{4},\frac{3}{5},\frac{4}{6},\frac{5}{7},...\right\}$$
Each fraction after the first is found by adding 1 to the preceding fraction's numerator and denominator. What is the product of these 30 fractions?

A. $\frac{1}{187}$
B. $\frac{1}{176}$
C. $\frac{2}{33}$
D. $\frac{1}{17}$
E. $\frac{1}{13}$

31. Carol is inventing a new notation in math for integers. She decided to use $n\boxplus$ means you square n and subtract the sum of all integers less than n. For example, $4\boxplus$ means $4^2 - (3+2+1)$. Carol has written 3 statement she is investigating as properties of $n\boxplus$.

  I. $n\boxplus +(n+1)^2 = (n+1)\boxplus$
  II. $n\boxplus -n^2 = (n-1)\boxplus$
  III. $n\boxplus -(n-1)\boxplus = n$

Which of these statements, if any, is(are) true for all positive integers n ?

A. I only
B. II only
C. III only
D. I, II, and III.
E. None

32. An order of 150 books, each 1.25 inches think, will be placed into boxes to ship to a customer. Each box can hold books with a combined thickness of no more than 18 inches. All but one box will hold the maximum number of books. What is the combined thickness, in inches, of the books in the partially filled box?

A. 15.0
B. 12.5
C. 10.0
D. 7.5
E. 3.75

33. When $(2x-5)^4$ is expanded and the like terms are combined, what is the coefficient of the x^3 term?

A. -160
B. -40
C. 16
D. 40
E. 600

34. A certain neighborhood has 90 houses, 60 of which have a pool. Of the houses with a pool, 47 have a dog. There are 18 houses that do not have a pool and also do not have a dog. If one house from the neighborhood is selected at random, what is the probability that the house selected will have a dog?

A. $\frac{47}{90}$
B. $\frac{59}{90}$
C. $\frac{60}{90}$
D. $\frac{65}{90}$
E. $\frac{72}{90}$

Practice ACT and Diagnostic Sheet

One of the best ways to prepare for test day is to complete a practice ACT. **The ACT provides 1 free practice ACT in their "Preparing For The ACT Test" Guide.** You can find a link to this free practice ACT at www.preppros.io/free-resources.

After you complete the practice ACT, use the diagnostic sheet below to identify what concepts and chapters you need to complete. The diagnostic sheet lists the topic and corresponding chapter for all questions on the practice test.

*Important note: One practice ACT is not enough to fully diagnose all your weaknesses. Completing any topics/chapters the correspond with the questions you answered incorrectly on this practice ACT is a great place to start, but you should not stop there. There are only 60 questions on each practice ACT. This practice ACT does not include all topics tested on the ACT. To be fully prepared for test day, you should complete the study guides for your level at the front of this book.

2022-2023 Preparing For the ACT (Form 2176CPRE)

Question	Question Type	Chapter Number
1	Probability	22
2	Algebra Skills - Combine Like Terms	7
3	Algebra Skills - PEMDAS	7
4	Absolute Value	18
5	Quadratics - Multiplying Binomials	16
6	Fractions	6
7	Exponential Growth and Decay	28
8	Word Problems	26
9	Geometry Part 2 - Shapes (Similar Triangles)	4
10	Ratios, Unit Conversion	10, 29
11	Probability	22
12	Lines - Midpoint Formula	5
13	Word Problems	26
14	Word Problems	26
15	Simple Percentage, Scientific Notation	9, 29
16	Algebra Skills - Combine Like Terms	7
17	Trigonometry - SOH-CAH-TOA	17
18	Exponents	13
19	Geometry Part 2 - Shapes (Pythagorean Theorem)	4
20	Basic Statistics	34
21	Geometry Part 2 - Shapes	4
22	Lines - Slope	5
23	Fractions	6
24	Number Theory - Least Common Multiple	8
25	Geometry Part 1 - Angles	3
26	Scientific Notation	29
27	Mean, Median, and Mode	12
28	Geometry Part 2 - Shapes	4
29	Geometry Part 2 - Shapes	29
30	Mean	12

31	Vectors	32
32	Fractions	6
33	Geometry Part 2 - Shapes, Unit Conversion	4, 29
34	Circles	21
35	Word Problems	26
36	Percentage	9
37	Word Problems	26
38	Probability	22
39	Matrices - Matrix Multiplication	19
40	Geometry Part 2 - Shapes	4
41	Quadratics – Factoring	16
42	Trigonometry	17
43	Geometry Part 2 - Shapes	4
44	Percentages	9
45	Fractions	6
46	Pronouns	5
47	Permutations	23
48	Geometry Part 2 - Shapes	4
49	Lines	4, 5
50	Functions	11
51	Fractions, Percentages	6, 9
52	Repeating Patterns	20
53	Composite Functions, Factoring Quadratics	11, 16
54	Absolute Value	18
55	Complex Numbers	25
56	Inequalities, Circles	27, 21
57	Number Theory	8
58	Trigonometry - Graphing Sine/Cosine Functions	17
59	Trigonometry - Law of Sines	17
60	Word Problems	26

Answer Key

Chapter 1: Backsolving

Pages 2-3:

1. D
2. D
3. C
4. B
5. D
6. C
7. D
8. C
9. C
10. B
11. C
12. B
13. D
14. C
15. A

Chapter 2: Substitution

Pages 5-6:

1. A
2. E
3. D
4. C
5. A
6. B
7. C
8. B
9. C
10. B
11. A
12. C
13. A

Chapter 3: Geometry Part 1 – Angles

Pages 10-13:

1. C
2. C
3. C
4. E
5. E
6. B
7. A
8. D
9. B
10. E
11. A
12. C
13. E
14. D
15. D
16. E
17. B
18. D
19. C
20. B
21. D
22. E

Chapter 4: Geometry Part 2 – Shapes

Pages 23-30:

1. C
2. C
3. C
4. B
5. B
6. D
7. D
8. B
9. C
10. E
11. E
12. B
13. E
14. D
15. A
16. B
17. A
18. E
19. A
20. B
21. A
22. C
23. B
24. D
25. E
26. D
27. A
28. E
29. E
30. D
31. A
32. D
33. C
34. B
35. C
36. E
37. B
38. B
39. D

40. B
41. B
42. C
43. E
44. D
45. C
46. D
47. A
48. B
49. C
50. A
51. C
52. E
53. B
54. C
55. B
56. A

Chapter 5: Lines

Pages 36-40:

1. A
2. D
3. A
4. B
5. C
6. A
7. D
8. C
9. B
10. D
11. E
12. D
13. D
14. D
15. E
16. D
17. B
18. D
19. E
20. E
21. C
22. A
23. B
24. A
25. B
26. A
27. C

Chapter 6: Fractions

Pages 46-50:

1. $\frac{17}{6}$
2. $\frac{7}{20}$
3. $\frac{11}{8}$
4. $-\frac{11}{6}$
5. $\frac{11}{21}$
6. $\frac{57}{10}$
7. $\frac{11}{6}$
8. $\frac{9}{20}$
9. $\frac{3}{2}$
10. $\frac{4}{15}$
11. 4
12. D
13. D
14. E
15. C
16. D
17. D
18. B
19. C
20. C
21. A
22. C
23. C
24. C
25. C
26. D
27. D
28. B
29. D
30. C
31. A
32. B
33. A
34. C
35. E
36. A
37. E
38. C
39. D
40. B
41. D
42. B
43. C
44. D

Chapter 7: Algebra Skills

Pages 57-60:

1. C
2. A
3. C
4. D
5. E
6. E
7. B
8. D
9. A
10. D
11. D
12. D
13. E
14. B
15. E
16. D
17. D
18. A
19. E
20. B
21. C
22. B
23. D
24. B
25. B
26. C
27. C
28. D
29. B
30. C
31. B
32. D
33. D

Chapter 8: Number Theory

Pages 68-71:

1. C
2. D
3. E
4. B
5. B
6. D
7. A
8. B
9. E
10. E
11. A
12. D
13. B
14. E
15. D
16. A
17. B
18. A
19. E
20. D
21. D
22. A
23. E
24. E
25. C
26. D
27. D
28. B
29. A
30. D
31. C
32. E
33. E
34. A
35. C

Chapter 9: Percentages

Simple Percentages

Pages 73-75:

1. C
2. E
3. B
4. C
5. C
6. D
7. E
8. A
9. C
10. B
11. C
12. C
13. B
14. A
15. B

Percent Increase and Decrease

Pages 77-81:

1. E
2. C
3. B
4. B
5. B
6. C
7. E
8. D
9. D
10. B

11. D
12. C
13. B
14. B
15. B
16. C
17. B
18. D
19. D
20. C
21. A
22. E
23. E
24. E
25. C
26. A
27. E
28. E

Chapter 10: Ratios and Proportions

Pages 85-88:

1. A
2. D
3. C
4. E
5. C
6. E
7. B
8. C
9. E
10. D
11. C
12. D
13. E
14. A
15. E
16. D
17. C
18. B
19. D
20. E
21. D
22. B
23. A
24. C
25. D
26. D
27. B
28. D

Chapter 11: Functions

Pages 97-101:

1. 25
2. 103
3. 193
4. -22
5. $18x^2 - 7$
6. $-3x + 19$
7. 117
8. 29
9. 36
10. $-18x^2 + 9x + 17$
11. -2
12. -7
13. 5 and -5
14. 7
15. 52
16. $8x^2 - 24x + 11$
17. 91
18. $-6x^3 + 20x^2 + 21x - 70$
19. -184
20. $-3x^2 + 13x - 14$
21. 11
22. $-\frac{2x}{8x^2-24x+11}$
23. $\frac{1}{3}$
24. $-54x^2 + 31$
25. E
26. C
27. D
28. A
29. D
30. C
31. B
32. E
33. E
34. D
35. D
36. D
37. C
38. C
39. D
40. E
41. D
42. B
43. A
44. E
45. C
46. B
47. B
48. E
49. A
50. E
51. B
52. A
53. D

Answer Key

> Want video explanation for how to solve all 1,250+ practice questions in this book? Go to page i to learn how to sign up.

54. D
55. B
56. E
57. B
58. E
59. E
60. B

Chapter 12: Mean, Median, Mode, and Range

Pages 107-111:

1. D
2. B
3. D
4. A
5. B
6. D
7. B
8. A
9. E
10. C
11. C
12. B
13. D
14. C
15. B
16. C
17. A
18. D
19. B
20. D
21. A
22. C
23. C
24. E
25. B
26. B
27. E
28. E
29. B
30. D
31. E
32. A
33. D
34. C
35. A
36. C

Chapter 13: Exponents and Roots

Page 114:

1. $x^6 y^3$
2. $3x^5$
3. $24x^3 y^7$
4. $4x^2 y^6$
5. $\frac{3y^5}{x^2}$
6. $9x^4$
7. $\frac{9y}{x^3 z^2}$
8. $\frac{1}{x}$
9. $\frac{z}{x^4}$
10. $\frac{9x^{10} z^2}{y^4}$
11. $16xy^3$
12. $\frac{25x^{17}}{8y^7}$
13. 1
14. 8
15. 5, −5
16. 1
17. $\frac{11}{6}$
18. 6
19. 6
20. 8

Page 117:

1. $2\sqrt{15}$
2. $7\sqrt{6}$
3. $2\sqrt{5}$
4. $7\sqrt{2}$
5. $5\sqrt[3]{6}$
6. $\sqrt{3}$
7. 1
8. $2b^2 \sqrt{2a}$
9. $4x\sqrt{y}$
10. $a^3 \sqrt{b}$
11. $(2x^2 y)\sqrt[3]{3y}$
12. $4x^5$
13. $\frac{20}{3}$
14. 45
15. 3
16. 90
17. 6
18. $\frac{45}{2}$ or 22.5
19. 4
20. 5

Pages 117-122:

1. C
2. C
3. C
4. B
5. E
6. E
7. C
8. B
9. C
10. A
11. D
12. B
13. D
14. C
15. A
16. C
17. C
18. B
19. C
20. D
21. B
22. C
23. E
24. E
25. D
26. E
27. B
28. B
29. A
30. E
31. A
32. A
33. B
34. C
35. B
36. B
37. D
38. B
39. C
40. E
41. D
42. D
43. D
44. E
45. B

Chapter 14: Logarithms

Pages 126-128:

1. E
2. E
3. E
4. D
5. B
6. C
7. A
8. D
9. B
10. B
11. D
12. A
13. C
14. C
15. D
16. B
17. E
18. C
19. B
20. C
21. B
22. C
23. B
24. C
25. E
26. B
27. E
28. C
29. C

Chapter 15: Systems of Equations

Pages 142-145:

1. D
2. B
3. C
4. B
5. D
6. B
7. A
8. C
9. E
10. D
11. D
12. A
13. D
14. B
15. D
16. C
17. E

Answer Key

18. B
19. E
20. A
21. D
22. E
23. A
24. C
25. B

Chapter 16: Quadratics

Pages 142-145:

1. C
2. E
3. D
4. D
5. B
6. E
7. C
8. D
9. A
10. D
11. A
12. D
13. C
14. B
15. C
16. D
17. E
18. B
19. C
20. E
21. A
22. C
23. E
24. E
25. C
26. A
27. A
28. D
29. C
30. C

Chapter 17: Trigonometry

Pages 164-172:

1. D
2. D
3. C
4. D
5. B
6. C
7. D
8. C
9. C
10. B
11. B
12. E
13. C
14. B
15. D
16. B
17. B
18. A
19. D
20. B
21. C
22. B
23. D
24. E
25. A
26. D
27. D
28. B
29. A
30. C
31. E
32. B
33. B
34. A
35. E
36. D
37. E
38. E
39. D
40. A
41. E
42. D
43. C
44. D
45. C
46. B

Chapter 18: Absolute Value

Pages 176-178:

1. B
2. C
3. E
4. D
5. E
6. C
7. C
8. E
9. B
10. A
11. B

12. B
13. D
14. D
15. E
16. E
17. E
18. C
19. E
20. B
21. B
22. D
23. E
24. D

Chapter 19: Matrices

Pages 187-190:

1. D
2. D
3. A
4. C
5. A
6. B
7. C
8. C
9. A
10. D
11. A
12. B
13. B
14. C
15. C
16. D
17. A
18. B
19. A
20. B
21. C
22. D
23. E

Chapter 20: Repeating Patterns

Pages 195-197:

1. B
2. D
3. C
4. E
5. E
6. E
7. A
8. D
9. B

10. D
11. C
12. C
13. E
14. D
15. D
16. A
17. C
18. E
19. A
20. B

Chapter 21: Circles, Ellipses, Hyperbolas

Pages 206-209:

1. C
2. C
3. E
4. E
5. A
6. D
7. A
8. D
9. C
10. A
11. C
12. B
13. C
14. B
15. A
16. C
17. A
18. C
19. E
20. A
21. D
22. A
23. C
24. B
25. D
26. D
27. D
28. A
29. D

Chapter 22: Probability

Pages 218-223:

1. A
2. E
3. B
4. B
5. B
6. B
7. B
8. B
9. E
10. A
11. C
12. A
13. A
14. E
15. B
16. B
17. E
18. C
19. C
20. D
21. D
22. E
23. B
24. D
25. E
26. C
27. E
28. B
29. D
30. C
31. B
32. D
33. D
34. C
35. B

Chapter 23: Factorial, Permutations, Combinations, and Organized Counting

Pages 230-234:

1. D
2. E
3. D
4. E
5. D
6. B
7. A
8. D
9. C
10. D
11. C
12. A
13. C
14. C
15. A
16. D
17. E
18. C
19. B
20. A
21. C
22. A
23. D
24. C
25. B
26. B
27. D
28. C
29. D
30. D
31. B

Chapter 24: Sequences

Pages 239-240:

1. D
2. C
3. B
4. B
5. E
6. B
7. B
8. A
9. E
10. E
11. D
12. B
13. D
14. B
15. E
16. C
17. E

Chapter 25: Complex Numbers

Pages 246-249:

1. C
2. C
3. A
4. D
5. C
6. B
7. C

8. D
9. A
10. B
11. B
12. D
13. C
14. E
15. E
16. B
17. C
18. E
19. B
20. D
21. E
22. C
23. D
24. B
25. B
26. D
27. A
28. C

Chapter 26: Word Problems

Pages 251-255:

1. D
2. B
3. C
4. C
5. A
6. E
7. C
8. A
9. C
10. B
11. D
12. D
13. E
14. C
15. C
16. B
17. D
18. C
19. C
20. D
21. C
22. D
23. B
24. A
25. C
26. C
27. B
28. A

Chapter 27: Inequalities

Pages 261-263:

1. A
2. D
3. C
4. D
5. B
6. A
7. B
8. B
9. E
10. A
11. C
12. D
13. C
14. D
15. B
16. C
17. C
18. A
19. B
20. D
21. E
22. A
23. D

Chapter 28: Exponential Growth and Decay

Pages 268-270:

1. A
2. E
3. D
4. A
5. A
6. D
7. B
8. C
9. A
10. D
11. A
12. B
13. E
14. E

Chapter 29: Unit Conversion

Pages 274-276:

1. B
2. A
3. C
4. B
5. C
6. E
7. B
8. C
9. E
10. B
11. C
12. A
13. C
14. B
15. A
16. E
17. E
18. C
19. B
20. C
21. D
22. B
23. B
24. D

Chapter 30: Scientific Notation

Pages 278-279:

1. C
2. B
3. B
4. E
5. A
6. D
7. D
8. A
9. E
10. B
11. C
12. A
13. B
14. D
15. B
16. E

Chapter 31: Arcs and Sectors

Pages 282-284:

1. A
2. B
3. B
4. A
5. C
6. D
7. C
8. C
9. B
10. B
11. E
12. D
13. A
14. E
15. B
16. B

Chapter 32: Vectors

Pages 288-290:

1. C
2. B
3. E
4. E
5. D
6. C
7. A
8. A
9. B
10. B
11. B
12. B
13. A
14. A
15. D

Chapter 33: Shifting and Transforming Functions

Pages 294-295:

1. B
2. D
3. E
4. C
5. C
6. D
7. A
8. E
9. E
10. B
11. C
12. C

Chapter 34: Basic Statistic

Pages 302-304:

1. C
2. A
3. D
4. A
5. A
6. E
7. B
8. C
9. A
10. C
11. D
12. D
13. B
14. C
15. E
16. B
17. C
18. C

Chapter 35: Miscellaneous Topics

Pages 316-320:

1. B
2. B
3. C
4. E
5. A
6. C
7. C
8. C
9. B
10. D
11. A
12. C
13. D
14. E
15. B
16. A
17. C
18. B
19. C
20. D
21. D
22. C
23. B
24. E
25. E
26. A
27. B
28. A
29. B
30. B
31. C
32. B
33. A
34. B

Made in the USA
Middletown, DE
06 March 2025

72358214R00208